EARLY MODERN PHILOSOPHY OF RELIGION

THE HISTORY OF
WESTERN PHILOSOPHY OF RELIGION

VOLUME 1: ANCIENT PHILOSOPHY OF RELIGION

VOLUME 2: MEDIEVAL PHILOSOPHY OF RELIGION

VOLUME 3: EARLY MODERN PHILOSOPHY OF RELIGION

VOLUME 4: NINETEENTH-CENTURY PHILOSOPHY OF RELIGION

VOLUME 5: TWENTIETH-CENTURY PHILOSOPHY OF RELIGION

EARLY MODERN PHILOSOPHY OF RELIGION

Edited by Graham Oppy and N. N. Trakakis

VOLUME 3

THE HISTORY OF WESTERN PHILOSOPHY OF RELIGION

ACUMEN

First published in 2009 by Acumen
First published in paperback by Acumen in 2013

Acumen Publishing Limited

4 Saddler Street
Durham
DH1 3NP

ISD, 70 Enterprise Drive
Bristol, CT 06010, USA

www.acumenpublishing.com

ISBN: 978-1-84465-683-7 (paperback Volume 3)
ISBN: 978-1-84465-679-0 (paperback 5 volume set)
ISBN: 978-1-84465-222-8 (hardcover Volume 3)
ISBN: 978-1-84465-181-8 (hardcover 5 volume set)

British Library Cataloguing-in-Publication Data
A catalogue record for this book is available from the British Library.

Typeset in Minion Pro.

CONTENTS

Editorial Introduction vii
Contributors xi

1. Early Modern Philosophy of Religion: An Introduction 1
PETER ANSTEY

2. Niccolò Machiavelli 19
MARY G. DIETZ AND ILYA WINHAM

3. Martin Luther 33
THEODOR DIETER

4. John Calvin 47
MICHAEL SUDDUTH

5. Michel de Montaigne 65
MARC FOGLIA

6. Francisco Suárez 75
BERNARDO J. CANTEÑS

7. Thomas Hobbes 89
SHARON LLOYD

8. René Descartes 101
GARY STEINER

9. Ralph Cudworth 113
BENJAMIN CARTER

10. Blaise Pascal 127
WILLIAM DAVID WETSEL

11. Baruch Spinoza 141
MICHAEL A. ROSENTHAL

12. John Locke 153
VICTOR NUOVO

13. Gottfried Wilhelm Leibniz 167
JACK D. DAVIDSON

14. George Berkeley 183
ROOMET JAKAPI

15. Voltaire 197
DAVID WILLIAMS

16. The Deists 211
PETER BYRNE

17. Jonathan Edwards 223
SANG HYUN LEE

18. Thomas Reid 235
RYAN NICHOLS

19. David Hume 249
PAUL DRAPER

20. Denis Diderot 263
DAVID ADAMS

21. Immanuel Kant 277
ECKART FÖRSTER

22. Gotthold Ephraim Lessing 289
DAVID BELL

23. William Paley 303
ROGER WHITE

Chronology 313
Bibliography 321
Index 335

EDITORIAL INTRODUCTION

Bertrand Russell's *History of Western Philosophy* (1946; hereafter *History*) provides a model for *some* of the significant features of the present work. Like Russell's more general history, our history of Western philosophy of religion consists principally of chapters devoted to the works of individual thinkers, selected because of their "considerable importance". Of course, we do not claim to have provided coverage of all of those who have made important contributions to Western philosophy of religion. However, we think that anyone who has made a significant contribution to Western philosophy of religion has either seriously engaged with the works of philosophers who are featured in this work, or has produced work that has been a focus of serious engagement for philosophers who are featured in this work.

Like Russell, we have aimed for contributions that show how the philosophy of religion developed by a given thinker is related to that thinker's life, and that trace out connections between the views developed by a given philosopher and the views of their predecessors, contemporaries and successors. While our primary aim is to provide an account of the ideas, concepts, claims and arguments developed by each of the philosophers under consideration, we think – with Russell – that this aim is unlikely to be achieved in a work in which "each philosopher appears as in a vacuum".

Again like Russell, we have only selected philosophers or religious writers who belong to, or have exerted a significant impact on, the intellectual tradition of the West (i.e. western Europe and the Anglo-American world). We realize that this selection criterion alone excludes from our work a number of important thinkers and religious groups or traditions, such as: Asian philosophers of religion, particularly those representing such religions as Hinduism, Buddhism, Confucianism and Taoism; African philosophers of religion; and individuals, texts and traditions emanating from indigenous religions, such as those found in the native populations of Australia and the Pacific Islands. Clearly, the non-Western world has produced thinkers who have made important, and often overlooked, contributions to the philosophy of religion. We have decided, however, not to include any entries on these thinkers, and our decision is based primarily on the (admittedly not incontestable) view that the Asian, African and indigenous philosophical and religious traditions have not had a great impact on the main historical narrative of the West. It would therefore have been difficult to integrate the various non-Western thinkers into the five-volume structure of the present work. The best way to redress this omission, in our view, is to produce a separate multi-volume work that would be dedicated to the history of non-Western philosophy of religion, a project that we invite others to take up.

Where we have departed most significantly from Russell is that our work has been written by a multitude of contributors, whereas Russell's work was the product of just one person. In the preface to his *History*, Russell claimed that:

> There is … something lost when many authors co-operate. If there is any unity in the movement of history, if there is any intimate relation between what goes before and what comes later, it is necessary, for setting this forth, that earlier and later periods should be synthesized in a single mind. (1946: 5)

We think that Russell exaggerates the difficulties in, and underestimates the benefits of, having a multitude of expert contributors. On the one hand, someone who is an expert on the work of a given philosopher is bound to have expert knowledge of the relation between the work of that philosopher, what goes before and what comes after. On the other hand, and as Russell himself acknowledged, it is impossible for one person to have the expertise of a specialist across such a wide field. (Indeed, while Russell's *History* is admirable for its conception and scope, there is no doubt that it is far from a model for good historical scholarship.)

Of course, Russell's worry about a multiplicity of authors does recur at the editorial level: the editors of this work have no particular claim to expertise concerning any of the philosophers who are featured in the work. In order to alleviate this problem, we invited all of the contributors to read drafts of neighbouring contributions, acting on the assumption that someone who is an expert on a particular philosopher is likely to have reasonably good knowledge of contemporaries and near contemporaries of that philosopher. Moreover, each of the five volumes comes with an expert introduction, written by someone who is much better placed than we are to survey the time period covered in the given volume.

Obviously enough, it is also the case that the present work does not have the kind of narrative unity that is possessed by Russell's work. Our work juxtaposes contributions from experts who make very different theoretical assumptions, and who belong to diverse philosophical schools and traditions. Again, it seems to us that this represents an advantage: there are many different contemporary approaches to philosophy of religion, and each of these approaches suggests a different view about the preceding history. Even if there is "unity in the movement of history", it is clear that there is considerable disagreement about the precise nature of that unity.

Although our work is divided into five volumes – and despite the fact that we have given labels to each of these volumes – we attach no particular significance to the way in which philosophers are collected together by these volumes. The order of the chapters is determined by the dates of birth of the philosophers who are the principal subjects of those chapters. While it would not be a task for a single evening, we do think that it should be possible to read the five volumes as a single, continuous work.

* * *

Collectively, our primary debt is to the 109 people who agreed to join with us in writing the material that appears in this work. We are indebted also to Tristan Palmer, who oversaw the project on behalf of Acumen. Tristan initially searched for someone prepared to take on the task of editing a single-volume history of Western philosophy of religion, and was actively involved in the shaping of the final project. He also provided invaluable advice on the full range of editorial questions that arise in a project on this scale. Thanks, too, to the copy-editors and others at Acumen, especially Kate Williams, who played a role in the completion of this project, and to the anonymous reviewers who provided many helpful comments. We are grateful to Karen Gillen for proofreading and indexing all five volumes, and to the Helen McPherson Smith Trust, which provided financial support for this project. We also acknowledge our debt to Monash University, and to our colleagues in the School of Philosophy and Bioethics. Special thanks to Dirk Baltzly for his suggestions about potential contributors to the volume on ancient Western philosophy of religion and for his editorial help with the chapter on Pythagoras.

Apart from these collective debts, Graham Oppy acknowledges personal debts to friends and family, especially to Camille, Gilbert, Calvin and Alfie. N. N. Trakakis is also grateful for the support of family and friends while working on this project, which he dedicates to his nephew and niece, Nicholas and Adrianna Trakakis: my prayer is that you will come to share the love of wisdom cultivated by the great figures in these volumes.

Graham Oppy
N. N. Trakakis

CONTRIBUTORS

David Adams is Professor of French Enlightenment Studies at the University of Manchester. He has published widely on the French Enlightenment, and on Diderot in particular. In addition to numerous articles, his books include *Diderot* (1986), a study of the author's early works, and a critical edition in translation of Diderot's *Thoughts on the Interpretation of Nature* (1999). He is also the author of a standard work of reference on Diderot, the two-volume *Bibliographie des œuvres de Denis Diderot, 1739–1900* (2000).

Peter Anstey is Professor of Early Modern Philosophy at the University of Otago, New Zealand. He has published widely in the field of early modern philosophy and, in particular, on the thought of Robert Boyle and John Locke. The topics of God and nature, the nature of causation and laws of nature, and the influence of Reformed theology on early modern natural philosophy are important focuses of his research. His books include *The Philosophy of Robert Boyle* (2000) and *The Science of Nature in the Seventeenth Century* (edited with J. Schuster, 2005). He is an associate editor of the *Australasian Journal of Philosophy*.

David Bell is Senior Lecturer in German Studies at the University of Manchester. His monograph *Spinoza in Germany* (1984) addresses the history of the reception of Spinoza's thought and examines the crucial role played by Lessing and the *Spinozastreit*, alongside the key contributions by Herder and Goethe in this process. He has also written on Goethe's religious thought and his poetic cycle, the *West-östlicher Divan*.

Peter Byrne is Professor of Ethics and Philosophy of Religion at King's College London. He is the author of *Natural Religion and the Nature of Religion* (1989) and seven other books in ethics and philosophy of religion, including *Prolegomena to Religious Pluralism* (1995), *The Moral Interpretation of Religion* (1998) and *Kant* *on God* (2007). He is also editor of *Religious Studies: An International Journal for the Philosophy of Religion*.

Bernardo J. Canteñs is Associate Professor of Philosophy at Moravian College, Bethlehem, Pennsylvania. His areas of specialization are late medieval philosophy (Suárez), American philosophy, metaphysics and Hispanic issues. Recent publications include "The Relationship Between God and Essences and the Notion of Eternal Truths According to Francisco Suárez" (*The Modern Schoolman*, 2000), "Ultimate Reality in the Metaphysics of Francisco Suárez" (*Ultimate Reality and Meaning*, 2002) and "What Kind of Beings (*entia*) Are Beings of Reason and What Kind of Being (*esse*) Do They Have? Suárez on Beings of Reason" (*American Catholic Philosophical Quarterly*, 2003).

Benjamin Carter is an Honorary Fellow of the Department of Theology attached to the Network for Religion in Public Life, University of Exeter. He has published on Cudworth, the Cambridge Platonists and early modern philosophy and theology, and has written a monograph on Cudworth's Trinitarian theology for the Peeters series *Studies in Philosophical Theology*. Between 2003 and 2008 he taught history and philosophy at the University of Bristol. He is currently an Ordinand in the Church of England.

Jack D. Davidson is currently Visiting Assistant Professor at Rice University, Houston. He has written on Leibniz's conception of freedom and punishment in two early texts, how the biblical doctrine that humans are imitators of God influenced his account of freedom, Leibniz's commentary on Locke's conception of freedom, Leibniz's adjudication of the middle knowledge controversy, and his view that the source of moral wrongdoing is the intellect and not the will.

Theodor Dieter studied philosophy and Protestant theology in Heidelberg and Tübingen, writing his dissertation on "The Philosophical Theses of Luther's 'Heidelberg Disputation'" and his habilitation on "The Young Luther and Aristotle" (published together as *Der junge Luther und Aristoteles*, 2001). He taught systematic theology in Tübingen for many years, was appointed Research Professor at the Institute for Ecumenical Research in Strasbourg in 1994, and has served as Director of this Institute since 1998. His main areas of research are Luther's theology, Roman Catholic theology, ecumenical theology, the relations between philosophy and theology, and social ethics.

Mary G. Dietz is a member of the Faculty of Political Science and Gender Studies at Northwestern University and currently editor of *Political Theory: An International Journal of Political Philosophy*. Her areas of research in political theory include democratic theory, feminist theory and the history of Western political thought, with emphasis on Aristotle, Machiavelli, Hobbes and Arendt. Among other works on Machiavelli, Dietz has authored "Trapping the Prince: Machiavelli and the Politics of Deception" (*American Political Science Review*, 1986) and "Working in Half-Truth: Habermas, Machiavelli, and the Milieu Proper to Politics" (in her *Turning Operations*, 2002).

Paul Draper is Professor of Philosophy at Purdue University. He has devoted much of his career to developing and defending various Humean arguments from evil against theism. He has also written several articles on the design argument, including "Hume's Reproduction Parody of the Design Argument" and "Cosmic Fine-Tuning and Terrestrial Suffering: Parallel Problems for Naturalism and Theism". A former President of the Society for Philosophy of Religion, he is editor of *Philo: A Journal of Philosophy*, co-editor of the second edition of *A Companion to Philosophy of Religion* and editor of *God or Blind Nature? Philosophers Debate the Evidence.*

Marc Foglia studied at the École Normale Supérieure in Paris, later publishing his PhD as *The Formation of Judgment in Montaigne* (2007). He taught for five years as an assistant professor in the history of philosophy and political philosophy at Paris-I Sorbonne. He contributed the article on Montaigne for the online *Stanford Encyclopedia of Philosophy*, and he presently works as a speechwriter and political advisor for the French government.

Eckart Förster is Professor of Philosophy, German, and the Humanities at Johns Hopkins University, Baltimore, and Honorary Professor of Philosophy at the Humboldt Universität Berlin. He is the author of *Kant's Final Synthesis* (2000), and editor of *Kant's Opus Postumum* (1993) and *Kant's Transcendental Deductions* (1989).

Roomet Jakapi is a Senior Researcher in the Department of Philosophy at the University of Tartu, Estonia. He is the author of many articles on George Berkeley's religious philosophy. He has published in the *British Journal for the History of Philosophy*, *Archiv für Geschichte der Philosophie*, *The Modern Schoolman* and *Berkeley Studies.* He has translated Berkeley's *Three Dialogues Between Hylas and Philonous* into Estonian and is the editor of the journal *Studia Philosophica Estonica.* His current research concentrates on various theological problems in early modern metaphysics.

Sang Hyun Lee is Kyung-Chik Han Professor of Systematic Theology at Princeton Theological Seminary, Princeton, and is the author of *The Philosophical Theology of Jonathan Edwards* (1988), the editor of the *Princeton Companion to Jonathan Edwards* (2005), and a member of the editorial board of the Yale edition of *The Works of Jonathan Edwards*, as well as the editor of volume 21 of that edition.

Sharon Lloyd is Professor of Philosophy, Law and Political Science at the University of Southern California. She is the author of *Ideals as Interests in Hobbes's Leviathan* (1992) and *Morality in the Philosophy of Thomas Hobbes* (2009). Formerly review editor of *Philosophy and Public Affairs*, she is editor of the *Pacific Philosophical Quarterly "Special Issue on Recent Work on the Moral and Political Philosophy of Thomas Hobbes"*. Her blog, *Hobbes Today*, provides a forum for discussion of applications of Hobbes' moral and political philosophy to issues of contemporary concern.

Ryan Nichols is Professor of Philosophy at California State University Fullerton. He is the author of *Thomas Reid's Theory of Perception* (2007). His published papers include "Natural Philosophy and Its Limits in the Scottish Enlightenment" (*The Monist*, 2007), "Reid's Inheritance from Locke, and How He Overcomes It" (*Journal for the History of Philosophy*, 2003) and "Reid on Fictional Objects and the Way of Ideas" (*The Philosophical Quarterly*, 2002). He has guest edited a special issue of the *Journal of Scottish Philosophy* on Reid and serves on its board of editors.

Victor Nuovo is Charles A. Dana Professor of Philosophy Emeritus, Middlebury College and Senior Research Fellow, Harris Manchester College, Oxford. He is the editor of *John Locke* (2002) and *John Locke* (2009); and the author of *John Locke, The Philosopher as Christian Virtuoso* (forthcoming).

Michael A. Rosenthal is Associate Professor of Philosophy at the University of Washington in Seattle. Some of his numerous articles include "Why Spinoza Chose the Hebrews: The Exemplary Function of Prophecy in the *Theological-Political Treatise*" (*History of Political Thought*, 1997), "Spinoza's Dogmas of Universal Faith and the Problem of Religion" (*Philosophy and Theology*, 2001) and "Spinoza's Republican Argument for Tolerance" (*Journal of Political Philosophy*, 2003). He is currently co-editing a volume of essays on the *Theological-Political Treatise*, and completing a monograph on the role of religion in Spinoza's political philosophy.

Gary Steiner is John Howard Harris Professor of Philosophy at Bucknell University, Lewisburg. He is the author of *Descartes as a Moral Thinker* (2004), *Anthropocentrism and Its Discontents* (2005) and *Animals and the Moral Community* (2008).

Michael Sudduth is a lecturer in the philosophy department at San Francisco State University, where he also serves as the director of the department's Religion programme. His main area of philosophical interest is philosophy of religion, where he has focused on religious epistemology and natural theology. He has published numerous articles in philosophy of religion, including articles in *Faith and Philosophy*, *International Journal for Philosophy of Religion* and *Religious*

Studies. His first book *The Reformed Objection to Natural Theology* is forthcoming in 2009.

William David Wetsel is the author of *L'Écriture et le reste* (1981) and *Pascal and Disbelief* (1994), and co-editor of *Pascal, New Trends in Port-Royal Studies* (2002). He was President of the North American Society for Seventeenth-Century French Literature in 2001–2.

Roger White is Associate Professor of Philosophy at the Massachusetts Institute of Technology. He specializes in epistemology and the philosophy of science. His work has focused on epistemological issues concerning probability and explanation in science. He has written on issues concerning the argument from design, particularly in connection with cosmology ("Fine-tuning and Multiple Universes" [*Noûs*, 2000]), and during 2006–2008 he contributed to an academic workshop on science and religion funded by the Mellon Foundation.

David Williams is Emeritus Professor of French at the University of Sheffield. He is a French Enlightenment specialist with particular interests in Voltaire and Condorcet. He is an ex-president of the British Society for Eighteenth-Century Studies, a member of the editorial board of the *British Journal for Eighteenth-Century Studies*, a vice-president of the editorial board of the new Oxford edition of Voltaire's *Complete Works*, and a research associate at the Voltaire Foundation. He has a major editorial role in the *Complete Works* project, and his most recent critical editions (2008) of Voltairean essays and treatises relating to religion include *Du Fanatisme* and *Sur le théisme.*

Ilya Winham is a doctoral student working on Machiavelli in the Department of Political Science at the University of Minnesota.

1

EARLY MODERN PHILOSOPHY OF RELIGION: AN INTRODUCTION

Peter Anstey

The early modern period is one of the richest, perhaps the richest, period in the history of relations between philosophy and religion. The chapters in this volume bear this out again and again, dealing as they do with some of the foremost thinkers of modern times, such as René Descartes, John Locke, David Hume and Immanuel Kant. Each of the following chapters is organized around the contributions of one of these philosophers or a group of philosophers, some of whom lived centuries apart, so it is important at the outset to get a bird's-eye view of the broad contours of the relations between philosophy and religion in the early modern period. This introduction aims to provide just such an overview by taking a thematic approach to the subject.

It goes without saying that Christianity was the dominant religion within Europe throughout the early modern period and almost all of the philosophers and religious thinkers who appear in these pages developed their views in relation to the Christian religion. Even those, such as Baruch Spinoza, who were not nurtured within a Christian community, found that Christian theology and Christian ecclesiastical structures were a dominant force in the polemical context in which they worked. To claim that Christianity was the dominant religion of the period is not, however, to claim that it faced no rivals or internal divisions. In fact, the internal ructions of the period were some of the most intense that the religion has ever faced. From 1517, when Martin Luther posted his ninety-five theses on the church door in Wittenberg and set off the Protestant Reformation, through the Counter Reformation and the Thirty Years War ending with the Peace of Westphalia in 1648, to the revocation of the Edict of Nantes in 1685, Christianity underwent massive changes and challenges. It is hardly surprising, therefore, that this coincided with such a fertile period of philosophical engagement with religion. However, interesting as these issues are, the socio-religio-political background to developments in philosophy and religion are not explored in any depth in this volume. Rather the approach is what historiographers call an 'internalist' one, focusing on the actual ideas and arguments of the leading philosophers and theologians of the period. There are, however, a number of historiographical issues that are worth highlighting before we commence our general survey.

HISTORIOGRAPHY

Any attempt to understand early modern thought must first come to terms with the question of periodization: when was the early modern period and why is it distinctive? Normally the term 'early modern' refers to the period spanning from the late sixteenth century to the early eighteenth century. In this volume, however, the term is used a little more broadly to encompass thinkers from the Protestant Reformation in the early sixteenth century through to the late eighteenth century. Thus, the centuries covered in this volume encompass other periods that historians have found to be distinctive, namely the Reformation, the late Renaissance, the Scientific Revolution and the Enlightenment. Although this may seem overambitious, it will become clear that there is a genuine continuity of thematic content in the issues that were discussed throughout these three centuries. Of course, all of these terms, 'early modern', 'Reformation', 'Scientific Revolution' and so on, are to a large extent the creations of historians rather than terms used by those living in the respective eras, and at times one needs to be careful not to let these historiographical categories obscure or unduly influence one's interpretation of the writings and events of these periods. But as long as we remain self-conscious of our categories, they can be of great use.

The same can be said of the sorts of disciplinary categories and boundaries that we use in philosophy and theology today and which we tend to read back into early modern thought. We speak, say, of Berkeley's *epistemology* or Leibniz's *metaphysics* meaning Berkeley's theory of knowledge and Leibniz's account of what there is, respectively. However, the branch of philosophy called 'epistemology' is a relatively new discipline, even if many of the questions it seeks to answer can be traced back to the Presocratics. Likewise, the term 'metaphysics' had quite a different semantic range in the early modern period than what it has today. When Jean Le Rond d'Alembert (1717–83) says in the *Preliminary Discourse* to Denis Diderot's *Encyclopédie* that Locke "created metaphysics, almost as Newton had created physics" (d'Alembert 1995: 83) a student of contemporary philosophy might find this puzzling; after all, Locke is normally thought to have made a major contribution to epistemology and only secondarily to metaphysics. However, d'Alembert is referring to the study of the understanding or pneumatology, something to which Locke did make a major contribution.

Likewise, we tend to speak of *science* when the early moderns referred instead to *natural philosophy*, and we speak of *scientists* where the latter would refer to *natural philosophers*. For most of the early modern period, theology was still the queen of the sciences where 'science' is derived from the Latin *scientia*, a term with quite a different semantic range to our modern term 'science'. Moreover, it has even been argued that the concept of *religion* is itself a product of the early modern period (Harrison 1990). All of this needs to be borne in mind as we approach the subject of the relations between philosophy and religion in the early modern period.

THEISTIC PROOFS

Undoubtedly the most famous and challenging development in the relations between philosophy and religion in the early modern period was the development of a series of rational arguments for the existence of God, often called 'theistic proofs'. There is a sense in which the theistic proofs are foundational to any philosophical theology. While all of these arguments predate the sixteenth century and while they were subject to important innovations and developments in the hands of Anselm and Aquinas, the high-water mark of the articulation and polemical deployment of this cluster of arguments occurred in the seventeenth and eighteenth centuries.

Luther and Calvin held a rather low view of rational theology in general, preferring to appeal to what they regarded as the revealed word of God rather than vain human ratiocinations (Calvin, *Institutes*, I. ii–v). However, theistic proofs were debated among scholastic theologians throughout the sixteenth and early seventeenth centuries and provide an important backdrop for the discussions of the leading seventeenth-century philosophers who made the arguments famous. In a rough and ready sense there is a discernible progression in the development of the theistic proofs from the ontological arguments, as spelt out by Descartes and Gottfried Wilhelm Leibniz, through to the cosmological arguments enunciated by the English natural philosopher Robert Boyle (1627–91), Samuel Clarke (1675–1729) and Leibniz, to the teleological argument championed by William Paley (1743–1805). This is not to say that these were the only theistic proofs discussed in the period, but these were the dominant and philosophically most interesting attempts to establish the existence of God by the use of reason.

It should also be stressed that by the end of the early modern period the value of the whole project of rational theology had become highly contentious. This was in part a result of the fact that the theistic proofs had ceased to be evaluated within the framework of Christianity itself, but were rather studied, at least up to the time of Hume's essay on "The Natural History of Religion" (1757), as a constituent of natural religion. Yet this is not to say that there were not strident promoters of the proofs within Christian ranks: Paley, for one, continued an apologetical tradition inaugurated by Boyle in the English-speaking world. And yet on the Continent Kant's attack on the theistic proofs in his *Critique of Pure Reason* (1781/87) marked a watershed in the debate and a natural terminus for early modern rational theology.

Once the existence of God has been argued for on rational grounds, it is then incumbent on the theist (or polytheist) to establish the manner in which God interacts (or the gods interact) with the material world. This brings us to another central concern of philosophy and religion in the early modern period: the relation between God and nature.

GOD AND NATURE

The question of God's relation to nature was far more widely discussed than the theistic proofs. This is in part because the issue impinged very closely on the new natural philosophy that emerged in the period. The predominance of the mechanical philosophy in the mid- to late seventeenth century set the problem of how God interacts with nature in sharp relief. The new conception of laws of nature, the widely held view that matter is completely inert and explanations of change in terms of the contact criterion – one body colliding with another – forced philosophers to articulate just what role God had in everyday events. Did causal interactions occur independently of God or was God involved in some or all physical causes? The problem was particularly acute in Cartesianism because Descartes' philosophy could be interpreted as not requiring divine intervention in material causal interactions, or as a form of occasionalism, that is, as requiring God's constant causal intervention. Moreover, the problem only intensified when it came to accounting for the interaction of immaterial entities and bodies and the nature of miracles.

Some philosophers, notably the Cambridge Platonists, augmented the doctrine of inert matter with an all-pervading World Soul that gave a basic form of perceptivity to matter and accounted for its law-like behaviour. Easily the most radical solution to the problem of God and nature, however, was that of Spinoza, who denied that God is a transcendent being and asserted instead that God is identical with nature herself. By collapsing the God and nature dichotomy, Spinoza presented a new set of problems in philosophical theology, but while he had his admirers, it is true to say that few took up his denial of God's transcendence. Thomas Hobbes, on the other hand, denied that there are any immaterial substances and claimed that everything can be explained using the principles of matter and motion. Not surprisingly, Spinoza and Hobbes were quickly marked out by their contemporaries as proffering philosophies that tended to atheism, and to be dubbed a Spinozist, as Lessing was more than a hundred years after Spinoza's death, was tantamount to being called an atheist.

Among the Cartesians, however, the favoured response was some form of occasionalism. Nicolas Malebranche (1638–1715) held undoubtedly the most radical form of this doctrine, claiming that God is the sole causal agent in the physical universe. Others, such as Antoine Arnauld (1612–94) and Boyle adopted a *via media* between the deistic (in the popular sense of the word) view that God is disengaged from his creation and occasionalism. It was a form of nomic occasionalism whereby matter has some limited causal powers, but God is required to guarantee that it obeys the laws of motion.

In the eighteenth century occasionalism was defended by Jonathan Edwards, but on the whole the doctrine remained a minority position. The opponents of occasionalism, on the other hand, denied that matter was causally impotent and asserted that the nature of matter and the laws of motion are sufficient for the emergence of the current fabric of the world and its continued existence. If they were right, what grounds are there for supposing that God communicates with human beings? Does humankind even need a revealed religion? And is there a form of knowledge that can be acquired only through special revelation? This brings us to another contested field within early modern philosophy: the nature and scope of knowledge and the relation between faith and reason.

KNOWLEDGE, FAITH AND REASON

In the early modern period the scope and limits of human reason were subjected to careful and sustained analysis by philosophers. Of particular importance in their reflections was the relation between religious faith and human reason. In fact, the debate over the powers of human reason and its relation to faith was conceptually prior to the enterprise of establishing arguments for the existence of God. Thus, natural theology was pursued as a consequence of an acceptance that human reason could make a contribution to reasons for believing in religious doctrines.

A cluster of doctrines fed into these discussions, some theological and others derived from Hellenistic philosophy. In particular, the doctrine of epistemic impairment or fallen knowledge and the clever use of argument forms derived from Pyrrhonian scepticism put important constraints on the development of many accounts of the power and scope of human reason. As for the former, the central idea is that at the Fall humankind was corrupted both morally and epistemically. In its most common form, the doctrine of epistemic impairment maintained that human beings had lost knowledge, particularly knowledge of the essences of natural objects. In its more radical form, the doctrine also claimed that the reasoning powers of human beings were irrevocably corrupted. This corruption was thought by some to be manifested in the ascendency of the passions over reason. Compounding the problem for the status of human reason was the deployment of sceptical arguments concerning the fallibility of the senses in the writings of Michel de Montaigne and others.

Philosophers from the period can be roughly grouped along a continuum of views ranging from belief in a highly depraved and negative view of human reason to a more moderate and optimistic account of the effects of the Fall. For those philosophers with a low view of the post-lapsarian condition of human reason, a form of what has come to be called fideism was the inevitable consequence of the Fall. That is, some philosophers, such as Blaise Pascal, and possibly Montaigne, argued that it is futile, or even impossible, to come to believe in the truth of the Christian religion on the basis of human reason. So, while Pascal's Wager was an attempt to give probabilistic reasons for the rationality of belief in God, it should be stressed that the wager does not concern probabilistic reasons for the truth of that belief (Pascal 1931: §233). By contrast, Descartes, in spite of his deployment of sceptical techniques of argumentation in the first two *Meditations* (Descartes 1984: 12–23), tended to downplay the doctrine of epistemic impairment and sought to complement the coherence and evidential basis of the Christian religion with natural theology. Others, such as Francis Bacon, believed that a new approach to natural philosophy would offer an opportunity to overcome the epistemological consequences of the Fall by opening up the 'book of nature' by using the correct method and by the use of newly invented instruments such as the microscope (Bacon 2004: 2–5; Hooke 1665: preface). In England this promotion of the complementarity of natural philosophy and religion led to the emergence of the vocation of the Christian virtuoso, epitomized by Boyle, who instituted in his will an annual series of Boyle Lectures for the defence of the Christian faith, which provided a major impetus to the development of natural theology in eighteenth-century Britain. Boyle promoted what he and others called 'physico-theology' in which natural philosophy served to augment the truths revealed in Scripture (Harrison 2005).

Philosophical reflection on the role of witnesses and testimony in the new experimental natural philosophy of the mid-seventeenth century naturally extended to a reflection on the role of testimony in establishing Christian belief, particularly belief in the miracles of the New Testament. Discussions on the nature and credibility of miracles spanned the period from Pietro Pomponazzi to the Cambridge Platonist Ralph Cudworth, Locke, Spinoza, Leibniz, the deists and Hume. Hume's treatment of miracles in his *An Enquiry Concerning Human Understanding* (1748) is perhaps the most widely discussed early modern treatment today (Earman 2000).

Not surprisingly, doctrinal divisions emerged within the Christian church as to the correct way to articulate the powers of human reason and the relation between reason and special revelation. When natural philosophical knowledge was to the fore, hermeneutical principles became the point of contention. This is perhaps best illustrated in Galileo's (1564–1642) marvellous *Letter to the Grand Duchess Christina* (1615) in which he claims that "nothing physical which sense-experience sets before our eyes, or which necessary demonstrations prove to us, ought to be called in question (much less condemned) upon the testimony of biblical passages which may have some different meaning beneath their words" (Galileo 1957: 182–3). When special revelation was to the fore in the seventeenth century, a series of fine-grained distinctions emerged around which theologians and philosophers were grouped, from the latitudinarians and Socinians, who held a high view of the powers of human reason in matters pertaining to special revelation, to those who argued that human reason should submit to revelation.

Indeed, the period is characterized by sects and 'enthusiasts' who believed that they still received revelation, and who were harshly censured by Locke and others. But contemporary revelation was not the only sort of revelation to come under attack by philosophers, for the late seventeenth century saw the emergence of a new form of biblical criticism in which the traditional belief in the Mosaic authorship of the first five books of the Old Testament was seriously challenged in the writings of Hobbes, Isaac La Peyrère (1596–1676) and Spinoza (see Malcolm 2002: ch. 12).

Furthermore, in the late seventeenth century, among those who accepted special revelation, there was an intense debate as to whether and in what sense parts of that revelation can be above reason but not contrary to reason (see Wojcik 1997; Antognazza 2006; Stewart 2006). This is the context in which Locke's famous discussion in book IV of the *Essay Concerning Human Understanding* (hereafter *Essay*) "Of Faith and Reason, and their Distinct Provinces" should be interpreted. With the rise of deism in the eighteenth century, reason was in the ascendancy. The deists of the eighteenth century are properly characterized as those who believed that all that can be known about God is able to be derived from human reason alone. The doctrine spread from Britain to the Continent and America, in spite of the countervailing impact of Bishop Joseph Butler's *Analogy of Religion* (1736) in Britain and Edwards' claims for a 'spiritual sense' of the heart. On the Continent, deism was advocated by Voltaire and Rousseau in France, and in America by Thomas Paine.

Finally, for the first time since the Hellenistic era, we find in the early modern period the philosophical development of forms of unbelief. This unbelief was found in various guises: unbelief in God's involvement in the created order; unbelief in God's revelation; unbelief in God as a personal being; and even the denial of the existence of God. From the time of the Reformation a new vocabulary emerged to describe various forms of unbelief. It is important, however, that one does not read the strict contemporary meaning of 'atheism' back into the early modern period, for the use of the term and its cognates was far looser then than it is today (see Hunter & Wootton 1992). The scepticism of Pierre Charron (1541–1603) and Montaigne, the materialism of Hobbes, the biblical criticism of Spinoza and his rejection of divine teleological agency, the deism of Pierre Bayle (1647–1706), Charles Blount and John Toland, Hume's critique of natural religion and the overt critique of religion by Baron d'Holbach (1723–89) are all important reference points for mapping the growth and articulation of unbelief as a disparate and yet in some sense progressive movement that contributed in a profound way to the secularization of Western societies in the modern era.

MORAL AND POLITICAL PHILOSOPHY[1]

Moral and political philosophy also made enormous advances in the early modern period. So rich and interwoven with religion were these developments that it is

1. A useful anthology of early modern writings on moral and political philosophy is Schneewind (1990).

difficult to prise them apart and to treat any theme in isolation from the others. Perhaps the best way to survey the manner in which early modern moral and political philosophy interlocked with religion is by an examination of three recurring themes. First, there is the tension between theories of free will and causal determinism and their implications for the problem of evil. Secondly, there is the manifestation of what moral philosophers often call 'the Euthyphro dilemma': the question as to whether the basis of morality is objective or determined by the divine will. Thirdly, there is the question of epistemic access to moral knowledge. Each of these issues arose again and again from the early Reformation in the writings of Erasmus (*c.*1466–1536), Luther and Calvin through to Kant at the end of the Enlightenment.

The question of the freedom of the will became particularly acute in the reformers' attempts to articulate the role of the will in the process of Christian salvation. In his *Bondage of the Will* (1525) Luther argued against Erasmus that the human will is incapable of choosing good and that it is free only in matters that are morally indifferent. Luther's motivation here was to preclude even the slightest hint that human beings might make some sort of contribution to their salvation, rather than to mark out a position in the debate over the compatibility of free will and determinism (Poppi 1988). Yet Luther's view of the impassivity of the will and Calvin's doctrine of predestination had serious theological and philosophical implications that were debated throughout the period.

Among Protestant theologians, the Arminians throughout the seventeenth century attempted to reconcile human freedom with divine providence by arguing for an ineliminable role for the will in salvation. Among the Catholics, Luis de Molina (1535–1600) and Francisco Suárez advanced a novel solution to the problem by claiming that God has a kind of 'middle knowledge'. That is, God knows what every possible free creature would freely do in every possible situation and that God causes circumstances in which he knows that we will freely act according to his plans. However, a significant number of the leading seventeenth-century philosophers were compatibilists about human freedom: they accepted that every event is causally determined and yet that human actions can be free. Descartes, Hobbes, Spinoza, Locke and Leibniz were all compatibilists of varying sophistication, and their writings, particularly those of Locke and Leibniz, are a fertile source of philosophical reflection on the issue of human freedom (Sleigh *et al.* 1998). Surprisingly, however, none of these philosophers, with the exception of Leibniz, gives extended treatment to the problem of evil and its consequences for the doctrine of freedom of the will. It is in the writings of Bayle and Voltaire's *Candide* (1759) that we find some of the most sustained discussion of the problem of evil in the eighteenth century.

The really distinctive feature of early modern moral and political philosophy, however, is the development of natural law theory. This provided the philosophical terms of reference for the emergence of early modern divine command theories and for theories of rights, sovereignty and international law. While natural law theory had a long pedigree in the Christian West stemming from the writings of Aquinas, it was only in the late sixteenth century that it became the dominant framework within which moral and political philosophy were discussed. Suárez, as in so many areas, made an important contribution to Catholic natural law theory, but it was the Protestant natural law theorists, beginning with Hugo Grotius (1583–1645), who dominated moral philosophy throughout much of the seventeenth and early eighteenth centuries. Hobbes, Nathaniel Culverwell (1619–51), Richard Cumberland (1631–1718) and Locke were the leading natural law theorists in England, while Samuel Pufendorf (1632–94) was a seminal influence in Germany and beyond. And this brings us to the second of the recurring themes in early modern moral philosophy, the Euthryphro dilemma.

Throughout the natural law tradition there is a recurring tension between those intellectualists, such as Grotius, who regarded the law of nature as arising out of human nature itself and the voluntarists, such as Suárez, who grounded the law of nature in the will of God. In fact, even among those philosophers whose moral thought was not developed within a natural law framework, such as the Cambridge Platonists Cudworth and Henry More, the issue was discussed in the most forthright terms. Cudworth was adamant that "it is universally true that things are what they are not by will but by nature", so that just as an omnipotent God cannot make white things black without changing their natures, neither can God arbitrarily make a just action unjust (Schneewind 1990: vol. 1, 279).

Most natural law theorists were in agreement that human reason could detect the moral law of nature unaided by revelation because it was founded in human nature itself, although for some the divine law found in Scripture was taken to be an important complement or short cut to moral knowledge. For others, divinely revealed law was absolutely necessary because of the corruption of human reason. Indeed, one of the core issues that concerned early modern natural law theorists was the relation between divine law, natural law and civil law. This issue naturally fed into the question as to the status of the sovereign and the sovereign's laws and the relation between church and state.

The early modern period witnessed the emergence of sovereign states, that is, territories ruled by a supreme authority. It also saw an extraordinarily intense and sustained debate about the justification, scope and powers of the sovereign. Of particular importance in these discussions was the relation between civil and ecclesiastical authority. Writing at the beginning of the sixteenth century, the secular Niccolò Machiavelli and the reformer Luther both sought to drive a wedge between secular and ecclesiastical power. Machiavelli was not opposed to religion *per se*, for it could be used by the prince to achieve the end of maintaining the state, just as it was so used in the Roman republic. However, to Machiavelli the Church of Rome had become corrupt and was partially responsible for the political ills of the city-states of the Italy of his day. Luther, too, was severely critical of the church of Rome, although his arguments for the radical separation between the two kingdoms of the people of God and the secular authority were theological rather than political or pragmatic. By stressing that civil authorities are instituted by God and by demarcating between their respective spheres of authority, Luther was able to articulate a political philosophy that had a profound impact on the actual development of relations between church and state throughout the early modern period. In his mature political theory he allowed the right to resist secular authority, while at the same time stressing the individual's political obligations under an authority instituted by God.

In Hobbes' discussion of the relation between civil and ecclesiastical authority in his *Leviathan* (1651) the emphasis shifts from God to the sovereign. The sovereign's power extends to the regulation of the worship of his subjects and determines uniformity in worship, a uniformity that is required to avoid interfaith and sectarian squabbles. The authority of the sovereign, for Hobbes, derives from a contract among all those who through their own self-interest seek to avoid the state of nature by forfeiting their right of nature to the sovereign. The final two parts of Hobbes' four-part work are given over to discussing the outworking of his political theory in a Christian commonwealth and the status of the present-day church. Surprisingly, for Hobbes, the very canonical authority of the Bible itself at any particular time derives from the sovereign who rules at that point in time.

But Hobbes' was not the only view of the origins of political authority in the seventeenth century. Robert Filmer (1588–1653) argued for the divine right of kings, claiming that the monarch had been delegated authority in an unbroken chain of patriarchal authority to Adam and originating in God himself. Locke, famously, attacked this view based on a close reading of the book of Genesis in the first of his *Two Treatises of Government* (published in 1690), and developed an alternative in his "Second Treatise". For Locke, universal consent is required to form political society and majority consent is required for the establishment of a sovereign. Like Hobbes, Locke develops his account of the formation of civil government by exploring the necessary and sufficient conditions required to pass from the state of nature to a safe and just society in which the rule of law is followed. But unlike Hobbes, Locke's theory is predicated on a concept of property that involves a right of disposal that is, in turn, limited by the law of nature instituted by God himself.

It may seem surprising to a twenty-first-century reader that these two leading early modern works on political philosophy should contain so many appeals to and discussions of biblical texts. There is no doubt that for both Hobbes and Locke the Bible provided a rich source of historical examples of the application of political principles. But could it provide more than that? This brings us to the third recurring theme of the moral and political philosophy of the period, namely, the sources of moral knowledge.

That Scripture could be a source of moral knowledge was the dominant view until the end of the seventeenth century, and yet there was heated disagreement as to what other sources of such knowledge were available. Locke, for his part, argued strongly against the existence of innate moral principles and claimed that human reason could deliver a demonstrative moral theory, although he never provided one. The question of our epistemic access to sources of moral knowledge and the law became particularly acute in the face of information gleaned from the New World, which revealed moral codes and mores that differed from those of Christianized Europe.[2] Fear of moral relativism and scepticism sharpened the debate. As confidence in the powers of human reason grew, however, it seemed to the deists that revelation was superfluous to the task of determining how to live well. Interestingly, in a development roughly simultaneous with the emergence of deism, some philosophers began to claim that the human understanding possessed a particular faculty or sensory power for experiencing moral sentiments. Beginning with the 3rd Earl of Shaftesbury (1671–1713), this moral sense theory reached its highpoint in the writings of Francis Hutcheson (1694–1746) in the 1720s.

Hutcheson sought to augment recent accounts of human moral psychology, and in particular the hedonism of Hobbes and Locke, by the addition of a moral sense. This is indicative of a broader shift within the early modern period in theories of moral knowledge and moral motivation from a largely theological context to a strongly psychologistic one. Where the reformers conceived of human propensities for moral action with reference to the doctrines of original sin and grace, by the mid- to late seventeenth century new conceptions of the understanding, and in particular new conceptions of the relation between reason and the passions, provided the locus within which theories of moral motivation were developed. The secular manifestation of this trend is seen in Hume's theory that desire alone can be the motivating reason for action. But far and away the most innovative account of moral motivation is Kant's discussion of the 'categorical imperative'. For Kant, a rational and autonomous agent will act on the categorical imperative irrespective of pre-existing desires or ends that they might have in mind. Moreover, reflection on and pursuit of the highest moral good, for Kant, rationally justify the belief that there is a God.

Questions of moral motivation in the sixteenth and seventeenth centuries were frequently set in the context of the examination of conscience and casuistry that was widely practised by Catholics and Protestants alike. Moreover, classical approaches to ethics, such as Aristotelian virtue ethics, Stoicism or Epicureanism, were widely read, but were evaluated and filtered through the lens of Christian ethics. By the end of the seventeenth century, however, moral philosophers had begun to discuss the manner in which it was possible for the non-religious or the unbeliever to become virtuous and, in particular, whether or not a virtuous society of atheists was possible. Following the lead of Bayle, it was argued by Shaftesbury, Hutcheson, Adam Smith (1723–90) and Thomas Reid that, contrary

2. For a recent study of reactions to moral and cultural diversity from Locke to Hutcheson, see Carey (2006).

to the Calvinist view, our moral sentiments are naturally inclined to virtue and this independently of religious belief (Harris 2003). For Bayle, the possibility of a whole society of virtuous atheists became an argument for toleration.

The issue of religious toleration was a particularly vexed one in the sixteenth and seventeenth centuries, given the ructions within Christendom and their political outworkings in the wars of religion. Among the important pro-tolerationists were Montaigne, Spinoza, Bayle and (the later) Locke. The latter's *Letter Concerning Toleration* (1689) is arguably the most important philosophical treatment of the issue before John Stuart Mill's *On Liberty* (1859).

HISTORY AND CREATION

In the early modern period there was much discussion about the origins, development and structure of the universe. One of the fruits of Aquinas' grafting of Aristotelian philosophy on to Christian theology was the ability to exploit all the advantages of Aristotelian cosmology and physics while retaining the biblical account of the origins of the universe. It was but a small step to accept the geocentric model of the universe (in which the earth is at the centre of a set of concentric spheres) and yet to say that the spheres had their origin in the creative word of God.

But Aristotle's was not the only Greek cosmological theory in play after the revival of ancient learning in the Renaissance. And from the late sixteenth century Epicurean atomism began to be taken up by philosophers and natural philosophers as one of a whole array of competing matter theories and cosmologies. The openness to new matter theories in the early seventeenth century was in part a result of the flowering of alchemy or 'chymistry', a flowering stimulated by the influential writings of the reformer of chymistry and pedagogy, popularly called Paracelsus (1493–1541). In the eyes of many, however, Epicureanism was tainted with atheism because of its account of the eternity of the universe, the chance formation of the current cosmological arrangement and its positing of a plurality of worlds.

It was not until the writings of the French philosopher Pierre Gassendi (1592–1655) that Epicurean atomism was 'baptized' and became a serious alternative to the plenist and continuist theories of the scholastics. Boyle, however, still felt the need to compose a work against Epicurean atheism in the 1670s, a work that remained unpublished in his lifetime (MacIntosh 2005: ch. 4). At a time when the predominant Aristotelian cosmology and its accompanying physics was under serious challenge as a result of the writings of Copernicus (1473–1543), Kepler (1571–1630) and Galileo, Descartes took it upon himself to provide a new cosmology and cosmogony. The Cartesian vortex theory, in effect, filled the placeholder that had been left by the failure of Aristotelian cosmology until the triumph of Newtonianism in the mid-eighteenth century. Descartes argued that the universe consists of an indefinite number of contiguous vortices or whirlpools of matter and at the centre of each vortex is a star. But this new theory had its own problems, not least because it did not appear to harmonize well with the Genesis account of creation. Thus, not only was Descartes' matter theory attacked for being inconsistent with the doctrine of transubstantiation, but his supposed unbiblical cosmogony cast serious doubt on the veracity of his whole system. Descartes' system was a stimulus to the emergence of a new genre of cosmological writing in England and France. Some of these writings defended Descartes' vortex theory and others offered cosmogonies and cosmologies of their own. Many, such as the Cambridge Platonist More and the neo-Cartesian Géraud de Cordemoy (1626–84), wrote with an eye to harmonizing the Cartesian cosmogony with the Genesis account (Harrison 2000).

Three other facets of the theory of the history of creation complement these speculative accounts of the formation of the world. First, there was renewed interest in the age of the earth and in the chronology of creation and human history. James Ussher (1581–1656), for example, on the basis of a literal interpretation of the Old Testament, calculated that the earth was created in the year 4004 BCE. Secondly, a natural concomitant to the interest in cosmogony and chronology were new theories of the history of salvation, including millenarian doctrines that flourished in the early to mid-seventeenth century. For example, in England in the 1640s the belief that the conversion of the Jews would usher in a new age had implications for the debate on religious toleration and led to utopian schemes for implementing the new science (Webster 2002). Thirdly, there was intense speculation in the seventeenth century about God's creation of species and the mechanisms of generation, that is, on the existence of protoplasts, seminal principles, preformation and spontaneous generation.

METAPHYSICS

Of all the philosophical disciplines, metaphysics underwent the most radical change during the early modern period. In the time of Luther and Calvin, scholastic Aristotelianism provided the basic resources for addressing the central problems of metaphysics: the nature of the soul; the theory of properties; cosmology and physics; the nature of God and angels; and so on. Just how developed scholastic metaphysics was at the beginning of the early modern period can be seen in the commentaries of the Coimbran school in Portugal that flourished in the sixteenth century. But this tradition of metaphysics found its hegemony eroded from the early decades of the seventeenth century. The last great scholastic metaphysician was the Jesuit Francisco Suárez, whose *Disputationes metaphysicae* (1597) was widely used and quoted throughout the seventeenth century. However, the advent of the new science, and in particular the mechanical philosophy as elaborated in the writings of Descartes, Gassendi, Hobbes and Boyle, brought profound change to all areas of metaphysical discussion. By the end of the early modern period many of the traditional scholastic ontological categories had changed: old metaphysical terms had been invested with new meaning. For example: the theory of properties had undergone a radical transformation; some core Christian metaphysical doctrines had been undermined or radically rearticulated; and new metaphysical questions were being asked, questions that had important theological implications.

In the order of being it is best to start with substance, that which depends on nothing for its existence and which is the bearer of properties or attributes. Throughout the early modern period almost all philosophers and theologians were committed to some form of substance/attribute ontology. Not only did the doctrine of substance lie at the heart of some of the central doctrines of Christianity, such as the doctrine of the Trinity and of the Eucharist, but it was also fundamental to the leading natural philosophies of the period ranging from scholastic Aristotelianism to mechanism. This is not to say, however, that the traditional ontological categories such as substance were not deployed in new and innovative ways. Descartes, for instance, argued for two radically different types of substance: material substance was defined by the essence of extension and thinking substance by the essence of thought. Locke took a rather deflationary line on our epistemic access to the nature of substance, claiming that apart from its role as a bearer and unifier of properties we can know nothing about it. Edward Stillingfleet responded to Locke by claiming that Locke had "almost discarded *Substance* out of the reasonable part of the World" (1697: 234), the implication being that since, according to Locke, we cannot have a clear and distinct idea of substance, it is a notion that is above reason. Spinoza and Leibniz developed radically different accounts of substance, the former identifying substance with God and positing a substantial monism, the latter arguing for a return to something akin to Aristotelian substantial forms and arguing for an infinity of soul-like substances or monads. George Berkeley and Hume, in turn, were severe critics of the doctrine of substance.

The theory of properties also saw important innovations in the early modern period, innovations that in some cases had deep ramifications for Christian theology. In fact, the mechanical philosophers achieved a complete reorientation of the theory of qualities. What on the Aristotelian scheme had been the *explanans* in the theory of qualities, the primary qualities (*primae qualitates*) of hot, cold, wet and dry, turned in the hands of the mechanical philosophers into the *explananda*: rather than hot, cold, wet and dry being used to explain the theory of elements and the accidental qualities of bodies, they became the subject of natural philosophical investigation themselves. In Locke's *Essay*, a new set of primary qualities was christened, the mechanical qualities of shape, size, motion and texture, and Locke's new primary and secondary quality distinction became the centrepiece of the post-Aristotelian theory of properties.

The theological implications of this shift surfaced early. For example, the matter theory of Descartes, including Descartes' denial of the intelligibility of real qualities, was seen as incompatible with the Catholic doctrine of transubstantiation and was the main motivation behind the listing of Descartes' works on the Catholic Church's *Index librorum prohibitorum* (List of prohibited books) in 1663 (Watson 1982). The reconciliation of the Cartesian matter theory with the doctrine of the Eucharist became a *desideratum* for some of the leading 'radical' Cartesians later in the seventeenth century (Schmaltz 2002). Real qualities were akin to junior substances (to use A. J. Ayer's phrase) that could exist while separated from a substance. They had been posited by Suárez and others in order to account for the persistence of the attributes of the bread and wine through the priestly act of consecration during the celebration of the Eucharist. Suárez also introduced the notion of modes as a new ontological category and this was taken up by Descartes, Boyle and others in their corpuscular matter theories.

The doctrines of substance and attributes did not exhaust the early modern ontological categories, for Gassendi argued that space itself was neither a substance nor an attribute but something of intermediate ontological status. Aristotelian and Cartesian physics had denied the possibility of empty space both beyond the world and within it. However, developments within the new philosophy in the work of Evangelista Torricelli (1608–47) and Boyle had deep implications for theories of space, which branched out to the doctrine of the omnipresence of God. This is witnessed in the way in which More's view that God is three-dimensional and extended throughout infinite space and that space inheres in God appears to have influenced Newton, who posited an absolute theory of infinite space (Grant 1981: 221–47). The issues of the absolute versus relative conceptions of space and the relation of space to God were later taken up in the debate on the nature of space in the Leibniz–Clarke correspondence, which contains a rich blend of natural philosophy and natural theology (Alexander 1956). Even more important was philosophical reflection on the nature of the soul in the early modern period. Luther and Calvin, like most Christian thinkers of the sixteenth century, accepted the tripartite division of the soul into vegetative, sensitive and rational souls. This division was a scholastic development of Aristotle's theory in his *On the Soul*. Descartes was the first of the leading early modern philosophers to change the terms of reference by which the soul came to be understood. Following a trend that had already developed in the late Renaissance, that of mechanizing animal physiology, Descartes attempted to give a fully mechanistic account of all the vegetative and sensitive functions of the material human body using explanations that ultimately referred only to extended substance and its modes and not to the soul. The rational soul, however, according to Descartes, was not reducible in these terms because it was immaterial.

A close reading of Descartes' theory, however, reveals a systematic ambiguity in the attribution of sensitive functions of the mind, such that they are attributed both to the body and to the rational soul. It has even been argued that Descartes' final position is not one of a mind–body dualism, but a form of trialism in which the mind–body union is a substantial one (Cottingham 1985). Regardless of how

Descartes is best interpreted, his substantial distinction between body and mind set the terms of reference for much of the ensuing debate over the nature of the soul in the early modern period. The theological implications of Descartes' theory were, on the whole, acceptable to Christian philosophers and theologians: after all, the theory could account for the soul's immortality and its identity over time, and it provided a clear demarcation line between human beings and animals – it was in virtue of the possession of a rational soul that human beings were in the image of God.

However, the theory also gave rise to some pressing problems. One consequence of Descartes' mechanistic analysis of animal physiology was the doctrine of the *bête machine*: the view that all animals are merely very sophisticated automata. This doctrine, in turn, prompted heated debate about the moral status of animals and our actions towards them. Another problem for Descartes' theory of the mind concerned mind–body interaction. Princess Elizabeth of Bohemia rightly sought from Descartes an account of just how an immaterial substance can causally interact with a material one. Did the soul have spatial location and if so where was it located? When was the soul implanted into the foetus and at what point did it leave the body? Was it reunited with the very same body at the resurrection or just a closely resembling one? Where were souls located between death and the resurrection? And so on. Hobbes' way out of the problem of interaction was to argue that the soul is material. Locke stressed our deep ignorance of the true nature of thinking substance and claimed that the case for 'thinking matter' was just as strong as that for thought being instantiated in an immaterial substance (Locke, *Essay* IV.iii). His comments became notorious and proved to be a major stimulus for reflection on the nature of the soul throughout the eighteenth century (Yolton 1983, 1991). It was only natural to follow Locke's suggestion and to generalize the Cartesian thesis of the *bête machine* to human beings. The man–machine doctrine as expounded by Diderot and Julien Offray de La Mettrie (1709–51) was seen by many as a legacy of Locke's view.

One positive doctrine to which Locke (and Hobbes before him) was committed was mortalism: the view that the soul dies when the body dies. Locke also contended that the resurrection body is not the same as the mortal body and that the identity of a person over time does not consist in any underlying substance, but in the identity of consciousness. Needless to say, each of these doctrines provoked reactions from the clergy. Stillingfleet attacked Locke's view of the resurrection, and Butler and Reid, in turn, raised famous objections against his account of personal identity.

The immaterial status of the soul might have been a hotly contested issue in the latter stages of the early modern period, but many philosophers and theologians throughout the period accepted the existence of other immaterial beings such as angels and demons. Indeed, interest in paranormal phenomena, miracles, witchcraft and second sight was widespread, and it is not difficult to find discussions of these issues in the writings of the leading philosophers of the age. Some philosophers argued from the great chain of being to the conclusion that creatures of higher epistemic, moral and ontological status are above human beings in the order of being. Great chain of being arguments were also used in early modern discussions of species and plenitude.

On the question of the nature of species, Aristotelian essentialism had been undermined at an empirical level by advances in the study of botany in the seventeenth century, and, in particular, what was called the degeneration of species. It was increasingly becoming clear that God had not made a determinate number of immutable species, but that species were, in many cases, variable and subject to ill-defined boundaries. This had implications not only for the doctrine of creation, but also for accounts of generation. Descartes, Malebranche, Locke and Leibniz all discussed the nature of generation with an eye to recent developments in natural philosophy (see Smith 2006). Debates over the nature of species continued well into the eighteenth century, most famously in the exchange between Carl Linnaeus (1707–78) and Comte de Buffon (1707–88).

The great chain of being and the question of plenitude came to the fore in the writings of Leibniz. In articulating his theory of possible worlds and his principle of sufficient reason, Leibniz opened a Pandora's box of issues in modality, teleology and the problem of evil. Where the mechanism of Descartes had, in effect, precluded knowledge of final causes from natural philosophy, Leibniz sought to reintroduce them at the most basic ontological level in his theory of formal atoms or monads. To be sure, Boyle had countered the Cartesian view of teleology in his earlier *A Disquisition about the Final Causes of Natural Things* (1688), arguing for teleology on the basis of the structural arrangement of natural objects. But in the philosophy of Leibniz, teleology was built into the most basic constituents of being, the monads themselves. This is another respect in which Leibniz's philosophy invoked a kind of neo-Aristotelian approach to nature, an approach that in turn had theological implications.

CONCLUSION

In many respects, however, Leibniz is the exception rather than the rule among early modern philosophers. For one of the salient shifts from the opening of the early modern period to its close is the shedding of many scholastic categories and, indeed, the superstructure of scholasticism itself. The intellectual worlds of Luther, Calvin and Suárez were markedly different from those, say, of Hume, Kant and Lessing, even if clear lines of development and influence can be traced from one end of the period to the other. Gone were the geocentric universe, the tripartite soul, the Aristotelian ontological categories. And where the old terminology remained, it was invested with new meanings and mobilized in new contexts. No doubt the creative interplay between theologically oriented philosophers and the new natural philosophy of the period played an important role here, but so did the multifarious changes and upheavals in the ecclesiastical and political power structures throughout the period.

The relations between philosophy and religion throughout the early modern period are, therefore, best characterized by the terms 'adaptation', 'innovation' and 'development'. The theistic proofs were reworked with great rigour, the theory of the soul was subject to radical changes, accounts of the relation between church and state were worked out in the harsh realities of the contingent political machinations of the period, and new philosophical debates emerged with deep theological implications, such as discussions of the nature of personal identity. In many cases these innovations and developments arose in response to specific issues in historical contexts, such as the Lisbon earthquake in 1755 that stimulated Voltaire's *Candide*. But the period is also replete with the fruits of abstract speculation and theorizing. The legacy of the early moderns' reflections on philosophy and religion may appear to have diminished in the post-Darwinian and more secularized age of the late nineteenth century and beyond. Yet the terms of reference and argument forms developed by the likes of Leibniz, Hume and others are still very much a part of the contemporary philosophical landscape. Currently, philosophical theology owes a debt to the thinkers of the early modern period. Perhaps it always will.

2

NICCOLÒ MACHIAVELLI

Mary G. Dietz and Ilya Winham

Some seventy-five years after the death of Niccolò Machiavelli (1469–1527), Francis Bacon lauded the author of *The Prince* and *The Discourses* for having the confidence to charge "in almost plain terms" that the Christian faith had left "good men" to the predations of those that are "tyrannical and unjust" (Bacon 2002: 363). That Machiavelli deserved credit for his writings on the political failures of Christianity was a view that other thinkers of Bacon's time and stature did not share; nor would it be the verdict of commentators for many centuries to come. In fact, on issues concerning religion, Christianity, morality and politics, Machiavelli was and "to some extent remains", as Najemy (1999: 659) observes, "a convenient scapegoat often blamed for the decline of religion in the modern world". Within Machiavelli studies, however, the question of the Florentine's view of religion is by no means settled, much less reducible to a version of paganism or devilish immorality. Rather, the religion question in Machiavelli remains a multifaceted problem eliciting among scholars a wide range of arguments, interpretations and debates. In what follows, we shall turn to Machiavelli's two most significant works of political theory, *The Prince* (1532) and, more extensively, *Discourses on the First Ten Books of Titus Livy* (1531), to assess the continuing scholarly interest and political significance of Machiavelli's treatment of religion.[1]

THE EXERCISE OF POWER AS THE RELIGION OF POLITICS: *THE PRINCE*

Machiavelli provides no extended discussion of religion in his most famous political work. Nevertheless, threaded through his allegedly immoral advice to princes are references that provoked later writers to condemn 'Machiavel' for desecrating

1. Translations from *The Prince* are taken from Machiavelli (1988), while translations from the *Discourses* are taken from Machiavelli (1970).

the supremacy of God's truth, the principles of Christian religion, the ethics of the Roman Church and the conduct of the godly ruler of the state.[2] In particular, *The Prince* registers two generally notorious points that privilege the pursuits of politics over the possession and exhibition of moral rectitude. The first point is related to the question of how rulers should keep their promises (XVIII). Machiavelli's answer famously elaborates the decisive argument begun in chapter XV, namely, that politics is a form of life wherein the principled practice of moral conduct can be catastrophic for the lives of princes and states, whereas vicious things may "strengthen one's position and cause one to flourish". Good deeds as well as bad may incur hatred, and the latter, once projected toward the prince, is devastating to maintaining the state (XIX). Thus in the political realm, a ruler who wishes to succeed cannot rely on being trustworthy but "must know how to act like a beast", always ready to break "peace treaties and promises" if he wishes to preserve the state (XVIII). Machiavelli allows that this advice would not be sound "if all men were upright"; but because they are not, a prince should not consider himself bound to keep promises to them. Furthermore, the basic circumstances of politics requires the ruler to keep the support of groups (whether nobles, soldiers or the people writ large) who may be irremediably base or corrupt, a compromising condition that makes "good deeds inimical" to the prince (XIX) and prohibits the possibility of his "living a completely virtuous life" (XV). In this realm, where a prince is often forced "to act treacherously, ruthlessly, or inhumanely", the precepts of religion must therefore be subordinated to prudent calculations of power if the principality is to survive (XVIII).

Bold as it is, Machiavelli's argument does not merely *register* the brute realities of politics; it also *recommends* behaviours that embrace cruelties, aggressions, deceptions and deceits as active expressions of princely acumen. The key term that *The Prince* innovates in order to capture the enactment of these princely capacities is *virtù*, the ability of the man (*vir*) of power to gain and maintain a state, achieving the goals of honour and glory. With this terminology to hand, Machiavelli abandons the governing assumption of classical humanism, namely, that princes must exemplify virtue (*virtus*) as honesty, exhibiting in full the four 'cardinal' traits of wisdom, justice, courage and temperance (Skinner 1981: 36). Even more notoriously, the primary tenets of Christian morality (e.g. goodness, piety, humility, faith, righteousness) are no longer privileged as the qualities required for princely success. In these shocking departures from the "methods of others" (XV), Machiavelli defies the entire genre of classical and contemporary humanisms, advising the *virtù*-ous prince to "be prepared" and "be capable" of acting irreligiously and immorally

2. See, for example, the *Anti-Machiavel* (1740) by Frederick of Prussia, for whom Machiavelli was "the enemy of mankind," and the earlier *Anti-Machiavel* (1576) by Innocent Gentillet, who argued that *The Prince* brought pernicious doctrines to France, perverting religion and policies of state. For contemporary accounts of Machiavelli as a "blasphemer" of Christianity, see Strauss (1958) and Mansfield (1979).

because the "winds of fortune" will require him to "be capable of entering upon the path of wrongdoing when this becomes necessary" (XVIII). Although *The Prince* allows that "it cannot be called virtue" to perform "treacherous, merciless, and irreligious" deeds as had Agathocles the Sicilian who gained power "but not glory" (VIII), Machiavelli steadfastly maintains that politics, if it were nothing more than the practice of Christian moral virtue, would not in fact be politics. In essence, the power of (Christian) religion, including its theological or scriptural significance, must be wholly subordinated to the religion of power. What power demands of political *virtù* is moral flexibility, not moral probity.

Machiavelli offers a second, even more notorious point about religion in the domain of politics. *The Prince* renders religion *complicit* with politics in a complex game of appearances, implicating it in the exercise of power as the effective exertion of mastery and control. Far from evacuating religious precepts *from* politics, Machiavelli incorporates them into the exercise of power, advising the prince to be "very careful" always to *display* five qualities of goodness: mercy, trustworthiness, humaneness, uprightness and devotion. Indeed, "it is most necessary of all to seem devout" (XVIII), since religious devotion upholds and sanctifies moral norms and popular values that secure the unity of the state. Not a blunt tool of mass control, religion is culturally and socially intricate, reflecting "a concern for a moral *fides* which, though certainly not transcendent, is nevertheless necessary to the construction of a political order based on *virtù*" (Fontana 1999: 657). Still, within this very same moral context, Machiavelli counsels the prince against "having and always cultivating" the five qualities, as opposed to being able to appear to have them and project them. If he does the former, his subjects will think him averse to or incapable of doing things that may be required to preserve the state. If he does the latter, he will know himself to be prudently prepared to do terrible things, while still remaining admired by all for his seeming goodness and devotion. On this Machiavellian political terrain, where "everyone can see what you appear to be, whereas few have direct experience of what you really are", we encounter a pragmatic approach to religiosity and moral character that places both in the service of the power and "the majesty of the ruler's position" (XVIII).

THE CRISIS OF REPUBLICS AND THE POLITICS OF RELIGION: THE *DISCOURSES*

Machiavelli's magnum opus, *Discourses on the First Ten Books of Titus Livy* (hereafter *Discourses*), presents his most direct and multifaceted observations on religion, past and present, material and symbolic. What emerges most clearly is religion's *secular* function in maintaining a civilized society and crafting the public spirit of the people in order to secure obedience to rule and the unity of the state. Machiavelli's "civil religion" is inspired by the pagan city built by Aeneas (I.1) and constituted through the laws, rituals and observances introduced by Romulus and

Numa, the rulers of ancient Rome. This complex of elements, whereby religion is theorized as a legislative device shorn of all Christian appurtenances, inspired by Roman paganism, and subjugated to the secular and political interests of the city, has led many commentators to characterize Machiavelli's view as oppositional if not hostile to Christianity (Strauss 1958; Berlin 1982; Hulliung 1983). Accordingly, the *Discourses* is taken to present "exclusively functional" or utilitarian calculations for securing the political order of rule (Preus 1979: 172). In this view, religion is, as Machiavelli himself allows, "the instrument necessary above all others for the maintenance of a civilized state" facilitating "whatever enterprise" that "great men" wish to undertake (I.11). However plausible, it would do disservice to the complexity of Machiavelli's analysis to reduce religion to a bare "political function". To appreciate the deeper significance that religion bears in Machiavelli's political thinking, we need to approach the *Discourses* as a historical interpretive project. Only on the historical field of modern Italian republics and on the political field of action is it possible to grasp Machiavelli's distinctive approach to religion.

Although Machiavelli begins the *Discourses* by acknowledging "the weak state to which the religion of today has brought the world", it is not modern Christianity as such that poses for him the deepest threat to freedom and effective political action. The danger he identifies is one more in keeping with a *hermeneutic deficit* that the *Discourses* seeks to rectify, namely, "the lack of a proper appreciation of history, owing to people failing to realize the significance of what they have read, and to their having no taste for the delicacies it comprises" (preface). The real crisis for modern republicans lies in their persistent failure to engage in the mental exercise of reading historical works of the past as guides for interpretation and action in the present. Responding to this deficit, Machiavelli seeks to induce in his readers a historico-political identification, reaching down to the deepest layers of solidarity, so they might discover new routes to "save the life and preserve the freedom" of their cities and states (III.41). The sense of present crisis that permeates the *Discourses* receives its most explicit articulation in II.2.2, where Machiavelli observes that Italian (Tuscan) cities (the most tarnished example is Florence) are burdened by "patterns of life" that have in fact weakened the entire world. Citizens are unable "to pull themselves together" to establish genuinely free constitutional regimes capable of invoking liberty against servitude and defending self-government so as to give tyranny no peace. The graveness of the present condition – where we see in the world "fewer republics than there used to be of old" (II.2.2) – demands that entrenched habits be broken and radically new measures of enquiry undertaken, before love of liberty is forgotten and servitude takes hold of all.

In noticing that what "history" has to say is "shunned by everybody", the *Discourses* resolves to confront contemporary vices through a recovery of contrastive events and circumstances from Italian antiquity (I, preface). The text nominally at the heart of this hermeneutic project is books I–X of Titus Livy's *History of Rome*; but the plan has nothing to do with producing either a memorial to the authority of Livy or another historical narrative of Rome (II, preface). What is really afoot in Machiavelli's text is an attempt to vitalize among living Italians a thinking awareness of "the harm that servitude has done to peoples and to cities" and to summon "the same love of liberty" that once animated the republics of old (II.2.2). Embarking on this "new way", Machiavelli forces an encounter between modern (Christian) Italy with ancient (pagan) Rome that will produce "practical lessons" for the political present (I, preface). Thus Machiavelli's history transgresses the dichotomy between Rome 'then' and Italy 'now' in service of thinking politically under the pressure of a contemporary moment "besmirched with filth of every kind" (II, preface). Let us turn, then, to Machiavelli's analysis of the role of ancient Roman and modern Christian religion as he imagines new routes, institutions and orders (*ordini nuovi*) for the "Tuscans of today" (II.4).

"OUR RELIGION" AND THEIRS

To suggest that modern Christianity is not for Machiavelli the primary problem posed to political freedom does not mean that he absolves it of blame. Indeed, *Discourses* II has barely begun before he turns to catalogue the irreducible differences between "bygone times" and "our religion" (II.2) in order to identify values and attitudes that make contemporary Italians weaker and less fond of liberty than were the pagan peoples of the republics of old. The fatal differences between "ours and theirs" can be figured in terms of their respective "highest goods": modern Christianity values humility, abnegation and contempt "for mundane things"; the pagan religion rewarded magnanimity, bodily strength "and everything else that conduces to make men very bold". Pagan rituals were suffused with ferocity and bloodletting, lacking neither pomp nor magnificence. Christian ceremonials are "delicate rather than imposing", lacking due regard for individuals "replete with worldly glory", such as the commanders of armies or the rulers of republics. The consequences of this lack can be readily observed on the contemporary field of battle, where Christian forces are so weak in discipline that they "can withstand but one attack". The ancients, by contrast, were schooled in the magnificence of their ferocious sacrifices and displays of courage, extraordinary in strength and *virtù*, their armies able to re-form three times during a battle and withstand multiple assaults (II.16).[3] In a comparative summation of these religious contexts worthy of Nietzsche's later insight into modernity's transvaluation of values (*see*

3. In *The Art of War*, Machiavelli has the commander Fabrizio Colonna observe that "the Christian religion has wrought such a change in the way of life and values of mankind" that peoples no longer defend themselves as they once did. The "terrible apprehensions" of slavery or death in the ancient world having passed, "men now no longer care to submit to the rigor and continual hardships of military discipline to ward off evils which they are but little afraid of". The "continual anxiety" once associated with military discipline has decreased, inclining states toward indolence. Petty states seek protection under the "wings

Vol. 4, Ch. 18, "Friedrich Nietzsche"), Machiavelli notes that what was considered strength in antiquity is now devalued, while what was formerly thought weakness is now revered as strength. "[I]f our religion demands that in you there be strength", he writes, "what it asks for is strength to suffer rather than strength to do bold things". The implications of this reversal, whereby one religion's valorization of strength as boldness is superseded by another's idealized conception of strength to suffer, carry considerable historical political significance for the citizens and soldiers of modern Italian republics.

Because all religions function as "a kind of education" (II.2.2) they produce orientations, attitudes and cultures of life that carry political consequences and generate profound worldly effects. Thus Christianity's glorification of humility and suffering as the willingness to bear injury and misfortune are not just *cultural* differences between ancients and moderns, between 'their' religion as a mode of life and 'ours'. The differences must also be assessed *politically*, against the backdrop of human history as a field of struggle and within a context where, as Machiavelli reminds all who will listen, men are "ungrateful, fickle, feigners and dissemblers, avoiders of danger, eager for gain" (*The Prince* XVII). Reviving a theme from *The Prince,* he contends that the religion that preaches (and practises) humility weakens the world and emasculates republics, ceding them to "the wicked" who are "well aware that the generality of men, with paradise for their goal, consider how best to bear, rather than how best to avenge, their injuries" (*Discourses* II.2.2). Worlds in which the vast majority of people abjure boldness and embrace suffering are ripe for domination by "men who are moved by their own appetites" (II.15), not the country's common good. To absorb this fact is to begin not only to challenge modern Christianity's paradisiacal transvaluation of values, but also to assert republican commitments to terrestrial self-governance, the rule of law and freedom from domination on earth.

Although in *Discourses* II.2.2 Machiavelli does not specify by name "the wicked" that prey on the weak of the world, it is evident elsewhere in the text (I.12) that this force is none other than the Roman Court. Against its "evil ways" and "bad example" he lodges two sardonic denunciations in the form of "debts" that Italians "owe" to the Church and its priests (I.12). First, the Italian people have become "more irreligious and perverse". Secondly, Italy is divided, "the prey not only of barbarian potentates, but of anyone who attacks it" (I.12). Priests educate their flocks to hold in contempt the very "mundane things" (*cose umane*) that they themselves covet and seek to control, provoking innumerable "inconveniences" and "disorders" (I.12) that inexorably sap the real religiosity of the Italian people and drain the strength of the Italian states. This *corrupting* condition is not simply a debilitating ethos born of ceremonials, rituals and sacrifices through which the

of the strong" and even the powerful ones are seemingly oblivious to, and thus unprepared for, "utter ruin" ([1521] 2001: 79–80).

Church counsels its sheep to disdain this-worldly things. It is the geopolitical fact of a temporal power of insufficient strength to unite Italy on its own, yet nonetheless strong enough to call on external powers to defend it against unruly people and city-states. The Court of Rome, as Machiavelli summarizes, "has neither been able to occupy the whole of Italy, nor has it allowed anyone else to occupy it". If it were possible to transport it to the territories of the Swiss (the only people of the present whom he regards as living "as the ancients did") it would cause "before long more disorders in that country" than anything else in its history or experience (*ibid.*).[4]

The impression that the *Discourses* is engaged in its own act of transvaluation whereby the Christian schema is coded 'bad' and the pagan schema re-encoded 'good' is further reinforced in II.5. There, Christianity's coming into being "*vis-à-vis* Paganism" is likened to the effects of "floods, pestilences and famines" that obliterate "the records of times gone by". Just as these forces purge whole generations and all knowledge of antiquity, Christianity "abolished all pagan institutions, all pagan rites, and destroyed the records of the theology of the ancients." Although Machiavelli acknowledges that the changes wrought by Christianity did no more to paganism than paganism did "to the religion that preceded it", he underscores how the "heads of the Christian religion" managed to destroy images and spoil everything else "that betokened in any way antiquity" (II.5) through a variety of ideological mystifications that obliterate the past. Their success in so doing has fashioned a population of survivors akin to "rude mountain-dwellers" who, although alive, possess no "knowledge of antiquity and so cannot hand it down to posterity". The hermeneutic strategy behind the *Discourses* is to undertake a project of historical knowledge recovery in order to pose a direct and educated challenge to the conventions and attitudes indoctrinated into the Italian people by the modern Roman Church.

THE CAUSE OF GREATNESS IN REPUBLICS

The restitution of knowledge of Roman paganism gets underway in book I, after eight discourses on the constitution of the Roman Republic (I.1–8) and a ninth in tribute to "the founders of kingdoms and republics": Moses, Lycurgus, Solon, Agis the King of Sparta and Romulus the founder of Rome (I.9). Machiavelli grants highest honour, however, to those leaders "who have played the chief part

4. An equally contemptuous critique of the temporal power of the papacy and the Roman Court appears in *The Prince*, chapter XI ("Ecclesiastical Principalities"). Given that the ecclesiastical principalities are sustained "by ancient religious institutions" that maintain their rulers in office no matter how they act, Machiavelli treats them outside the "inventory" (Althusser 1999: 69–70) of principalities deserving attention. In essence, they pose no interesting questions in history about either *virtù* or luck.

in founding a religion" (I.10). In the case of Rome this order of rank belongs to the priestly king Numa Pompilius, who is credited with taming a "ferocious" people with "the instrument necessary above all others for the maintenance of a civilized state" (I.11). At issue is neither the theological nor the doctrinal dimensions of the Roman religion, but rather how Numa deployed this "instrument" as a finely honed secularized device, utilizing "the fear of God" and the "appeal to divine authority" to keep the people in thrall. These strategic manipulations made it easy to "impress on [the people] any new form" of institutions required for the preservation of the state (I.11). Machiavelli in turn deploys Numa to interpret for his readers how pagan religion provided the resources for sustaining in the Roman people strength of devotion to the sacredness of their body politic. Numa fortified Romulus' act of founding by directing the populace's allegiance towards a higher, immortal, authority in such a way that bound them to the laws and institutions of the Roman state. Having made the point that the innovations introduced by Numa must be considered among "the primary causes of Rome's success", Machiavelli leaps to insist that as "the observance of divine worship", religion is "the cause of greatness in republics" (I.11). The *Discourses*' (considerably edited and condensed)[5] appropriation of Livy's interpretation of Numa allows us to specify two features of the Roman religion that are of particular significance for the practical lessons Machiavelli wishes his contemporaries to draw concerning the cause of the origin of the greatness of the Roman republic. The first feature is religion's function as an instrument of discipline directed toward insuring the republic's political and military *virtù*. The second is its embodiment as a repository of certain values, feelings and dispositions that generate good conduct in the people and foster cultural unity and civic *virtù*.

Machiavelli does not underestimate the extent to which religion (whether archaic or modern) functions as a disciplinary mechanism to induce the populace to consent to existing relations of power, accept military and executive decrees, obey legal–juridical regulations and submit voluntarily to various forms of repression. Thus Numa enabled "whatever enterprise the senate and the great men of Rome designed to undertake" (I.1) by manipulating the effects of religious ceremonies and rituals. To further this point, *Discourses* I.13 appropriates Livy to emphasize how the Roman nobility effectively played on the plebeians' fear of the gods to "remedy" potential threats that the consular power of the tribunes posed to the rule of elites. Through the seizure and deployment of various means of divination and communication, including the interpretation of oracles and the sacred Sibylline books, the swearing of oaths to the gods, the diagnosis of auspices and the expounding of auguries, the nobles were able to manipulate the plebeians'

5. Entirely eliminated from Machiavelli's interpretation is Livy's repeated characterization of Numa (in contrast to Romulus) as the "jealous guardian of *peace* even more than of power", which he considers "the grandest achievement of [Numa's] reign" (Livy 1960: 55, emphasis added).

"reverence for religion" to secure their acquiescence to decisions that the tribunes themselves adamantly opposed. Such was the case with the deferral of the question of the Terentillian law (I.13). Machiavelli appreciates, as Althusser observes, how religion operates as "part of state ideology, not to say an *ideological state apparatus*" (1999: 92), infusing into the populace certain ways of thinking that contribute to the well-being of the republic's institutional organs of order and control (I.14).

Nowhere is religion's ideological function as a disciplinary mode of education more vital or important to the state than in matters pertaining to the prosecution of war. This includes the inculcation of *virtù* and discipline (*disciplina*) in those who follow in the profession of arms. Without military power, as Machiavelli notes in *The Art of War*, "the best ordinances in the world will be despised and trampled under foot" (2001: 4). Archaic religion offers examples of how military commanders instilled discipline by means of rites and ceremonies that harnessed "ferocity" and fostered in soldiers "an obstinate will to conquer" (*Discourses* I.15). Religion was used by Roman generals in the siege of Veii "in order to keep the troops keyed up for attack" (I.13). Auguries, "in large part the basis of the ancient religion of the gentiles", were also conjured to order the army to fall in for battle (I.14).[6] Just as the nobles of Rome appealed to divine authority to command popular opinion and channel the passions of the plebs, so the Roman commanders would never set forth on an expedition "until they had convinced the troops that the gods had promised them victory" (I.14). In both contexts, Machiavelli provides an account of the Roman pagan religion that underscores its earthly instrumentality and its practical political utility. When effectively operationalized, religion achieved a *double disciplinary effect*: it converted a potentially unruly populace into *citizens* obedient to the rule of aristocratic nobility and *soldiers* regimented and organized under the command of the state.

Notwithstanding its prodigious disciplinary properties, Roman religion in Machiavelli's analysis does not reduce to "a mere tool in the hands of the political rulers" (Cassirer 1946: 138). It serves a second earthly function by creating powerful forces for "producing good men" and "shaming the bad" (I.11), thereby keeping the republic "good and united" (I.12). Primary among these forces were means of interpretation and communication in the form of oracles and "a body of soothsayers and diviners" that transmitted messages from the gods and generated the activity of belief in miracles and divine worship. People were led to believe

6. The *Discourses* offers an example of the malleability of religious symbols in its account (I.14) of when the Roman general Papirius strategically managed the portents of religion on the field of battle, in the affair of the fraud perpetrated by the chicken-handlers (*pullarii*). Machiavelli interprets Papirius's actions "by attributing to him the motive of making 'the result correspond to the prophecy'", acknowledging that the consul knew "full well how to fit his plans to the auspices" (Najemy 1999: 676), thereby appearing to honour religious precepts while at the same time manipulating them.

that a god who can predict your future "could also bring it about" (I.12). On this psychological foundation of tremulous anticipation arose great temples in which "the gods were venerated by sacrifices, supplications and ceremonies of all kinds". A society induced to worship the divine thereby produces people who habituate themselves to "wonder and devotion": dispositions that productively harness unbridled ferocities and aggressions while strengthening the nation's moral fibre. Thus "respect for religion" promulgates habits of "goodness" and "good conduct", which are in turn reinvested in divine observances (I.55). Machiavelli offers an example of precisely this sort of habituation in a story linked to the Roman army's sacking of the city of Veii. On entering the temple of Juno, the Romans "did not create a disturbance but behaved devoutly and displayed the greatest reverence", asking the divine image, "*Do you want to come to Rome?*". To all of them the goddess seemed to answer yes because "the men were so deeply imbued with religion" that it seemed to them that they "heard the answer they wanted the goddess to give and had taken for granted when they approached her" (I.12). Geared toward certain choices and outcomes through the inculcations of divine worship, the soldiers of Rome performed acts of "good conduct" of the sort to which they had been habituated through ritualized exercises of veneration of the gods. However deeply internalized such dispositions toward goodness may have been, Machiavelli nevertheless reminds us that they were "studiously fostered and encouraged" by the rulers and commanders of Rome (I.12). Hence even when functioning well as a repository for moral values, the pagan religion operated as an instrument for controlling the passions of the people and the army, in order to promote the greatness of the Roman republic.

INTERPRETING RELIGION

The extended treatment that Machiavelli gives to the religion of the Romans in *Discourses* I demonstrates his "pragmatic approach" (Skinner 1981) to the power of religion as a political, cultural and social force. What is far less certain among scholars is whether he considered religion indispensable to politics, thus anticipating a return to the pagan religion of Rome as an antidote to the crisis of republics in his own time. If the latter is the case, then the *Discourses*' project of knowledge recovery of antiquity might be a subversive scheme intent on wiping out all of the appurtenances of Christianity so as better to advance worldly republican goals. On this question (as on many others) Machiavelli scholars disagree, variously contending that the Florentine is: (i) admiring of the salutary political effects of Roman paganism while relentlessly hostile to Christianity (Pocock 1975; Berlin 1982; Hulliung 1983); (ii) positively disposed toward transforming Christianity into a new and superior conception of the world (Viroli 1998; Fontana 1999); (iii) alert to the "pernicious" effects of both ancient pagan and modern Christian religions and attuned toward the construction of a hybridized "third

Rome" (Sullivan 1996); (iv) secularizing Christianity for a world where politics and religion are now separated (Vatter 2000); or (v) revitalizing the ancient virtue of Roman modes and orders but uncertain about what to do with the existing Christian ones (Coby 1999). Without attempting to adjudicate these various interpretive disagreements, we might note the significance that *interpretation itself* plays for Machiavelli's appropriation of Livy's text and his treatment of religion in the *Discourses*.

If we accept the possibility that the *Discourses* is not simply a homage to Livy's history of Rome's past but rather a *hermeneutically strategic project* aimed at changing things in the Italian present, then we might imagine the text also wishing for results that are realistically located in sixteenth-century modern Italian republics and able to alter the balance of forces that define and dominate them. Facing this pressing political imperative, Machiavelli apprehends Christianity quite literally and terrestrially, as "our religion", a material historical possession of the people, desperately in need of a different mode of interpretation and means of communication.[7] From this starting-point Machiavelli approaches Italy's religious code of Christian values not as transcendent or fixed in stone but instead as subjected over time to distortion and "the pusillanimity of those who have interpreted [it] in terms of *laissez faire*, not in terms of *virtù*" (II.2). Thus "our religion" does not *have* to be interpreted in terms hostile to the pagan virtues of bodily strength, magnanimity, boldness and valour, but can in fact be resuscitated by way of a solidarity forged with the Roman past and secured by republican *virtù*. In its active creating of an affinity between the living and the dead, contemporaneity and antiquity, ours and theirs, the *Discourses* endeavours to defeat the hegemonic interpretation of the Roman Court which has forced Christians into complicity with a debilitating "pattern of life" (*d'ozio*) (II.2). Indeed, the catalogue of moral values and attitudes that Machiavelli enumerates as aspects of the weakness of the modern Christian way of life are the effluvia of the "grave misinterpretations" (II.2) of popes, prelates and priests, that bear no necessary relationship to the people. Accordingly, Machiavelli offers present-day Italians the chance to free Christianity from its domination by imbuing it with the *virtù* that is a recoverable part of its own national historical past. At this interpretive conjuncture of present and past, Italian republicans can imagine a Christianity of *virtù* that, with all the powers of pagan antiquity, induces modern citizens "to love and honour" their countries and train themselves to provide for their defence (II.2).

7. Machiavelli brackets many issues that form key elements of early modern Anglo-European political thought and circulate around questions of natural law, natural right and moral and political legitimacy. He does not attempt to adjudicate or even raise the question of whether citizens are morally obligated to obey a sovereign power that violates the divine laws of God or the precepts of Christianity. A sovereign power that generates such questions has already lost its effectiveness by failing to harness religion in such a way as to elicit popular support, obedience and consent.

Thus Machiavelli insists on the necessity for all republics to return from time to time to the "original principles" of their religious and state institutions in order to achieve renovations and reconstitutions for the good of each. St Francis and St Dominic previously restored to strength the weakened moral fibre of the religion of Christianity in Italy, convincing the populace that "it is an evil thing to talk evilly of evil doing" and if they did otherwise "it must be left to God to chastise them" (III.1). Actively reinvesting the higher power of God's immortal authority and reinterpreting Christian values and attitudes, Francis and Dominic in effect revived them, even in the minds of those Italians who were convinced that their religion was dead.[8]

That Machiavelli does not pursue in any depth what a reinterpreted Christianity, shorn of its "effeminacy" and powerlessness, requires in order to imbue it with a commitment to *patria* and power is perhaps an indication of the hermeneutic project's defeat in the face of the impenetrable reality of the victorious and corrupting domination of Italy under the Church of Rome. Perhaps also at issue, thanks to the Court of Rome, is the ecclesiastical calcification of Christianity's hermeneutic flexibility, the diminishment of its capacities as a religion to embrace alternative political worlds. Or perhaps the problem that besets the *Discourses* has less to do with the exhaustion of Christianity in Italy than with the lack of any fertile political ground in Tuscany from out of which a new religion could grow, encouraging citizens to love their native cities more than their souls, as Machiavelli professes of himself. With that bleak possibility before his eyes, Machiavelli faces up to the reality that, notwithstanding their damaging effects, the "grave misinterpretations" of Christianity were not, in fact, what brought an end to the love of liberty that had exemplified the ancient, "obstinate" and "well-armed" Tuscan states. In truth, the Roman Empire itself, "with its armed forces and its grandiose ideas", wiped out these republics, leaving behind peoples who have not been able "to pull themselves together" since then (II.2). The Roman pagan religion that Machiavelli so deeply admires is also that which brings to an end the liberty of the Tuscan republics that he loves. From out of these extreme conditions of conquest and defeat an ameliorative religion emerged, eschewing politics and all objects of this-worldly attachment, and counselling quietude and acceptance of what Machiavelli calls "the servitude that now is" (II.2).

8. A recommendation to imitate St Francis (and St Jerome), who "undertook to mortify the flesh and so prevent it from forcing them into evildoing", also appears in "The Exhortation to Penitence", Machiavelli's (undated) discourse to a Florentine religious society, perhaps the Company of Piety into which he was inducted in 1495. To escape "the gripe of the devil", Machiavelli advises, "we must have recourse to penitence … we must weep bitterly, and repent of all the faults we have committed" (1992: 122). The address ends by invoking Petrarch in tones considerably different from those that conclude *The Prince* (XXVI): "Repent and tune ourselves to this one theme/That worldly pleasure is a short-lived dream" (*ibid.*).

Against the horizon of nearly non-existent civic freedom and republican citizenship in Italy, the best a reinterpreted Christian religion might be able to do is help shape the moral selves of private persons as members of modern secular states. Without doubt this is not a situation that Machiavelli would have embraced. He would have nevertheless insisted on keeping all religion open to interpretation, while holding fast to the thought that it is "beyond question" that only in republics is the common good looked to properly and "all that promotes it is carried out" (II.2).

FURTHER READING

Boyle, M. 2004. "Machiavelli and the Politics of Grace". *MLN Italian Issue Supplement* **119**: 224–46.

Colish, M. 1999. "Republicanism, Religion, and Machiavelli's Savonarolan Moment". *Journal of the History of Ideas* **60**: 597–616.

De Grazia, S. 1989. *Machiavelli in Hell.* Princeton, NJ: Princeton University Press.

Dietz, M. 1986. "Trapping the Prince: Machiavelli and the Politics of Deception". *American Political Science Review* **80**: 777–99.

Kahn, V. 1994. *Machiavellian Rhetoric: From the Counter-Reformation to Milton.* Princeton, NJ: Princeton University Press.

Lefort, C. 1990. "Machiavelli: History, Politics, Discourse". In *The States of "Theory"*, D. Carroll (ed.), 113–24. New York: Columbia University Press.

Nederman, C. 1999. "Amazing Grace: Fortune, God, and Free Will in Machiavelli's Thought". *Journal of the History of Ideas* **60**: 617–38.

Pitkin, H. 1999. *Fortune is a Woman: Gender and Politics in the Thought of Niccolò Machiavelli: With a New Afterword.* Chicago, IL: University of Chicago Press.

Prezzolini, G. 1970. "The Christian Roots of Machiavelli's Moral Pessimism". *Review of National Literatures* **1**: 26–37.

Wright, P. 2005. "Machiavelli's *City of God*: Civic Humanism and Augustinian Terror". In *Augustine and Politics*, J. Doody, K. Hughes & K. Paffenroth (eds), 297–336. New York: Lexington Books.

On MORALITY see also Chs 8, 12, 14, 21, 22; Vol. 2, Ch. 12; Vol. 4, Chs 4, 12, 18; Vol. 5, Ch. 6. On PAGANISM see also Vol. 2. Ch. 8. On POLITICS see also Ch. 11. On SOCIETY see also Vol. 4, Chs 14, 21; Vol. 5, Ch. 4.

3

MARTIN LUTHER

Theodor Dieter

Martin Luther (1483–1546) was a Christian theologian through and through. For Luther, this meant focusing all theological work on God's revelation in Jesus Christ: "in the crucified Christ there is true theology and knowledge of God" (WA 1: 362,18–19; LW 31: 53).[1] Thus one cannot expect to find in his work a philosophy of religion in a narrow sense, a general theory of God or a concept of religious consciousness that does not explicitly refer to the revelation of God in Jesus Christ. However, one will encounter in Luther's thought a highly elaborate and sophisticated self-interpretation of Christian faith that demonstrates a number of both creative and conflictive interactions between theology and philosophy. This study will focus primarily on this interface.

According to Luther's understanding, the essence of theology is interpretation of the Bible. In Luther's time, this book was viewed as the singular authoritative horizon for the construction of human self-understanding. Thus Luther's fresh interpretation of crucial aspects of Holy Scripture deeply changed the self-interpretation of many of his contemporaries, and, what is more, made world history. The Lutheran reformation originated in the university, and therefore Luther's theology developed through critical engagement with a variety of traditions: scholastic (especially Ockhamist), mystical, humanist and Augustinian. The university was the institutional setting within which theology, understood as a rational account of the Christian faith, interacted with the findings and claims of philosophy. Nevertheless, Luther had become convinced that the comprehensive reception of philosophical thoughts in theology during the Middle Ages made it difficult for Christian theologians adequately to present the truth expressed in the biblical texts. Aristotle was the main target of his criticism, but in his critical comments on 'Aristotle' or 'reason',

1. The following abbreviations are used for Luther's works: WA, *D. Martin Luthers Werke: Kritische Gesamtausgabe* (Luther 1883–2005), cited by volume, page and line numbers; LW, *Luther's Works*, American Edition (Luther 1955–86), cited by volume and page numbers.

Luther had a number of different things in mind: (i) philosophical propositions and concepts that one can find in Aristotle's writings; (ii) medieval interpretations of Aristotelian texts; (iii) theological doctrines that assimilated Aristotelian propositions and concepts; and (iv) institutional 'Aristotelianism' – the organization of academic education and learning in late medieval times. These four meanings of 'Aristotle' must be carefully distinguished (Dieter 2001). This chapter intends to show, first, some aspects of Luther's approach to the doctrines of God and humanity and to the complex cluster of problems associated with God's relation to human beings, and, secondly, Luther's evaluation of the conflicts between theology and philosophy and his theological deployment of philosophical insights and methods in theology (White 1994).

A COMMON CONCEPT OF GOD

According to Luther, all human beings have knowledge of the existence and nature of God. This is evident, he argues, in the normal human response to situations of emergency: namely, the turning to God for help. This shows that, in common human experience, God is considered to be a being from whom persons can expect help or from whom they might hope to receive good things. Nevertheless, people are quite uncertain *who* this being is and *how* they can gain access to him. In his *Large Catechism*, Luther states: "A 'god' is the term for that to which we are to look for all good and in which we are to find refuge in all need. Therefore, to have a god is nothing else than to trust and believe in that one with your whole heart … For these two belong together, faith and God" (Kolb & Wengert 2000: 386).

This understanding has far-reaching consequences. According to Luther, the basic religious relation to God is trusting, rather than thinking or willing (acting), though trusting of course involves cognition and leads to willing and acting. Thus Luther is not very interested in arguments for the existence of God. This also means that Luther does not deal only with *God in himself*, but rather always considers the *relation* both of God to human beings and of human beings to God:

> Anything on which your heart relies and depends, I say, that is really your God. (*Ibid.*)

> It is the trust and faith of the heart alone that make both God and an idol. If your faith and trust are right, then your God is the true one. Conversely, where your trust is false and wrong, there you do not have the true God. (*Ibid.*)

Whether a trust is right or false depends on whether the 'object' of this trust is the true God. But the fact that an object can be called 'God' is always related to a person, and, more precisely, to that person's trust.

Thus Luther's theology must be called 'existential' in so far as he focuses not only on the truth of propositions but also on the truth of the persons who hold true propositions. He is concerned with the fact that, and the manner in which, persons relate their lives both to those true propositions and to that to which those propositions refer. The 'I' of thinking is always present in a reflective way in Luther's considerations of theological matters. What God is *in himself* he should also become *for me* (*pro me*). The question of the identity of God is therefore the question of who or what ultimately defines basic human self-understanding and basic trust.

TWO TYPES OF THEOLOGY: THEOLOGY OF GLORY AND THEOLOGY OF THE CROSS

In his *Heidelberg Disputation* (1518), the young Luther distinguishes two types of theology: the theology of glory and the theology of the cross (WA 1: 361,31–363,37; LW 31: 52–5). As the first two of the twelve philosophical theses of this disputation (WA 59: 409,1–410,12) reveal, Luther insists that philosophy must be treated in the same way as the theology of glory. Without the theology of the cross, Luther says, the human being uses even the best goods in the worst way (WA 1: 363,25–6; LW 31: 55). This indicates that the two contrasting theologies do not merely have different contents and methods, but rather represent different ways of existing altogether.

A widespread conviction among scholastic theologians was that the human being who loves the higher good more than the lesser good is able also to love the highest good – God – most and above all. They thus conceived of an ascent from the good to the better and finally to the *summum bonum*. The one who loves his native country more than his life, for example, will be able to transcend self-love in order to arrive at a love of God for God's sake. Many scholastics accordingly interpreted the apostle Paul's assertion that the invisible God is known to all human beings (Romans 1:19–20) in the following way. In creation we perceive God as *our good*, but from what is created we come to a knowledge of the goodness of God *in himself*. But what is true for cognition is also true for love, and, therefore, whereas human beings often love God *for their own sake*, they are able to follow the way of cognition, overcome their self-love and love God *for God's sake*. Luther, however, observed that Paul in fact states that human beings, while knowing of God's divinity, have not acknowledged God as God. Luther therefore asserts: "By nature, a human being is not able to will that God is God, rather he or she wills that he or she is God and God is not God" (WA 1: 225,1–2; LW 31: 10). That God is the final goal of one's life is both a religious and a metaphysical requirement. A human being who does not love God as his or her final goal will see himself or herself as the final goal and thus seek his or her own interest in everything. This is to be understood in a *transmoral* sense, not as the moral accusation of egoism. For human beings can and do seek their own interests even through good moral agency, for example by applauding themselves for their moral accomplishments. In addition to biblical argumentation, Luther offers numerous other examples from human life to demonstrate that this is true. This cluster of issues leads to one basic definition of sin offered by Luther: sin is seeking one's interest in everything. When people seek their own interest in everything they will also use God, the highest good, for their own sake.

But, Luther insists, God refuses to be used by human beings in this way, and instead reveals himself to them in the crucified Christ: the *summum bonum* at the cross! This is the crisis for all who wish to appropriate God for their own sake. God hides himself, but not simply so. While human beings attribute strength, wisdom and all other perfections to God, God is in fact present in the weakness, foolishness and so on that human beings experience. Just so, God hides himself in his opposite (*sub contrario*). Thus, either a human being turns away from such a God, or his or her striving and willing will be changed. Such a change cannot be a matter of human decision, since human striving and willing is determined by self-seeking in everything. Thus the transformation of a human being can happen only in suffering and passivity.

Luther applies this argument to both theologians and philosophers. For him, the Aristotelian concept of happiness as the final goal of human beings (*see* Vol. 1, Ch. 5, "Aristotle") conceptualizes the self-seeking character of human beings. Philosophical activity is a good, and this activity becomes better the higher the value of its object(s). Again, when God is viewed as the highest object of cognition, this activity becomes the most valuable human enterprise. God, as the highest object of love and the highest object of knowledge, appears to be the highest realization of human self-love. But there is the inner contradiction in this line of thought in so far as the metaphysical concept of the highest good requires that God is loved for his own sake and not for the sake of human self-realization. Luther's theology of the cross, following the understanding of the apostle Paul, recognizes this inner contradiction and offers an alternative.

In his lecture of the Summer Semester 1921 ("Augustine and Neoplatonism"), Martin Heidegger, referring to the above-mentioned passage from Romans 1:20, offered the following analysis:

> For the early Fathers [of the Church], this text provided a Pauline confirmation for a graded Platonic ascent in thought from the sensory to the supersensory world. But this is a basic misunderstanding. The young Luther was the first to see what the text really means in its own context (Romans 1:20–23), and so opened up the possibility for a renewed understanding of primitive Christianity and a return to the original Christian life. The theses of his Heidelberg Disputation (1518) likewise provide crucial insights into the long-standing historical relationship over the centuries between Christianity and culture.
>
> (Heidegger 1995: 281–2; trans. in Kisiel 1993: 206)

JUSTIFICATION AND FREEDOM

Luther is known as the theologian who developed a doctrine of justification that is radically oriented to God's grace and its correspondence in human faith. He claimed that this doctrine of justification is the true centre of theology. This created serious conflicts with other, more traditional theologians. In addition, Luther regarded this doctrine as being in conflict with philosophy, in particular concerning the understanding of and relation between the person and his or her acts. It is not very easy to understand this aspect of Luther's criticism primarily because he perceives philosophy from a theological point of view and thus expects philosophy to make theological claims. For the most part philosophy does not do this. However, in Luther's time many elements of moral philosophy were integrated into theological systems, and Luther's criticism makes sense, particularly in regard to these philosophical–theological systems.

Moreover, when Luther uses the term 'reason' he often has in mind the everyday self-understanding of human beings and not a particular faculty of the soul or a philosophical concept. According to Luther, these beings are in need of 'justifying' their own existence. They must relate to themselves, either by accepting or by denying themselves. They respond, so to speak, to the question: why *am* I, rather than *not* at all? Luther distinguishes between three different contexts or forums before which human beings practise this justification: the forum before oneself (*coram seipso*); the forum before other human beings (*coram hominibus*); and the forum before God (*coram Deo*). With reference to these forums, judgements are made about what persons are and what they desire, will and do. The criteria for making, and the structures of, judgements in these forums are quite different. Acts that seem to be good in the eyes of others may appear quite differently in one's conscience; acts that seem to be morally good according to the judgement of one's conscience may be bad or sinful in a theological perspective. Offering such distinctions is quite typical of Luther, for he wishes to take seriously the complexity of reality and to clarify and safeguard the distinctive character of theology.

This structural motif of Luther's theology is quite important for understanding his doctrine of justification. We consider a human judge to be just when he or she punishes the evildoer and rewards the doer of good (*iustitia distributiva*). It is Luther's decisive theological insight that God's 'justice' or 'righteousness' is quite different from that of a human judge. The righteousness of God is a *communicative* divine attribute: God is righteous in that he conveys his righteousness to human persons so that they themselves, in receiving this righteousness, also become righteous. In his *Treatise on Christian Liberty*, Luther examines mystical traditions in order to describe justification. He expresses the relation between the soul and Christ with the image of a marriage between the two, with faith being the wedding ring. According to marriage laws, the possessions of the bridegroom become the possessions of the bride, and vice versa. In the case of justification, the possession of the bridegroom is righteousness, while the possessions of the bride are her sins. In this marriage, the soul receives the bridegroom's righteousness and loses her sins. Thus freedom is established, since there is no obligation to work in order to realize justification. Righteousness is not the result of one or many appropriate acts, as Luther is convinced that philosophers hold; rather, it is a gift that the person can only receive. "A Christian is a perfectly free lord of all, subject to none" (WA 7: 49,22–3; LW 31: 344). Being liberated from the need to justify oneself, the person spontaneously acts for the sake of the good alone or for the sake of one's neighbour's needs. Thus, for Luther, love and the 'servitude' of love correspond to the freedom of faith.

This mystical image illustrates a conceptual structure commonly found in Luther's thought. He conceives of unities between two entities (e.g. Christ and soul) that can also be seen in and for themselves, but, in the context of unity, mutually determine each other so that a communication of their respective properties takes place. The unity does not therefore consist of an addition or an aggregation of separate entities, but is rather a real unity realized in the exchange of properties. It is precisely this perceiving of the human person in relation to Christ that shapes Luther's theological approach to anthropology. This relation is not something additional to human being but is rather constitutive for human being (even if the individual negates this relation). 'Freedom' here signifies something different from freedom as the property of will and choice that is the subject of philosophy.

PHILOSOPHY AND THEOLOGICAL ANTHROPOLOGY

In the disputation *De homine* (On humankind), Luther defines the relation between theology and philosophy with regard to anthropology as follows. Philosophy places the human being as *animal rationale* in the horizon of all animals from which the human being differs by possessing reason. Thus the topic of philosophy is the *mortal* human being or the human being of *this* life. Accordingly, it is reason that receives Luther's highest praise as something quasi-divine, concerning the relation of human beings to the world. He understands reason as the "inventor and guide (*inventrix et gubernatrix*) of all arts, medicine, law, and whatever in this life of wisdom, power, virtue and glory is possessed by human beings" (WA 39I: 175,11–13). This perception of the achievements of reason corresponds to the biblical creation account that describes the human being as a ruler over the non-human animals. Nevertheless, what philosophy does not recognize are – and here Luther uses the model of the four causes – the effective cause (the creator) and the final cause, since it sees as the goal of human beings only 'the peace of this life'. That philosophers are far from a consensus in knowing the human soul indicates that they understand the formal cause in an insufficient way, since only by looking into the source (God) can human beings recognize what they are, namely, images of God (WA 39I: 175,24–176,4).

Unlike philosophy, claims Luther, theology defines the "whole and perfect human being" (WA 39I: 176,5–6). The horizon of this definition is God, and the human being is understood as a counterpart of God. Thus a traditional definition using *genus proximum* and *differentia specifica* is not possible for theology. Rather, the human being is defined by an event between God and the human being, that is, by his or her justification by God.

The human being is defined as the being that is in need of being justified. This implies that the human being is a sinner, a being that lives in contradiction to his or her original purpose (not trusting God and thus seeking his or her own interest in everything) and unable to achieve this purpose by his or her own means. Thus justification cannot depend on any conditions on the part of human beings. It requires an action from God's side that has the structure of creation. Human receptivity corresponds to this creative action. Both this action and its reception are communicative, mediated through human words. Since human words must be understood, the human reception of God's action involves the activity of understanding. And since these words aim to create trust in the human being, this reception is *understanding trust*.

What Luther says about the basic relational structure of the human being is also crucial for his theological understanding of eternal life. For him, immortality is based not on the quality of the soul – its simplicity or indivisibility – but rather on God's relation to human beings: "Where and with whomever God speaks, whether in anger or in grace, that person is surely immortal. The Person of God, who speaks, and the Word point out that we are the kind of creatures with whom God would want to speak eternally and in an immortal manner" (WA 43: 481,32–5; LW 5: 76). Since the 'speaking' of God has its origin in the eternity of God, this communication will never end. Therefore those who have been addressed – all human beings – will not come to an end (not even in death) since God's talking is creative and life-giving.

DOES LUTHER HOLD THE DOCTRINE OF THE DOUBLE TRUTH? LUTHER'S CONCEPT OF DIFFERENT REALMS

In the disputation "The Word Was Made Flesh" (1539), Luther criticizes the Sorbonne: "The Sorbonne, the mother of errors, very badly laid down [*definivit*] that the same thing is true in philosophy and theology" (39II: 3,7–8; trans. in White 1994: 125). This thesis has been taken by some as an indication that Luther holds the so-called 'doctrine of the double truth' (Frank 2003: 44–51). The concept of the double truth is mentioned in the Prologue of the Bishop of Paris, Stephan Tempier, to the text of his condemnation of 219 theses in 1277: some members of the faculty of arts talk errors, claiming "that they are true according to philosophy, but not according to the Catholic faith, as if two contrary truths existed and as if a truth in the writings of some damned pagan people stood against the truth of Holy Scripture" (quoted in Flasch 1989: 89). In accord with this very condemnation, Luther's philosophy teacher at Erfurt, Arnoldi von Usingen, stated in his

Exercitium Physicorum (Exercises in physics; 1507) that, "the principles of natural reason and light do not contradict the theological principles and truths. Therefore what is true in theology is also true in philosophy" (quoted in Frank 2003: 47 n.85). While some of the philosophers in Paris toward whom the bishop directed his critique tried to claim autonomy for philosophy over against theology, Luther appears to be making a claim for the autonomy of theology (*ibid.*: 49).

But Luther does not have the doctrine of the double truth in mind. He emphasizes that every truth agrees with every truth: that is, every true proposition agrees with every true proposition (WA 39II: 3,1–2). Nevertheless, there are different areas of truth, such that a proposition that is true in one area does not necessarily make sense in another. Luther offers many examples (WA 39II: 5,13–36). 'Humidity moistens' is true in the area of air, but not in the area of fire. One may hang a weight from a material point: this is true, but if we are referring to a mathematical point or line then this would not be true (WA 39II: 5,29–30, 15–16). One may consider different arts and their respective works and see that the same proposition is never true in all of them. This is even more the case with the relation of philosophical and theological propositions. Luther thus argues that the realm of objects of philosophy differs in character from the realm of objects of theology. "Thus we would do better if we leave dialectic or philosophy in their realm and learn to talk in new tongues in the reign of faith outside of the sphere of those disciplines" (39II: 5,35–6; corrections according to Schwarz 1966: 338 n.164).

There is a correspondence between this difference in the realms of philosophy and theology and the need for theology to practise a new language. To be sure, theology employs words of ordinary language and even words also used in philosophy, but these words receive a new meaning in theology. Luther develops this idea in his reflections on the proposition that 'Jesus Christ is a human being'. The being for which the name 'Jesus Christ' supposits in this proposition is a true human being. Thus the term 'human being' in the proposition contains elements of meaning that allow one to identify the being to which it refers as a human being. At the same time, the term 'human being' in this proposition contains elements of meaning that do not apply when the same term is used, for example, in the proposition 'Socrates is a human being'. When 'human being' refers to individuals like Socrates, one is able to make the inference that 'they are beings which are not God but are separated from God'. Such an inference is not allowed when 'Jesus Christ' is part of the proposition. Rather, 'human being' here refers to a being that is intimately connected with God. Thus, according to Luther all words that refer to Jesus Christ gain new meaning when compared to the meaning they have when used in philosophy (White 1994: 299–348).

Along the same lines, Luther takes up and further develops an old tradition of predication about Jesus Christ: *communicatio idiomatum* (communication of the properties of Christ's divine and human natures). This concept encapsulates the notion that a predicate that belongs to the human nature of Jesus Christ is also true about God (e.g. 'suffering' – 'This God [Jesus Christ] suffered and died'), or, vice versa, that a predicate that belongs to God is also true about the human being (e.g. 'creating' – 'This human being created the world'). This is an interpretation of the Creed of the Council of Nicaea, according to which Jesus Christ is true God and true human being. Luther insisted on the difference between the realm of theology and the realm of philosophy precisely because the special character of Jesus Christ would otherwise be downplayed or negated.

Another area of conflict between theology and reason – another indication for the need to distinguish the realms of theology and philosophy – is the doctrine of the Trinity. The basic proposition of this doctrine is the thesis that "God is one and triune, the one creator of all things outside of him" (39II: 287,13–14), or "One indistinct thing is three distinct things" (39II: 254,5–6). All of this is to say that the one God is Father, Son and Holy Spirit. In God there are three distinct persons, but one essence, and each of the three persons is the whole God. Luther emphasizes that it is impossible for reason to understand this, since the area to which reason is related and where it is developed is the realm of creatures. In this realm one does not find the structure 'three things are one thing'. In that sense, speaking about the Trinity appears to be improper speech. Trinitarian language, however, is established not by empirical realities but by the revelation to which Holy Scripture bears witness. Recognizing that the Trinity is seldom delineated explicitly in Scripture, Luther nevertheless claims to follow its implications with his Trinitarian doctrine.

But even though reason is not able to grasp the doctrine of the Trinity, there is a need to distinguish between false and correct propositions in the doctrine. In order to do so, one must give particular reasons for or against this or that proposition. Offering reasons for this purpose, Luther demonstrates a particular way of using reason in theology. What reason is has to be adjusted to the state of affairs with which it deals. This is precisely what Luther does in the academic disputations on this doctrine. On the one hand, he is rejecting a use of reason that he regards as misleading for theology because it would impose a way of thinking in terms of creaturely structures on theological matters. On the other hand, this very criticism of reason aims at establishing an appropriate use of reason in the realm of theology.

The standard tool for making and analysing arguments is logic. But in Trinitarian doctrine, logic, especially syllogistic logic, creates problems. For example, there is the so-called *syllogismus expositorius*: "The divine Father generates [the Son] [1]. The Father is the divine essence [2]. Therefore the conclusion: 'The divine essence generates', is valid [3]" (39II: 4,24–5). Theology, however, must not conclude that the one divine essence generates, for in this case there would be two Gods. In the above proposition, both of the two premises are true and the conclusion is *formally* correct, but it is incorrect in terms of *content*. This was a shocking experience for medieval logicians. Since they did not doubt the truth of the propositions, they had to doubt the formality or universality of logic. Thus they tried to refine and sharpen the conditions for syllogisms, so that syllogisms like the one mentioned could no longer be regarded as formally correct (Dieter 2001: 380–90).

Luther asserted that the syllogistic form of argumentation is not valid in propositions concerning God. It is interesting that he also offered an explanation for this: "The 'thing' itself is equivocal" (39II: 316,24). This is reflected in the fact that the word 'essence' can be employed in two different ways: 'substantially' or 'personally' (i.e. 'essentially' or 'relatively'). Used in the first way, 'essence' refers to the divine essence; understood in the second way, it refers to the respective persons of the Trinity. The syllogism mentioned above is a paralogism because its propositions mix up the different ways in which the word 'essence' can be used. In consequence, Luther proposes, as he often does, to first analyse the semantics of propositions before applying logic to them. The truth-value of propositions varies depending on the reference of the words used in them.

Luther gives a list of true propositions that apply to the doctrine of the Trinity. It is not a complete list. Rather, he offers examples in support of his overall argument, and in doing so employs the tools of logical and semantic analysis. Two examples may be given. Luther often discusses the question as to whether or not the proposition that 'The (divine) essence generates the (divine) essence' is true. This refers to a famous conflict in the Middle Ages between Peter Lombard and Joachim of Fiore about how to correctly speak about the essence of God. The Fourth Lateran Council of 1215 declared that the essence of God does not generate. But Luther argues that the Council of Nicaea confessed the Christian faith with reference to Jesus Christ by saying that he is "God from God, light from light, true God from true God". This is, as he insists, only true if 'God' and 'light' are understood personally and not essentially, again taking up the distinction just mentioned of two ways of using the term 'essence'. Thus, Luther argues, 'essentia' can also be understood personally when used with reference to the person of the Father and the person of the Son: the Father – the essence – generates the Son – the essence. "If we take [God] personally, then it is true that 'God generates God'; but, if it is taken essentially, then God neither generates himself nor another God. The essence does not generate, but a person does" (39II: 370,8–14; trans. in White 1994: 191).

We now turn to a second example. Luther describes the relation of essence and persons in God by employing two propositions: (i) "Any of these (divine) persons is the whole God", and (ii) "Nevertheless it cannot be said that any of these persons exclusively is God" (39II: 253,4–6). Again, Luther uses an element of medieval semantic theory, the so-called 'exponibles' (*exponibilia*): syncategorematic terms that determine how subject or predicate terms in a given proposition supposit for things ('every', 'whole', 'except' are such exponibles). By applying this analytical instrument, Luther is able to more precisely determine the relation between persons and essence in God (Helmer 1999: 113–18). Luther's attentiveness to the semantic and logical analysis of propositions and his concern for the evaluation of propositional truth indicate that he follows some basic lines of late medieval Ockhamism (White 1994).

A third indication for the need to distinguish different realms of theology and philosophy are the problems that the words of institution in the Eucharist ('This is my body', said by the priest on behalf of Jesus Christ) create for all theologians. Luther describes these problems as follows.[2] The priest points to the bread in his hands, saying 'This is my body'. Now, the truth-condition for propositions, according to Ockham, is that the subject term and the predicate term supposit for the same thing. Obviously, this is not the case here, for 'this' supposits for the bread while 'my body' supposits for the body of Christ, which is believed to be present in the sacrament. Thus there are two different beings – bread and the body of Christ – but not one, identical thing. Thus the truth-condition of the so-called identical predication (*praedicatio identica*) is not fulfilled. Luther acknowledges this objection and explicitly states that both reason and Holy Scripture do not allow any exception. Two different things cannot be one identical thing. There appear to be only two ways out of this dilemma. In order to guarantee the truth of the proposition 'This is my body', one can either assume that bread is not present in the Eucharist (at least not the substance of the bread), or that the body of Christ is not present (the bread is a sign for the body of Christ, which is not present). The first way is the one taken by the scholastics, who presuppose a transubstantiation of the bread so that only the accidents of bread – that is, the properties but not the substance – remain at the altar. The second way is the one taken by Wyclif, and also Luther's contemporary and opponent Zwingli. For Luther, it is clear that one cannot achieve one, identical entity if one starts with two entities that are identical in themselves. As such, only an aggregate of entities is possible.

Luther proposes to consider the grammar and rhetoric of the sentence 'This is my body', and other sentences that are comparable, before any logical analysis is applied. While logic takes 'bread' and 'body' as a reference to different entities identical in and for themselves, Luther understands the grammar of the sentence to be 'speaking together' (*zusammensprechen*) two entities as one, such that the unity of the sentence constitutes and expresses the unity of the object. Accordingly, both 'this' and 'my body' refer to the one unity 'body–bread'. One could speak of a grammar and, following the grammatical analysis, also of a logic of communion where the bread and Christ's body mutually communicate their respective properties to each other: they determine themselves mutually and thus constitute a new unity. It is therefore still possible to say 'This is bread' and 'This is the body of Christ'. At the same time, bread and body are perceived as one entity.

Luther offers some examples both from everyday life and from Holy Scripture in order to show that the logic of the communication of properties applies to numerous binary pairings. One example is red-hot iron as the unity of fire and iron. Luther thus claims to overcome the alternative between transubstantiation

2. In fact, the situation is more complicated (Hilgenfeld 1971: 13–182, 387–426), but what follows may suffice in order to understand Luther's option.

(the substance of the bread disappears, only the accidents remain) and signification (the bread that is on the altar only signifies the body of Christ). Both the bread and the body of Christ are on the altar, but in a newly constituted unity of mutually communicated properties.

CONCLUSION

From its beginning, Christian theology has been engaged in an intense dialogue with philosophy. In part, both theology and philosophy deal with the 'same' topics by approaching them from different perspectives, and both claim to proceed in a rational way. Since Christian theology focuses on revelation, and revelation is seen to have culminated in the person of Jesus Christ, some particular areas of conflict between theology and philosophy have emerged. There are theological propositions such as 'God is human being', 'God is one and triune' and 'This is my body' (the priest pointing to the bread in Eucharist) that are difficult to understand from a philosophical point of view. These objections are not alien to Christians, since they too share in human rationality. But they are convinced that in Jesus Christ they are confronted with an exceptional reality that cannot be understood by employing a rationality that is related only to the field of philosophical enquiry. Nevertheless, theology claims that from this exceptional reality a new light is thrown on all reality. Conflicts over domination between theology and philosophy have their origin in this state of affairs, so that from time to time both theology and philosophy have felt alienated by being too strongly influenced by the other discipline.

Even though Aristotelian philosophy was received in medieval times in a critical and highly constructive way by Christian theology so that not only theology but also philosophy was further developed, Luther was very critical of such a reception. He argued: what help can theology expect from a philosophy that holds that the world is eternal and denies that there is a creator, from a philosophy that sees the human soul as mortal and denies that human beings have to live their lives in the horizon of being accountable to God, from a philosophy whose concept of happiness is related only to life on earth? These were traditional arguments, but Luther took them up in order to criticize fundamentally the syntheses of 'Aristotelian' philosophy and Christian thought (Dieter 2001: 431–631).

In Luther's view, human sinfulness affects cognition in two ways. First, he sees the *act* of cognition as compromised by the self-seeking orientation of human beings: sinful self-interest affects human acts of perception. Secondly, according to this sinful self-interest, the human perception of God, of human beings and of the relationship between them is misleading with regard to its *content* and does not bring human beings into the right relationship to God and to others. The alternative that Luther offers is his 'theology of the cross'. Nevertheless, Luther not only criticizes reason and philosophy, but also argues for the distinction of different realms of theology, philosophy, arts and sciences. By doing so he attempts to develop a rationality specific to theology. This takes place mainly in the university disputations: "There is no clearer way to show how Luther regards the positive role of reason in investigating the theological subject matter than by studying his use of the *disputatio*" (Helmer 1999: 42). Thus both rejection and reception of philosophical thoughts and methods belong together in Luther, both sharp criticism of philosophical claims and creative adaptation: for the goal is a theology that is a faithful *and* rational account of God's revelation in Jesus Christ.

FURTHER READING

Andreatta, E. 1996. *Lutero e Aristotele*. Padua: Cusl Nuova Vita.

Ebeling, G. 1977. *Disputatio de homine. Erster Teil: Text und Traditionshintergrund*. Tübingen: Mohr.

Ebeling, G. 1982. *Disputatio de homine. Zweiter Teil: Die philosophische Definition des Menschen*. Tübingen: Mohr.

Ebeling, G. 1989. *Disputatio de homine. Dritter Teil: Die theologische Definition des Menschen*. Tübingen: Mohr.

Junghans, H. 1985. *Der junge Luther und die Humanisten*. Göttingen: Vandenhoeck & Ruprecht.

Kolb, R. 2005. *Bound Choice, Election, and Wittenberg Theological Method: From Martin Luther to the Formula of Concord*. Grand Rapids, MI: Eerdmans.

Lohse, B. 1999. *Martin Luther's Theology: Its Historical and Systematic Development*. Edinburgh: T&T Clark.

Wicks, J. 2007. "Luther and 'This Damned, Conceited, Rascally Heathen' Aristotle: An Encounter More Complicated Than Many Think". *Pro Ecclesia* **16**: 90–104.

Zur Mühlen, K.-H. 1980. *Reformatorische Vernunftkritik und neuzeitliches Denken*. Tübingen: Mohr.

On THE EUCHARIST see also Vol. 2, Ch. 15. On LOGIC see also Ch. 3; Vol. 2, Chs 2, 4, 17; Vol. 4, Ch. 19. On THE PROTESTANT REFORMATION see also Ch. 4. On SCRIPTURE see also Chs 4, 15; Vol. 1, Chs 9, 13, 17; Vol. 2, Ch. 19; Vol. 4, Ch. 3; Vol. 5, Ch. 12. On THE TRINITY see also Chs 9, 17; Vol. 1, Chs 14, 17, 20; Vol. 2, Chs 2, 8, 15; Vol. 4, Ch. 4; Vol. 5, Chs 12, 23. On TRUTH see also Chs 8, 13; Vol. 1, Ch. 13; Vol. 2, Ch. 17; Vol. 4, Chs 8, 18; Vol. 5, Ch. 4.

4

JOHN CALVIN

Michael Sudduth

The French Genevan reformer John Calvin (1509–64) holds an important place in the development of the theology of the Protestant Reformation. Building on insights articulated by other reformers such as Philipp Melanchthon, Martin Bucer and Huldrych Zwingli, Calvin is perhaps best known for his careful and penetrating biblical exegesis and the production of a compendium of Christian theology that strongly influenced the emergence of Reformed orthodoxy in the latter part of the sixteenth century. Calvin's teachings on divine providence and predestination, the doctrine of sin and the Christian's union with Christ were among his influential contributions to Reformed theology. But Calvin is also known for his doctrine of the natural knowledge of God, roughly, the idea that human beings have some knowledge of God from the light of nature and independent of scriptural revelation. The relationship between this doctrine and traditional natural theology (i.e. arguments for the existence and nature of God) has been a point of controversy among Calvin commentators and philosophical theologians in the Protestant tradition. In this entry I outline this controversy and show why Calvin should be regarded as having made an important, positive contribution to natural theology.

INTRODUCTION

Calvin's educational background and theological work

The structure of Calvin's thought and his influence as a Protestant reformer must be viewed in the light of his own intellectual development and background as a humanist thinker educated in classical literature and law.[1] In 1523, at fourteen

1. The historical information in this section of the paper is drawn from Battles (1996: 47–85), Wendel (1963: 15–68) and Steinmetz (1995: 3–22).

years of age, Calvin began his college education (ostensibly in preparation for the priesthood) in Paris at the Collège de la Marche. Here Calvin came under the instruction of the Latinist and rhetorician Mathurin Cordier, an important influence on the development of Calvin's Latin writing style and an inspiration for the pedagogy Calvin sought to implement in the schools in Geneva many years later. Calvin's stay at the Collège de la Marche was brief, though, and within several months he transferred to the Collège de Montaigu, where he completed his licentiate in arts in 1527. Beginning in 1528 Calvin took up the study of civil law, first at the University of Orléans and then at the University of Bourges, universities where Calvin was taught by influential legal scholars of the day such as Pierre de l'Estoile and Andrea Alciati. Calvin's humanist educational background was evident in his first published book, a commentary on Seneca's *De Clementia* (On clemency; 1532). Calvin's Seneca commentary demonstrated his acquaintance with classical culture, history and philosophy, but also revealed the philological skills on which he would later rely to produce an impressive series of commentaries on nearly the entire Bible.

Calvin's conversion and break from the Catholic Church, some time between 1532 and 1534, precipitated the redirection of his humanist education and skills toward the efforts of Protestant reform. Calvin directed these efforts initially in Geneva (1536–8), for a short period of time in Strasbourg (1538–41), and then again in Geneva (1541–64), where he served as pastor until his death. In 1536 he published the first edition of his *Institutes of the Christian Religion*, which functioned as both an introductory theology text and a defence of the Protestant reform movement. Modelled largely on Luther's catechisms, the *Institutes* would undergo significant expansion and many revisions over the years, first during Calvin's Strasbourg years and later in Geneva, by which time the text had blossomed into a complete theological compendium. The 1559 Latin edition (1560 French edition) arguably represents Calvin's culminating and definitive theological statement. On returning to the pastorate in Geneva in 1541, Calvin embarked on a rigorous schedule of in-depth preaching on various parts of the Bible. He had already produced an important commentary on the Epistle to the Romans (in 1540), which allowed him to provide a thorough exegetical engagement with the doctrine of justification by faith, a pillar of Reformation theology. Before his death in 1564, Calvin would produce commentaries on twenty-four of the books of the Old Testament and all but three books of the New Testament, as well as a large number of treatises on theological topics such as predestination, the sacraments and church polity.

Calvin's ambivalence toward philosophical theology

Since Calvin's primary interests were in biblical exposition and in the development of an ostensibly biblically controlled theology, the interests of 'philosophical theology' and 'philosophy of religion' appear foreign to both the letter and spirit of Calvin's theology. Not surprisingly, Calvin's attitude toward philosophical enquiry about God ranges from disinterest to hostile criticism. His assessment of what the pagan philosophers have achieved with respect to the knowledge of divine things is bleak, partly because of the distorting effects of sin on the human intellect and partly because the pagans lacked the illumination of Scripture. The medieval scholastics, too, despite their possession of the Bible, were a frequent target of Calvin's criticisms. Calvin's humanist background no doubt contributed to his largely negative assessment of philosophical enquiry as represented by 'the Schoolmen'. However, he also saw in the scholastic use of human reason the resources for theological doctrines he judged to be without biblical warrant, if not incompatible with the teachings of Scripture. His general opposition to rational speculation about God is fundamentally rooted in his belief in the incomprehensibility of God, which renders reason intrinsically incapable of knowing the divine essence. Hence, beyond the defects of reason incurred by the Fall, reason has a crucial boundary imposed by the creator–creature distinction. Finally, Calvin's interest in the 'knowledge of God' is governed by a powerful ethical orientation. The knowledge of God should engender and sustain love and worship of God, not simply satisfy our intellectual curiosity or some set of theoretical interests.

However, despite Calvin's widely advertised opposition to philosophical enquiry about God, there are aspects to Calvin's thought that suggest a more optimistic conclusion concerning the interface between philosophy and the Christian faith. Calvin does quote approvingly from pagan philosophers such as Plato, Seneca and Cicero. His concept of God at least unconsciously appropriates aspects of the Greek philosophical tradition, largely mediated through patristic theology, especially that of Augustine (*see* Vol. 1, esp. Ch. 18). However, the most important connection between Calvin and philosophy of religion is found in Calvin's discussion of the natural knowledge of God, most systematically developed in the opening chapters of his *Institutes of the Christian Religion*. The idea that there are truths about God that may be known by human reason, without the light of Scripture, divine revelation or dogmatic theology, is an essential epistemological presupposition of natural theology, the project of developing rational arguments for the existence and nature of God. Given the importance of natural theology to the philosophy of religion, a proper evaluation of Calvin's views at this juncture will illuminate his position on, and potential contributions to, the nature and role of philosophical enquiry about God.

THE NATURAL KNOWLEDGE OF GOD

In the opening chapters of his *Institutes of the Christian Religion* (hereafter *Institutes*), John Calvin claimed, "There is within the human mind, and indeed by natural instinct, an awareness of divinity ... God himself has implanted in all men a certain understanding of his divine majesty" (*Institutes* 1.3.1).[2] Closely related to this *sensus divinitatis* (sense of divinity) is an external manifestation of God in creation. God "not only sowed in men's minds that seed of religion of which we have spoken but revealed himself and daily discloses himself in the whole workmanship of the universe. As a consequence, men cannot open their eyes without being compelled to see him" (1.5.1). This knowledge is aptly designated a *natural* knowledge of God. It is derived from "the order of nature" (1.2.1), and Calvin links it to "natural instinct" (1.3.1) and the "light of nature" (1.3.2). Furthermore, he says that it is "naturally implanted" (1.3.3), "by nature engraven" (1.4.4), "taught by nature" (1.5.12), and "sown in [men's] minds out of the wonderful workmanship of nature" (1.5.15). So Calvin affirms both a *sensus divinitatis* and knowledge of God derived from the *opera Dei* (God's works – of creation and providence).

Like other reformers (e.g. Melanchthon, Bucer and Vermigli) Calvin's acceptance of a natural knowledge of God was based on his exegesis of Scripture, especially Romans 1 and 2:

> God is in himself invisible; but as his majesty shines forth in his works and in his creatures everywhere, men ought in these to acknowledge him, for they clearly set forth their maker ... He does not mention all the particulars which may be thought to belong to God; but he states, that we can arrive at the knowledge of his eternal power and divinity, for he who is the framer of all things, must necessarily be without beginning and from himself. (Calvin 1979b: 70)[3]

Calvin is careful to contrast the natural knowledge of God with knowledge of God that is given by way of sacred Scripture (*Institutes* 1.2.1, 1.6.1). Whereas the natural knowledge of God is the knowledge of God as creator, Scripture communicates knowledge of God as both creator and redeemer. Since the latter is necessary for salvation, the natural knowledge of God is both incomplete and non-saving. Moreover, as will be discussed below, Calvin's doctrine of sin provides another important constraint on the knowledge of God available from nature. Not everything that can *in principle* be known about God from nature may be known *in fact* because of the effects of sin on the human mind. Scripture, then, not only augments but also corrects the natural knowledge of God. Hence, for Calvin, the primary function of the natural knowledge of God is to establish the moral inexcusability of the human race (1.5.14–15). Since God has revealed himself, if there is ignorance of God, the ignorance is culpable.

2. All quotations from Calvin's *Institutes* are from Calvin (1960), cited by book, chapter and paragraph numbers.
3. See Steinmetz (1995) for an account of the exegesis of Romans 1 and 2 among other Protestant reformers.

Calvin's affirmation of natural knowledge of God marks an important point of continuity between Calvin and earlier theologians of the patristic and medieval periods (e.g. John Chrysostom, Augustine, John of Damascus, Bonaventure, Thomas Aquinas). In fact, since Calvin draws heavily on classical sources such as Cicero's *De natura deorum* (On the nature of the gods), there is arguably continuity between Calvin and the larger Western philosophical tradition. Of course, Western philosophy and philosophical theology have often emphasized rational *arguments* for the existence and nature of God: so-called *natural theology*. Should Calvin's affirmation of natural knowledge of God be read as an endorsement of natural theology? Calvin commentators have not spoken with one voice here. One tier of the debate is largely epistemological: according to Calvin, is the natural knowledge of God inferential? The other tier of the debate is at least partly theological: does the influence of sin in the human personality negate, distort or significantly limit the knowledge of God that would otherwise be acquired from the natural order? The prospects for natural theology in Calvin depend on the answers given to each of these questions.

TWO INTERPRETATIONS OF CALVIN'S ACCOUNT OF THE NATURAL KNOWLEDGE OF GOD

Beginning with the earliest abridgments to Calvin's *Institutes* in the latter part of the sixteenth century, Calvin commentators have typically interpreted Calvin's account of the natural knowledge of God as at least including an inferential element, specifically inferences to the attributes of God from empirically accessible features of the world such as its beauty and order.[4] While the *sensus divinitatis* refers to the nearly universal conviction that there is some sort of divinity, by means of God's manifestation of himself in creation we are able to *infer* the goodness, wisdom and providential power of this deity. On this traditional view the natural knowledge of God is both naturally *implanted* and *acquired* discursively from observable features of the world. Traditionally, this has provided a two-step justification for natural theology. First, by virtue of affirming a *natural* knowledge of God, Calvin accepts a crucial epistemological presupposition of natural theology, namely, the epistemic accessibility of the divine being. Secondly, the natural knowledge of God acquired from the *opera Dei* entails that the divine being is epistemically accessible by way of logical inference. This second point is crucial. It links Calvin's discussion of natural *knowledge* of God to the more specific project of theistic *argument*. Either Calvin's account of the acquired natural knowledge of God involves the actual presentation of theistic arguments or the arguments of

4. See Dowey (1994: 72–81), Sudduth (1995), Warfield (2000: 39–44), Adams (2001: 280–92) and Muller (2003a: 275; 2003b: 173–4).

natural theology formalize inferential elements in the natural knowledge of God. So Calvin either explicitly or implicitly endorses natural theology.

However, despite the long-standing and widespread acceptance of the traditional interpretation of Calvin, a number of twentieth-century philosophers of religion have proposed that Calvin's account of the natural knowledge of God can plausibly be interpreted as involving no inferential element at all.[5] As they see things, for Calvin the natural knowledge of God is exclusively immediate. We simply have an innate disposition to form various theistic beliefs, and these beliefs are formed when the disposition is trigged by experiential circumstances such as the observation of the beauty or orderly nature of the cosmos. The position does not deny the conceptual mediacy of the natural knowledge of God, nor that the knowledge of God is mediated by creation in some way. The idea is rather that we do not arrive at belief in God by way of argument or inference from other beliefs or knowledge. The *opera Dei* trigger an innate disposition to believe in God. They do not form the content of beliefs from which we infer truths about God. So natural knowledge of God is analogous to widely held accounts of sensory perceptual knowledge, knowledge of other minds and knowledge of self-evident truths. The knowledge is spontaneously and non-inferentially formed in us in certain experiential circumstances. This interpretation of Calvin undercuts the traditional justification for natural theology by removing the inferential element in the natural knowledge of God. Some authors argue that the immediacy of the natural knowledge of God at least partly explains Calvin's alleged rejection of theistic arguments.[6]

CALVIN AND THEISTIC ARGUMENTS

Advocates of the non-traditional interpretation of Calvin emphasize that Calvin provides nothing like Aquinas' Five Ways, nor the philosophical argumentation of Gottfried Wilhelm Leibniz, René Descartes or Samuel Clarke. This seems correct. However, unless we adopt a fairly narrow conception of inference or argument, this fact does little to prove that Calvin presents no theistic arguments at all, much less that he construes the natural knowledge of God as exclusively non-inferential in character.

Rhetorical and demonstrative types of natural theology

John Platt (1982) and Richard Muller (2003a,b) have each carefully documented the distinction in early Protestant theology between *rhetorical* theistic arguments

5. See Parker (1959: 9 n.1), Plantinga (1980; 2000: 171–7), Hoitenga (1991: 155–7) and Helm (1997: 180–82).
6. See LeCerf (1949: 242–5), Parker (1959: 7–9) and Helm (1997: 181–2).

(arguments from universal consent, providence, simple appeal to design) and *demonstrative* theistic arguments (arguments from final and efficient causality).[7] The latter kinds of argument would eventually dominate Enlightenment and post-Enlightenment philosophical theology. Whether as a result of their humanist training or practical desiderata, the reformers shared a preference for more rhetorically styled theistic arguments classically expressed in Cicero's *De natura deorum*, an important influence on the Reformation doctrine of the natural knowledge of God. The fundamental goal of rhetorical arguments is to persuade, not to satisfy the demands of philosophical clarity and syllogistic rigour. Calvin must be read over against this background of the Reformation preference for a particular kind and style of argumentation. Hence, while "no long or toilsome proof [*demonstratio*] is needed to elicit the evidences [*testimonia*] that illuminate and affirm the divine majesty" (*Institutes* 1.5.9), the knowledge of God is inferentially acquired from the *opera Dei* and may be set forth by way of argument.

Calvin's innumerable evidences and theistic inferences

Calvin speaks of the "innumerable evidences (*documenta*)" in the fabric of the world that declare the wisdom, power and goodness of God. These evidences are drawn from careful observation in astronomy, medicine, and the natural sciences, as well as the more obvious evidences of design in the cosmos that are available to the uneducated, for example the movement and structure of the celestial bodies. "Likewise," he says:

> in regard to the structure of the human body one must have the greatest keenness in order to weigh, with Galen's skill, its articulation, symmetry, beauty, and use. But yet, as all acknowledge, the human body shows itself to be a composition so ingenious that its Artificer is rightly judged a wonder-worker. (*Institutes* 1.5.2)

Notice that Calvin does not say that these evidences declare the *existence* of God. These innumerable evidences declare the attributes of a being whose existence is already known by way of a *sensus divinitatis*.

How exactly does the physical world show or declare God's wisdom, power and goodness? With respect to Psalm 19, Calvin says: "David shows how it is that the heavens proclaim to us the glory of God, namely, by openly bearing testimony that they have not been put together by chance but were wonderfully created by the Supreme Architect" (1979c: vol. 4, 309). How do they bear such testimony? Not by automatically engendering theistic beliefs, but by exhibiting the properties of

7. For a detailed examination of the historical evolution of such arguments in the Reformed tradition, see Sudduth (forthcoming: ch. 1).

order and beauty that are taken as indications of intelligence, power and goodness. The Psalmist is said "to extol the matchless wisdom God has shown in creating the heavens; for the sun, moon, and stars are not confusedly mixed together, but each has its own position and station assigned to it, and their manifold courses are regulated" (*ibid.*: vol. 4, 305). Consequently knowledge of God is *derived from* the contemplation of these features of the world, not merely *occasioned by* the experience of them. There is a logical relation between order and the divine attributes. The inference may be spontaneous, but it is an inference nonetheless, depending on beliefs to the effect that the world exhibits order, beauty and utility in the arrangement of things, and that these properties are indications of wisdom, goodness and power.

Calvin summarized the natural theistic inference in his commentary on Romans:

> God has presented to the minds of all the means of knowing him, having so manifested himself by his works, that they must see what of themselves they seek not to know – that there is some God; for the world does not exist by chance, nor could it have proceeded from itself. (1979b: 71)

Calvin here alludes to the design argument, on which he elaborates with greater detail in the *Institutes* 1.5.2–3, 6–8, and in his commentaries on Psalms 19 and 104. The inference to God takes the form of a disjunctive argument that eliminates chance and natural principles as alternative explanations for the data in question.

Finally, Calvin finds a sanction for theistic arguments in Paul's preaching to pagans in the Book of Acts. When confronting the people of Lystra in Acts 14, Paul proved the oneness and providence of God by way of "natural arguments" (*naturalibus argumentis*). Although Paul did not rigorously reason "after the manner of philosophers", since his audience was not highly educated, Calvin claims that Paul nonetheless relied on the principle that "in the order of nature there is a certain and evident manifestation of God" (1979a: 19, cf. 16). Paul develops and clarifies this manifestation by way of arguments. Similarly, in connection with Paul's appearance before the Stoic and Epicurean philosophers in Acts 17, Calvin says that Paul "showeth by natural arguments (*naturalibus argumentis*) who and what God is, and how He is rightly worshipped" (*ibid.*: 154). Calvin adds, "Furthermore, because he hath to deal with profane men, he draweth proofs from nature itself; for in vain he should have cited the testimonies of Scripture" (*ibid.*: 157–8).

Melanchthon and Calvin

One can better appreciate the link between logical argument and Calvin's appeal to testimonies to God in nature by comparing Calvin's account with Melanchthon's treatment of the natural knowledge of God. In his 1532 *Commentary on Romans* (of which Calvin was both familiar and spoke favourably), Melanchthon affirms the natural knowledge of God: "For in some manner reason naturally understands and possesses signs (*signa*) and arguments (*argumenta*) collected from God's works in the whole of natural order. Hence we infer (*rationcinamur*) the existence of God, by whom the natural order was founded" ([1532] 1965: 73, trans. in Platt 1982: 18–19). Melanchthon adds that this ability to draw inferences about God from the created order depends on a preconception (*prolepsis*) of God naturally implanted in the human heart. Although Melanchthon briefly listed some examples of the *signa* and *argumenta* in the 1532 edition of his Romans commentary, in the 1540 edition he greatly expanded his treatment, listing nine arguments for the existence and nature of God. Most of these arguments are rhetorically styled arguments, but at least two are metaphysical and demonstrative in character. The rhetorically styled arguments follow a general pattern: (i) there is some observational datum *O*; (ii) *O* could not have come about through chance; therefore (iii) some intelligent, powerful or good being is the cause of *O*.

The similarities between Melanchthon and Calvin at this juncture should be clear. Calvin's appeal to the movement of the heavenly bodies, the arrangement of the parts of the human body and the punishment of wrongdoers in society forms the essential content of nine of Melanchthon's theistic arguments. In Melanchthon, however, the inferential nature of appeals to cosmic and social order is seen in clear relief because these rhetorical arguments are placed alongside causal or metaphysical arguments, which were the stock-in-trade of natural theology in the medieval period. This is obscured by Calvin's omission of the metaphysical proofs and his exclusive concentration on rhetorical arguments grounded in the Stoic tradition and expressed in Cicero's *De natura deorum*. Nonetheless, sixteenth-century readers would have recognized the continuities between Calvin and Melanchthon at this juncture.

Immediacy and inference

It is important to clarify that on the traditional interpretation the natural knowledge of God is not exclusively inferential, for there is a distinction between the *sensus divinitatis* and the external witness. Some knowledge of God (e.g. a creator who ought to be worshipped) is naturally implanted in us by nature. This *sensus divinitatis* can be taken as immediate knowledge, but it is fairly minimal in content. As Dowey (1994) indicates, Calvin introduces the divine attributes of wisdom, power and goodness only in connection with the visible manifestation of God in creation (*Institutes* 1.5), not in the context of the affirmation of the *sensus divinitatis* (1.3). While the attributes of God are plausibly contained in the concept of God as creator, the idea of God implicated in the *sensus divinitatis* needs to be tethered to the revelation of God in creation. Inferences from creation serve both to confirm and refine a native belief in God. These inferences presuppose an antecedent *sensus divinitatis*.[8] From this vantage point, the project of natural theology reflectively elaborates and systematically develops the natural knowledge of God. Yet this knowledge first comes to people in a spontaneous manner in their experience of and reflection on the world. Natural theology as theistic argument presupposes natural theology as natural knowledge of God.

THE NOETIC EFFECTS OF SIN

While it would appear that Calvin unambiguously asserts that human beings possess some natural knowledge of God, even an inferential natural knowledge of God, a sanction for natural theology in Calvin also depends on Calvin's understanding of the relationship between the natural knowledge of God and the noetic effects of sin.

Calvin and the noetic effects of sin

Calvin argued that inherited and personal sin corrupts the *sensus divinitatis* and blinds human beings from seeing the revelation of God in the created order. Calvin speaks of this knowledge as "the primal and simple knowledge to which the very order of nature would have led us *if Adam had remained upright*" (*Institutes* 1.2.1). This suggests that the natural knowledge of God is a reality only before the Fall of Adam and the entrance of sin into the world. After discussing the corruption of the natural knowledge of God due to the "blindness of the human mind", Calvin says, "if men were taught only by nature, they would hold to nothing certain or solid or clear-cut, but would be so tied to confused principles as to worship an unknown god" (1.5.12). Calvin ends the discussion of the natural knowledge of God by saying, "men soon corrupt the seed of the knowledge of God, sown in their minds out of the wonderful workmanship of nature", and "we lack the natural ability to mount up unto the pure and clear knowledge of God" (1.5.15). The chapter that follows the discussion of the natural knowledge of God and its corruption by sin asserts the necessity of Scripture as a guide, not merely to knowledge of God as redeemer but equally to rectify the knowledge of God as creator.

On the basis of this sort of textual evidence, some prominent Calvin commentators, including Karl Barth, Peter Barth, G. C. Berkouwer and T. H. L. Parker,

8. For example, knowledge of God as creator presupposes a being with power, but it does not analytically entail the exercise of power in providential control over the world. When Calvin speaks of the power of God manifested in the created order, it is typically power exercised in providence (*Institutes* 1.16.1–3). So the visible works of creation may be viewed as augmenting the content of a preconception of God implanted in human nature. Cf. Cicero, *De natura deorum* 2.13, and Sextus Empiricus, *Adversus mathematicos* (Against the professors) 9.61.

conclude that, according to Calvin, the natural knowledge of God is nothing more than an abstract *possibility* for fallen and sinfully corrupted human reason.[9] According to these thinkers, Calvin maintained that the noetic effects of sin have *in fact* completely extinguished the natural knowledge of God. So there is no basis in Calvin for any *actual* natural theology. However, the plausibility of such an argument depends crucially on just how we understand Calvin's view of the epistemic consequences of sin.

The knowledge of God

To this end, it is important to be clear about just what Calvin *means* by 'knowledge of God'. He begins his entire discussion on humanity's knowledge of God in the *Institutes* by clarifying this.

> Now, the knowledge of God, as I understand it, is that by which we not only conceive that there is a God, but also grasp what befits us and is proper to his glory, in fine, what is to our advantage to know of him. Indeed, we shall not say that, properly speaking, God is known where this is no religion or piety. Here I do not yet touch upon the sort of knowledge with which men in themselves lost and accursed, apprehend God the Redeemer in Christ the Mediator, but I speak only of the primal and simple knowledge to which the very order of nature would have led us if Adam had remained upright. (1.2.1)

The natural knowledge of God, then, embraces several different elements. It includes (i) propositional content: (a) conceiving that there is a God and (b) grasping what benefits us and is proper to his glory. Calvin links the perception of various divine attributes to (b), for example the perception of God's goodness, power and wisdom as they are manifested in the works of creation and providence. He links the perception of our duties to God to both (a) and (b). But Calvin's 'knowledge of God' is not merely *propositional* knowledge of God. Calvin emphasized a second element, (ii) piety. Calvin defines piety as "that reverence joined with love of God which the knowledge of his benefits induces" (1.2.1). While one might be tempted to see (ii) as an effect of knowledge of God, Calvin links them more closely. Calvin says that God is not known where there is no piety or religion, and "all right knowledge of God is born in obedience" (1.6.2). Calvin disparages knowledge that is disinterested or merely theoretical in nature: "And here again we ought to observe that we are called to a knowledge of God: not

9. See Barth (1935), Parker (1959: 27–39), Berkouwer (1979: 30–31, 46–7, 152–3), Beversluis (1995) and Barth & Brunner (2002: 106; cf. 107–9). Parker actually allowed a remaining, although corrupted, *sensus divinitatis* but denied knowledge of God derived from the *opera Dei*. For a response to Beversluis, see Sudduth (1998).

that knowledge which, content with empty speculation, merely flits in the brain, but that which will be sound and fruitful if we duly perceive it, and if it takes root in the heart" (1.5.9). Hence, Calvin emphasizes that "our knowledge should serve first to teach us fear and reverence" (1.2.2) and "knowledge of this sort, then, ought not only to arouse us to the worship of God but also to awaken and encourage us to the hope of the future life" (1.5.10; cf. 2.13.1). Again, he writes: "the knowledge of God does not rest in cold speculation, but carries with it the honoring of him" (1.12.1). "True knowledge of God", then, is a matter of the intellect and the will (i.e. choices and affections).[10]

In several passages where Calvin draws attention to the effects of sin on the natural knowledge of God, he focuses on the impact of sin on the ethical aspects of humanity's knowledge of God, not its propositional content. *Institutes* book I, chapter 4, which introduces the corruption of the natural knowledge of God, links this corruption very closely to the absence of piety, false worship and disobedience to God. The post-lapsarian "confused knowledge of God" is contrasted with the "piety from which religion takes its source" (1.4.4; cf. 1.4.1). Calvin goes on to elaborate:

> For where they ought to have remained consistently obedient throughout life, they boldly rebel against him in almost all their deeds, and are zealous to placate him merely with a few paltry sacrifices … while their trust ought to have been placed in him they neglect him and rely on themselves. (1.4.4)

God's revelation of himself in nature is said to "flow away without profiting us" (1.5.11) and "in no way lead[s] us into the right path" (1.5.14). So, for example, we "ought, then, to break forth in praises of him but are actually puffed up and swollen with all the more pride" (1.5.4). Hence, Calvin concludes, "we lack the natural ability to mount up unto the pure and clear knowledge of God" (1.5.15). In these important passages, Calvin contrasts the pre-lapsarian moral and religious efficacy of the knowledge of God with its post-lapsarian failure in this regard. This ethical emphasis is perhaps more readily apparent in the 1536 edition of the *Institutes*, in which Calvin introduced 'knowledge of God' only as a short preface to his extended discourse on the law of God.

The retention of epistemic elements

Calvin clearly affirms the retention of *some* correct propositional content in humanity's natural knowledge of God.[11] Calvin refers to an instinctual "awareness

10. See Parker (1959: 107; cf. 106), Wendel (1963: 152–3) and Dowey (1994: 3; cf. 24–31).
11. See Postema (1992), Bouwsma (1992), Dowey (1994: ch. 3), Steinmetz (1995: 28–32), Warfield (2000: 44–5) and Muller (2003a: 273–6).

of divinity" by which "all" perceive that "there is a God" and that "He is their maker". He also speaks of a "deep-seated conviction that there is a God" (1.3.1), "a sense of deity inscribed on the hearts of all" (1.3.1), "some conception of God is ever alive in all men's minds" (1.3.2), people's minds as "imbued with a firm conviction about God" (1.3.2) and "this conviction … that there is some God" (1.3.3). He goes as far as to claim that "the unity of God has been engraved on the hearts of all" (1.10.3). In each case the context indicates that Calvin is speaking of *fallen* and *unregenerate* human beings. For instance, Calvin says, "to prevent anyone from taking refuge in the pretense of ignorance, God himself has planted in all men a certain understanding of his divine majesty" (1.3.1). Again, there is "no nation so barbarous, no people so savage, that they have not a deep-seated conviction that there is a God" (1.3.1). "The impious themselves", he says, "exemplify the fact that some conception of God is ever alive in all men's minds" (1.3.2). He says that this sense of divinity "can never be effaced" (1.3.3), nor "uprooted" (1.4.4). Hence a "general knowledge of God doth nevertheless remain still in them" (1979a: 170). While this knowledge is "unstable and fleeting" (*Institutes* 1.3.3) and a "confused knowledge of God" (1.4.4), it is knowledge nonetheless.

THE LIMITS AND RECONSTRUCTION OF NATURAL THEOLOGY

There is a remaining concern, however. The retention of some correct propositional content in man's natural knowledge of God might be insufficient to ground any *system* of natural theology. So the *de facto* validity of natural theology may be a hallow sort of validity. In Calvin's view, just *how much* can the natural light of human reason know about God in its fallen, corrupted state?

The limited scope of propositional knowledge of God

While a *sensus divinitatis* remains in nearly all, sin nonetheless negatively impacts the content of the natural knowledge of God. Human beings fall into a "huge mass of errors" in their thoughts about God (*Institutes* 1.4.4), especially when it comes to their thoughts about the nature of God (1.4.2–3, 1.5.4, 1.5.11–12). Speaking of the manifestation of God's wisdom, power and goodness in creation, Calvin says:

> most people, immersed in their own errors, are struck blind in such a dazzling theater … however much the glory of God shines forth, scarcely one man in a hundred is a true spectator of it! (1.5.8)
>
> Human reason, therefore, neither approaches nor strives toward, nor even takes a straight aim at, this truth: to understand who the true God is or what sort of God he wishes to be toward us. (2.2.18)

Human beings "do not therefore apprehend God as he offers himself, but imagine him as they have fashioned him in their own presumption" (1.4.1). Moreover, the noetic effects of sin are often mediated by personal sins, so epistemic blindness is in many instances self-inflicted (1.4.2). Finally, Calvin does not deny "competent and apt statements about God here and there in the philosophers", but he claims that they merely happen upon these truths (2.2.18).

In several places Calvin parses the ignorance of the unregenerate mind in terms of an ignorance of *who* or *what* God is, where this is compatible with a knowledge *that* God is. With respect to Romans 1:20, Calvin wrote: "We conceive that there is a Deity; and then we conclude, that whoever he may be, he ought to be worshipped: but our reason here fails, because it cannot ascertain who or what sort of being God is" (1979b: 71).[12] So while the noetic effects of sin leave the knowledge that there is some God intact, they infect with confusion and error the knowledge of who or what sort of being God is.[13] Perhaps Calvin's contrast cannot be too strictly followed here, but his intent I believe is to restrict the *scope* of the natural knowledge of God in fallen people, going as far as to say that some sinful minds do not recognize the divine attributes of eternity, wisdom, justice and goodness, although these are manifested throughout creation. The propositional content of the *sensus divinitatis* is simply the knowledge that there is some creator and that he ought to be worshipped. While this self-evidently entails the existence of a being with power and knowledge, it does not necessarily entail the existence of an all-wise and all-good being who exercises complete providential care over the world, but these latter concepts are essential to Calvin's doctrine of God. What post-lapsarian minds grasp by nature, then, is fairly general, perhaps supplemented to varying degrees by some knowledge of the divine attributes from the *opera Dei*.

Unregenerate and regenerate natural theology

However, while Calvin was keenly aware of the ways in which fallen humans corrupt the content of the natural knowledge of God, he was also careful to draw a distinction between reason as it functions in fallen, *unregenerate* persons and reason as it operates in fallen *regenerated* persons guided by the Holy Scriptures.[14]

---

12. See Muller (2003b: 155–9) on the Reformed distinction between *an deus sit* (whether there is a God), *quid sit* (what he is), *quails sit* (what sort of being he is).
13. Calvin explicitly draws attention to this in connection with Acts 17; he says that the apostle Paul attempted to show the men at Athens by natural arguments *who* and *what* God is, and thus *how* he should be worshipped, "for they were persuaded that there was some divinity … [but] there remaineth a confused opinion concerning the nature of God" (1979a: 158).
14. See LeCerf (1949: 388), Dowey (1994: 73–7, 131–46), Moroney (2000: 9–12) and Warfield (2000: 68–70).

First, regeneration entails an illumination of the mind that enables the Christian to see God's natural revelation more clearly:

> Men's minds therefore are wholly blind, so that they see not this light of nature which shines forth in created things, until being irradiated by God's Spirit, they begin to understand by faith what otherwise they cannot comprehend ... the faithful ... to whom he has given eyes, see the sparks of his glory, as it were, glittering in every created thing.
> (1979e: 265–6; cf. *Institutes* 2.1.9, 3.2.33)

Secondly, the Christian has the Scriptures, which function like a pair of spectacles, assisting those with weak eyesight to perceive more clearly the manifestation of God in his works: "For by the Scripture as our guide and teacher, he [God] not only makes those things plain which would otherwise escape our notice, but almost compels us to behold them; as if he had assisted our dull sight with spectacles" (1979d: 62; cf. *Institutes* 1.6.1, 1.14.1). Finally, as a restoration of the image of God, regeneration entails a restoration of the distinctly affective or ethical elements in the natural knowledge, which Calvin maintained was lost through the Fall. For the believer, natural theology will be integrated into the distinctly practical sphere of piety.

While the natural theology of the unregenerate is unsound in principle and in fact, Calvin can point positively toward the appropriation of natural theology by the Christian. Here natural theology represents the reflective exploration, presentation and clarification of the revelation of God in the created order in the context of faith. In his commentary on Psalm 19, Calvin says: "David, with a view to encouraging the faithful to contemplate the glory of God, sets before them, in the first place, a mirror of it in the fabric of the heavens, and in the exquisite order of their workmanship which we behold" (1979c: vol. 4, 307). Calvin too urges the believer to consider the *opera Dei*, not to speculate into the secret essence of God but to consider the nature of God as revealed in the workmanship of the universe (*Institutes* 1.5.9). Hence, while Calvin was critical of rational theological enquiry by the philosophers, he sees such enquiry as more than appropriate in the context of faith:

> It is vain for any to reason as philosophers on the workmanship of the world, except those who, having first been by the preaching of the gospel, have learned to submit the whole of their intellectual wisdom (as Paul expresses it) to the foolishness of the cross (1 Corinthians 1:21).
> (Calvin 1979d: 63)

Indeed, Calvin is explicit that divine grace should not "prevent us from applying our senses to the consideration of heaven and earth, that we may thence seek a confirmation in the true knowledge of God" (*ibid.*: 64).

Calvin's commentary on Psalm 104 provides a good illustration of this. At some points Calvin's reasoning simply provides illustrations accessible to natural reason of the observable benefits that result from the temporal and spatial order that the Psalmist declares God has established. In other places Calvin goes further to outline natural arguments that have as their conclusion what is explicitly affirmed by Scripture itself. For example, in Psalm 104:5–9 the Psalmist affirms that by his power God has laid the foundations of the earth so that it remains stable, and God has fixed boundaries between the oceans and dry land so that each remains in its place. Calvin, however, reasons *to* this testimony of Scripture *from* observation and principles of natural philosophy. Calvin argues roughly as follows. It is evident to the senses that (1) the oceans do not overflow their banks and flood the entire earth. (2) If there is no God who by his power restrains the oceans, then the oceans would overflow their banks and flood the entire earth. We know (2) since it is a principle of natural philosophy that (3) the tendency of water – owing to its unstable and fluid properties – is to flow over the boundaries set by the dry land. Therefore, (4) there is a God who by his power restrains the oceans.[15] In this way, Calvin reasons to the testimony of Scripture on the basis of observation and principles of natural philosophy. While Scripture affirms (4), and perhaps suggests that there is a cogent inference from (1) to (4), Scripture does not provide the argument from (1) to (4).

For Calvin, then, the *de facto* validity of natural theology is not undermined by the limits imposed on reason by the noetic effects of sin. While it is impossible for the unbeliever to erect an adequate system of theology relying solely on the resources of natural reason, the epistemic constraints on the natural knowledge of God point to the need for recontextualizing natural theology, placing it in a Christian context. First, on Calvin's view, the believer, in whom the image of God is being restored, is in the best position to consider the manifestation of God in the works of creation and providence. Secondly, rational reflection on general revelation must be situated within the larger framework of biblical theology, so that it plays a role in the systematic development of the doctrine of God. Of course, the Christian reconstruction of natural theology is compatible with the apologetic deployment of theistic arguments. An abiding *sensus divinitatis* provides a point of contact with the unbeliever, as demonstrated in Paul's preaching in the Book of Acts. Paul can argue with unbelievers about the nature of God because they possess a *sensus divinitatis*. So a natural theology that emerges in the context of biblical revelation may direct itself to those situated outside biblical revelation, but this is possible only because Calvin believes there is a universal, innate religious impulse. But natural theology remains fundamentally a rational excursion in the larger journey of biblical and dogmatic theology.

---

15. Calvin develops this argument, a form of inference to best explanation, in his comments on Psalm 104, verses 5, 6 and 9. See Calvin (1979c: vol. 6. 148–52).

CONCLUSION

In this chapter I have examined two prominent features of Calvin's account of the natural knowledge of God that illuminate his positive contributions to philosophical reflection on God. Like many of the reformers, it was Calvin's biblical theology that grounded his acceptance of a natural revelation and the actuality of a natural knowledge of God based on this natural revelation. It was also this biblical theology that set important constraints on the extent to which reason could, of its own resources, develop any systematic account of the being and attributes of God. Hence, for Calvin, rational reflection on the being and attributes of God must be situated in a Christian context, where it will retain its proper ethical orientation and avoid the stultifying 'labyrinth' of reason. This stands in sharp contrast to how natural theology would be conceptualized by the end of the seventeenth century. For Calvin, natural theology must be an aspect of the system of revealed theology, not a rational preface to it. Natural theology provides a clarification and confirmation of faith, not a rational basis for it.

It is not surprising that twentieth-century theologians have often viewed Calvin as an opponent of natural theology. They – unlike Calvin – have typically assumed a one-dimensional view of natural theology as a rational system of theological truth placed alongside, and prior to, revealed or dogmatic theology. While clearly rejecting *this* sort of natural theology, Calvin endorses a very different kind of natural theology. In suggesting the contextual nature of reason itself, the possibility of a Christian natural theology is introduced, for natural theology can now be construed as a product of natural reason functioning in a distinctly Christian context. In this way, Calvin may be read as sanctioning a Protestant project of *fides quaerens intellectum*, a project that at the hands of subsequent Calvinists would prove instrumental to the development of a system of Reformed theology and a theologically inspired philosophy of the Reformed faith.

FURTHER READING

Adams, E. 2001. "Calvin's View of Natural Knowledge of God". *International Journal of Systematic Theology* **3**: 280–92.

Dowey, E., Jr 1952. *The Knowledge of God in Calvin's Theology*. New York: Columbia University Press.

Helm, P. 2004. "Natural Theology and the *Sensus Divinitatis*". In his *John Calvin's Ideas*, 209–45. Oxford: Clarendon Press.

Parker, T. 1952. *Calvin's Doctrine of the Knowledge of God*. Grand Rapids, MI: Eerdmans.

Schreiner, S. 1995. *The Theater of His Glory: Nature and the Natural Order in the Thought of John Calvin*. Grand Rapids, MI: Baker Book House.

Steinmetz, D. 1991. "Calvin and the Natural Knowledge of God". In *Via Augustini: Augustine in the Later Middle Ages, Renaissance and Reformation*, H. Oberman (ed.), 142–56. Leiden: Brill.

Sudduth, M. (forthcoming). *The Reformed Objection to Natural Theology*. Aldershot: Ashgate.

Thomas, J. 1958. "The Place of Natural Theology in the Thought of John Calvin". *Journal of Religious Thought* **15**: 107–36.

Vos, A. 1985. *Aquinas, Calvin, and Contemporary Protestant Thought: A Critique of Protestant Views on the Thought of Thomas Aquinas*. Grand Rapids, MI: Eerdmans.

Warfield, B. 2000. *Calvin and Calvinism*, The Works of Benjamin Breckinridge Warfield, vol. 5. Grand Rapids, MI: Baker Book House.

On NATURAL RELIGION/THEOLOGY see also Chs 6, 7, 11, 12, 13, 19, 23; Vol. 4, Chs 8, 12; Vol. 5, Ch. 23. On THE PROTESTANT REFORMATION see also Ch. 3. On SCRIPTURE see also Chs 4, 15; Vol. 1, Chs 9, 13, 17; Vol. 2, Ch. 19; Vol. 4, Ch. 3; Vol. 5, Ch. 12. On SIN see also Vol. 1, Chs 10, 13.

5

MICHEL DE MONTAIGNE

Marc Foglia

Michel de Montaigne (1533–92) came from a rich bourgeois family that acquired nobility after his father fought in Italy in the army of King Francis I of France. For his grandfather and father the sixteenth century was a period of remarkable social ascent. Yet, from 1562 onwards, France became "a disturbed and sick state" (III.8, F.719)[1] as the wars of religion between Catholics and Huguenots were fought with varying intensity to 1592. In fact, religious faith was only one aspect of the crisis; family clans and friendships did not always correspond to confessional differences. A number of his family members and friends converted to Protestantism, but Montaigne remained faithful to the Catholic Church. Replicating Petrarca's choice in *De vita solitaria* (On the solitary life), he chose to dedicate himself to the Muses. In his library, which was quite large for the time, he had wisdom sayings carved on the wooden beams. These sayings were drawn from the Book of Ecclesiastes, Sextus Empiricus, Lucretius and other classical authors, whom he read intensively.

In spite of a tradition rooted in the nineteenth century, which tended to relegate his work to the expression of a frivolous subjectivity, Montaigne shook some fundamental aspects of Western thought, such as the superiority we assign to human beings over animals (II.12), to reason over custom (I.23), to reason over the world and to European civilization over others (such as the "Barbarians" of Brazil, I.31). He put his judgement to trial, drawing not only from the classics or from historians, but also from his own experience, examining varied opinions, facts or customs in critical sequences he called 'essays'. This literary form, to which Montaigne himself gave birth, calls for hermeneutical subtlety. The reader cannot pick up a passage and simply assert, 'Here is what Montaigne believes'. In

1. References to Montaigne's *Essays* are cited by book (Roman numerals, corresponding to one of the three books of the *Essays*) and chapter numbers; the letter F indicates the Donald M. Frame translation and edition (Montaigne 1948), and the subsequent number is a page number in that work.

the *Essays*, statements are reported opinions, which need to be re-examined by the reader, as they were first by their author.

RELIGION AS CUSTOM

Montaigne tackles all sorts of questions, including religion, with a cultivated freedom of thought. Thus, religion is often depicted as one of the many customs in which we are raised. "We are Christians by the same title that we are Perigordians or Germans" (II.12, F.394; see on this subject the contemporaries Boemus [1520, 1556], Belleforest [1570] and Münster [1575]). Religious ideas and observances deserve to be criticized as any of our customs, but they equally call for the same kind of respect that society deserves. Far from considering human customs as a mere collection of whims, Montaigne sees them as a mould of behaviour and mind (I.23; III.13, F.1008), the other great educator being philosophy (I.26, F.148). Custom enables us to live our lives, yet its hold on us is such that it also frustrates our wish to base our lives on absolute grounds, be they the force of reason or the "laws of conscience" (I.23, F.100). Humanity appears deprived of the absolute, according to a Socratic approach to life formulated at the very end of the *Essays*: "You are as much god as you will own/That you are nothing but a man alone" (III.13, F.1044).

Montaigne has often been mistaken by critics as a 'free thinker', as such people came to be known in the seventeenth century. Liberty of thought is neither an absolute for Montaigne nor a dangerous Utopia. The authority of individual judgement and the desire for new things should be carefully balanced by custom (I.23). It would be dangerous for social order to allow critical judgement free rein: as a first reaction to the bloody religious strife of his time, Montaigne believes that the exercise of critical judgement can open the door to much trouble (II.12: Introduction). Protestants have erred in allowing all and sundry to discuss the interpretation of the Bible, which has only exacerbated the problems within the Church. Religion is something changeable and frail; nevertheless, the will to protect religion by 'human means', such as prosecution or censorship, also adds to the trouble as religious wars all too clearly show (II.12, F.395ff.). Obedience, which implies a respect for tradition and submission to it, is a religious virtue, for if we were to determine our duties through reason, we would soon end up practising cannibalism (II.12, F.436).

CRITICIZING NATURAL THEOLOGY

Montaigne's longest essay is called the "Apology of Raymond Sebond" (hereafter "Apology"); it is a paradoxical defence of a Catalan theologian who in the fifteenth century undertook to reconcile Christian faith with universal reason.

Indeed, Montaigne leads a fierce attack against 'natural theology' and a naive conception of reason, which his father had enjoined him to defend. According to Sebond's *Theologia naturalis sive liber creaturarum* (Natural theology or the book of creatures; 1484), human reason can discover in the 'book of nature' that Christian faith is the true religion. Sebond endeavoured to show that the existence of God and the perfection of God are to be grasped without revelation, and the true principles of faith can be known spontaneously, without the mediation of the university teachers. His thought, inspired by Aquinas, exerted a strong influence on Nicholas of Cusa, Charles de Bovelle and later Hugo Grotius. Montaigne's father entrusted his son with the task of translating the book into French, in order to counter Luther and his 'innovations', which, according to the father, would soon cause the ruin of society. The young Montaigne's translation was published in 1569. Later, as he gathered his thought on reason and religion, Montaigne takes the opposite view: religion escapes reason, and reason is unable to direct human life. Drawing from the classics, such as the writings of Lucretius, Cicero and Laertius, Montaigne asserts that the religion we grasp is only the one we can imagine. He does not trust reason any longer as an alleged universal standard. His position against natural theology will give birth to the religious trend called 'fideism' during the seventeenth century (Popkin 1979).

In a chapter originally intended to defend this heritage, Montaigne comes paradoxically to criticize Aristotelian philosophy and Thomistic theology. He thus writes: "Reason does nothing but go astray in everything, and especially when it meddles with divine things" (II.12, F.469). His reflections on reason and religion lead to a famous praise of scepticism as the philosophy best adapted to the human condition. He ostensibly scorns theological debates, in which he detects an intellectual will of domination: "in the disputes we have at present in our religion … they will tell you quite shamelessly that it is not in God's power to make his body in paradise and on earth, and in several places at the same time" (II.12, F.477). The faculties of human beings are not fit for achieving the knowledge of God. We have better things to do than to quarrel about the supernatural, which will not improve our condition. As a consequence, religion is on many occasions brushed aside in the *Essays* as a source of trouble, an unwarranted diversion from the human condition (see e.g. I.32; I.56; II.12, F. 553ff.), or an astonishing testimony to our foolishness.

Religion as we know it cannot be the recipient of a transcendent gift, since in it we are unable to separate the wheat from the chaff. We corrupt religious matters as soon as we handle them (II.12). The possibility is to be excluded that we could receive religion as an "extraordinary and privileged favor"; Montaigne doubts that "purely human means are at all capable of this" (II.12, F.389). After having brought true religion back to faith, Montaigne asks if it would not be better to speak about "simple belief", rather than about a "faith" (F.393) that urges us to believe in a divine intervention. One might therefore ask whether there is a valid notion of religion at all in the *Essays*. In any case, if religion is a human matter, as it is, we have to exert our judgement on it. We cannot blind our minds to the vices, violence, unjustified sacrifices and social catastrophes religion sometimes fuels. Montaigne's intention is obviously to protect himself and his readers against any kind of fanaticism. He judged scepticism among the whole range of philosophies as the best way to prepare for faith (II.12), but we can question his willingness to pass from scepticism to faith. "It presents man naked and empty, acknowledging his natural weakness … annihilating his judgment to make more room for faith" (II.12, F.455). Montaigne never fails to notice and criticize human arrogance when we invest the divine greatness with our humours, faculties and most shameful needs (F.470) or submit God to our endless speeches and debates. To have a look at one's religion is also a way to know oneself, as Plato had noticed in *Alcibiades*, and a way to purify one's mind from undue pretence. The perspective of annihilation of thought does not really appeal to the author, who prefers the formation of a stronger and more flexible judgement.

FREE JUDGEMENT AND THE AUTHORITY OF THE CHURCH

In reference to considerations of social order, Montaigne thinks that the authority of the Church in religious matters should be kept intact. Yet, the authority of theologians should not extend beyond religious matters, allowing for freedom on simply human or non-religious matters: "the divine doctrine keeps her rank better apart, as Queen and mistress" (I.56, F.284). One might therefore assume that Montaigne's profession of religious obedience is somehow a strategy to secure his liberty of judgement, although this submission has been taken at face value by some commentators. "And I submit them [my thoughts] to the judgment of those whose concern is to regulate not only my actions and my writings, but even my thoughts" (I.56, F.278). The scope of this submission is reduced by the claim that, in matters other than religious ones, human judgement should be freely exerted: "I set forth notions that are human and my own, simply as human notions considered in themselves, not as determined and decreed by heavenly ordinance … as a matter of opinion, not a matter of faith" (I.56, F.284). Montaigne thus dismisses the scholastic conception of philosophy as *ancilla theologiae*. Philosophy, as the exercise and formation of judgement, is not to be ruled by such authorities as schools, universities (see I.25, "Of Pedantry"), science or established disciplines, which Montaigne often thrusts aside as "the doctrine". Is not entrusting spiritual matters to the Church also a way of removing a bone of contention from human society?

Montaigne does not deny that there is such a thing as sainthood, but we would be mistaken to think it could be reached by force or will. Does this mean that our natural faculties are useless in religion? As the example of Socrates shows, the more we accomplish ourselves as human beings, the more enjoyable, and the more akin to the divine, human life proves to be (III.13, F.1044). Book III delivers a more optimistic message than the "Apology". The word 'God' retains a meaning, although we cannot grasp it through reason: it means the fullness, the being and the eternity in comparison with which we can conceive of our nothingness (II.12, F.555). A French critic and philosopher, Marcel Conche (1996), has noticed that the consecrated words 'Holy Trinity', 'Incarnation' and 'Redemption' do not appear in the *Essays*. Since these words refer to mysteries reserved for the Church, Montaigne carefully avoids their use. Nevertheless, the word 'God' occurs 331 times, indicating that Montaigne takes it to be a word properly used in secular investigations. As the key term in Montaigne's investigations of religions, the word 'God' does not betray a commitment to any particular belief or doctrine. In this sense, there is at least an attempt in the *Essays* to conceive of God in a very general way, and as the limit of human thought.

Indeed, the *Essays*, far from reducing God to a human whim, challenge the limits of our understanding of God. If we were able to see the world as God sees it, we would not admit the notion of evil. For example, we would accept that a child be stuck to another child with only one head. "What we call monsters are not so to God, who sees in the immensity of his work the infinity of forms that he has comprised in it" (II.30, F.654). Notions such as 'evil', 'false' and 'impossible' are relative to our limited knowledge, not to the world itself or to God (I.27, F.161). Montaigne thus seems to adopt the neo-Stoic view of an orderly world infused with God, in which all things are as they should be. He experiences a religious feeling of gratitude towards nature, which he expresses by reference to classical sources rather than Christian ones. Nature, as a 'gentle guide', deserves a thankful prayer (III.13, F.1042). This intellectual and emotional prayer is both a personal feeling and a rational conception, which borrows from the 'natural right' developed by Cicero and Seneca, and assimilates with discretion the heritage of Sebond. Montaigne does not try to build a theology or a philosophy to justify his attitude; he rather looks to nature as a kind of lost paradise: "I seek her footprints everywhere. We have confused them with artificial tracks ..." (III.13, F.1042). In his quest for a norm, the author of the *Essays* knows he can rely only on feeble human strengths.

FROM ROMAN CENSORSHIP TO SOCRATES' GOD

Indisposed by the use of the notions of 'nature' and 'fortune' in the *Essays*, the censors in Rome ordered Montaigne to strike them out and substitute 'God' and 'Providence' (see the *Travel Journal to Italy* [hereafter *Journal*] in Montaigne 1948). Once back in France, Montaigne disregarded the Censors' judgement, letting the text stand as it was. Contrary to the decisions of the Council of Trent, he refused in the chapter "On Prayers" (I.56) to give prayer full efficacy, which he knew would elicit particular attention from religious authorities. Montaigne's view becomes quite clear in the following statement: "We must have our soul clean, at least in that moment in which we pray to him [God], and be rid of vicious passions" (I.56, F.279). In other words, prayer cannot act as a substitute for the work of moral effort. This opinion, which the Roman censors condemned, could have brought Montaigne some trouble during his travels in Italy. His courage should be stressed, as he brought his book with him to Rome and had it confiscated. The offensive aspect of Montaigne's thought should not be undervalued, although it stands in contradiction with his willingness to support religious customs.

As to the personal religious convictions of Montaigne, great controversy has long reigned between specialists, some taking him to be a sincere Christian, others as a precursor of libertinism, or even a veiled Jew or Huguenot. In any case, this ambiguity does not mean that Montaigne was indifferent to religion, whether as a theoretical problem or as a range of human practices. The *Journal* relates that he was keen on observing religious mores; thus, for example, he headed towards the synagogue in Rome and spoke with rabbis. Some critics also point to the fact that Montaigne's mother came from a family of *convertos*, who emigrated from Spain around 1492.

Montaigne's attitude toward religion, which was primarily one of curiosity rather than one of reverence, could also be interpreted as a pragmatic approach: the best way to approach religion is to learn how it is practised. Religion, deprived of its claim to truth, is nevertheless an important part of human customs and practices. This view is supported by the figure of the god Apollo, who would have taught this to Socrates and his contemporaries:

> How could that ancient god more clearly accuse human knowledge of ignorance of the divine being, and teach men that religion was only a creature of their own invention, suitable to bind their society together, than by declaring, as he did … that the true cult for each man was that which he found observed according to the practice of the place he was in? (II.12, F.530)

Montaigne finds in antiquity (for example, in Plutarch and Cicero, whom he read intensively) a notion of religion as a major element of civil life. For Montaigne, however, religion does not appear any longer as a structuring civil force, but rather as an occasion for division and war. Religion is thus cut off from its divine and civil foundations, while the interior dimension of religion does not really appear, being inferior to the moral requirement. We should not be surprised, therefore, that on the subject of religion the modernity of the *Essays* has been obvious to many commentators. At the end of the nineteenth century, Montaigne is accepted (by e.g. Compayré 1879; Lanson 1929; Villey 1933) as an author compatible with the laicism of the Third Republic, and apt to offer readers a general rather than merely specialized understanding. Montaigne's scepticism, however, was considered dangerous, and led the pedagogues to classify him as a writer, not a philosopher. At the end of the twentieth century, Montaigne receives praise as the founding father of ethnology, and critic of Western civilization and cultural relativism (see Lévy-Strauss 1981; Lestringant 1990; Todorov 2000). In the first case, Montaigne is the patron for all gentlemen to come, setting a kind of universal human standard; one century later, he is the philosophical counterpart of Columbus, denouncing the Western will to eradicate other people. Nevertheless, in both cases, the conspicuous part played by Montaigne in the history of thought includes a breach with religion as a higher value. The humanist thinker is first defined outside his traditional medieval environments, the Church and the university, which Montaigne presents as places of subjection (II.12). He is also the herald of a new humanity, which educates itself through a new relationship to classical knowledge that is personal and vivid, and forbids itself to consider others as 'barbarians' in virtue of not sharing the same religion or because they "would not wear socks" (I.31).

A HUMANIST APPROACH TO RELIGION

Seeing clearly that religion all too often serves as a pretext for giving free rein to tyrannical passions, for oppressing or killing those who do not think the same as we do, Montaigne sets it down as a rule that we should not commingle the name of God with our human passions (I.32, F.194), or with our changing interests. It is necessary to neutralize the tyrannies of religion and the stupidity of some religious believers:

> I leave aside the gross impostures of religions, with which so many great nations and so many able men have been seen to be besotted, for since this matter is beyond the scope of our human reason, it is more excusable for anyone who is not extraordinarily enlightened by divine favor to be lost in it. (I.23, F.95)

Indeed, many passages in the *Essays* can be read as a fierce critique or even dismissal of religion, as if their author had been eager to warn his readers of the dangers of religion. Should we not also consider religion as a possible incentive toward virtue, or, if not, as a custom that enables people to live together? Montaigne is looking for solutions to a world overcome by crisis and despair, and he shows benevolence towards religious feelings that can bring people in harmony with nature (III.1, III.13). God is synonymous with nature, as Montaigne accepts "everything that Nature has made for him" (III.13). At the end of the *Essays*, the critical enquiry of judgement is superseded by a feeling of reconciliation with life, which combines Stoic approval of the world order with Christian gratitude towards the "almighty Giver".

As human phenomena, religions are at the intersections of many intellectual and psychological faults, such as the ones that today go by the names of 'anthropocentrism' and 'ethnocentrism', from which violence easily results. The task is difficult, since it implies a resistance of judgement against our very wish to believe and against our tendency to claim the possession of truth. Therefore, education of judgement comes to the forefront as an uncertain path towards peace, happiness and moderation. It is worth noticing that this education is conceived by Montaigne without reference to the Bible or to any particular school of thought and without any reference to the Bible (I.25, I.26; see Porteau 1935). Willingness to engage in dialogue and an attitude of open-mindedness are the main requirements: "Wonderful brilliance may be gained for the human judgment by getting to know men. We are all huddled and concentrated in ourselves, and our vision is reduced to the length of our nose. Socrates was asked where he was from. He replied not 'Athens', but 'the world'" (I.26, F.140). Obviously, the teachings of any specific religion do not fit within this cosmopolitan manifesto.

In order to examine the diversity of religious conceptions and approaches in a rich and variegated literature, we mirror the behaviour of bees, which flit from flower to flower gathering pollen. Montaigne intensively practised this '*butinage*' method in his private library, following the 'innutrition' doctrine elaborated by humanist scholars such as Erasmus and Bembo (Grafton & Jardine 1986). In order to keep religions at a distance, it is best to consider their diversity. The humanist approach, when applied to religion, manifests a deep philosophical meaning. Our judgement should make an effort to transcend our usual narrow-mindedness: "When the vines freeze in my village, my priest infers that the wrath of God is upon the human race" (I.26, F.141). Similarly, in order to escape religious partiality, let us shift our point of view from our village or country to the world at large: "This great world … is the mirror in which we must look at ourselves to recognize ourselves from the proper angle" (I.26, F.141). Thus, Montaigne seems to assert his Christian faith only when necessary, as a tribute to the society he lives in; but he prefers to think of himself as, like Socrates, a citizen of the world. The problem is that religion counts precisely among the highest obstacles one can face on the road towards universal dialogue.

AGAINST SPIRITUAL ARROGANCE

In order to free people's minds of their religious prejudices, Montaigne uses religion against religion, drawing on Christian and antique religious literature in order to destroy human pretentiousness, of which theological systems and philosophical doctrines stand out as the most splendid but fictitious and credulous expressions (II.12). We find on the beams of his library this quotation from the Bible: "If anyone thinks he is something when he is nothing, he deceives himself" (Galatians 6:3). Marguerite de Navarre, sister of King Francis I and famous supporter of the Reformation, wrote in the middle of the century: "God confuses the glory of those who claim to be something and are nothing" (1558: XXII). Montaigne similarly expatiates on this Christian theme of human nothingness in the "Apology".

Nevertheless, he manages to divert this spiritual trend from its usual meaning: the thought of the absolute is so far removed from life that we should soon seek to reconcile humanity with itself. In a more optimistic way, Montaigne thus comes to write: "Of the opinions of philosophy I most gladly embrace those that are most solid, that is to say, most human and most our own" (III.13, F.1042). Thus, the reader might notice a continuity when Montaigne enumerates conceptions of God, on the one hand even making fun of the ancient philosophers – "to make gods ourselves, like antiquity, passes the utmost bounds of feeble-mindedness" (II.12, F.466) – while, on the other hand, taking pleasure in describing his favourite dishes, seasons, hobbies or atmospheres – "I am not excessively fond of either salads or fruits, except melons" (III.13, F.1031). Many circumstances that the shadow of religion had deprived of any value become in the *Essays* occasions for writing, reflection and enjoyment, as they can be in real life. Melons, but also lemons, rabbits and glasses, become the objects of painting, an art reconciled with the modest frailties and beauties of human life (Todorov 2000).

As our religious attitudes and observances are part of the world of custom, they must fall under the scrutiny of human judgement. Islam is several times severely criticized (II.12, F.467, F.482) and Montaigne correspondingly does not fail to criticize the behaviour of Christians on many occasions (II.5, II.11). Whereas the nature and powers of God are not subject to critical appreciation, since they escape the power of our understanding, Montaigne criticizes as boldly as prudence allows him a Father of the Church, namely, Tertullian: "This arrogance of trying to discover God with our eyes made a great man of our religion give the deity bodily form" (II.12, F.478). The same scathing remarks apply equally to Christian and pagan dogmas: "Because our occupations burden us, Strato endowed the gods with total immunity from duties" (II.12, F.478). It is obvious, from a mere lexical point of view, that the author of the *Essays* escapes a Christian frame of thought, being more familiar with Plato, Cicero and Seneca than with the Bible, and quoting more liberally from the classics than from Scripture. He also draws happily on the criticisms of pagan religion he found in Augustine, applying this anthropological critique to all types of religion. "In short, the construction and the destruction of the deity, and its conditions, are wrought by man, on the basis of a relationship to himself. What a pattern and what a model!" (II.12, F.481). Brought back to the needs and imaginations of humanity, religion becomes an object of philosophical enquiry, as all other phenomena are. We thus find a rich and genuine philosophy of religion in the *Essays*.

CONCLUSION: A COPERNICAN PHILOSOPHY OF RELIGION

In the "Apology", Montaigne welcomed the thesis of Copernicus, which displaced humanity from its central position in the order of the universe. The previous scientific tradition may have been a mere reflection of our arrogance. Similarly, religion is much better understood when we assign humanity as its centre and true origin. On the verge of modernity, Montaigne appears as the Copernicus of human religion, re-assigning the central role around which all else revolves. "The powers of the gods are detailed according to our need: one cures horses, one men, one the plague ..." (II.12, F.483). Religious representations are indeed the warehouse of human wishes, where one sometimes exerts real power over other people or experiences real feelings. "It is a pity that we fool ourselves with our own monkey tricks and inventions. 'They fear their own imaginings' like children who take fright at that very face that they have smeared and blackened for their playmate" (II.12, F.479, quoting Lucan). It may be that religions have never taught us about God, but only about ourselves.

Montaigne advocates a sceptical reservation of judgement whenever we are confronted with claims to truth. However, the study of religions, miracles (III.11) and religious virtues such as chastity (II.12; III.12) can be a way of enlarging one's experience and knowledge of human life. Without a philosophy of religion, the Socratic project of 'know thyself' would remain incomplete. This lesson will exert a strong influence on Blaise Pascal, who will rely on Montaigne's 'essays' on religion as a springboard for his own thinking in the *Pensées*.

FURTHER READING

Auerbach, E. 1953. *Mimesis: The Representation of Reality in Western Literature*, W. Trask (trans.). Princeton, NJ: Princeton University Press.

Carraud, V. & J.-L. Marion (eds) 2004. *Montaigne: scepticisme, métaphysique, théologie*. Paris: PUF.

Crouzet, D. 1990. *Guerriers de Dieu: La violence au temps des troubles de religion, vers 1525–vers 1610*, 2 vols. Seyssel: Champ Vallon.

Friedrich, H. 1949. *Montaigne*. Bern: Francke.

Hoffmann, G. 1998. *Montaigne's Career*. Oxford: Clarendon Press.

Imbach, R. 1983. "'Et toutefois nostre outrecuidance veut faire passer la divinité par nostre estamine', l'essai II,12 et la genèse de la pensée moderne. Construction d'une thèse explicative". In *Paradigmes de théologie philosophique*, O. Höffe & R. Imbach (eds), 199–219. Fribourg: Editions universitaires.

Kallendorf, C. (ed. & trans.) 2002. *Humanist Educational Treatises*. Cambridge, MA: Harvard University Press.

Langer, U. (ed.) 2005. *The Cambridge Companion to Montaigne*. Cambridge: Cambridge University Press.

Supple, J. 1984. *Arms Versus Letters: The Military and Literary Ideals in the "Essays" of Montaigne*. Oxford: Clarendon Press.

On FIDEISM see also Vol. 5, Ch. 13. On HUMANISM see also Ch. 16; Vol. 2, Ch. 19; Vol. 5, Ch. 6. On PRAYER see also Vol. 1, Chs 13, 18; Vol. 5, Ch. 21. On SCEPTICISM see also Vol. 1, Ch. 12; Vol. 4, Ch. 11.

6

FRANCISCO SUÁREZ

Bernardo J. Canteñs

Francisco Suárez was born on 5 January 1548 in Granada, Spain. At the age of thirteen he set out with his older brother to the University of Salamanca, where he began his studies in canon law. After three years, on 16 June 1564, he entered the Novitiate of the Society of Jesus (Jesuits), which had been founded by Ignatius of Loyola in 1540. He was ordained a priest in 1572. Suárez taught philosophy and theology for forty-four years at some of the most prestigious international universities of his time: Avila (1571), Segovia (1575), Valladolid (1576), Rome (1580–85), Alcalá (1585–92), Salamanca (1592–7) and Coimbra (1597–1616). He died in Lisbon on 25 September 1617. He was nicknamed *Doctor eximius et pius* (Most exalted and pious teacher) by Pope Paul V.

Suárez was a prolific writer and his *Opera omnia* consists of twenty-six volumes. A list of his most notable publications include (in chronological order): *De mysteriis vitae Christi* (On the mysteries of the life of Christ; 1592); *De sacramentis I* and *II* (On the sacraments; 1595/1602); *Disputationes metaphysicae* (Metaphyscial disputations; 1597); *De censuris* (On censures; 1603); *De Deo uno et trino* (On God, one and triune; 1606); *De virtute et statu religionis I and II* (On the virtue and state of religion; 1608/9); *De legibus* (On laws; 1612); and *Defensio fidei catholicae* (Defence of the Catholic faith; 1613). The following works appeared posthumously: *De gratia I* and *III* (On grace; 1619); *De angelis* (On the angels; 1620); *De anima* (On the soul; 1620–21); *De opera sex dierum* (On the works of the six days; 1621); *De fide, spe, et caritate* (On faith, hope and charity; 1621); *De virtute et statu religionis III* and *IV* (On the virtue and state of religion; 1624/25); *De ultimo fine* (On the final end; 1628); *De gratia II* (On grace; 1651); and *De vera intelligentia auxilii efficacies* (On the true understanding of efficacious cause; 1655).

While much of his work centred on theology, he wrote an important and influential philosophical work called *Disputationes metaphysicae* (Metaphysical disputations; hereafter *DM*) in 1597. There are five elements that characterize Suárez's *DM* as a pre-eminent philosophical work. First, it is one of the few scholastic works of such an enormous size to be devoted only to metaphysics; secondly, it is, even today, one of the most well-structured and systematized metaphysical treatises; thirdly, it is one of the most comprehensive works on metaphysics; fourthly, its style is historically rich, including a wide spectrum of ancient and medieval philosophical sources; and finally, its style is philosophically rigorous, providing detailed arguments for the views he rejects and defends. To illustrate the structure and completeness of the *DM*, as well as the place of Suárez's natural theology within this work, a brief description of it is in order.

Suárez's *DM* is composed of fifty-four disputations, which are divided into two main parts. The first part (disputations 1–27) studies the concept of being, *qua* real being. It analyses the properties of being (i.e. unity, goodness and truth) and the causes of being (i.e. material, formal, efficient and final causes). The second part (disputations 28–54) investigates four different kinds of beings: infinite being; finite substantial being; finite accidental being; and beings of reason. While this succinct description leaves out many of the details, it provides some idea of the methodical and systematic rationality driving its orchestration.

SUÁREZ'S NATURAL THEOLOGY

Suárez's natural theology is expounded primarily in his *DM*, particularly disputation 29, "About God, the First Being and Uncreated Substance, as He Can by Natural Reason Be Known to Exist", where he develops arguments for the existence of a first, uncreated being, and disputation 30, "On the First Being, Insofar as He Can Be Known Through Natural Reason, His Essence and Attributes", where he examines the essence of the first uncreated being. Before proceeding to examine these in more detail, let us explore four general elements that permeate the spirit of Suárez's natural theology.

First, Suárez's natural theology does not use doctrines of faith or claims based on revelation to support philosophical arguments. Secondly, Suárez viewed the human intellect as having a limited capacity to know and understand the divine nature. He held that a person could not obtain knowledge of God's essence as it is in itself through natural reason directly and immediately; instead, the best the human intellect could do is to know about God through God's effects, which are accessible through natural faculties of sense-perception. Thirdly, Suárez's natural theology relies heavily on negative theology for understanding and describing the nature of God. He argued that since God's essence cannot be positively grasped by the human intellect, we mostly talk about God through negations. For instance, the claim that God is a being that exists through its own being, "although it seems to be positive, *only adds a negation to being as such* … Through this negation we state a positive and simple perfection of that being, which thus in itself and its own essence includes existence itself, in a way that it receives it from no other" (Suárez 2004: 5–6, emphasis added). Finally, Suárez concurred with Thomas Aquinas that the existence of God was not self-evident and thus that a metaphysical demonstration was necessary to prove the existence of a first cause and creator of all things. He accepted the distinction between a proposition being self-evident *in itself* and a proposition being self-evident *for us*. Suárez believed that the proposition 'God exists' is self-evident in itself but not for us.

DISPUTATION 29: METAPHYSICAL ARGUMENT FOR THE EXISTENCE OF GOD

Disputation 29 has three sections. In the first section, Suárez presents and defends the metaphysical argument for the existence of a first uncreated being. In the second section, he proceeds to demonstrate *a posteriori* that there can only be one uncreated being and thus that this uncreated being is the one true God. In the third section, he presents an *a priori* demonstration that there can only be one uncreated being and thus that this uncreated being is the one true God.

Suárez's metaphysical argument for the existence of a first cause

Suárez rejects the validity of arguments for the existence of God based on natural philosophy. He considers two physical arguments, one from motion and another from the rational soul, and he rejects both, showing that they either fail to demonstrate the existence of a first, uncreated, immaterial substance or have to rely on metaphysical principles to produce merely probable conclusions for God's existence. He concludes that arguments for the existence of an uncreated, immaterial substance belong properly to the science of metaphysics, as opposed to the science of natural philosophy. Nevertheless, he maintains that the physical sciences prepare the way for the metaphysical proofs. In this sense, then, natural philosophy and metaphysics can work together toward developing an argument for the existence of God.

The difference between an argument from natural philosophy and one from metaphysics can be reduced to the basic principles on which these arguments rest. An argument from natural philosophy is based on the principle that "Every thing that is moved is moved by another" (P1). An argument from metaphysics is based on the principle that "Everything that is produced is produced by another" (P2). Suárez argues that the necessity of the truth of P2 is more evident than the necessity of the truth of P1. He introduces counter-examples in which something is moved but not by another, such as acts moved by one's will, to demonstrate that P1 is not absolutely necessary. On the other hand, he argues that P2 is absolutely necessary, since there are only three explanations for how a thing can come into being: from another, from itself or from nothing. The last is impossible because something cannot come from nothing, and the second is impossible because before a thing exists it is nothing. Therefore, it is evident and necessary that everything that is produced is produced by another. P2 is the foundation for Suárez's metaphysical argument for the existence of God.

The argument goes as follows:

[1] Every being is either made or not made, that is uncreated.
[2] All beings in the totality [of being] cannot be made [i.e. not all beings in the totality of being can be made].
[3] Therefore, it is necessary that there be some being which is not made, or which is uncreated [i.e. necessary being].
(Suárez 2004: 66)

Why can all beings not be made? Suárez argues that if a being is made by another, then that other being is either made by another (a third being) or it is an uncreated being. If it is an uncreated being, then we have derived our conclusion. If it is made by a third being, then that being is either an uncreated being or it is made by another being (a fourth being). This series of efficient causes can have only three possible outcomes: (i) arrive at a first uncreated being, (ii) go on to infinity or (iii) move in a circle. Suárez defends the view that both (ii) and (iii) are impossible and therefore (i) must be true.

Why can a series of dependent beings not be infinitely circular?

Reasoning in a circle, with respect to efficient causes, is to suppose a scenario like the following: B1 produces B2, B2 produces B3, and B3 produces B1. This, Suárez argues, contradicts the metaphysical principle P2 (everything produced must be produced by another). The effects caused by a being cannot also be the cause of the existence of that being (e.g. B1), since its power to cause anything already presupposes its existence. However, Suárez raises an interesting objection: it is true that if B1 produces B2, then B2 cannot produce B1 if their existences overlap in time; however, why could B1 not produce B2, and B2 produce B3, and, after B1 goes out of existence, B3 produce B1? This is conceivable given a metaphysical hypothesis such as the Pythagorean conception of reincarnation, where souls return to new bodies continuously. Suárez points out that such a metaphysical view is impossible because it would rest on the supposition that there can be an infinite series of dependent beings, or on outcome (ii), which is impossible. In other words, an infinitely circular series of beings would have no first uncreated being (i), but would consist in an infinitely circular series of contingent beings (iii), which in turn presupposes an infinite series of dependent causes (ii).

Why can a series of dependent beings not go on infinitely?

Suárez deliberately excludes arguments that prove the impossibility of an actual infinite; instead, his line of argumentation proves the impossibility that the whole collection of beings in the world is made or dependent. The argument, therefore, defends the minor premise 2:

[4] If [2] were false, that is, if all beings in the totality of being were made, then the world would be a collection made up entirely of dependent beings.
[5] "It is impossible that the whole collection of beings or of efficient causes [in the world] be dependent in its being and its operations.
[3] [Therefore] It is necessary that among them there is something necessary [i.e. not made or uncreated]" (Suárez 2004: 69).

The weight of the argument shifts from premise 2 to 5, that is, if 5 is true Suárez believes his argument for 3 is sound. Premise 5 emphasizes the impossibility that the world consists only of a collection of dependent beings. However, the question remains: why is it impossible that the whole collection of beings or of efficient causes in the world be dependent in its being and its operations? Suárez continues:

[6] [I]f, therefore, the whole collection of things [in the world] were dependent [i.e. 5 were false], it [the whole collection] would necessarily depend upon another. [from P2]
[7] Outside the [*whole*] collection [of things in the world] there is nothing else. [by definition]
[3] [Therefore] It is necessary that among them there is something necessary [i.e. not made or uncreated]. (*Ibid.*)

Here the weight of the argument shifts again from premise 5 to 6, that is, if 6 is true Suárez believes his argument for 3 is sound. Suárez is aware that there is an implicit premise missing in the argument, which he stands ready to defend, namely, 6′ that "if every being taken separately or distributively would be dependent and made, the whole collection also would be dependent and made" (*ibid.*: 71).

Is a collection of dependent beings dependent?

Suárez presents an objection (similar to the one David Hume presents many years later) when he argues that if the whole comprises its parts, then the causal explanation of each part should satisfy an explanation of the whole. Therefore, the total sum of the causal explanation of each particular individual is also the causal explanation of the collection itself. As a consequence, we may conclude that if there is an efficient cause for every dependent being, then an independent cause for the collection itself is not necessary. Suárez admits that this line of reasoning works for some concepts of causes, such as material and formal causes, or what he refers to as "second efficient causes". However, he defends the view that "if some total multitude as such depends efficiently, it is necessary that it depend upon something not included in that multitude" (*ibid.*: 70).

Suárez distinguishes two notions of efficient cause. The first is understood "adequately and according to its whole self" (*adeaequate et secundum se totam*) and is the one he intends to use in his metaphysical argument. Let us refer to this notion as 'total efficient cause'. Suárez views a total efficient cause as having an explanatory value that extends over an entire species of events and things. The second notion of cause is understood as a relative efficient cause and its explanatory value extends only to the events and things it immediately engenders. For instance, the relative efficient cause of a fire is the previous existing fire that produced it. A first fire, then, may be said to be the relative efficient cause of a second fire, if it produced that fire; and a second fire is the relative efficient cause of a third, if it produced that fire. However, neither the first nor the second fire – independently or conjoined – can be said to be the total efficient cause of fire in general. Instead, the total efficient cause of the fire entails a broader notion of causality, necessarily requiring an explanation not only of why there is this (e.g. second) or that (e.g. third) particular fire but also why there is fire in general. The total efficient cause, therefore, encompasses the cause of the first fire and all subsequent fires, and it is not limited to a particular fire; it requires an explanation of the making of fire as such, that is, an explanation of the generator of the fire. This notion of total efficient cause is evidently different and more fundamental, since:

> the whole generated fire is said to depend upon a generator, because without the action of that [generator], in fact the whole [fire] would not have existed; ... when, therefore, we say that the whole collection of beings cannot be dependent [and thus there must be an independent being], we understand it in this way. (*Ibid.*)

This is the key to Suárez's defence of 6′ and consequently of 3. If Suárez's argument is successful in demonstrating 3, that there must exist an uncreated or necessary being, then it also demonstrates 3′, that "we cannot go on in that progression [of causes] to infinity, but we must stop at an unproduced being which is also independent in its causing" (*ibid.*: 69–70).

SUÁREZ'S *A POSTERIORI* DEMONSTRATION THAT THERE CAN BE ONLY ONE UNCREATED BEING

Having demonstrated that there must be at least one independent being, Suárez goes on to demonstrate that this being is God. To accomplish this, he believes it is necessary to show that there can be only one necessary being; since if it is possible that there are many necessary beings then we have not shown that the one true God exists. On the other hand, if it can be shown that the first cause and necessary being must be one and unique, then we have shown that this one necessary being must be the cause of all things and thus the one true God.

Suárez claims that we must first describe what is meant by the name 'God' in order to consider God's existence. He argues that in arriving at a first definition of God we should be neither too elaborate nor too vague. If we assign too many attributes to God from the start, we would have to demonstrate that a necessary being with the said attributes exists, making matters more difficult than necessary. On the other hand, if we are too vague, then we leave the door open for many things, which we would not consider to be the Supreme Being, to satisfy the definition. He proposes the following middle ground: "the name [God] signifies a certain most noble being which both surpasses the rest and from which as a first author *all the rest depend*" (*ibid.*: 85, emphasis added). According to this definition, then, what is required is to show that the independent being that was demonstrated to exist above is the unique source of all things.

Suárez formulates an interesting teleological–aesthetic argument for the uniqueness of a necessary being by arguing that if we consider the beauty, order, structure and intricate connections of parts of the universe, then our minds will be led to the conclusion that that "there is one first being, by whom all things are governed and from whom they draw their origin" (*ibid.*: 87). He then presents four objections to this argument. Suárez's fourth and most interesting objection is the possibility that there is more than one universe and more than one first uncreated being. He argues, *contra* Aristotle, that it is possible that there be matter distinct from the matter in this universe and that "the bodies of distinct worlds not have an order between them and therefore neither would desire to be under another or over another" (*ibid.*: 112). He concedes, then, that even if the teleological–aesthetic argument could demonstrate that there exists one unique necessary being for our world, since it is possible that there be many unrelated worlds it is also possible that there be many necessary beings, each unique in its own world.

SUÁREZ'S *A PRIORI* DEMONSTRATION THAT THERE CAN BE ONLY ONE UNCREATED BEING

The arguments in this section do not constitute an *a priori* demonstration for the existence of God in the traditional sense; instead, they demonstrate that an uncreated, necessary being must be singular. Suárez presents six arguments. The discussions below are limited to the fourth and fifth arguments, which he considers to be sufficient for the demonstration that the uncreated being can only be one and thus must be the one true God.

Suárez's fourth argument claims that if the property of singularity were essential to the nature of a necessary being, then such a nature could not be multiplied; hence, there could be only one necessary being. Since existence is part of the essence of a necessary being, and the existence of any being entails its singularity, singularity is also a part of the essence of a necessary being. If singularity is part of the essence of a necessary being, then it is impossible for there to be more than one necessary being. To understand the force of the argument, two things must be kept in mind. First, existence and singularity are inseparable. Secondly, since existence is part of the essential properties of a necessary being, a necessary being cannot be multiplied. Compare the case of God to that of angels. The essence of angels does not entail existence and thus does not entail singularity; and so there can be various species of angels.

Suárez's fifth argument claims that if there are two or more necessary beings, then they would be either of the same species or of diverse species. The first horn of the dilemma cannot be true because two necessary beings cannot be of the same species, since (as was argued above) the nature of a necessary being is essentially singular and it cannot be multiplied. The same argument can be made as follows. If two or more necessary beings are of the same species, then they would have the same essence. However, if they have the same essence, then they would have the same existence, since existence is part of the essence of a necessary being. Hence, if they have the same existence they would be the same being. On the other hand, if existence is not part of their essence, then they would not be necessary beings. Therefore, it is impossible to have two or more necessary beings of the same species.

Suárez also contends that if more than one necessary being of the same species exists, then there would have to be an actual infinite number of necessary beings. Why? Suárez reasons that if it is possible for there to exist more than one necessary being within the same species (i.e. the existence of another necessary being presents no contradiction), and, since necessary beings exist necessarily (i.e. they have no potentiality), then there must be an infinite number of necessary beings. Suárez claims that since the idea of an actual infinite number of necessary beings is impossible, there cannot be more than one necessary being of the same species.

Suárez also rejects the second horn of the dilemma, namely, that there may be two or more necessary beings of distinct species. If there are two or more species of necessary beings, then the two or more species are either equal in perfection or unequal in perfection. They cannot be equal in perfection, because a necessary being has the greatest perfection of all, namely, it encompass all other perfections. If there are two or more perfect beings of different species, then none could encompass all perfections and thus none would be absolutely perfect. As a consequence, there cannot be two or more necessary beings of distinct species that are all absolutely perfect.

A second argument claims that if there are two or more necessary beings of distinct species, then they would be either equal in absolute perfection or unequal in absolute perfection. If they are equal in absolute perfection and no inequality can be attributed to their perfect essence, then they would be the same absolutely perfect necessary being, and therefore there could not be two or more necessary beings of distinct species. If they are unequal in perfection, then there would be either one who would be supremely perfect (the most perfect of all) or an infinite multitude of necessary beings of distinct species of unequal perfections. In the first case, if there is one supremely perfect being, then the rest would be finitely absolutely perfect, which makes no sense. In the second case, if there is an infinite multitude of beings unequal in absolute perfection, then there could be no being that is supremely perfect and thus all beings would be finitely absolutely perfect, which makes no sense. We must conclude, therefore, that if there is a necessary being, there can be only one that is absolutely perfect. Suárez concludes that this one uncreated, perfect being, on which all other beings depend, is God.

DISPUTATION 30: THE ESSENCE OF GOD

The central purpose of disputation 30 is to provide an analysis of God's essence and attributes. Suárez's philosophical analyses are guided by several epistemological principles. First, he does not believe that through natural reason alone one can come to know God's essence or attributes as they are in themselves. Secondly, he does not believe that it is possible that one can come to know God's essence or attributes *a priori*, since our knowledge of God comes through God's effects. However, he notes that once we have knowledge of some of God's attributes, then it becomes possible to derive *a priori* other attributes, as one derives one concept from another *a priori*. So where does one begin? Suárez argues that the first attribute we can determine of God is that God is essentially a necessary being (*Deo est esse ens per necessarium*) and that God is his own being through his essence (*suum esse per essentiam*) (see arguments above in disputation 29). Therefore, the first attribute we know of God is that God's existence is identical to his essence (*ipsum ergo esse Dei est quidditas eius*). From this property of God, Suárez derives most of the other properties of God. Suárez's analysis of God's essence in disputation 30 is divided into seventeen sections; it is a long treatise that contains an extensive historical survey of arguments and views about the attributes of God. Below is a list and summary of the properties and topics Suárez discusses, which can serve as a guide for further investigation.

Topics in disputation 30:
Section 1: God is perfect
Section 2: God is infinite
Section 3: God is pure act and absolute simplicity
Section 4: God lacks substantial composition
Section 5: God lacks accidental composition
Section 6: Divine attributes are part of God's essence
Section 7: God is omnipresent
Section 8: God is immutable and eternal
Section 9: Harmonizing immutability of God with divine liberty
Section 10: God is one
Section 11: God is invisible

Section 12: God is incomprehensible
Section 13: God is ineffable
Section 14: God is living substance, essentially intellectual, and self-sufficient
Section 15: On divine knowledge
Section 16: On divine will
Section 17: On divine potentiality and action

God is absolutely perfect

According to Suárez, perfection is said of that which is missing nothing. Perfection can be understood in two ways: (i) as relative to a thing's nature, and (ii) as absolute perfection. In the first way, perfection is said of that which lacks nothing that the completeness of its nature requires. In this way, many things can be called perfect in their genus or species without being called absolutely perfect in the realm of all beings. In the second way, perfection is said of that which lacks *absolutely* nothing and thus includes all perfections in the realm of all beings. Suárez understands God to be absolutely perfect, so that God's nature includes all possible perfections. God, therefore, is a being so perfect that none other can be conceived greater, and as a consequence God embraces all possible perfections.

God is infinite and omnipotent

When Suárez speaks of God as an infinite being, he is not referring to mass or quantity, since God is not a material being. Instead, our first understanding of infinite ought to be with respect to duration. Thus, to say that God is infinite means that God is eternal. However, the question of God's eternal nature is resolved in disputation 29. Here, therefore, Suárez is concerned with 'infinite' as it refers to God's essence and power. He views the relationship between the essence of a creature and its power to be proportional, so that a being that has an absolutely, infinitely perfect essence would also have infinite power. To say that God is infinite, then, means that God's essence is not restricted or limited to any one genus found in creatures; rather, God's perfect essence transcends all genera and thus includes all possible perfections. Moreover, it also means that God has the power to do anything that is logically possible.

God is pure act and simple

For Suárez, 'act' refers to existence. Pure act, then, is said of a being whose being (*esse*) excludes any potentiality with respect to its state of existence. God is pure act in so far as he is a necessary being and thus God must exists in all possible worlds. Since this concept of pure act describes a perfection of God in terms of what is excluded from his essence, it is classified as a negation. Suárez also considers God as simple, and this concept is also a negation since it adds no reality to the thing of which it is said; instead, it excludes the notion of composition. Suárez acknowledges that simplicity is not always a great-making property. For instance, an accident is simpler than substance and yet an accident is less perfect than a substance. Moreover, a part is simpler than a whole and yet a part is not more perfect than a whole. Nevertheless, Suárez argues that all things being equal simplicity makes a being more perfect than composition. He argues that, in the case of God, simplicity is a great-making property and therefore, in God, there is neither substantial composition (e.g. essence and existence, form and matter, genus and difference) nor accidental composition. Moreover, he argues that from God's simplicity we can deduce that God cannot have accidental properties. Hence, all of God's attributes are essential properties and thus part of the essence of God.

God is immense (omnipresent)

Suárez understands God's immensity as the divine attribute that describes God's presence in the world. In what sense is God omnipresent? Is God present in all things and in all places? If he is, in what way is he present? Suárez defends the Thomistic arguments that conclude that God is present in all things and in all places. Suárez reconciles God's attribute of omnipresence with simplicity, indivisibility and spirituality by uniquely defining the meaning of presence. God is present in all things but not in the way that created beings are present, particularly physical beings, since such an understanding would limit God's infinite nature. Therefore, Suárez asserts that we should not understand God 'to be present' in the world as 'next to' or 'alongside', but rather more like 'same with'. Moreover, Suárez maintains that God's presence is never partial but always complete in his substance. Finally, location or place should not be understood as an accident when attributed to God, as when it is of created beings; instead, it is part of God's intrinsic nature.

God is immutable

Suárez argues that the immutability of God cannot be demonstrated through *a posteriori* arguments. However, given the divine attributes that have already been shown to belong to the divine nature, it can be demonstrated *a priori* that God is immutable. For change to take place in a substance, the substance must have some form of composition. By definition, change requires that an underlying subject remain between the two termini of the change. The subject either loses or adds something as a result of the process of change. This can occur only if the subject is a composite being. It was demonstrated above, however, that God is a simple being who lacks both substantial and accidental composition. Therefore, God must be immutable. Even if change is understood in a broader sense to include creation and annihilation of a substance, it could not be attributed to God, since, given God's nature as a necessary being, God could not come into being nor could his being be terminated. Therefore, no accidental or substantial change can take place in God.

The problem of divine freedom and immutability

Suárez argues that there is an apparent contradiction between the attribute of divine freedom and immutability. If God is free, then any action God undertakes, for instance the act of creation or the act of loving his creation, is one that God may have chosen not to undertake. Thus it is possible that God could have been different and thus God is not immutable. Suárez discusses four attempts at reconciling God's freedom and immutability, but he claims that none is completely successful. Indeed, he concedes that the difficulty of this problem is so great that no solution is completely satisfactory.

Suárez claims that the solution to this mysterious and paradoxical problem should ultimately be guided by the concept of God's perfection. He claims, therefore, that there are three things we must affirm. First, we must affirm that God truly and not metaphorically wills and loves the things he wills and loves, and does so freely; so that it might have been the case that he not have willed or loved them. Secondly, we must affirm that God loves creatures through a real act of his will. Thirdly, we must affirm that God wills all things he wills and does not will those he does not will through the same and absolutely identical act, which is simple and indivisible. Moreover, in this process he does not add or lose anything (i.e. God is immutable).

God is invisible, incomprehensible and ineffable

Suárez argues that not only is God invisible to human perception, but his essence is also invisible to the natural understanding of all created intellects. Therefore, no created intellect through its natural powers can grasp the concept of the divine as it is in itself. If the essence of God is not visible to the intellect of created beings, then God cannot be comprehended. Therefore, God is also incomprehensible. Suárez notes that while God is incomprehensible for created beings, God is not incomprehensible as such, since God comprehends himself. At the same time, this does not mean that we cannot know anything about God's essence, since, as it has already been shown above, we can know much about God's attributes. So even if we cannot know about God directly, through immediate contact with his essence, we can know about God indirectly, through concepts that represent him or one of his perfections.

Finally, Suárez argues that God is ineffable. By this he does not mean that the divine being cannot be named or properly spoken of; instead, he means that God, in all his perfection, cannot be explained with words. In addition, God's nature, as it is in itself, cannot be expressed by a name. The understanding of God's ineffability follows from God's attributes of invisibility and incomprehensibility; since, if names are signs of concepts, then just as we cannot conceive of God's essence in and of itself, we cannot give names or express God's perfection with words.

FURTHER READING

Canteñs, B. 2000. "The Relationship between God and Essences and the Notion of Eternal Truths according to Francisco Suárez". *The Modern Schoolman* **72**: 127–43.

Canteñs, B. 2002. "Ultimate Reality in the Metaphysics of Francisco Suárez". *Ultimate Reality and Meaning* **25**: 73–92.

Canteñs, B. 2003. "What Kind of Beings (*entia*) Are Beings of Reason and What Kind of Being (*esse*) Do They Have? Suárez on Beings of Reason". *American Catholic Philosophical Quarterly* **77**: 171–87.

Davis, D. 1993. "Suárez on the Problem of Positive Evil". *American Catholic Philosophical Quarterly* **67**: 361–72.

Fichter, J. 1940. *Man of Spain: Francis Suárez*. New York: Macmillan.

Gracia, J. 1992. "Suárez and the Problem of the Transcendentals". *Topoi* **11**: 121–33.

Koren, J. 1993. "The Importance of the Concept of Substantial Unity in Suárez's Argument for Hylomorphism". *American Catholic Philosophical Quarterly* **67**: 335–59.

Suárez, F. 1947. *On The Various Kinds Of Distinction* (Dist. VII), C. Vollert (trans.). Milwaukee, WI: Marquette University Press.

Suárez, F. 1964. *On Formal and Universal Unity* (Dist. VI), J. Ross (trans.). Milwaukee, WI: Marquette University Press.

Suárez, F. 1982. *Individual Unity and Its Principle* (Dist. V), J. Gracia (trans.). Milwaukee, WI: Marquette University Press.

Suárez, F. 1983. *On The Essence Of Finite Being As Such, On The Existence Of That Essence And Their Distinction* (Dist. XXXI), N. Wells (trans.). Milwaukee, WI: Marquette University Press.

Suárez, F. 1989. *Concerning Transcendental Good or Goodness* (Dist. X–XI, and passages of XXIII), J. Gracia & D. Davis (trans.). Munich: Philosophia Verlag.

Suárez, F. 1994. *On Efficient Causality* (Dist. XVII–IXX), A. Freddoso (trans.). New Haven, CT: Yale University Press.

Suárez, F. 1995. *On Beings of Reason* (Dist. LIV), J. Doyle (trans.). Milwaukee, WI: Marquette University Press.

Suárez, F. 2000. *On The Formal Cause of Substance* (Dist. XV), J. Kronen & J. Reedy (trans.). Milwaukee, WI: Marquette University Press.

On EXISTENCE OF GOD see also Vol. 1, Chs 18, 19; Vol. 2, Chs 5, 6, 13, 14; Vol. 3, Chs 6, 12, 13, 14, 15, 21; Vol. 5, Chs 11, 16. On FIRST CAUSE see also Vol. 1, Chs 15, 16; Vol. 2, Ch. 14; Vol. 3, Ch. 6. On NATURAL RELIGION/THEOLOGY see also Chs 4, 7, 11, 12, 13, 19, 23; Vol. 4, Chs 8, 12; Vol. 5, Ch. 23.

7

THOMAS HOBBES

Sharon Lloyd

Thomas Hobbes (1588–1679), whose writings span the period of intense political conflict surrounding the English Civil War and Restoration, is best known for the absolutist political theory articulated in his masterwork, *Leviathan* (1651), and in its earlier incarnations, *De cive* (The citizen; 1642) and *The Elements of Law* (1650). Because he thought a proper understanding of religious duty is essential for structuring and maintaining a stable political society, Hobbes devoted an increasing percentage of each of these works to discussion of the profession and practice of Christianity. In addition, Hobbes wrote several works devoted primarily to discussion of religion, including his Latin poem recording the history of religion, *Historia ecclesiastica* (Ecclesiastical history; 1688), his *Historical Narrative Concerning Heresy and the Punishment Thereof* (1680); works arguing the compatibility of his views on free will and necessity with Christian doctrine, his *Of Libertie and Necessitie a Treatise Wherein all Controversie Concerning Predestination, Election, Free-will, Grace, Merits, Reprobation, etc. Is Fully Decided and Cleared* (1654), *The Questions concerning Liberty, Necessity, and Chance Clearly Stated and Debated between Dr Bramhall Bishop of Derry, and Thomas Hobbes of Malmesbury* (1656) a history of the English civil wars analysed largely as resulting from religious conflict, *Behemoth* (1679); and some works attempting to defend Hobbes' own piety and doctrines, including *Considerations upon the Reputation, Loyalty, Manners, and Religion of Thomas Hobbes of Malmesbury* (1662). Hobbes' political and religious views engendered significant hostility. In 1666 there were threats in parliament of an enquiry into Hobbes' religious views, and in 1683 Oxford condemned and burned *De cive* and *Leviathan*.

Hobbes holds that religion is so natural to human beings as to be ineliminable. Its 'natural seeds' are a curiosity about the causes of events, and a fearful desire to affect the course of events, which lead us to posit, or imagine, invisible causal agents whose actions we may hope to influence through our behaviour toward them. Some have nourished these seeds of natural religion according to God's direction, but other ambitious impostors have exploited them in order to gain a following that would secure temporal power for themselves. We can assure ourselves of the bare existence of God by realizing that the causal chain of events we observe must have had an originating cause, and by observing the admirable order and design of the world. Because Hobbes holds that the religious impulse cannot be repressed, it is essential that it be properly channelled. Although Hobbes appears to offer a somewhat deflationary account of natural religion in purely psychological terms not underwritten by a robust ontology, he does insist that his account is perfectly compatible with taking revealed religion seriously.

In order to manage the religious interests of his readers so that those interests will support rather than undermine the state's authority and operation, Hobbes attempts to show that all of the authoritative sources of religious knowledge available to Christians not only permit but require them to submit their private judgements in all matters, including the interpretation, profession and practice of religion, to the public judgement of a civil sovereign. Hobbes argues that both natural reason and Scripture, understood as the compilation of the personal revelations of the true prophets, direct us to treat as authoritative the judgement of a single authority over temporal and spiritual matters alike. This project requires Hobbes to redescribe and rationalize his readers' religious interests, and to reinterpret Scripture. He does this through a painstaking engagement with the canonical texts of the Bible, along with philosophical analysis, for: "though there be many things in God's word above reason, that is to say, which cannot by natural reason be either demonstrated or confuted; yet there is nothing contrary to it; but when it seemeth so, the fault is either in our unskilfull interpretation, or erroneous ratiocination" (*Leviathan* 409–10).[1]

It is striking that across all three versions of his political theory, Hobbes increasingly expands his discussion of religion to the point that more than half of *Leviathan* is consumed in that project. Indeed, in the final chapter of part II of *Leviathan*, just halfway through that work, after having laid out what most commentators regard as his complete theory of political obligation, Hobbes acknowledges that nothing he has argued so far will suffice to give us knowledge of our civil duties without our coming to a correct understanding of our religious duties. He writes:

> That subjects owe to Soveraigns, simple Obedience, in all things wherein their obedience is not repugnant to the Lawes of God, I have sufficiently proved in that which I have already written. There wants onely, for the entire knowledge of civill duty, to know what are those Lawes of God. For without that, a man knows not, when he is commanded any thing by the Civill Power, whether it be contrary to the Law of God, or not: and so, either by too much civill obedience

1. Quotations from *Leviathan* are taken from Hobbes (1968), with page numbers from that edition.

> offends the Divine Majesty, or through feare of offending God, transgresses the commandements of the Common-wealth. To avoid both the Rocks, it is necessary to know what are the Lawes Divine.
> (*Leviathan* 395)

In the Dedicatory Epistle to *Leviathan*, Hobbes insists that his scriptural exegesis is essential to his project, acknowledging:

> That which perhaps may most offend, are certain Texts of Holy Scripture, alleged by me to other purpose than ordinarily they used to be by others. But I have done it with due submission, and also (in order to my subject) necessarily; for they are the Outworks of the Enemy, from whence they impugne the Civill Power. (*Leviathan* 76)

Unaided natural reason allows us to discover God's existence, but nothing of his properties:

> Whatsoever we imagine is finite. Therefore there is no idea, or conception of anything we call infinite … And therefore the name of God is used, not to make us conceive him (for he is incomprehensible, and his greatnesse and power are unconceivable); but that we may honour him. (*Leviathan* 99)

To think God finite or limited in power or goodness would be to think him less than he could possibly be; while to deny his care for humanity would be to deprive us of any incentive to honour him. To honour God is to think as highly of his goodness and power as is possible. Worship is just the external expression of honour, and is naturally expressed by thanks and obedience, which praise God's goodness and magnify his power, and by prayers. These are natural forms of worship because they are the natural external expressions of those human passions – hope, love and fear – that arise from the belief that God is infinitely good and powerful. We honour God by the same sorts of actions we use to honour human beings: obedience, thanksgiving, praise, public worship and considerate speech. However, natural reason is silent on the question of the particular ceremonies, words and gestures to be used in worship, and this silence suggests that these are a matter of indifference. What does matter is that worship be public, if we wish ours to be a Christian commonwealth. Public worship requires uniformity:

> for those actions that are done differently, by different men, cannot be said to be a public worship. And therefore, where many sorts of worship be allowed, proceeding from the different religions of private men, it cannot be said there is any public worship, nor that the commonwealth is of any religion at all. (*Leviathan* 405)

Natural reason requires obedience to God's laws, but what does it tell us about the content of those laws? Hobbes argues that natural reason instructs us to form political communities by authorizing a single public judgement – a sovereign – to interpret all laws and adjudicate all disputes, including those concerning the proper public profession and practice of religion. To understand how it does this, it is necessary to appreciate Hobbes' method.

Hobbes distinguishes between prudence and sapience, or wisdom. Prudence is correct extrapolation from experience to predict future events or to identify past causes of current events. This sort of practical know-how depends on experience, is also possessed by many non-human animals and is, like claims based on occurent sensory experience, fallible. Sapience is scientific knowledge of what conduces to human good, and science is a system of demonstrated truths deduced from universal propositions that are true by virtue of the definitions of their component terms, along with any propositions that, although not analytic, are indubitable on introspection by every person who considers them. Hobbes defends a conventionalist view of science as a purely formal system modelled on Euclidean geometry, with the addition of indubitable introspectables (or universal intuitions, one might say).

"The science of the Lawes of Nature is the true Morall Philosophie" (*Leviathan* 215–16), according to Hobbes, and these laws of nature are those of God's laws discernible by unaided natural reason. Using the method just described, Hobbes argues that human beings are rational, and that rationality requires offering justifying considerations for one's actions; but to offer considerations as justifying one's own action commits one to accepting those same considerations as justifying the like actions of others, *ceteris paribus*. Thus the reasons we offer to others for imposing constraints on their actions we too must accept as imposing the same constraints on our own. Hobbes conceives of this reciprocity requirement of rational agency as the 'sum' of the law of nature, and says that it is captured in "that law of the Gospell; Whatsoever you require that others should do to you, that do ye to them. And that Law of all men, *Quod tibi fieri non vis, alteri ne fecris*" (*Leviathan* 190).

From this core law of nature Hobbes argues that a rational person is required to submit to government. Introspective consideration of our human nature reveals to each person that the situation that would result if every person remained free to exercise their 'right of nature' to do whatever they think useful for their own preservation is so dangerous to the lives, fortunes, liberty and effective agency of others that no rational person can be willing to allow others such an extensive right. Each must demand that others transfer a portion of their natural right to a political authority who is authorized and empowered to adjudicate disputes and enforce decisions over contested matters; but what one demands of others one must also do oneself, hence Hobbes' second law of nature: "That a man be willing, when others are so too, as farre-forth, as for Peace and defence of himselfe he shall think it necessary, to lay down this right to all things; and be contented with so much liberty against other men, as he would allow other men against himself"

(*Ibid.*). This is done by authorizing a sovereign. In this way, natural reason tells us that God requires us to submit to government. Hobbes goes on to argue that any effective government must necessarily enjoy the right to interpret all laws and adjudicate all disputes over contended matters, including those concerning the profession and practice of religion; and indeed must insist on uniformity in religion if the commonwealth is to exhibit the public worship natural religion demands.

Personal revelation and prophecy are further sources of religious knowledge. Both are forms of supernatural revelation: in the first, God speaks to a person immediately; in the second, he speaks to them by the mediation of some other person, to whom he has formerly spoken immediately. The methods by which God reveals his will to individuals are dreams and visions resulting from the immediate intervention of God. This makes revelation *essentially private*, and *inaccessible* to others. Because most dreams and visions have perfectly naturalistic causal explanations, people are entitled to doubt whether one who claims to have received a personal revelation has in fact done so; Scripture explicitly directs that we should reject such claims unless the claimant both performs miracles and teaches the established religion. A miracle, as Hobbes defines it, is "a work of God (besides his operation by the way of nature, ordained in the Creation) done for the making manifest to his elect, the mission of an extraordinary minister for their salvation" (*Leviathan* 473). God does not make mistakes, and does not change his mind, so he is not going to direct his prophets to preach against the religion he has formerly established. And because God wants us to *believe* his prophets – and since what we believe is a function of our reason and experience – he requires the performance of an experience for which our reason can give no naturalistic account. And so:

> it is manifest that the teaching of the religion which God hath established, and the shewing of a present miracle, joined together, were the only marks whereby the Scripture would have a true prophet, that is to say, immediate revelation to be acknowledged; neither of them being singly sufficient to oblige any other man to regard what he saith.
>
> (*Leviathan* 414)

However, there have long since ceased to be any miracles, and so we are no longer required to acknowledge the doctrine of any pretended prophet "farther than it is conformable to the Holy Scriptures, which since the time of our Saviour, supply the place, and sufficiently recompense the want of all other prophesy" (*ibid.*). Because what counts as naturalistically inexplicable to one person may not so count to another of greater scientific sophistication, and because frauds may conspire to stage apparent miracles for their own gain, the individual's judgement of whether a miracle has been performed is unreliable. If we cannot know a miracle when we see one, it is as if, for us, miracles had ceased; and miracles ceasing, we can no longer be assured that anyone who now claims to be a prophet truly is. For this judgement, "we must have recourse to God's Lieutenant, [sovereign] to whom in all doubtful cases wee have submitted our private judgments" (*Leviathan* 477). And because judgement of whether the new doctrine alleged does or does not conform to the established religion also properly belongs to the sovereign, personal revelation ceases to be, for all practical political purposes, an independent source of religious knowledge.

Although a person who genuinely believes that God has immediately spoken to her ought to do whatever she believes she has been directed to do, such permission can have little effect on social stability when the rest are justified in following her only if the sovereign approves her claim. She may permissibly and perhaps ought to follow her conscience, even if it means her martyrdom. "It is true", Hobbes writes, "that God is the soveraign of all soveraigns, and therefore, when he speaks to any subject, he ought to be obeyed, whatsoever any earthly potentate command to the contrary" (*Leviathan* 415). But ordinary subjects who have not enjoyed immediate divine revelation need have no scruples of conscience in obeying even the erroneous religious commands of their sovereigns, for those commands are the sole responsibility of the sovereign; whereas the responsibility of the subject is, as analysis of Scripture shows, first and foremost to obey the civil sovereign in all of its commands. Of course, *if* obeying a sovereign command would damn one to eternal death, "it would be madnesse" to obey. But Hobbes argues from Scripture that the necessary conditions for salvation are but two: belief that Jesus is the Christ, and a will to obey God's laws, which will we exhibit by the internal intention to comply, and repentance for our failures. God accepts the will for the deed, so faith in this single article, along with a will to obey, are all that God requires of us.

In his extended interpretation of Scripture, Hobbes aims to show that this source of religious knowledge, when properly interpreted, confirms rather than undermines civil authority. He seeks to prove out of Scripture: (1) that one's duty to God is properly identified by an appropriate religious authority, and thus that everyone ought to profess and practice religion as that appropriate religious authority dictates; (2) that any given group of Christians is subject to only one authority in both civil and religious matters; and (3) that the appropriate authority in both secular and religious matters is one's national civil sovereign. In fact, Hobbes' arguments carry him only so far as (3′) that the appropriate authority is *either* one's national civil sovereign *or* the pope, understood as the sovereign of a universal commonwealth of Christians; but considering his English audience, and his subsequent efforts in part IV of *Leviathan* to unmask Catholic pretensions as biblically unsupported power grabs, conclusion (3′) suffices for his purpose.

There are, however, limits on credible claims as to the content of revealed religion. As noted, natural reason, along with our experiences "are the talents which He hath put into our hands to negotiate till the coming again of our blessed Saviour, and therefore not to be folded up in the napkin of an implicate faith, but employed in the purchase of justice, peace, and true religion" (*Leviathan* 409).

This commitment shapes Hobbes' scriptural interpretations. If the Bible offers mutually contradictory accounts of some concept, we are to interpret at least some of those accounts metaphorically, because our readiness to honour God requires that we refuse to believe that God makes mistakes or contradicts himself. So, for instance, we should not take literally the biblical claim that hell is a bottomless pit in the earth, because no thing of finite size (as is the earth) could contain anything of infinite size. Surveying all the conflicting characterizations of hell he finds in Scripture, Hobbes employs his own natural reason to conclude that 'hell' must be a metaphor for *final* death.

Hobbes interprets Scripture to say that human beings do not by their nature have immortal souls existing separately from their bodies. "The soule in Scripture", writes Hobbes, "signifieth always, either the life, or the living creature and the body and soule jointly, the body alive" (*Leviathan* 637–8). It is true that had Adam not sinned, he and his posterity, eating from the tree of life, would have lived eternally in their bodies on the earth; but since by sinning Adam forfeited eternal life, God has withheld from human beings the tree that would have allowed them to overcome their natural mortality. Jesus cancels that forfeiture of eternal life for those who believe in him, and at the Second Coming they will be resurrected, body, brain and mental life, to live in their incorruptible bodies on the earth forever. Establishing this conclusion is essential to Hobbes' political project of showing that there can be only one sovereign at a time over any given Christian because there do not exist two coexistent realms, one spiritual and the other temporal: "It is true that the bodies of the faithful, after the resurrection, shall be not onely spirituall, but eternall: but in this life they are grosse, and corruptibile. There is therefore no other government in this life, neither of state, nor religion, but temporall" (*Leviathan* 499). Furthermore, a correct interpretation of Scripture shows that the commission of ecclesiastics was merely to convert people to belief by teaching, and so never included coercive authority, such as must be held by sovereigns. Citing Peter's admonition to, in Hobbes' words, "obey the king and his governors, for this is God's will" (1 Peter 2:13–14), and Paul's instruction to "put men in mind to be subject to their principalities and powers, and to obey magistrates" (Titus 3:1) even though they were infidels, Hobbes argues that Scripture established that Christians are to recognize the judgements of their civil sovereigns in all matters, religious and civil, as authoritative, whether those judgements are ultimately correct or incorrect. God will sort the wheat from the chaff.

Hobbes insists that part of the problem of the Schools is that they demand that Christians abandon their natural reason to embrace conceptual impossibilities, such as the bodiless body that they term 'immaterial substance'. These sorts of nonsensical concepts that defy natural reason are designed, Hobbes argues, by the Schools as weapons of war against civil authority. They are 'verbal forks', which Hobbes characterizes as "meaningless distinctions that signify nothing, but serve only to confuse and astonish the multitude of ignorant men" which the Schoolmen use for "imposing what they list upon their readers, and declining the force of true reason" in order to bring them to heel to the Church's authority (Hobbes 1990: 41). Many of these are imported out of Aristotle, whom Hobbes systematically condemns as employing nonsense concepts that have perverted Christian doctrine. The now familiar engraving Hobbes commissioned for the frontispiece of *Leviathan* pithily to depict its theme of the problem posed for peace by the duplication of temporal and spiritual sovereignties contains under the title banner a frame showing various "verbal forks". The most important of these is the temporal–spiritual distinction, which Hobbes says "makes men see double and mistake their lawfull sovereign" (*ibid.*). Hobbes wryly labelled a set of *horns* from which this verbal fork springs "Di-lem-ma". These spiritual weapons are contrasted with ordinary weapons and equipment of war, such as bayonets, guns, drums and standards, in the corresponding temporal frame.

The reason different people embrace differing religious views is that they have been differently taught, or trained. Hobbes thinks that because our beliefs result from our experience and education in conjunction with our bodily constitutions, *what* we believe will be a fairly straightforward function of *whom* we believe, and so shaping the content of religious belief is importantly a matter of having one's authority accepted. This implies that uniformity of religious education will be essential for the maintenance of sovereign authority in any commonwealth, and so Hobbes expends considerable effort discussing how religious education ought to be conceived and disseminated:

> The greatest part of Man-kind … received the notions of their duty chiefly from Divines in the pulpit … and the Divines … derive their knowledge from the Universities … It is therefore manifest, that the instruction of the people dependeth wholly on the right teaching of Youth in the universities. (*Leviathan* 384)

It is the duty of the sovereign under the law of nature to procure the good of the people, and so to educate all subjects in the fundamentals of religious duty contained in those laws. This duty to educate does not, however, imply that the sovereign must enquire into subjects' religious beliefs and root out dissidents and disbelievers, nor even that such inquisition and persecution are permissible under the law of nature. They are not permissible. Belief not being subject to the will, the most a sovereign may reasonably require from subjects is outward conformity in profession and practice. "There ought to be no power over the consciences of men, but of the word it selfe, working faith in every one…according to the purpose of God himself", particularly because "it is unreasonable of them who teach there is such danger in every little error, to require of a man endued with reason of his own, to follow the reason of any other man" (*Leviathan* 711).

The most difficult structural issue in understanding Hobbes' religious views is thinking about how Hobbes reconciles natural divine law and the possibly whimsical pronouncements of any sovereign's positive law. Hobbes is not a value subjectivist. He notes that most people 'call' right and wrong, good and bad, by their own likings and dislikings, but he expressly disapproves of that use of language and condemns the "Schools of the Grecians" for it in these words:

> Their morall philosophy is but a description of their own passions. For the rule of manners, without civill government, is the Law of Nature; and in it, the law civill; that determineth what is ... good and evill: whereas they make the rules of good and bad by their own liking and disliking: By which means, in so great diversity of taste, there is nothing generally agreed on; but every one doth (as far as he dares) whatsoever seemeth good in his owne eyes, to the subversion of commonwealth.
> (*Leviathan* 686)

There is an objective fact of the matter about what is right or wrong, good or evil; people may "*misrepresent*" to others what is good as evil or vice versa, and even though they judge conscientiously, may "*err*" on such matters. Hobbes explicitly acknowledges that the Sovereign may, in fact, err on such matters: "There is no judge, subordinate, nor sovereign, but may erre in a judgment of equity" (*Leviathan* 323). And:

> Suppose that a Christian king should from this foundation *Jesus is the Christ,* draw some false consequences ... and demand the teaching of the same ... *Christian kings may err in deducing a consequence*, but who shall judge? Shall a private man judge, when the question is of his own obedience? (*Leviathan* 624–5)

God's laws of nature tell us that no private man is to judge. Despite the fallibility of all sovereigns, God prefers that we should comport ourselves in compliance with the commands of even so fallible an authority, than that we should run amok, each marching to their own distinct drummer.

God will burn away the erroneous "superstructions of hay or stubble", the correct from the incorrect, in due time, and it is not the subjects' business to try to make that judgement. Hobbes titles his major political treatise '*Leviathan*', drawing on the Book of Job, precisely because he wishes to humble us prideful human beings. Each of us supposes that our own private judgements are authoritative, that we know right from wrong, good from bad, just from unjust, and that we are justified in fighting for the claims of our little conscience, no matter the costs to other people, to peace, to civilization. Hobbes insists that we are not justified. We were nowhere when God laid the foundations of the world; we cannot know his purposes or judge his justice. To think otherwise is mere hubris. A Leviathan is needed to rule "over all the children of pride" (*Leviathan* 362).

But how can a Christian, in good conscience, obey commands concerning religion that they believe with full conviction to be wrongful? Hobbes argued for a *hierarchy of responsibility*, according to which subjects are answerable to God for their obedience to the commands of their governors, while those governors are answerable to God for their substantive commands. In his discussion in *Leviathan* explaining how Naaman, a Syrian converted to the God of Israel, could guiltlessly bow before his master's heathen gods, Hobbes explains that whatever one does in obedience to the command of constituted authority is blameless, so long as one holds in one's heart a different belief, and obeys only because commanded to do so by an authority whom God requires him to obey, whether the command is substantively right or wrong. (Indeed, Hobbes goes further, arguing that to deny a "Mohemetan" the same protection of conscience and action against a Christian master would be to violate both the law of nature and the saviour's directive under the Golden Rule.)

Some will dismiss this position of Hobbes' as a form of *Nuremberg defence*: a claim that anything goes for those who were 'just following orders'. Such a judgement would not be fair to Hobbes. For Hobbes, the uniquely correct interpretation of the authoritative Christian religion directs us to submit our private judgement to the public – whether we think it right or wrong – *as a matter of religious principle*. There is thus a *self-effacing* character to Hobbes' religious argument: both the law of nature and divine positive law as revealed in Scripture direct individuals to treat as authoritative the interpretations of those laws' requirements laid down by their civil sovereigns.

How did Hobbes reconcile his naturalistic, scientific, determinist conception of the world with morality and Christian theology? Hobbes held that every event is strictly determined in a causal chain beginning in the actions of God. Most of these actions are set in motion by God's ordination of natural physical laws; others by his extraordinary suspension of those laws. But all are strictly causally necessitated. This fact neither abridges human freedom nor invalidates human practices of praise and blame. A free human person is one who is not stopped by external impediments from doing that which they have the will and capability to do. A person is responsible – and so liable to praise or blame – for those of their actions that result from their will, that is, from their own deliberation. Although a person is not free to choose how they will, they are properly said to be free when they can do as they will, and are properly held responsible for those of their doings that result from their willing. Hobbes articulates a genuinely compatibilist position, judging that no other position permits us to honour God as both omnipotent and just.

Hobbes' tone in writing has prompted many readers to wonder about the sincerity of his religious beliefs, and whether he adequately appreciated the sensibilities of religious persons with regard to religious duty and virtue. Seeing Hobbes' mode of operation in systematically viewing religion with an eye to establishing and maintaining civil authority, one may reasonably wonder whether Hobbes was himself a Christian believer. He always insisted that he was, and his biographer Aubrey provides some evidence for his claim. But even Hobbes' definition of religion in chapter 6 of *Leviathan* invites the question. Hobbes defines

'RELIGION' thus: "Feare of powers invisible, feigned by the mind, or imagined from tales publiquely allowed, RELIGION; not allowed, SUPERSTITION", although adding that "when the power imagined, is truly such as we imagine, TRUE RELIGION" (*Leviathan* 124). This talk of what we "imagine" seems already deflationary, even before we notice that on this account, even true religion would count as superstition in any society in which it was not authorized. However, attention to Hobbes' concern with disagreement in private judgements, as just discussed, permits us to interpret these remarks consistently with the possibility of veridical religion.

Hobbes' anti-clericalism is absolutely clear and undeniable, as is his hostility to the "Romish" religion. Was Hobbes a respectable Lutheran, a would-be, if unconventional, orthodox Protestant Christian, a deist, an early advocate of religious toleration or a closeted atheist with designs to pull down an evil empire? Hobbes scholars part company on this question. Some have argued that he is an orthodox Anglican, or Lutheran; others that he was a sceptic; still others that he intended to overthrow religious belief altogether by a sneaky programme of rhetorical 'avowal by disavowal'. Hobbes' texts are very rich, and each reader will take pleasure in pursing this question.

But we can ask some further questions about why Hobbes proceeds the way he does. He opts for authoritarianism in religion rather than for toleration. This may seem to us to be unnatural, and we may wish to enquire why. Hobbes seems wistfully to have acknowledged the attractions of toleration and free faith in his remark in chapter 47 of *Leviathan* that "the independency of the primitive Christians to follow Paul, or Cephas, or Apollos, every man as he liketh best ... if it be without contention ... is perhaps the best" (*Leviathan* 711). Still, Hobbes did not believe that the psychological commitments required to sustain a system of toleration existed in his day. Religious toleration is a significant achievement of human society. It requires us to respect and protect those whom we think mistaken about the most fundamental matters, as a point of principle, and not just because we cannot stably impose our beliefs on them. Hobbes saw no prospect for this for his own society. In the same way that we might suppose that some barbarous peoples will fight themselves out of existence unless their passions are tamped down by a strongman, so Hobbes seems to have believed that until humanity follows the train of its God-given natural reason, it does best in a sort of receivership, parented by a trustee appointed by the divine court.

FURTHER READING

Darwall, S. 2000. "Normativity and Projection in Hobbes's *Leviathan*". *Philosophical Review* **109**: 313–47.

Lloyd, S. 1992. *Ideals as Interests in Hobbes's Leviathan*. Cambridge: Cambridge University Press.

Lloyd, S. (ed.) 2001. "*Special Issue on Recent Work on the Moral and Political Philosophy of Thomas Hobbes*". *Pacific Philosophical Quarterly* **82**: 227–474.

Martinich, A. 1992. *The Two Gods of Leviathan: Thomas Hobbes on Religion and Politics*. Cambridge: Cambridge University Press.
Martinich, A. 1999. *Hobbes: A Biography*. Cambridge: Cambridge University Press.
Pasquino, P. 2001. "Hobbes, Religion, and Rational Choice: Hobbes's Two Leviathans and the Fool". *Pacific Philosophical Quarterly* **82:** 406–19.
Ryan, A. 1988. "A More Tolerant Hobbes?". In *Justifying Toleration: Conceptual and Historical Perspectives*, S. Mendus (ed.), 37–59. Cambridge: Cambridge University Press.
Springborg, P. 1996. "Hobbes on Religion". In *The Cambridge Companion to Hobbes*, T. Sorell (ed.), 346–80. Cambridge: Cambridge University Press.
Tuck, R. 1990. "Hobbes and Locke on Toleration". In *Thomas Hobbes and Political Theory*, M. Dietz (ed.), 153–71. Lawrence, KS: University of Kansas Press.
Tuck, R. 1992. "The Christian Atheism of Thomas Hobbes". In *Atheisim from the Reformation to the Enlightenment*, M. Hunter & D. Wootton (eds), 111–30. Oxford: Clarendon Press.
Wright, G. 2002. "Curley and Martinich in Dubious Battle". *Journal of the History of Philosophy* **40**: 461–76.

On NATURAL RELIGION/THEOLOGY see also Chs 4, 6, 11, 12, 13, 19, 23; Vol. 4, Chs 8, 12; Vol. 5, Ch. 23. On REVELATION see also Chs 11, 16; Vol. 1, Ch. 14; Vol. 2, Ch. 11; Vol. 4, Chs 5, 11; Vol. 5, Chs 8, 23.

8

RENÉ DESCARTES

Gary Steiner

In his *Lectures on the History of Philosophy*, Hegel declared that:

> Descartes is in fact the true inaugurator of modern philosophy, which makes thinking into a principle. Here thinking in itself is distinguished from philosophical theology, which distances itself from thinking ... The influence of this man on his time cannot be overestimated. He is a hero who embarked upon the subject entirely from scratch and established a new foundation for philosophy. (Hegel 1982: 123)

Descartes recognized that the mind innately possesses the rudiments of truth, and that these rudiments form the foundation of an edifice of knowledge that promises to render human beings "the masters and possessors of nature" (Descartes 1985: 141–2). In pursuing this programme, Descartes established a rigorous distinction between articles of faith and systematic insights of reason, thereby unwittingly setting up an opposition between reason and faith that was inconceivable to the likes of Augustine and Thomas Aquinas. That Descartes did not intend to establish such an opposition is evident from his efforts to argue for an inner compatibility between faith and reason, as well as from a reflection on the Christian roots of his programme for the mastery of nature. Descartes sought to correct the mistakes and misconceptions of a tradition of medieval philosophy that had commingled faith and reason in a manner that prevented genuine progress in the sciences. In doing so, he did more than any other single modern thinker to advance the historical process of secularization, which in the centuries after Descartes continued to refine Descartes' insights into the autonomy of reason and effected a detachment of reason from faith so complete that faith became marginalized to the point that European philosophers such as Kant sought to establish even the discipline of ethics on a purely secular foundation.

Descartes was born in La Haye (subsequently renamed Descartes), Touraine in 1596. From 1607 to 1615 he studied at the Jesuit College of La Flèche, where he excelled in mathematics and was exposed to Loyola's *Spiritual Exercises*, which influenced the conception of meditation at the methodological core of Descartes' *Meditations on First Philosophy* (hereafter *Meditations*; 1641), and to Stoic philosophy, which influenced the development of Descartes' moral thought. From 1615 to 1616 he studied law at Poitiers and passed the examinations for the *baccalauréat* and the *license* with honours. In 1618 he travelled to Breda, Holland, and enlisted as a volunteer in the army of Maurice of Nassau, the Prince of Orange. During his brief tenure in Maurice's army, Descartes made the acquaintance of Isaac Beeckman, who inspired Descartes to seek practical applications for mathematics. In November 1619, Descartes is said to have had a powerful trio of dreams in which he envisaged for the first time the ideal of a *mathesis universalis* (universal mathematics or learning) that would serve as the foundation for the unification of all the sciences. Descartes explored the prospects for such a *mathesis universalis* in *Rules for the Direction of the Mind* (1619–28), but left this text uncompleted and never sought to publish it in his lifetime. During the early 1630s he worked on the text *Le Monde* (The world), in which he sought to give a systematic account of natural phenomena; but the condemnation of Galileo in 1633 for advocating Copernicanism so frightened Descartes that he suppressed *Le Monde*, a text that made clear Descartes' commitment to the proposition that the earth moves, and in subsequent texts Descartes was careful to treat Copernicanism as a mere hypothesis. In 1637 he published *Discourse on Method* (hereafter *Discourse*), together with texts on geometry, optics and meteorology; the *Discourse* presented Descartes' criticisms of traditional approaches to learning, particularly scholasticism, and articulated for the first time Descartes' mature conception of method and his notion of absolute cognitive certainty, which he subsequently applied in the *Meditations*. In 1644 he published *Principles of Philosophy*, which presented his metaphysical and scientific views in a form meant to be suitable for use in scholastic universities. In 1649 he published *Passions of the Soul*, which articulated his views about the relationship between soul and body, views that had been shaped by his correspondence with Queen Christina of Sweden and Princess Elizabeth of Bohemia during the mid- to late 1640s. Descartes died in 1650 in Stockholm.

A recurring theme in Descartes' writings is the need for theoretical knowledge with specific practical applications. In this respect he is at odds with Aristotle, who believed that theory is a pure discipline in the sense that it has no practical applications; for Aristotle, theory is directed at eternal verities that are to be contemplated for their own sake. For Descartes and early modern contemporaries such as Francis Bacon, on the other hand, the value of theory lies in its applicability to earthly existence and the prospects it provides for improving our material circumstances. Thus Descartes defines wisdom as "not only prudence in our everyday affairs but also a perfect knowledge of all things that mankind is capable of knowing, both for the conduct of life and for the preservation of health and the discovery of all manner of skills" (1985: 179). Descartes conceives of wisdom as being based entirely on reason; the pursuit of the supreme earthly good specifically excludes any appeals to divine revelation. For Descartes, as for Galileo before him, reason informs us about the workings of material processes, whereas faith pertains exclusively to matters of eternal salvation.

This secular conception of wisdom informs Descartes' characterization of the proper aims of earthly existence. He characterizes the pursuit of earthly wisdom in terms of a tree metaphor, according to which:

> the roots are metaphysics, the trunk is physics, and the branches emerging from the trunk are all the other sciences, which may be reduced to three principal ones, namely medicine, mechanics and morals. By 'morals' I understand the highest and most perfect moral system, which presupposes a complete knowledge of the other sciences and is the ultimate level of wisdom. (*Ibid.*: 186)

Metaphysics, the roots of the tree, consists in an "explanation of the principal attributes of God, the non-material nature of our souls and all the clear and distinct notions which are in us" (*ibid.*). Metaphysics for Descartes thus includes epistemology, the study of the rudiments of knowledge, as well as reflection on the nature of God and the human soul or mind. A study of the former will reveal that every human mind possesses ideas that are impervious to doubt and hence can function as the basis for knowledge in physics and all the other sciences. Once we have established the metaphysical foundations of science, we may proceed to establish physics on a solid foundation unknown to the ancients and the medievals, and in turn we will be able to use this knowledge in physics to exert systematic control over natural processes. In particular, we will be able to use this knowledge to advance medicine, which Descartes considers to be "the chief good and the foundation of all the other goods in this life" (*ibid.*: 143). Moreover, by securing knowledge on this new and solid foundation, we will be able to get past the petty disputes so common in the Schools and obviate "the major cause of the heresies and disagreements which now plague the world" (*ibid.*: 188).

Fundamental to Descartes' conception of reason is the idea that all human beings possess reason more or less equally. In contrast with Aristotle, who believed that different types of people possess fundamentally different rational capacities – free men are fully rational, whereas women's reason "lacks authority" and slaves are just rational enough to apprehend a rational rule but cannot generate it for themselves – Descartes asserts an essential equality of minds (Aristotle 1995: 1999). Descartes extends the scope of Martin Luther's rejection of hierarchy in the pursuit of truth. Where a hundred years earlier Luther argued that each individual possesses the capacity to contemplate the meaning of Scripture for himself or herself and thus is not subject to the putatively superior insight of members of the Church hierarchy, Descartes argues that each individual is able to use his or her own reason to determine the truth or falsity of any matter that can be subjected to rational scrutiny. If different people appear to be superior to others in the exercise of their reason, this is not because "some of us are more reasonable than others but solely because we direct our thoughts along different paths and do not attend to the same things. For it is not enough to have a good mind; the main thing is to apply it well" (Descartes 1985: 111). Thus differences in education, the assiduousness with which we apply ourselves and so on will influence the extent to which we develop our rational capacity; but each individual's innate rational capacity is the same as any other individual's.

From this principle of the equality of minds follows the proposition that we must be ever on guard lest our sense of the truth be distorted by the influence of "example and custom" (*ibid.*: 116, 119). One should not accept a proposition as true simply because a supposed authority, say a Jesuit professor, asserts that it is true. Instead, one must accept the truth of a proposition only once one has subjected it to rigorous scrutiny. Implicit in this assertion is a criticism of the medieval Christian method of university teaching, which proceeded with the imparting of a lesson that the students were to memorize by rote; henceforth, all learning must be an active process in which the learner establishes the rudiments of knowledge for himself or herself and proceeds to build up an edifice of knowledge in collaboration with others. Descartes, who was educated at the Jesuit college in La Flèche, France, writes that he "found [himself] beset by so many doubts and errors that [he] came to think [he] had gained nothing from [his] attempts to become educated but increasing recognition of [his] ignorance" (*ibid.*: 113).

A related cause of Descartes' former ignorance was the Aristotelian basis of learning in the medieval Christian universities. One focal point of Descartes' criticism of Aristotelianism is its reliance on the outward appearance of things, which led Aristotle to proclaim the fixed centrality of the earth in the cosmic scheme of things, a proclamation that made Aristotle's thought particularly congenial as a basis for scientific enquiry within the framework of a Christian worldview. Descartes, like Copernicus and Kepler before him, saw the need to move beyond the outward appearance of things and to constitute our sense of the order of the universe in acts of abstract reflection that project systematic mathematical order onto the world. This is how Copernicus was able to arrive at the insight that the earth is neither fixed nor the centre of things, and it is also how Kepler was able to distil Tycho Brahe's astronomical data into laws of planetary motion based on the geometric concept of the ellipse. Descartes follows this line of thinking in proclaiming the homogeneity of matter and the priority of rectilinear motion, and in proposing that nature can be modelled using pure geometry (*ibid.*: 232, 241, 247).

Another main focal point of Descartes' criticism of Aristotelian method is its reliance on syllogism. Descartes observes that syllogisms do not yield new knowledge, but simply derive logical implications of truths already known or presupposed. To prove the soundness of a syllogism, one must establish the truth of the major and the minor premise; but in order to do this using syllogistic method, one must derive the truth of each premise from two other premises in yet another syllogistic argument. The truth of the premises of that other argument must be established by yet other syllogisms, and so on *ad infinitum*. Thus syllogistic method involves us in an infinite regress with no prospects for an absolute foundation for establishing the truth of any particular proposition (*ibid*.: 36–7, 119; 1991: 222).

Descartes' solution to this problem is to propose an alternative logic of thought that yields insights whose truth can be certified without recourse to logical derivation. From his earliest writings, Descartes sees in mathematics an example of the power of the human mind to seize on "certain primary seeds of truth naturally implanted in human minds" that ground knowledge not only in mathematics but in all other areas of knowledge as well (1985: 18, 144). Against Aristotle, who believed that each field of knowledge had its own methods and basic concepts, Descartes advocates a foundationalism that provides one unified method and set of basic insights for all areas of knowledge; these basic insights are the first principles of metaphysics, which constitute the roots of the tree of wisdom. Descartes notes that the term 'mathematical' signifies not only mathematics in the straightforward sense of disciplines such as geometry and arithmetic, but more fundamentally *disciplina*, that which can be learned; at this more basic level, mathematics concerns all "questions of order or measure and ... it is irrelevant whether the measure in question involves numbers, shapes, stars, sounds, or any other object whatsoever" (*ibid*.: 19). Descartes proposes that the same "primary seeds of truth" that facilitate certainty in geometry and arithmetic can also provide certainty in the other areas of knowledge sketched in the tree metaphor. Thus perhaps we can achieve certainty even in disciplines such as ethics. Descartes considers it an embarrassment that the ancients gained insight into mathematics but established their moral thought on a foundation of nothing more than "sand and mud" (*ibid*.: 114).

Descartes proposes a method for the pursuit of truth that promises to yield the fundamental insights that are to serve as the first principles of all knowledge. In the *Discourse* he presents four rules for the pursuit of truth. The most important of these rules is the first, which states that one should "never ... accept anything as true" unless one has "evident knowledge of its truth", that is, one should accept as true only what presents itself to the mind "so clearly and so distinctly that [one has] no occasion to doubt it" (*ibid*.: 120). Descartes defines a clear insight as "present and accessible to the attentive mind", and a distinct insight as one that "as well as being clear ... is so sharply separated from all other perceptions that it contains within it only what is clear" (*ibid*.: 208). A clear and distinct perception presents itself so forcefully and singularly to the mind that it is absolutely impervious to doubt. Such perceptions are the "primary seeds of truth" of which Descartes sometimes speaks; they are not derived from experience but instead are implanted in our minds by God, that is, they are innate. Principally, these clear and distinct ideas concern God, the self (the nature of the mind or soul) and mathematics; thus they constitute the metaphysical foundation of the tree of wisdom and hold the promise of certainty in scientific fields such as mathematics.

In the *Meditations*, Descartes employs a technique known as the method of doubt to arrive at the indubitable first principles of knowledge. Through the persona of the individual meditator, who represents any rational individual interested in establishing the foundations for certain knowledge, Descartes subjects all traditionally accepted knowledge to doubt in order to determine which, if any, insights in the mind are so certain as to survive even the most intense scrutiny. Descartes likens this process to one in which a person has a basket of apples and wants to ensure that none of the apples is rotten: "We should first tip them all out, leaving none at all inside, and then pick up again (or get from elsewhere) only those apples in which no flaw can be detected" (1984: 349; see also 324). This is no everyday sort of doubt, as when I wonder whether I made sure to lock the door to my house when I left for work this morning. It is a radical or hyperbolic doubt designed to leave intact only those insights that are so absolutely certain and foundational that they can serve as a solid basis for the pursuit of knowledge in the sciences. The method of doubt thus requires us to subject to doubt all sorts of beliefs that we would never question in our everyday dealings.

In the First Meditation, the meditator proceeds through a series of increasingly hyperbolic doubts, concluding with the insight that we have no absolutely certain basis for our former belief that the external world exists: everything that we perceive with our sense organs could conceivably be a massive illusion placed in our minds by an evil deceiver. As counter-intuitive as such a supposition may be, it serves the methodological purpose of clearing away every perception that is subject to the slightest doubt, thereby making way early in the Second Meditation for the first indubitable insight in the order of reasons: "I think, [therefore] I am". The meditator observes that even if an evil genius is deceiving him or her about matters such as the existence of the material world, it is impossible to be deceived about one's own existence in the moment in which one contemplates it.

> Let him deceive me as much as he can, he will never bring it about that I am nothing so long as I think that I am something. So after considering everything very thoroughly, I must finally conclude that this proposition, *I am, I exist* [*ego sum, ego existo*], is necessarily true whenever it is put forward by me or conceived in my mind.
>
> (*Ibid.*: 17; 1985: 127)

More generally, to doubt, will, contemplate, question or wonder – in short, to engage in any act of thought whatsoever – is impossible unless I exist in the same instant that I engage in that act.

By itself, the so-called *cogito* ('I think') insight does not provide any concrete content to thought; instead it functions as the most immediate example of a clear and distinct insight, one so present and apparent to an attentive mind that it is absolutely impervious to doubt. What is certain is not that I think, nor that I exist, but rather the *connection* between thinking and existing: the most powerful evil genius could not make it such that I thought or was deceived while I did not exist. I can be absolutely certain about this connection, because no evidence could possibly be brought to bear that would undermine it. It is clear and distinct, evident, certain, indubitable. Further reflection on the *cogito* leads the meditator to a series of other clear and distinct insights, particularly the insights that my own existence is not possible except on the condition that God exists, that God exists necessarily and that God is not a deceiver. On the basis of this chain of indubitable reasons, the meditator concludes the *Meditations* by establishing that the material world does indeed exist, and by delineating the general terms of an approach to natural science that can promote human welfare.

A central question in the evaluation of Descartes' metaphysics concerns the sincerity of his appeals to divine veracity in securing the foundations of physics. In his own time Descartes was charged with dissimulating his secular intentions beneath the guise of appeals to the metaphysical primacy of God. Descartes was the object of virulent attacks by Gisbertus Voetius, professor of theology and later rector of Utrecht University, who charged Descartes with atheism and in 1642 moved the Utrecht academic senate to issue a formal condemnation of Cartesian philosophy.[1] Henry More and Julien Offray de La Mettrie maintained that Descartes' appeals to the idea of an immortal soul were disingenuous, and that he was really a metaphysical materialist. More recently, commentators alleging dissimulation have sought support for their allegations in the fact that Descartes expressed fear about the prospect of suffering Galileo's fate for supporting the Copernican hypothesis; Galileo was placed under house arrest for the last seven years of his life, and Descartes writes that he suppressed his text *Le Monde* because of its advocacy of Copernicanism (1985: 141–2, 145–6; 1976: 440–41). Charges of dissimulation have plagued Descartes ever since, accompanied by the suggestion that Descartes was interested purely in a physics with practical applications. And yet Maritain asserts that "Descartes was sincerely Catholic" (1944: 44), and Jaspers sees Descartes' Catholicism as "essential to the meaning of his entire philosophy and to the practical grounding of life" (1995: 8).

There can be no definitive resolution of the dissimulation question, but a reflection on the Christian roots of Descartes' programme for the mastery of nature makes charges of heterodoxy against Descartes considerably less forceful than they might otherwise appear. In accordance with Genesis 8 and 9, Augustine and Aquinas both proclaim human dominion over nature, and in the twelfth century Hugh of Saint-Victor anticipates Descartes' call for human beings to render themselves "the masters and possessors of nature" in the following words:

1. On the details of Descartes' dispute with Voetius, see Verbeek (1992).

"For, in truth, God the Creator first made the world, and then made man as the possessor and Lord of the world, so that man might rule over all things by right of his foundation, being subject with free will to Him alone by whom he had been made" (1951: 28). Descartes fulfils the promise of this ideal of human mastery by providing the methodological basis for the pursuit of truth in science generally, and then by articulating the basic principles of modern physics, which dispense with the Aristotelian reliance on the outward appearance of things as well as with Aristotelian final causes and substantial forms.

A key feature of Descartes' departure from Aristotle is his conception of matter as homogeneous, a conception endorsed later in the seventeenth century by Newton and adhered to ever since. Aristotle had conceived of the cosmos as consisting of heterogeneous domains, with the earth and its atmosphere consisting of the primary elements of fire, air, earth and water, and the heavens consisting of aether. Descartes asserts both the fundamental sameness of matter throughout the universe and the operation of universal laws that govern changes throughout the universe. Universal laws replace Aristotelian final causes and, together with Descartes' application of mathematics to the understanding of natural phenomena, facilitate the prediction and control of natural processes.

Descartes proposes a representation or reduction of particular sensible qualities in nature to unique geometric representations (Descartes 1985: 40–41).[2] By assigning a different geometric figure to each colour or shade of colour that can be perceived, we can give an objective representation of the phenomenon of colour. We can do the same with all other sensible qualities such as sounds. The mathematical representation of subjectively perceived qualities enables us to give objective descriptions of magnitudes and rates of change. In proposing this reduction of sensible qualities to mathematical representations, Descartes anticipates the digital revolution in its entirety: for what is, for example, the digitization of sound but an application of Descartes' principle? With the wax experiment in the Second Meditation, Descartes offers a different way to conceptualize the reduction of subjectively perceived qualities to objective descriptions. There the meditator proposes that no matter how many changes we witness in, say, a piece of wax – it has solidity and scent when we remove it from the hive, but loses both these qualities when we put it near the fire – our mind perceives clearly that the wax remains a selfsame substance whose essence is extension or the occupation of space. In other words, one feature of any material substance is the fact that it always occupies a determinate space, which can be described objectively in mathematical terms. The experiment in the Second Meditation happens to be performed on a piece of wax, but can be performed on any material object whatsoever; thus the wax experiment complements Descartes' proposal for the reduction of sensible

2. Francis Bacon offers a strikingly similar proposal a generation earlier in his *Valerius terminus: Of the Interpretation of Nature* (*c.*1603).

qualities to distinct geometric figures, providing the basis for an objective description of all observable phenomena in nature.

Descartes states that all natural phenomena are subject to laws of nature, ordained by God, that hold in all possible worlds; these laws are the same as the laws of mechanics (*ibid.*: 132, 139). Descartes' interest in conceiving of nature as a mechanistic system is born of his interest in mastery. To view nature as a mechanistic system is to see it as a nexus of cause-and-effect relations. We never observe causes in nature, but rather only particular effects. The goal of science is to reflect on the observed effects in an effort to postulate the unobserved causes that would be necessary to produce the effects. Once we comprehend the causes responsible for particular effects, we will be in a position to produce desired effects by bringing the necessary causes to bear. If, for example, we want to bring about particular effects caused by a magnet, we need only attain a clear and distinct grasp of the unseen phenomena responsible for those effects (*ibid.*: 49, 57). To use a more contemporary example, if we want to make it rain, we need to know what sorts of causes (such as iodine and pressure) need to be produced. The job of the scientist is to conduct observations of natural effects and deduce the necessary causes in the interest of harnessing natural powers to advance "the general well-being of mankind" (*ibid.*: 144). Descartes thus advances a fundamental principle of modern technology: that the prediction and control of natural processes depend on a theoretical comprehension of the antecedent causes required for the production of observed (or desired) effects.

In representing nature as a mathematically describable whole subject to universal laws, Descartes sets up a picture of nature as a clockwork mechanism. He explicitly posits the principle of inertia and the priority of rectilinear motion, and he advances a principle that roughly anticipates the principle of conservation of momentum (*ibid.*: 240–42).[3] Descartes' conviction that these laws are universal, innate in the human mind and sufficient as a basis for modelling all observable cause-and-effect relationships grounds his confidence that the principles of his new physics will eventually render human beings "the masters and possessors of nature".

Descartes devotes a great deal of attention to the human body as a mechanism, sometimes describing its functioning as comparable to that of a church organ. In the *Discourse* he advances a conception of the human heart as a machine; and while he offers a mistaken picture of the specific way in which the heart functions (he conceives of it as an oven rather than as a pump), his conception nonetheless paves the way for later medical innovations such as heart surgery and heart transplantation. Descartes also uses his mechanistic conception of the body to draw a fundamental distinction between human beings and animals. Human beings are

3. As Gottfried Leibniz would later point out, Descartes fails to grasp sufficiently the notion of force, mistakenly believing that the principles of geometry alone are sufficient to explain physical phenomena; see Descartes (1985: 247) and Leibniz (1989: 50).

a composite of mind (or soul) and body; but animals are pure mechanism, with no mind or inner experience whatsoever. This conception of animals underlies Descartes' advocacy of vivisection, which he describes on a number of occasions. If animals are machines subject to the same forces and principles as the human body, we stand to learn a great deal through animal experimentation that will be of great value to human beings; and given that animals cannot perceive or feel in any subjective sense, we need have no scruples whatsoever about experimenting on them, nor about killing and eating them.

Whereas animals are pure mechanisms, human beings on Descartes' view are a composite of mind or soul and body. Descartes subscribes to a dualism according to which the soul is ultimately independent of the body but is conjoined with it for the duration of our mortal existence; he writes that his discussion of dualism in the *Meditations* should be sufficient "to give mortals the hope of an after-life" (1984: 10). At the same time, Descartes attempts to adhere to the strict bifurcation between matters of faith and matters of reason asserted earlier by Galileo: religious concerns such as eternal salvation are not proper objects of philosophical reflection, since matters of revelation exceed the grasp of reason (Galileo 1957: 179–82). The ultimate value of philosophy lies in the foundations it can provide for the conduct of life in our earthly, mortal condition, that is, in our condition as a composite of mind and body. Descartes devotes the last text he wrote, *Passions of the Soul*, to an examination of the reciprocal relations between mind and body, and to the prospects for regulating our passions with the use of reason so that they promote rather than interfere with the pursuit of earthly goods.

Descartes' concern with the unity of (or interaction between) mind and body is a concern with the uppermost branches of the tree of wisdom: medicine, mechanics and morality. A central mystery in the interpretation of Descartes' thought is the exact status of his conception of morality: if morals are to be understood as a branch of science that presupposes physics, then what can he possibly envisage when he speaks of a "highest and most perfect moral system"? The only text in which Descartes writes at length about morals is the *Discourse*, in which he presents the principles of a "provisional morality" that is supposed to guide us until we have examined and re-established the foundations of knowledge. Descartes does not explicitly present this provisional morality as one that everyone should follow; instead, he presents it as the one that he chose to follow while he was establishing new foundations for knowledge, and the reader is implicitly invited to consider the usefulness of such a provisional moral code in his or her own life. Descartes relates that he respected the customs and laws of his country, sought to be moderate in his actions, and practised the religion of his birth; that he sought to act as resolutely as the circumstances permitted, never abandoning a particular course of action unless and until he settled on a superior course of action; that he endeavoured to restrict his concern to matters that were in his power; and that he chose what he considered to be the best occupation in life (1985: 122–4).

Implicit in the presentation of this provisional morality is the prospect of a definitive morality that will be firmly grounded in metaphysics and physics. What remains mysterious about this conception is how reason, as Descartes envisages it, is capable of adducing normative principles. If rational certainty is a matter of perceiving logical relationships, such as the connection between my thinking now and my existing now, then it is not clear that reason can arrive at definitive insights into right and wrong. A case in point is Descartes' call to master nature; such a call is not a matter of logical evidence, but instead, as noted earlier, is derived from a tradition of religious thinking about the propriety of human dominion. Indeed, the specific moral commitments that Descartes advances in his writings, such as the principle of devotion to community, have a pointedly Christian cast to them. Likewise, the basic virtues of a moral life as Descartes envisages it – charity, humility, compassion and repentance – are all Christian virtues that appear to be grounded not in reason but in the very religious tradition that Descartes sought to supersede with a definitive morality founded on reason. The influence of Christianity is also evident in Descartes' conception of the passion of generosity, which he considers pre-eminent in a virtuous life.

Descartes' legacy is that of a rationalist thinker who made a sharp break with medieval Christian tradition, thereby liberating European consciousness from the inappropriate encroachment of religious dogma into the domain of science and opening the way for a secular approach to science and technology. This interpretation of Descartes emphasizes his insights into the power of reason, and thereby provides an overly simplistic picture of a thinker whose thought reflects a profound *ambivalence* about the respective contributions that reason and faith can make to a life well led. To the extent that we today are in an important sense still Cartesians, to overlook this ambivalence is to misunderstand ourselves and the crisis in meaning with which we find ourselves confronted.

FURTHER READING

Curley, E. 1978. *Descartes Against the Skeptics*. Cambridge, MA: Harvard University Press.

Frankfurt, H. 1970. *Demons, Dreamers, and Madmen: The Defense of Reason in Descartes's "Meditations"*. Indianapolis, IN: Bobbs-Merrill.

Gaukroger, S. 1995. *Descartes: An Intellectual Biography*. Oxford: Clarendon Press.

Gueroult, M. 1984–5. *Descartes's Philosophy Interpreted According to the Order of Reasons*, 2 vols, R. Ariew (trans.). Minneapolis, MN: University of Minnesota Press.

Maritain, J. 1944. *The Dream of Descartes Together with Some Other Essays*, M. Andison (trans.). New York: Philosophical Library.

Rodis-Lewis, G. 1998. *Descartes: His Life and Thought*, J. Todd (trans.). Ithaca, NY: Cornell University Press.

Steiner, G. 2004. *Descartes as a Moral Thinker: Christianity, Technology, Nihilism*. Amherst, NY: Prometheus.

Williams, B. 1978. *Descartes: The Project of Pure Enquiry*. Harmondsworth: Penguin.

On FAITH see also Vol. 1, Ch. 13; Vol. 2, Chs 6, 12, 16, 18; Vol. 4, Chs 8, 10, 13; Vol. 5, Chs 7, 18. On MATHEMATICS see also Vol. 2, Ch. 17. On METAPHYSICS see also Vol. 2, Ch. 10. On MORALITY see also Chs 2, 12, 14, 21, 22; Vol. 2, Ch. 12; Vol. 4, Chs 4, 12, 18; Vol. 5, Ch. 6. On REASON see also Chs 12, 16, 21; Vol. 2, Chs 10, 11, 12, 16, 18; Vol. 4, Chs 4, 8. On TRUTH see also Chs 3, 13; Vol. 1, Ch. 13; Vol. 2, Ch. 17; Vol. 4, Chs 8, 18; Vol. 5, Ch. 4.

9

RALPH CUDWORTH

Benjamin Carter

Ralph Cudworth (1617–88) is one of the great overlooked figures in early modern philosophy. Despite the outpouring of contextual studies of early modern thought in recent years, Cudworth's work has been largely ignored. At first glance it is easy to see why. His overt Neoplatonism appears to place him at odds with the general trends of early modern thought and against the emerging empiricism of English seventeenth-century thought in particular. Also his style, owing, as it does, so much to the humanist scholarship of the Renaissance, seems more eager to look backwards than forwards. At best Cudworth is characterized as a middling figure, standing Janus-faced on the margins between antiquity and modernity. These traditional characterizations of Cudworth, however, fundamentally misinterpret Cudworth's thought. Despite the immediate problems presented by his thought, and his voluminous *The True Intellectual System of the Universe* (hereafter *Intellectual System*; 1678) in particular, Cudworth deserves a higher place within the history of philosophy. He, along with the other Cambridge Platonists, was one of the first English thinkers to engage systematically with Cartesian thought. Cudworth also provided some of the earliest criticisms of the thought of Thomas Hobbes and Baruch Spinoza. However, Cudworth should not simply be read as a commentator of contemporary thought. His thought, particularly in the philosophy of religion, provided innovative and progressive accounts of central terms in Christian theology, in particular the doctrine of the Trinity. These theological principles then underpinned his writings on epistemology, ethics and human agency. By constructing, if only in a partial and incomplete form, a comprehensive philosophical system on the principles of his theological insight, Cudworth's work deserves to be recognized as one of the defining contributions to early modern philosophy, and one of the finest works in – using the term that Cudworth himself invented – the philosophy of religion.

INTELLECTUAL ORIGINS

Cudworth is the heir to the tradition of moderate English religious thought that includes Richard Hooker, Lord Herbert of Cherbury and the Great Tew Circle. What unites the thinkers in this moderate tradition is not only their use of reason within religious discussion, but also their use of reason to distance themselves from orthodox Calvinism. This form of Calvinism stressed the omnipotent will of God above all things. High Calvinism dominated the theological outlook of English thought in the early seventeenth century, and became, as we shall see, the dominant theological influence on Cudworth's early life. What marks Cudworth and the Cambridge Platonists out from their moderate forebears is their reliance on the forms and structures of Platonic thought. Although Platonic and Neoplatonic thought was not a common thread in English thought, there had been an undercurrent of it in England from the sixteenth century, most notably in the humanism of Thomas More and Erasmus. There was also a strong Platonic theme within the metaphysical poetry of, among others, Edmund Spencer (from whom Henry More claimed to have first developed his Platonism) and Thomas Traherne.

Gilbert Burnet identifies Benjamin Whichcote as first introducing Platonism into the curriculum at Cambridge. There are several reasons why this development of Platonic thought is of interest. First, the Cambridge Platonists used Platonic philosophy to counter and grapple with many of the theological and philosophical principles of the day. In particular, the Cambridge Platonists commonly adopted an overtly Platonic position to the dominant scholastic education of the day. Secondly, the Platonism of the Cambridge men was, to all intents, a development of the Florentine Neoplatonism of Marsilio Ficino. Although Cudworth utilized a vast array of classical sources in his writings – Platonic, Presocratic, Aristotelian, Stoic –all these readings were coloured by his reading of Plotinus. In fact, so strong was this influence that Samuel Taylor Coleridge once pithily commented that the Cambridge men were "more truly Plotinists" than Platonists (Coleridge 1955: 366).

CALVINISM AND THE CAMBRIDGE PLATONISTS

Cudworth's use of Platonic thought was part of a conscious reaction to the strictures and rigours of English Calvinism. All of Cudworth's writings present a powerful defence of an intellectualist conception of God, in contrast to the dominant voluntarism of Calvinism. For Cudworth, as with the other Cambridge Platonists, the Calvinist preoccupation with the omnipotence of the divine will had distorted the conception of God, creating, in their opinion, an arbitrary and vengeful God who ruled by the dictates of an incomprehensible will, not the eternal precepts of love and justice.

One of Cudworth's earliest writings, his *A Sermon Preached before the Honourable House of Commons* of 1647, is an extended exposition on this theme. Preached in the Palace of Westminster, where the Calvinist-dominated Westminster Assembly was also meeting, Cudworth's sermon presents an extended rejection of the basic principles of Calvinist thought. Central to Cudworth's rejection of Calvinism, and a dominant theme in his later writings, is a belief in the role of human will in the economy of salvation. Cudworth argues that the Calvinist rejection of human agency in favour of the omnipotent power of God's will not only degrades God, but also downplays the responsibilities that human beings have in securing their salvation. Making a pointed reference to the Westminster Assembly, Cudworth states that human beings should not "perswade our selves that we are certainly elected to everlasting happiness: before we see the image of God, in rightousnesse and true holinesse, shaped in our hearts" (Patrides 1969: 94). In place of this, Cudworth argues that human beings come to God by experiencing the intellectual form of divine creation. Borrowing from Plato's *Euthyphro* Cudworth argues that "Vertue and Holinesse in creatures ... are not *therefore Good, because God loveth them* and will have them be accounted such; but rather, *God therefore loveth them because they are in themselves simply good*" (*ibid.*: 102). This participatory form of religious experience was available to human beings not in the form of spiritual enthusiasm, so popular with many of the religious reformers of the middle decades of the seventeenth century, but in the sober and measured reflections of the human mind. Cudworth places his understanding of religious experience within the overarching structure of his Neoplatonic intellectualist philosophical system. For Cudworth God is defined as good, just and above all rational. Therefore human beings, because they exist at least to a limited extent as rational creatures, are able to participate actively in the divine creation through the use of their rational faculties. Spiritual enlightenment comes, Cudworth argues, not from divine inspiration, but from intellectual and rational introspection.

The clearest defence of this rational introspection came in a series of letters written in 1651 between Whichcote, then provost of King's College, and the Calvinist divine Anthony Tuckney, who was Master of Emmanuel. In these letters Tuckney, who had acted as Whichcote's tutor at Emmanuel in the 1630s, counselled against the excesses of Whichcote's rational faith. For Tuckney, Whichcote's adherence to rationality in religious questions drew him away from the narrow path of Calvinist orthodoxy. In particular Tuckney criticized Whichcote's devotion to pagan and, particularly, Platonic philosophers in his writings and sermons. In doing so Tuckney accused Whichcote of undermining the efficacy of biblical revelation creating "a kinde of a Moral Divinitie minted; onlie with a little tincture of Christ added: nay, a Platonique faith united to God" (Whichcote 1753: 39). In response, Whichcote presented a spirited defence of the place of reason in religious discourse characteristic of the writings of all the Cambridge Platonists. Defending his use of pagan philosophy, Whichcote stated that "Truth is Truth;

whosoever hath spoken it" (*ibid.*: 57). Far from leading to heresy, Whichcote argued, reason is the true essence of religion, and "that religion is the truest and highest reason; as, on the contrarie, irreligion is sottishness" (*ibid.*: 43). Reason therefore acts not only as the principle that defines creation, but also acts as the principle by and through which human beings come to know God within creation.

This theme of rational participation defines the central dictum of the Cambridge Platonists: "the spirit of man is the candle of the Lord". This quote, although largely absent from Cudworth's writings, defines the form and nature of human participation in the divine creation. Taken from Proverbs 20:27, it illustrates three important themes that defined how the Cambridge Platonists placed humanity within creation. First, human beings are connected in all things to the light of God's creation; as Whichcote, in one of his many aphorisms, stated, "the *Spirit of Man is the Candle of the Lord*; Lighted *by* God, and Lighting us to God" (1930: 102). Secondly, it is important to note that the spirit of man is equated to the dim, flickering and essentially fragile light of a candle. Like the apostle Paul's "through a glass darkly", the candlelight of the human soul can only give us a partial illumination of God. The Cambridge Platonists therefore accepted that the human soul was limited, fallible and fallen. However, they did not accept, as Calvinists did, that human beings shared collectively and federally in the Fall of Adam. This point leads to the final characteristic of the candle of the Lord: the religious life requires the active and conscious participation of human beings. As a consequence, the candle of the Lord implies, in contrast to the teaching of Calvinism, a defence of human agency and free will.

THE TRUE INTELLECTUAL SYSTEM OF THE UNIVERSE

All these themes come together in Cudworth's *Intellectual System*. This was originally envisaged as a three-volume work, of which Cudworth published only the first part. The first volume is a compendious apology for the form of intellectual theism that lies at the heart of the writings of all the Cambridge Platonists. In great detail, and often wearisome and repetitive form, Cudworth denies the philosophical validity of atheism and determinism. In form and structure, the *Intellectual System* looks back to the humanism of the Renaissance. Cudworth's thought attempts to synthesize all philosophy into a *philosophia perennis* (perennial philosophy), in which all truth and wisdom find their origin in the example and teaching of Adam and Moses. This apologetic strategy had three chief aims. First, it allowed for the reconciliation of pagan and Christian sources, as we have already seen Whichcote defend, into one revealed truth. Secondly, Cudworth argued that the philosophical innovations of the seventeenth century were not 'new', but resurrections of ancient philosophical systems: so Descartes is praised for restoring the atomism of the Mosaic and Pythagorean traditions; Hobbes is derided for adopting the materialism of Epicurus and Democritus. Thirdly, Cudworth aimed to show that all forms of atheism lacked philosophical coherence or validity. Cudworth hoped that this project would create a definitive account of the origins, form and nature of not only theism, but also the Trinity as the definitive expression of true theism. As a result Cudworth spends as much time outlining and explaining those systems that he thought were in error (polytheism and atheism) as he did those theistic systems that he thought to be in truth. Despite these problems, what remains in Cudworth's *Intellectual System* is one of the first systematic works in 'philosophy of religion' in the English language (Cudworth 1678: xvii).

PROOF OF THE EXISTENCE OF GOD

Before Cudworth is able to account for his Trinitarian conception of God he first has to account for the natural knowledge of God held by all. Although the style and form of Cudworth's *Intellectual System* looks back to the Renaissance humanism of Marsilio Ficino and Agostino Steucho, Cudworth's writing mixes ancient learning with many of the key philosophical developments of the seventeenth century. In fact, Cudworth's apparent reliance on ancient learning should not mask the modernity of his thought. Cudworth's proof of the existence of God is a case in point, presenting as it does an extended commentary and development of Descartes' ontological proof.

Cudworth's proof accepts from the outset Descartes assertion that the human intellect can conceive of the existence of God from *a priori* principles alone. The ontological proof appealed to Cudworth because it made the idea of God a natural part of the intellectual capacities of the human mind. Cudworth, however, takes issue with Descartes, following although not necessarily relying on the criticisms of Gassendi and Arnauld, by stressing the essential circularity of Descartes' proof. For Cudworth the circularity in Descartes' argument is a direct result of Descartes' use of sceptical reason. Such a sceptical method necessarily brings human faculties into doubt, however the knowledge of the existence of God is, in ontological terms, founded exclusively on the supposition of these faculties that, in Cartesian terms, can be thought to be reliable only if the existence of God is assumed (Cudworth 1678: 717). By arguing that reason can doubt the existence of all things, Cudworth states that Descartes can effectively make claims with certainty only if the divine is first presupposed. Therefore the existence of God cannot be known with any certainty because this conclusion is based on a method that itself relies on God to create that certainty. Consequently, Cudworth argues that Descartes' proof relies on the "[*F*]*irmness* and *Solidity*, of such *Thin* and *Subtle Cobwebs*" (*ibid.*: 725).

In place of Cartesian scepticism Cudworth utilizes the metaphysical structure of Neoplatonism to account for the knowledge of God as known on *a priori* intellectual terms alone. Following Plotinus, Cudworth defines God not as an Aristotelian passive first mover, but in the Platonic form of thought thinking itself; in Plotinian terms, an overflowing and inexhaustible fountain. Consequently all creation is united in its relationship to the intellectual source of creation. Cudworth, following many of his Neoplatonic forebears, defines this relationship as an intellectual hierarchy, or scale of being. This hierarchy explains, for Cudworth, the intellectual form of the divine, the place of human beings in that creation and the superiority of the mind over the body. As Cudworth states:

> Wherefore there being plainly a scale or ladder of entity, the order of things was unquestionably, in way of descent, from higher perfection downward to lower; it being as impossible for a greater perfection to be produced from a lesser, as for something to be caused by nothing. Neither are the steps or degrees of this ladder (either upward or downward) infinite; but at the foot, bottom, or lowest round thereof is stupid and senseless matter, devoid of all life and understanding; so is the head, top, and summit of it a perfect omnipotent Being, comprehending itself, and all possibilities of things. (*Ibid.*: 435)

Human beings, therefore, have a natural knowledge of God because they exist within this continual scale of being. Cudworth therefore accepts the spirit of Descartes' proof, but rejects the method. In contrast to this, Cudworth argues that because God is a rational creative being, all truly rational thoughts cannot doubt God because reasoned acts, by definition, have their source and existence in the divine. Cudworth's version of the ontological proof, relying as it does on a cosmological element to overcome the circularity of Descartes' proof, is mirrored by More's version of the ontological proof in *An Explanation of the Grand Mystery of Godliness* (1660).

THE TRINITY

The apologetic form of Cudworth's *Intellectual System* extends from his intellectualist theism to what Cudworth understood as the true expression of the divine in the Trinity. Cudworth states that the Trinity is not only the central term of Christianity – "the Choke-pear of Christianity" – but also a recurring theme in all sound forms of pagan theism (Cudworth 1678: xii). Theologically, Cudworth's Trinitarianism is marked by a reversion to an 'immanent' interpretation of the Trinity against the dominant Calvinist 'economic' Trinity. Central to Cudworth's reassertion of the immanent Trinity is his definition of the unified intellectual form of the Trinity. In particular, Cudworth adopts the Cartesian definition of immaterial substance to assert the Trinity as an indivisible and intellectual substance. By beginning his understanding of the Trinity with the unified substance of God, Cudworth accounts for the existence of the different persons of the Trinity while still maintaining the unified form of the persons as being of one substance, or *homoousious*. Cudworth defines the Nicene term *homoousious* as "not a *sameness* of singular and Numerical, but of Common or *universal Essence* only; that is, the *Generical* or *specifical Essence of the Godhead*" (*ibid.*: 608). The persons of the Trinity exist, Cudworth argues, as the different and necessary expressions of the same unified essence.

Cudworth's specific definition of the Trinity rests on fundamentally Neoplatonic principles. At the source of the Trinity is God the Father. Cudworth defines the Father as "above *Mind* and *Understanding* and also … *Essence*, Ineffable and Incomprehensible". The Father is a simple light, a fountain, a source; consequently the Father has and needs no comprehension of himself. However, because human beings can comprehend the divine, this comprehending power must also derive from the divine. This power derives from the second person, the *Logos*. The *Logos* is "*Mind* or *Understanding*, *Reason* and *Wisdom*", the principle of reason and intelligibility that infuses and binds all creation together. The third person is the means of transport, "*Infinite Self-Activity* … *Infinite*, *Active*, *Perceptive*, and *Animadversive Power*" (*ibid.*: 582–3). Much of Cudworth's argument here, particularly his concentration on the unified substance of the Trinity, is used to counter the accusation that Neoplatonism lay at the heart of the Arian heresy. Cudworth argues that the Arian heresy was derived from later perversions of the Platonic tradition, whereas the genuine Platonism of Plato and Plotinus contained hidden within it the true form of the Trinity, later confirmed and revealed in the incarnation of Christ. Cudworth therefore asserts that his is a "*Platonick Trinity* … a certain Middle thing also, betwixt the Doctrine of *Sabellius* and that of *Arius*; it being neither a *Trinity of Words* only, or *Logical Notions*, or meer *Modes*; but a *Trinity* of *Hypostases*" (*ibid.*: 579). By implication, Cudworth's defence of the Trinity was also aimed at the seventeenth-century anti-Trinitarian heresy of Socinianism. However, despite Cudworth's reassertion of the immanent Trinity and his professed orthodoxy, his definition of the Trinity carries with it the problem of subordination, particularly with regards to the relationship between the singular principle of God the Father and the reflexive principle of the *Logos*. This problem led to Cudworth being accused of opening the door to Trinitarian heresies in his own time, and subsequently of being a pseudo-Arian himself.

FORM OF CREATION

Cudworth goes to great lengths to counter this implicit weakness in his Trinitarian thought, and is highly critical of those philosophical systems that accepted a version of subordination within the divine. In particular, Cudworth criticizes later Platonic thinkers who saw the persons of the Trinity as the beginning of a descent from the divine to the created world. God is, Cudworth argues consistently, defined by his unity expressed in the persons of the Trinity. That does not mean, however, that Cudworth thought of God as absent from, or indifferent to, the created world. Cudworth is at great pains to show that the created world does not exist as a by-product of the divine intellect, but is actively linked to and defined by its relation to God. It is therefore of great importance for Cudworth to establish the visible presence of God within creation. All the forms of atheism that Cudworth attacks in the *Intellectual System* essentially derive, he argues, from an incorrect understanding of the relationship between God and creation. Cudworth argues that these forms of atheism fall into four different types: *atomical* atheism held that creation came about by chance; *hylozoic* atheism asserted that life comes from matter; *hylopathian* atheism argued that there was a hierarchy of intelligent matter; and *cosmo-plastic* atheism, while accepting the existence of a divine soul, posited no ruling principle in creation.

In reaction to these forms of atheism, Cudworth defines a powerful and at times highly complex account of the immediate providential presence of God within creation. As with many of the principles within Cudworth's theology, the starting-point for this is an implicit rejection of the determinism of Calvinism. Cudworth equates the voluntarism implicit in Calvinism with an arbitrary and wilful conception of the divine. For Cudworth, the Calvinist doctrine of predestination removed from human beings any principle of moral or personal responsibility. As he states in his free will manuscripts, such a position assumes that "man, having hands, should not use them to blow or wipe his nose, but [instead] sit still expecting that God, by miracles, should do that office for him" (Cudworth n.d.: 4980, 38). Therefore Cudworth is adamant that human beings are not predestined because it is ridiculous to think that God would be concerned with every act, however minuscule, that occurs on earth. However, the problem remains of how to account for the presence of divine wisdom and goodness in creation, without making God immediately concerned with and directly responsible for every single act within creation. To counter this, Cudworth developed his doctrine of the 'Plastic Nature of Reality', fully developed in an extended "Digression" within the *Intellectual System*. This doctrine, broadly derived from the Platonic *anima mundi* (the idea that the world is locked together through a comprehensive immaterial spiritual principle), asserts the existence of a regulatory principle within the world derived from the intellectual principle of the divine rather than representing the immediate presence of the divine within nature. Plastic Nature, Cudworth states, "doth Drudgingly Execute the Part of his Providence, which consists in the Regular and Orderly Motion of Matter" (1678: 150). Plastic Nature allows Cudworth to account for the basic order and regularity of the universe while allowing God to remain separate from the mundane ordering of the universe. This distinction plays an important role in Cudworth's thought for several reasons. First, as stated, it allows Cudworth to show that the providential power of God exists in the regulatory principles of the universe. Secondly, it permits him to argue that when these principles become perverted or corrupted this is not directly the will of God, but a fault within the workings of these lower plastic principles. Thirdly, and most importantly, it allows Cudworth to argue that, although God's wisdom drives the mundane principles of creation, these plastic principles do not control all human actions. Importantly, Cudworth argues that "*Plastic Nature* cannot act *Electively* nor with *Discretion*", in the manner that human beings can (*ibid.*: iv–v). Cudworth therefore uses Plastic Nature to reject the determinism of Calvinism and, by implication, Hobbesianism. In both these systems, Cudworth argues, human beings are driven slavishly in their actions by the immediate presence of determining principles in all parts of creation; for Calvin through the will of God; for Hobbes through matter in motion. Cudworth accepts the existence of these regulatory principles but, through the doctrine of Plastic Nature, argues that they extend only as far as the mundane workings of creation. Therefore in the realm of human agency a different understanding of the providential will of God is at play.

ETHICS

Cudworth's intention was for the first part of the *Intellectual System* to provide the framework for two further volumes. The second volume, on ethics, would argue that there are things "Just *and* Unjust, *to us* Naturally", the third would outline the form of "Liberty … *in* Rational Creatures, *as may render them* Accountable, *capable of* Rewards *and* Punishments, *and so* Objects *of* Distributive *or* Retributive Justice" (1678: iv–v). For reasons that are now lost to us, Cudworth never completed this project in a published form. However, his *Treatise Concerning Eternal and Immutable Morality* (hereafter *Morality*), his *Treatise of Freewill*, and his unpublished free will manuscripts (which are now held in at the British Library) cover much of this intellectual ground. Although these works do not complete Cudworth's projected *Intellectual System*, they build on the theological and philosophical premises that have been outlined above.

Eternal and immutable morality

Cudworth's *Morality* holds a curious place in the history of ethical philosophy. Its publication in 1731 was part of the ongoing debates concerning ethical rationalism engendered by Samuel Clarke's *Boyle Lectures* of 1706 and 1707. Cudworth's text has therefore been commonly viewed in the context of this later debate on ethical theory. Certainly the publication of the *Morality* placed Cudworth at the heart of debates on ethical rationalism, and open to attack from, among others, David Hume (Hume 1896: 3.1.1).

It is, however, important to place Cudworth's *Morality* in the theological and philosophical context of his *Intellectual System*. Cudworth's concern with ethics was not removed from his theological concerns, but central to his understanding and definition of the workings of the divine within creation. It is possible to identify

Cudworth's interest in ethical questions in two published Latin orations, *Dantur boni et mali rationes aeternae et indispensabiles* and *Dantur substantiae incorporeae sua natura immortales*, published in 1651 and delivered for either Cudworth's degree of Bachelor of Divinity in 1644 or Doctor of Divinity in 1651. Certainly we know, from a letter that Cudworth wrote to his friend John Worthington, that he was working on a text on "Natural Ethicks" in the mid 1660s. As the manuscript that the published edition was prepared from is now lost, it is impossible to know with any certainty where the *Morality* fits into this historical picture. What seems certain is that the *Morality* is not the complete text on ethics that Cudworth intended to write, but a *prolegomenon* outlining how human beings come to know and recognize the existence of eternal and immutable moral truths. In this way Cudworth's *Morality* is as much a text on epistemology as it is on ethics.

Cudworth begins by assessing the means by which human beings come to knowledge of the world around them. Beginning with sense-perception, Cudworth argues that the "dull, confused, and stupid perception obtruded on the soul from without" lacks the necessary perceptive power needed for knowledge (1996: 53). Like the realm of Plastic Nature, sense-perception lacks the self-awareness needed to understand anything more than its immediate locality. For Cudworth, knowledge is not imposed on the mind from the outside, but formed by the mind comprehending itself:

> [K]nowledge is not a passion from anything without the mind, but an active exertion of the inward strength, vigor, and power of the mind displaying itself from within, and the intelligible forms by which things are understood or known are not stamps or impressions passively printed upon the soul from without, but ideas vitally protended or actively exerted from within itself. (*Ibid.*: 73–4)

This, however, is not to say that Cudworth thought all knowledge resided unborn in the mind and divorced from the experiences and impressions presented by the external world. Cudworth's epistemology, although borrowing from the traditional Platonic forms of recollection, rejects the suggestion that knowledge is simply the recollection of principles pre-existing in the human soul. Unlike More, Cudworth actively rejects the Platonic doctrine of the pre-existence of the soul, and the linked epistemological theory of *anamnesis*: that all knowledge is held in the soul from eternity (compare Cudworth [1678: 44] with More [1969: 119]). Instead, Cudworth argues that the divinely inspired, rational powers of the human mind are used by human beings to search out, identify and acknowledge the principle of the divine in all parts of creation. Cudworth's epistemology therefore employs the same structure as his proof of the existence of God; the internal workings of the mind comprehend the principle and truth of the divine, which is then confirmed and clarified by the application of this principle in encounters with the created world.

Like all of Cudworth's thought, this model of ethical epistemology drew on his intellectualist understanding of the divine. Moral truths were not asserted by the arbitrary will of God but woven, eternally and immutably, into the fabric of creation. Therefore, for Cudworth, moral certainties are arrived at by testing the assertions of the mind against the reality of the created world. Moral truths are "ectypal prints ... and derivative signatures ... from one archetypal intellect, that is essentially the *rationes* of all things and all verities" (Cudworth 1996: 131). In this manner Cudworth, like his mentor Whichcote and his daughter's friend John Locke, argues that morality can be asserted with the same surety as mathematical proofs. Cudworth's *Morality* therefore does not assert or seek to offer a programme of ethical norms; rather, it provides the framework within which human beings can develop as ethically self-determined individuals. The epistemology that Cudworth offers in the *Morality* mirrors that presented in the *Intellectual System*, and has been interpreted by many as one of Cudworth's most thoroughgoing philosophical innovations, one that even looks forward to the idealism of the Kantian critiques (Lovejoy 1908; Darwall 1995: 109). Certainly, Cudworth's ethical epistemology presents a fully developed account of the traditional Neoplatonic innatist theory of human knowledge that was so thoroughly undermined in the opening chapters of John Locke's *An Essay Concerning Human Understanding*.

Free will

Implicit in Cudworth's ethical theory is the assertion that ethical knowledge is achieved by the free exercise of the mind. Consequently Cudworth's ethical theory contains within it a defence of human free will. Like his ethical epistemology, we can find intimations of this defence within Cudworth's *Intellectual System*, particularly in the "Digression on the Plastic Nature of Reality". Cudworth's interest in questions of free will fits naturally into the wider seventeenth-century debate on human agency. For Cudworth these debates exist within two overlapping contexts: the implicit denial of free will in Calvinist theology; and the modification of Calvinist determinism in the materialist thought of Hobbes.

Cudworth's defence of free will is of interest for two reasons. First, Cudworth attempts to reconcile ideas of free will with principles of divine providence. In traditional determinist systems, human agency is denied because of the inexorable power of providence. In Calvinism this takes the form of the doctrine of predestination; in Hobbesianism this is modified to the determinism of physical necessity. Many defences of free will found in the seventeenth century, most notably that offered by Bishop Bramhall in opposition to Hobbes, are based on a de-coupling of cause and effect: an argument that although an action has a discernible and sufficient cause, this is only a contingent, and not a necessary relationship. Implicit in these defences of free will, therefore, is an undermining of the principle of a providential chain of events. By contrast, Cudworth's defence of free will relies not on an attack on providence but, as Cudworth sees it, an enhancement of providence.

Within Cudworth's published work this development of providence is found in his 'Digression' on Plastic Nature, particularly his assertion that although there are some actions that are determined by the principles of the divine intellect, these are merely the mundane actions. Therefore, above this mundane plastic realm exists a realm defined by the free actions of human beings. The realm in which free will is at play, however, is not divorced from the mind and knowledge of God. Rather, Cudworth argues that we need to recognize that the divine intellect is so vast that it not only knows all the form of all necessary future actions, as is asserted in traditional models of providence, but all possible and contingent future actions as well. So Cudworth argues, "the Comprehensiveness of the Divine Understanding ... Grasps and presents all futurity in it" (Cudworth n.d.: 4981, 50). Therefore Cudworth places human free will within the infinite web of possible future actions that are known to the mind of God.

The second area of interest in Cudworth's theory of free will is the linguistic innovations he employs. For Cudworth free will exists as the means by which human beings can come to know and participate in the higher truths of the divine intellect. Freedom exists not in a separation from or indifference to the created world, but in the active participation with the divine principle in all parts of creation. Cudworth first articulates this version of free will in a sermon he preached in the Chapel of Lincoln's Inn in 1664. Here Cudworth contrasts the limitations of Hobbesianism and Calvinism with the characterization of what he terms "God's freeman". The life of God's freeman is one of individual choice and ethical legislation in which human beings come willingly and freely to the love and righteousness of God (Cudworth 1664: 46–8). In Cudworth's manuscripts this process of individual moral regulation is defined using the language of Stoic moral philosophy. In particular, Cudworth develops the Stoic idea of individual self-government or *hegemonikon* to define not simply the foundation of moral responsibility, but also the defining principle of human individuality. Cudworth anglicizes the Stoic language through the use of 'self' constructs, of which 'self-determination' remains the most widely recognized and used in the lexicon of contemporary ethical philosophy (1996: 210). It is perhaps in this area that Cudworth's lasting philosophical influence can be most clearly recognized.

FURTHER READING

Cassirer, E. 1953. *The Platonic Renaissance in England*, J. Pettegrove (trans.). London: Nelson.

Cragg, G. (ed.) 1968. *The Cambridge Platonists*. Oxford: Oxford University Press.

Passmore, J. 1961. *Ralph Cudworth: An Interpretation*. Cambridge: Cambridge University Press.

Rogers, G., J. Vienne & Y.-C. Zarka (eds) 1997. *The Cambridge Platonists in Philosophical Context: Politics, Metaphysics and Religion*. Dordrecht: Kluwer.

Taliaferro, C. & A. Teply (eds) 2004. *Cambridge Platonist Spirituality*. Mahwah, NJ: Paulist Press.

Taliaferro, C. 2005. *Evidence and Faith: Philosophy and Religion since the Seventeenth Century.* Cambridge: Cambridge University Press.
Tulloch, J. 1874. *Rational Theology and Christian Philosophy in England in the Seventeenth Century*, 2 vols. Edinburgh: William Blackwood & Sons.

On CREATION see also Vol. 1, Chs 9, 13, 17; Vol. 5, Ch. 5. On ETHICS see also Vol. 1, Ch. 11; Vol. 2, Chs 4, 8; Vol. 4, Chs 13, 19; Vol. 5, Chs 12, 15, 21. On FREE WILL see also Ch. 15; Vol. 1, Ch. 18; Vol. 2, Chs 2, 7, 9, 19; Vol. 5, Ch. 22. On NEOPLATONISM see also Vol. 1, Chs 19, 20; Vol. 2, Chs 3, 4; Vol. 4, Chs 4, 9. On THE TRINITY see also Chs 3, 17; Vol. 1, Chs 14, 17, 20; Vol. 2, Chs 2, 8, 15; Vol. 4, Ch. 4; Vol. 5, Chs 12, 23.

10

BLAISE PASCAL

William David Wetsel

Blaise Pascal (1623–62) was a towering intellectual figure in seventeenth-century France, the last of the universal geniuses in European history. His discoveries and ideas still have great influence in modern intellectual and scientific life. A true polymath, he made contributions in physics, mathematics, philosophy and theology. Students of physics have heard of Pascal's vases; students of mathematics know of his triangle. It was he who established experimentally that the weight of the earth's atmosphere varies according to altitude and first gave theoretical embodiment to the idea of the vacuum. His ideas also gave rise variously to the concept of the calculator or computer and to inexpensive public transportation.

In 1646, at the age of 23, Pascal had a profound religious experience when he became associated with a group of disciples of Jean du Vergier, the Abbé de Saint-Cyran, who lived in the vicinity of Rouen. He accepted their doctrine of 'conversion' or abandonment of the world and submission to God, and even converted his family to Jansenism. This conversion, however, did not have an immediate effect on his work. One reason was that he became seriously ill in 1647 and returned to Paris, where his physicians advised him to find diversions from his work. That advice led him to relax the religious discipline.

Another profound mystical experience occurred in 1654 when Pascal became intimately associated with the Convent of Port-Royal, where his sister Jacqueline had become a religious initiate and where Saint-Cyran was spiritual director. He recorded this second, intense religious experience in his *Mémorial* (1654). This experience marked Pascal indelibly for the rest of his life, as is evidenced by the fact that the *Mémorial*, a document of simple physical appearance dominated by lines, dashes and exclamations, was sewn into the lining of his coat. In the following year, 1655, one of the many retreats that Pascal undertook at Port-Royal led to his *Conversation with M. de Sacy on Epictetus and Montaigne*.

In 1656 he composed his *Provincial Letters*, his contribution to the mass of pamphlet literature in the explosion of the Jansenist and Jesuit controversies on grace and predestination. In this genre of literature, a recondite dispute is thrust into the non-specialist arena of public opinion by means of a series of what we would now call literary instalments containing hilarious satires on the opponents of the Jansenists. To understand the *Provincial Letters* and Pascal himself requires knowledge of at least the major contours of Jansenism, the Roman Catholic reform movement that took its name from Cornelius Jansen (1585–1638).

Jansen had been Bishop of Ypres, and his immense, posthumously published *Augustinus* (1640) initiated an intense renewal of interest in Augustine among a group of theologians in close contact with the sisters of Port-Royal. The Jesuits, who found this renewed version of Augustinianism too harsh and its view of salvation too narrow, began to manufacture a kind of caricature of the Jansenists. As the slanders spread (for example, that the Jansenists did not believe in transubstantiation), Pascal's associates at Port-Royal asked him to write a polemic against the Jesuits. The result was the *Provincial Letters*. Although it is a text containing obscure theological disputes hardly relevant to modern Catholic theology, the *Letters* remain the greatest satirical and ironical work in the French language. They have evolved from religious polemic to a work central to French literature.

Even after a second spiritual experience, Pascal continued to maintain contact with his secular friends and attempted to win them over to Catholic belief. While thinking about two of those friends, Antoine Gombaud, the Chevalier de Méré (1607–84), and Damien Mitton (1618–90), Pascal decided to write an apology for the Christian religion. Gombaud and Mitton were leading young intellectuals in Parisian society whose views of life simply ignored or bypassed religion entirely. They were not active atheists but a new type of what in the nineteenth-century would come to be called 'agnostics'.

Pascal realized that their indifference was a much greater danger to the cause of Christianity than classical scepticism or traditional heresies. As preparation for writing his *Apology for the Christian Religion* (now rather incorrectly known as the *Pensées*), Pascal began to collect an extensive set of notes that he organized during the last years of his life, a life cut short by a recurrence of the illness that had befallen him in 1647. Before his death, Pascal had the time to organize and classify approximately the first half of his notes. The fragments of the second half, however, remain 'unclassified'. At least eighty per cent (or 800) of the fragments known as the *Pensées* were destined for the *Apology*.

In contrast to the relative unity of the first half, the reader finds in the second half notes on a great variety of topics – religion, style, political power, the nature of poetic language and so on – that contain *inter alia* references to Montaigne, Descartes and the Bible. Some of the most important *pensées* of the entire work are to be found in these sections. A fundamental problem in the interpretation of the *Pensées* is the relationship between these fragments and Pascal's overall apologetic endeavour. Unlike other apologists, Pascal does not mount a direct attack on those whom he considers his adversaries, what he perceives as the growing number of atheists and sceptics in Paris. Rather, he first gives an overview of their blindness (in fragment 681/427)[1] and lures them into an interest in whether God exists via the famous wager (680/418).

Pascal undertakes a lengthy anthropological analysis of the human condition designed to demonstrate that human experience is permeated with a fatal and universal flaw. Only after establishing the enigmatic and total defect in the human condition does he set out to explain the origin of the flawed human condition.

Why should the modern reader be fascinated by a Christian Apology written more than three hundred years ago? The answer partially lies in the fact that the text demonstrates how the most pertinent of all questions (the fate of the soul after death) never loses its power in the human mind. The appeal of the text to the modern mind is even stronger because Pascal's premature death left it in fragmentary form. This state and the fragmented strategy of writing are of fundamental interest to modern literary critics. Pascal's approach has the effect of deconstructing traditional notions of totality. While written by an intellectual of vast depth, the *Pensées* are characterized by the same direct involvement that marked the *Provincial Letters*. The text is replete with social, political and psychological insights expressed with rapier-like precision.

The influence of the *Pensées* on subsequent French literature has been enormous. Voltaire, while praising Pascal's exquisite mastery of French prose, sought to demolish his pessimism and theology in the *English Letters*. Baudelaire's *Les Fleurs du Mal* (The flowers of evil; [1857] 1991) is replete with resonances of the *Pensées*, as are the works of Albert Camus. In the field of sociology one of the most prominent thinkers of recent years, Pierre Bourdieu, in his *Méditations pascaliennes* (Pascalian meditations; 1997, 2000), constructs an anthropological theory of realism derived from Pascal. Charles Taylor repeatedly noted that Pascal was the first thinker to explore human incompleteness and imperfection in terms that remain relevant today. Historians set on tracing the very idea of 'self' cannot possibly ignore Pascal's acute meditations, which provide a powerful counter to Descartes' more familiar confidence in the possibility of attaining certain knowledge. The modern Continental tradition, with its interest in the key notion of the 'subject', finds itself fascinated by Pascal's influence on Freud's irreverent disciple, Jacques Lacan. His work is also the ultimate source of Althusser's theory of ideology.

While fueling much theoretical literary speculation, Pascal's unprecedented contribution to the history of religious philosophy has remained almost entirely neglected and unexplored in the English-speaking world.

1. The first fragment number refers to the Sellier edition (Pascal 1991). An English translation of this edition is due to be published by the Catholic University of America Press, with Pierre Zoberman as general editor. The second number refers to the Lafuma edition, as reproduced in the familiar Penguin edition (1995).

MANUSCRIPTS AND EDITIONS OF THE *PENSÉES*

Understanding Pascal's plan for his *Apology of the Christian Religion* is near impossible without reviewing the major contours of his manuscript text. Pascal set down his fragmentary notes (*pensées*) on large sheets of parchment. After having constituted most of his preliminary notes ('fragments'), he began cutting up and filing the notes in stacks (*liasses*) using needle and thread. Having completed a series of twenty-eight bundles that outline the major stages of his proposed *Apology*, his filing was interrupted by his final illness. The fragments that he had filed in the dossiers are known as the 'classed' dossiers. Those never sorted into separate files we know as the 'unclassed' dossiers, most of which have no discernible order.

Pascal's autograph manuscript, known as the *Recueil original* (Original collection) remains the ultimate arbiter of the words Pascal used. However, it is of almost no help in reconstituting the order and contours of the *Apology*. In 1711, the fragments were all trimmed and pasted in a manuscript completely at random, the spaces on the manuscript paper determining where each fragment would fit. This precious manuscript, in Pascal's own hand and that of his secretary, reposes in the Bibliothèque Nationale in Paris.

Just after Pascal's death, the as yet unmutilated original (along with other copies of Pascal's bundles) formed the basis of the first edition of the *Pensées*, the Port-Royal Edition (1670). This first edition was collated by Pascal's friends and the theologians at Port-Royal with the help of Pascal's nephew. These first editors thought it essential to rearrange Pascal's fragments into an order that they thought reflected Pascal's ultimate work. They also thought it necessary to polish and sometimes re-word Pascal's text in accordance with the dictates of classical style.

This edition, reissued in 1991, became the basis of all subsequent editions of the *Pensées* until the twentieth century. Editions in the Age of Enlightenment stressed the so-called 'philosophical' fragments and eliminated most of the 'religious' *pensées*. Editions compiled during the Romantic period tended to cast Pascal as a melancholy sceptic by attributing fragments expressing the plight of the unbelievers to Pascal himself.

In the early twentieth century, Léon Brunschvigg sought to produce the first scholarly edition of the *Pensées* by consulting the definitive *Recueil original* and correcting what had become a mutilated version of the Port-Royal Edition. However, Brunschvigg reorganized Pascal's entire text into what he thought would have been Pascal's final manuscript. This edition, while correcting the lexical and syntactical errors that had crept into the various successive editions of the *Pensées*, resulted in an edition that was at great variance from Pascal's original plan.

Two copies housed at the Bibliothèque National had been neglected since the Port-Royal Edition, because they were thought to be spurious and erroneous copies of Pascal's original manuscript deformed in 1711. Only in the 1940s and 1950s did the scholars Zacharie Tournier and Louis Lafuma examine these manuscripts and conclude that they were exact facsimile copies of the state in which Pascal left his papers at the time of his death. Long ignored was Pascal's nephew Etienne Perrier's notation of the exact state of Pascal's papers at the time of his death.

Correcting errors of transcription made by the copyists by using the *Recueil original*, Lafuma produced what remained for fifty years the definitive edition of the *Pensées*. However, because he used the first of the copies (L1), in which the unclassed fragments were grouped as entities on a single manuscript page, the order of the unclassed bundles remained incorrect. Only in the 1970s did Philippe Sellier realize that the order in which Pascal left his unclassed bundles was absolutely clear in copy L2. In this second copy, the copyist had run on the text from the bottom of one page to the top of the successive page. By using the second copy of Pascal's original papers – and by further correcting the copyist's transcription errors via consultation with the misarranged autograph (the *Recueil original*) – Sellier produced what is to date the definitive text of the *Pensées*.

Sellier's edition has gained widespread currency in France over the past decade and is now considered the standard edition for scholars. However, since the arrangement of the *Pensées* left at Pascal's death still represents a text of great difficulty for the non-specialist, Sellier has also produced a 'reader's version' of the *Pensées* based on Pascal's notes in the classed dossiers.[2]

Scholars now generally agree that the twenty-eight classified dossiers represent at least Pascal's tentative outline for his *Apology*. The first dossier, "Order", contains fragments that it is difficult to place anywhere in the *Apology*. However, and far more importantly, this dossier contains key fragments indicating the shape of the entire *Apology*. Fragment 40/6 outlines the principal parts of the anticipated *Apology*: an anthropological investigation of the enigma of the human condition and the successively potent theological proofs that explain this enigma.

> The pain of man without God
>
> ---
>
> The felicity of man with God

Even more importantly, fragment 45/11 shows that the highly polished fragment 681/427 (long ignored because it stands in the unclassified dossier) is in fact the preface to the entire *Apology*. It is followed by what is commonly called 'the wager'. Modern scholars have tended to see the wager as lying at the heart of the *Pensées*. In fact, like the preface, it is a kind of discourse designed to lure the unbeliever to read onwards.

2. While the Lafuma edition has been translated into English, along with many errors of transcription and translation, neither Sellier's scholarly edition nor his reader's edition has yet been translated into English. Under the aegis of the Catholic University of America Press and the editorship of Nicholas Hammond and David Wetsel, translations of both of these editions are underway.

THE PREFACE TO THE *APOLOGY*

Those who are not Pascal scholars would indeed do well to begin with fragment 681/427 as anticipated in the dossier "Order". The most nearly complete and polished of all the discourses, it received little attention until quite recently, both because it stands outside the classed dossiers and because it is missing from the *Recueil original.* It is obviously the preface to the entire *Apology for the Christian Religion*. Pascal first confronts the sceptics and atheists head-on. They argue that they see no evidence of God's hand in human society or in Scripture and this raises the 'problem of evil'. Pascal turns the tables on them by arguing that this is in perfect agreement with Christian doctrine and Scripture, which teach that God is a hidden God, a *deus abconditus.*

Pascal insists that the question of whether the human soul is immortal is the enigma that should preoccupy the entire human race. The sceptics' lack of interest in this question must have a "supernatural cause". Pascal sympathizes with those who seek but have not found the answer to this all-important question. However, those sceptics who neglect the question altogether are "monstrous" to him. They are not even motivated to investigate what is the most important question with regard to their own self interest:

> One does not need to have a very elevated soul to realize that this life is the source of no true or lasting happiness, that all our pleasures are but vanity, that our sufferings are infinite and that ultimately death, which menaces us every second, will in but a few years infallibly present us with the horrible necessity of being annihilated or unhappy.
> (681/427)

Pascal follows this analysis of the human condition with a series of portraits of sceptics and unbelievers. Because of the random nature of seventeenth-century citation marks, almost all editors and readers until recently have seen Pascal himself as expressing a profound scepticism that belongs not to him, but to the sceptics whose portraits he is painting. "The eternal silence of infinite space terrifies me" has been attributed over and over again to Pascal's own fears. However, Pascal places this passage in the mouth of a sceptic who is at least awed into seeking the truth. For Pascal, all of humanity can be reduced to three categories:

> Those who serve God having found him; those who make a concerted effort to seek Him, not having found him; then those others who live without seeking Him nor having found Him. Those in the first category are reasonable and happy. Those in the last category are insane and unhappy. Those standing in the middle are unhappy but reasonable. (92/160)

In the light of Augustinian theology, the last category is made up of those predestined to damnation. They merit being abandoned to their insanity. We must summon up all the charity required by Christianity so as to view the unbelievers, as long as they are still in this world, as capable of receiving that grace which can alone save them. God's will is inscrutable. In the twinkling of an eye, the unbeliever could be enlightened by more grace than believers have. Likewise, believers could fall into the very blindness of the unbelievers. However, in numerous fragments Pascal seems to make it clear that his *Apology* will be principally addressed to those unhappy souls who are at least seeking God, not having yet found him.

THE WAGER

In the fragment "Order", Pascal makes it clear that the foregoing preface was to be immediately followed by the long and highly incomplete fragment that has come to be called 'the wager'. Pascal himself designates it as a "Discourse on the Machine", designed to remove obstacles to belief and to prepare the 'machine' to search for God via reason. In light of Cartesian philosophy, the 'machine' is obviously the physical human body. As odd as it sounds to us, training the body to act as if the mind believed – praying aloud, genuflecting, taking holy water when entering a church, participating in the Mass – serves to prepare the machine so that obstacles to belief may be dissolved.

No argument in the whole of the *Pensées* is more well known – and more inaccurately misinterpreted – than what is inappropriately called 'the wager'. Going at least as far back as Voltaire in his *Philosophical Letters*, this "Discourse on the Machine" has been wrongly taken by both critics and readers alike as both the key to the *Pensées* and Pascal's ultimate argument for the existence of the Christian God. It is neither. Rather, standing as the opening chapter after the preface, its only purpose is to fascinate the reader and lure him into reading further into Pascal's *Apology*.

At best, it is an extremely flawed proof only of the existence of a deist God. "Deism", Pascal notes in fragment 690/449, "is almost as far removed from Christianity as is atheism". The so-called wager is in no way even pointing to a *proof* of the Christian God, whose existence is only found in sacred history and holy tradition. In fragment 702/463, Pascal remarks that no canonical writer ever used nature to prove God's existence. In fragment 690/449, in which the preface to part II of the *Apology* is adumbrated, Pascal reiterates that he will not undertake to prove either the existence of God nor the immortality of the soul by natural reason. Not only would such arguments not faze hardened atheists, but such arguments, "without Jesus-Christ, would be useless and sterile". So would the very mathematical argument proposed in the wager:

> Even if someone were convinced that the proportions between Numbers are immaterial, eternal truths depending on a first truth in

> which they subsist, called God; I would not conclude that he had made much progress towards his salvation. The Christian's God does not consist merely of a God Who is the author of mathematical truths and the order of the elements … But the God of Abraham, the God of Isaac, and the God of Jacob? The God of the Christians is a God of love and consolation who make them inwardly aware of their suffering and of his infinite mercy … All those who seek God apart from Christ [fall] either into atheism or deism, two things almost equally abhorrent to Christianity. (690/449)

In his *Philosophical Letters*, Voltaire had, given the gravity of the subject, called the idea of winning or losing indecent and puerile. In the light of Pascal's severe Augustinian schema in which so few would be saved, he argued, Pascal's Wager could only serve to produce conversions to atheism. In point of fact, Pascal's interlocutor in fragment 680/418 never seems overly impressed by the gravity of the subject of eternal life or death. Rather, he seems transfixed, at least at first, by sheer fascination with Pascal's theory of probability:

> Either God exists or he does not … Reason cannot decide this question. Infinite chaos separates us. At the far end of this infinite distance [between us and God], a coin is being spun which will come down heads or tails … You have two things to lose, the true and the good … two things to avoid, error and suffering … if you win, you win everything; if you lose nothing … Wager then that [God] does exist. (680/418)

Wagering that God exists entails only two possible consequences: (i) being wrong but never knowing it because consciousness is annihilated by death; or (ii) being correct and having the possibility of having an eternity of life and happiness. God's chief attribute is infinity. Wherever infinity is involved, rational behaviour depends on wagering on the infinite. Pascal then turns to the consequences in this life of the one who wagers on God's existence but might be wrong. He will be "honest, humble, grateful, and full of good works, a sincere and good friend" (680/418). Most importantly, he will act as though he believes.

Here Pascal brings into play the Cartesian idea of the 'machine' first set down in fragment 45/11. Repressing carnal passions will remove the "obstacles to belief". What follows is perhaps Pascal's most controversial fragment in all the *Pensées*: "That will make you believe mechanically, as does an animal" (680).[3] By training oneself to adopt reflexes of religious significance, one opens oneself to the

3. This sentence has long shocked readers and scholars. The French word *abêtira* means 'to reduce to the level of an animal'. According to Descartes, man is partly mechanical. For Pascal, this inherent human mechanism is subject to training, even with respect to belief.

possibility of receiving God's grace. The entire process, nevertheless, lies within the inscrutability of God's will.

Those who read only the one or two English translations of the *Pensées* would naturally assume that the text of the so-called wager was written out by Pascal in a fairly straightforward way. Were they to consult the various French editions of the text they would find a bewildering situation in which lines and paragraphs have been transposed in endlessly different ways. Moreover, they would find a multiplicity of words themselves changed according to the editor's reading of the text of the *Recueil original*. Pascal seems to have written the entire text in one sitting. The single page on which the text is written is partly written from top to bottom (with many lines and passages struck through), partly written in the margins (with many lines and crosses indicating where these pages were to be inserted) and partly written at the top (with the page turned upside-down). Moreover, the handwriting (blurred by ink smears) makes it one of the most difficult passages in the whole of the *Pensées* to transcribe. In other words, there exists no definitive text of the wager. Therefore, no definitive explication of this most popular Pascalian passage is possible.

ANTHROPOLOGY AND THE ENIGMA OF THE HUMAN CONDITION

In fragment 40/6 of the chapter "Order", Pascal very clearly sets down the outline of his *Apology*, which is to follow the preface ("The Letter Urging the Search for God") and then the "Discourse on the Machine" (the wager):

> Part One: the Suffering of Man without God.
> Part Two: the Felicity of Man with God.
>
> ---
>
> In other words
> Part One: that nature is corrupt, by nature itself.
> Part Two: that there is a Restorer, by Scripture.

The fact that the editors of the Port-Royal Edition prepared by those who knew Pascal set what we have called the 'preface' near the beginning of their edition probably indicates that they (and those whom they supposed would be their potential readers) were most interested in Pascal's text as an apology for the Christian religion. The multitude of eighteenth- to twentieth-century editions tended to divide the manuscript into a privileged 'philosophical' section and an often greatly reduced section of 'religious' thoughts. The Age of Enlightenment had particularly little use for the theological sections. The Romantic period mined the religious texts only to construct their picture of Pascal as a brooding Hamlet-like sceptic.

When Lafuma and Sellier returned to the First and Second Copies, recording the state in which Pascal left his papers at the time of his death, they found that with the exception of the preface and the wager (relegated to the unclassed dossiers), these dossiers indeed follow parts I and II as adumbrated in the chapter "Order". Chapters I–X present the enigma of the corrupt and fallen condition of humanity from an almost entirely anthropological perspective, via an examination of human nature. Chapters XII–XXIII carefully and gradually move toward a theological and scriptural explanation of human corruption, culminating with scriptural proofs of the restorative and salvific work of Christ.

Unlike Jacques-Bénigne Bossuet, who could not understand why the visible activity of providence was not perceived by the unbelievers, Pascal believes that the only reasonable attitude for an unbeliever is that of provisional agnosticism. How, many have asked over three centuries, is it possible to write an apology inviting conversion within the framework of the severe Augustinian doctrine of predestination? Pascal's answer is that the initiative leading to conversion is God's alone. If God does not grant the unbeliever a passion for truth, any presentation of proofs will be futile. They will be heard without interest or even mocked. As soon as the apologist meets a person aware of their condition and passionate about truth, he finds an invitation to be an instrument in the service of the progress of grace.

Pascal's sister Gilberte was fond of saying that when he conferred with atheists, her brother never began by preaching theology or Scripture. If they had their heart in the pursuit of truth, Pascal began by starting to build up his case that the human condition amounts to a disastrous enigma. Indeed, in the 'anthropological' chapters, Pascal hardly ever mentions theology or religion. Rather, he draws from the scepticism of Montaigne to provoke ever increasing doubt on the part of the unbeliever that the tragedy of the human condition can ever be explained by philosophy, nature or human experience. Pascal's mentor at Port-Royal, Monsieur de Sacy, was profoundly shocked by Pascal's plan to make use of Montaigne's dangerous scepticism. Once he heard Pascal's larger apologetic plan, perhaps in the discourse delivered by Pascal to his mentors "At Port-Royal" (ch. XII), he described Pascal as an extremely gifted physician who knew how to manipulate fatal poisons in order to effect miraculous cures.

The essential source of Pascal's 'anthropological' analysis is Augustine. From the late sixteenth century, philosophers became increasingly obsessed with death and the impermanence of the world. Christian philosophers, looking at the universe from the divine perspective (immutability, permanence, eternal rest), recognized in the universe only the painful absence of God. Pascal is undoubtedly the last of these baroque thinkers to perceive a totally fallen universe. The 'anthropological' chapters ("Vanity", "Philosophers", and so on), which avoid all mention of the theological dimension of the Fall, reach their climax in the chapter "The Sovereign Good". Without exception, human beings attempt over and over again without success to attain perfect happiness. At this point only the Christian doctrine of the Fall can make sense of this enigma: "what can the obvious power of this avidity and impotence be if not that humanity once possessed true happiness, which now remains only an 'empty print and trace,' an infinite abyss which can only be filled by something infinite and immutable, that is to say by God himself" (181/148).

Having moved from knowledge of humanity to that of God in chapters XII–XVI, Pascal turns to Islam as the perfect example of a false religion. In the following chapter, designed to urge the unbelievers to at least *wish* that Christianity were true, Pascal nevertheless feels obliged to enunciate Augustine's most severe doctrine: "One understands nothing of God's works if he does not accept the principal that [God] meant to blind some men and enlighten others" (264/232). God is hidden, but not, as the philosophers believe, in the human heart; rather, he has left signs in sacred history for those truly seeking to believe. However, in order to find and be converted by these signs, the unbeliever must know how to unlock the keys to holy Scripture.

All of the arguments of the theological chapters (XVII–XXVIII) build towards an ultimate and decisive argument. The fulfilment of the Old Testament prophecies in the New Testament validates the whole of holy Scripture as authentic and historically true. Thus, both the Fall and the Redemption are the key to the enigma of the human condition and how it may be transcended. Unfortunately, the past two hundred years of biblical scholarship has voided almost every single exegetical argument used by Pascal. Together with the fact that these chapters are far less complete and far more enigmatic than the 'anthropological' chapters, readers and scholars alike have almost universally ignored them.

Pascal's diagnosis of a flaw in the human condition is no less chilling and plausible for modern readers than it was for those of Pascal's own time. Even the theory of the Fall outlined in the chapter "A.P.R." is at least a plausible hypothesis if not taken literally. Surprisingly, very few modern theologians have dared to try to rescue the Fall from historicity. Indeed, in the Catholic intellectual world, only Pope Benedict XVI in his works *In the Beginning* and *Schoepfung und Evolution* (Creation and evolution) has seriously tried to make the case that evolution and Christian doctrine are not irreconcilable.

Nonetheless, we would be wrong to view Pascal as in any way a reactionary biblical exegete. No one in his time suspected that the world was over six thousand years old. The exegetical model he so carefully models is that of both the apostle Paul and the writers of the four Gospels, amended and hallowed by two thousand years of Christian scholarship. If anything, Pascal follows the more stringent exegetes at Port-Royal, who were returning to the Hebrew and Greek texts of holy Scripture. Both as traditional exegesis formulated in an exceptional literary form and as a revelation of Pascal's mode of thought, these chapters are vital to understanding the *Apology* as a whole. Indeed, without them, the *Pensées* themselves would not really amount to a precursor of an apology of the Christian religion.

PASCAL'S EXEGETICAL PROOFS

According to traditional Catholic exegesis, the Old Testament is a 'cipher' that only the seekers can hope to penetrate with the help of the apologists. Its veracity can be trusted because of the longevity of the Patriarchs: "Sem, who knew Lamech, who knew Jacob as well, knew those who knew Moses. Therefore the Flood and the Creation are true …" (327/296). Those able to penetrate the literal sense of the Old Testament will find that, figuratively, the entire Old Testament anticipates the New Testament:

> The Messiah has always been believed in. The tradition of Adam was fresh in the mind of Moses. He was predicted by the prophets, who foresaw the events which had to happen and the promises concerning the Messiah … Jesus Christ accomplished miracles which converted the pagans. Thus the prophecies being accomplished, the Messiah is inexorably proved. (314/298)

Unlike modern biblical scholars who stress the historicity of Jesus, Pascal's Christ remains hidden in his incarnation and 'secret' resurrection. Christ remained hidden in the person of Jesus of Nazareth, as he continues to be hidden in the Gospels, the poor, and the Eucharist. Yet, for those who had eyes to see him, he was "humble, patient, holy, holy, holy to God, terrifying to demons and with no sin whatsoever … For those who had the eyes of charity to perceive him, he came in prodigious magnificence" (339/309).

No chapter in the entire *Pensées* is more impenetrable than the chapter "Prophecies" (XXV/XXIIV). It is replete with notes referring to Scripture and obscure long passages difficult to penetrate. In addition to predicting the circumstances of the arrival of the Messiah, Daniel predicts the very date of his death (Daniel 9:24–7):

> The prophets having given diverse signs which were all supposed to come to pass at the coming of the Messiah, all these signs had to occur at the same time. So the fourth monarchy had to have come when the seventy weeks of Daniel ended, and the scepter had to then be removed from Judah. And all this came to pass with no difficulty. And then Jesus-Christ came, calling himself the Messiah. (371/339)

Pascal's proof remains indecipherable without the exegetical explanation given by Pascal's mentor, Monsieur de Sacy, in his preface to his monumental translation of the Bible into French. Sacy first explains that the four monarchies are those of the Chaldeans, the Persians, the Greeks and the Romans. The weeks in this prophecy are "weeks of years as in Leviticus". Sacy therefore multiplies seven times seventy to arrive at the number 490. He then subtracts four years since Daniel

9:12 specifies that the Christ will be put to death "in the middle of this last week". According to Daniel 9, this figure (i.e. 486) should be added to the date when the order went out for the rebuilding of Jerusalem. Consulting the *Holy Chronology* of his colleague Lancelot, Sacy finds that Artaxerxes issued this edict in the "Year of the World" 3550, that is, 3550 years after the creation. Adding 486 to 3550, Sacy comes up with the Year of the World 4036. Using 4000 BCE, the traditional date of Jesus' birth, Sacy interprets Daniel 9:24–7 as a prediction that Jesus would be put to death in the year 36 CE.

TRUE CONVERSION

Pascal then turns the tables on the seeker. He reveals that those, particularly the poor, effectively believe without having ever read the two Testaments: "These have a completely holy inner disposition. What they hear said about our religion conforms exactly to their beliefs. They want only to love God and hate themselves. It is God himself who inclines their hearts to believe" (413–14/381–2). Pascal ends the classified dossiers with a warning to those seekers at the point of conversion. They should not even imagine that true conversion means a two-way communication with God:

> True conversion means annihilating oneself in the presence of this universal being that one has nearly provoked to wrath so many times and who can legitimately damn you at any moment. It means recognizing that one can do nothing without him, and that one has merited only his withdrawal of grace. It consists of understanding that there is an invincible opposition between God and us, and that without a Mediator, approaching God is impossible. (410/378)

> How distant it is from the knowledge of God to the love of God. (409/377)

In saving the elect, God transcends his own hidden nature in order to reveal himself to those who seek him with all their hearts. Those whose hearts are fixed on temporal things will never penetrate the literal veil of revelation in holy Scripture. In Pascal's view, however, those who seek God sincerely must somehow have been already touched by grace, otherwise they would not be seeking God. As Christ tells Pascal in the *Mystery of Jesus*, "You would not be seeking me, if you did not already possess me".

A NOTE ON PASCAL'S SPIRITUALITY

Readers who delve into the vast world of Pascalian scholarship will find references to Pascal's several 'conversions'. They should not imagine that Pascal himself was converted from a sceptic to a Christian. From childhood, the apologist was already deeply, if not fanatically, a believer and polemicist. Pascal's sister Gilberte, in her *Life of Monsieur Pascal* (1684), veers so close to hagiography that the scenes she describes must not always be taken literally. When scholars speak of Pascal's 'worldly period', readers should not imagine Pascal frequently attending social events. His foray into gambling was both to test his theory of probability and to observe such agnostics as his friends Mitton and Méré. His many scientific experiments can hardly be called 'worldly'.

It is probably true, however, that the healing of Pascal's niece with a relic of the crown of thorns strengthened his resolve to write the *Apology*. Even more so, the remarkable mystical experience called the *Mémorial*, recorded by Pascal in fragment 913/742 and found sewn into his vest only after his death, must have profoundly deepened his private spirituality. His sale of all his belongings, furniture and books certainly represent a literal response to Jesus' admonition in Mark 10:21, as did his taking in an impoverished family afflicted with smallpox.

At this point even Gilberte intervened and insisted that the dying Pascal be transported to her house. Having received the Last Rites, he died two days later on 19 August 1662, at the age of thirty-nine. His last words were, "May God never abandon me".

FURTHER READING

Hammond, N. 1994. *Playing with Truth: Language and the Human Condition in Pascal's Pensées*. Oxford: Clarendon Press.

Hammond, N. (ed.) 2003. *The Cambridge Companion to Pascal*. Cambridge: Cambridge University Press.

Koch, E. 2003. "Blaise Pascal". In *Dictionary of Literary Biography, vol. 268: Seventeenth-Century Writers*, F. Jaouen (ed.), 272–89. New York: Thompson Gale.

Pugh, A. 1984. *The Composition of Pascal's Apologia*. Toronto: University of Toronto Press.

Wetsel, D. 1981. *L'Écriture et le reste: The Pensées of Pascal in the Exegetical Tradition of Port-Royal*. Columbus, OH: Ohio State University Press.

Wetsel, D. 1994. *Pascal and Disbelief: Catechesis and Conversion in the Pensées*. Washington, DC: Catholic University of America Press.

Wetsel, D. & F. Canovas (eds) 2002. *Pascal: New Trends in Port-Royal Studies*. Tübingen: Gunter Narr.

On AGNOSTICISM see also Vol. 5, Ch. 6. On IMMORTALITY OF THE SOUL see also Ch. 19; Vol. 1, Chs 2, 4; Vol. 2, Chs 12, 16. On THE FALL see also Vol. 4, Ch. 16.

11

BARUCH SPINOZA

Michael A. Rosenthal

Baruch Spinoza was born in Amsterdam on 24 November 1632. He was the son of a merchant family of Jews originally from Portugal. His family were 'conversos', that is, Jews from the Iberian Peninsula who had been forcibly converted to Christianity and had immigrated to the Dutch Republic at the end of the sixteenth century in order to live openly as Jews again. The Dutch had admitted them to Amsterdam because of their useful links to trade and their contribution to the economy. They were extended a limited but relatively generous toleration for their religious practices. But owing to the complex background of many of the members of the community there were numerous internal conflicts over beliefs. Spinoza himself received a traditional Jewish education and knew many of the important rabbis in Amsterdam, including Menasseh ben Israel, the kabbalist Isaac Aboab da Fonseca, and the rationalist Saul Levi Mortera. He also took advantage of the intellectual and cosmopolitan city, which afforded him other means to expand his education. He learned Latin and the classics, primarily with the radical former Jesuit, Franciscus van den Enden. His own unorthodox views eventually, on 27 July 1656, led the leaders of his congregation to pronounce a ban (*cherem*), which ostracized him from the Jewish community. Spinoza stayed in Amsterdam and deepened his relations with other freethinkers, many of whom were members of dissident Protestant sects, such as the Collegiants. Their questions prompted Spinoza to write a treatise on philosophical method, *The Treatise on the Emendation of the Intellect*, which, although it remained unfinished, articulated themes that would be present in all of his subsequent work. He then started work on the *Short Treatise on God, Man and His Well-Being*, which he continued when he moved to Rijnsburg, near Leiden, in 1661. His study of Cartesian philosophy culminated in a geometric presentation of Descartes' works with an appended commentary, which was the only work published under his own name during his lifetime. He moved from Rijnsburg to Voorburg, near The Hague, in 1663, and then several years later to the The Hague itself. While he laboured over the rest of his life on his *magnum opus*, the *Ethics*, Spinoza also devoted himself to other subjects. He acquired a reputation as a lens-grinder and conducted a variety of other scientific experiments. He returned to more controversial subjects when he interrupted his strictly philosophical labours to write the *Theological-Political Treatise*, which he published anonymously in 1670. He completed the *Ethics*, which was published only posthumously, and he worked on another political work, the *Political Treatise*, which remained unfinished at his death on 21 February 1677.

The question whether Spinoza is a profound philosopher of religion or a scathing critic of it has raged ever since he was banned from the Jewish community of Amsterdam owing to his supposed "evil opinions and acts" (Nadler 1999: 120). His work has enjoyed the most varied and contradictory reception among writers, artists and philosophers. On the one hand, Spinoza's view that there is but one substance in nature and that this substance is God was described by Pierre Bayle, the early modern sceptic, as "the most monstrous hypothesis", which is the cause of both immorality and impiety (1965: 300–301). Recent historians have cast Spinoza as the central figure in the 'radical' wing of the Enlightenment, whose goal it was to radically reform society and abolish religion (Israel 2001). On the other hand, Novalis and the German Romantics challenged the image of Spinoza as an atheist and described him instead as "a God-intoxicated man" (Moreau 1996). Albert Einstein was also inspired by Spinoza's vision of the universe. And despite his expulsion from the Jewish community, Spinoza has been taken up by numerous writers (e.g. I. B. Singer and Bernard Malamud) and even politicians (e.g. Israel's first prime minister, David Ben-Gurion) as a symbol of modern Jewish identity. In what follows we shall examine systematically the main themes in Spinoza's work that account for this surprising and contradictory history of reception. Spinoza is a far-reaching critic of many of the claims of revealed religion but at the same time he develops his own radical positions within a quite traditional philosophical framework.

THE CRITIQUE OF RELIGION

Spinoza first gained notoriety through the anonymous publication of the *Theological-Political Treatise* (hereafter *Treatise*) in 1670, which was banned by the Dutch authorities almost as soon as it appeared (Israel 2001). As he started to expand and develop his own philosophical thinking in the work that would eventually become the *Ethics*, he wrote to Henry Oldenburg in 1665 that he had started writing a treatise on Scripture for several reasons: to attack the prejudices of the theologians, which stand in the way of philosophizing; to avert the widespread perception held by the common people (*vulgus*) that he is an atheist; and to defend the freedom to philosophize (Spinoza 1985: letter 30). The purpose of this work clearly was to intervene in the ongoing struggles of the nascent Dutch Republic, in which the more tolerant States party was coming under attack by the aristocratic Orange party supported by the clergy. Spinoza's strategy was to undermine the authority of the Dutch Reformed clergy through a reinterpretation of Scripture and then to recommend a more tolerant policy on prudential grounds.

Spinoza based his critique of religion developed in the first part of the *Treatise* on four main points: the psychosocial origin of most religious belief; the epistemologically inadequate nature of the knowledge claimed by prophets through revelation; the metaphysics of God; and the historical account of Scripture itself. Spinoza was not the first to suggest that religion had a social origin. In the *Leviathan*, first published in 1651 and translated into Latin in 1668, Hobbes claims that natural religion springs from human ignorance. Not knowing the causes of things and endowed with a lively power of fantasy, human beings create all sorts of gods to explain what they do not know and to assuage their fears (Hobbes 1994). Spinoza develops this view in the preface to the *Treatise*, where he argues that the origin of superstition is found in our finite nature and our inevitable bondage to fortune, or the power of things external to us. Because we depend on many things over which we have little or no control, and that we do not understand, we tend to vacillate between hope that fortune will favour us and fear that it will not. Ambitious individuals take advantage of this wretched condition and offer specious explanations of natural phenomena in terms of signs and omens to convince the anxious masses of their power to control events. The masses then link their terrestrial destiny with the signs of a supernatural power above who orchestrates things to an end conveniently revealed to the special person of the prophet. In this way, the seeds of the growth – and also, as we shall see, the demise – of organized religion are sown.

The social explanation of the origin of religion leads naturally to the second point of critique, which is focused on the kind of knowledge found in revelation. The first point of critique is moot if the knowledge of natural events and the moral injunctions offered by the prophet to the masses turn out to be true. Some medieval philosophers, such as Moses Maimonides, had argued that the prophet was a philosopher, albeit one endowed with a special power of the imagination that allowed him to communicate abstract philosophical truths to the irrational masses in terms that were convincing to them (Maimonides 1963). Spinoza directly attacks this doctrine in the first two chapters of the *Treatise*, where he distinguishes between two kinds of revelation. On the one hand, there is natural revelation, which is acquired through reason. All human beings have the capacity to reason and what they discover through reason is universal and applicable to everyone. So this kind of revelation based on reason is not unique or specific to any one individual or group, and practitioners of this knowledge cannot, strictly speaking, be called prophets. On the other hand, there is prophetic revelation, which is given to only a few people, who possess an extraordinarily vivid imagination and who act for the good of others. Through this distinction Spinoza lays the foundation for a direct attack on the traditional allegorical method of interpreting Scripture, which claims that the sacred texts have two levels, one exoteric and meant for the masses, the other esoteric and meant for philosophers. Allegorical interpretation defends Scripture as a consistent source of philosophical knowledge while at the same time acknowledging apparent contradictions in its narratives. Spinoza claims that Scripture does not contain any hidden well of philosophical wisdom or universal natural knowledge because it was produced by individuals who predominantly understood the world through their imagination for the sake of a certain group of people in a specific time and place. If a reader is looking for philosophical wisdom they ought to look elsewhere.

If Scripture is based on the imagination, then the idea of God that it offers its readers is bound to be philosophically inadequate. In the famous appendix to the first part of his *Ethics*, Spinoza argues that the common idea of God found in theology is just a projection of our own ignorance onto the divine being itself. More specifically, he claims that because we conceive of ourselves acting for the sake of some end we imagine that God also must act for the sake of an end, and that nature was created by God to satisfy human ends in the service of some divine plan, which we call providence. We will have more to say about Spinoza's own idea of God below, but it will suffice to say that the philosophical conception of God as an eternal, necessary being, identical in some sense with nature, is inimical to the idea of God found in Scripture: a being who has created the world through a contingent act of will and rules over it as a king rules over his subjects, alternately jealous and benevolent. And since we have just ruled out the possibility that Scripture could be interpreted in a way that would make it compatible with philosophy, it follows that Scripture gives us a wholly inadequate idea of God. What reason teaches us about the nature of God is not compatible with what the imagination teaches us, and the philosophical truth is not going to be found in Scripture or in imaginatively revealed religions. The first readers of the *Treatise* already suspected that Spinoza was committed to such a heretical doctrine, but once the *Ethics* was published he was branded a pantheist, determinist and libertine who was committed to the destruction of God and morality (Bayle 1965).

Spinoza supported his critique not only through philosophical argument but also through a historical and philological analysis of Scripture itself. He claimed, among other things, that the Old Testament was not written by Moses but compiled from many sources, that there is an ineradicable obscurity in the text of the Hebrew Bible due to our ignorance and the nature of the language (e.g. ambiguities in vowels and tense system of verbs) and that, without a fuller understanding of the authors of the texts and their intentions, we cannot fully grasp their ends. Spinoza is far more cautious in relation to the New Testament and claims not to have the expertise to judge it in this manner. But it is fair to say that, although he was openly far harsher in his critique of the Old Testament than of the New, he raised questions that were just as problematic for the text of any prophetically revealed religion. And, to the extent that Christians depended on the Old Testament to explain the role of Jesus in the New, they would have been and were just as perturbed by the implications. Spinoza may not have been the first to apply methods that had been developed by humanist scholars to analyse classical texts to the Bible, but he was surely the most notorious and systematic of early modern biblical critics, and he helped inaugurate what came to be known as higher biblical criticism. His emphasis on the historical and philological analysis of the Bible was consistent with and supportive of his view that the Bible is imaginatively produced and related to the specific circumstances of the prophets. This would not, as we shall see, render the text useless in relation to human life, but it certainly limited the scope of its claims.

SPINOZA'S GOD

The view that Spinoza was an atheist was widespread in his time and has remained prevalent up to our time. But we have to take his words to Oldenburg at face value when he writes that one of the central purposes of the *Treatise* was to dispel the view of the multitude (*vulgus*) that he is an atheist. Part of the problem, of course, is that the charge of atheism can mean a variety of things and we must be careful to specify just what is meant by it. It might mean, as was common in the seventeenth century, that one's concept of God is unorthodox and potentially heretical. So, many Christian sects in the seventeenth century were deemed heretical in the sense that their views deviated from orthodox belief and would eventually *lead* to either practices deemed immoral or to a disbelief in God. Or it might mean, as it commonly does now, that the view itself directly denies the existence of God. Spinoza never denies the existence of God, although, as we have just seen, he is systematically critical of many traditional beliefs about God. This has led some interpreters to question the sincerity of his assertion that he is not an atheist. But if, as we have just seen, the charge of atheism is itself more nuanced than the charge of simply denying the existence of God, then instead of simply assuming that Spinoza's critique of traditional religious beliefs is incompatible with a sincere belief in the existence of God, we ought to look for another, less hypocritical defence against the charge.

In the *Ethics*, Spinoza uses quite traditional philosophical methods to establish the existence of a very unorthodox idea of God. Descartes had defined the most basic metaphysical entity, which he called 'substance', as that which does not depend on anything else for its existence. But he went on to use the term equivocally: there is true substance, or God, which creates two other kinds of substances, mind (*res cogitans*) and body (*res extensa*), which, although they depend on God, are the most basic things (first principles) in the created world (*Principles of Philosophy* I, 52–3). Spinoza insists on a single meaning for substance and argues not only that substance necessarily exists but that there can be only one such substance. This substance is expressed through infinitely many *attributes*, which express essential qualities of substance, such as thinking and extension, and also through infinitely many *modes*, which express non-essential qualities. The modes in turn are either *infinite*, such as the laws of nature, or *finite*, such as particular things like minds or bodies. What results is a completely interrelated and intelligible system. At its basis is the idea of a single, self-caused (*causa-sui*) being, on which all other things depend in some way. A finite thing depends on other finite things but also on the laws of nature that govern their interaction. Those laws of nature in turn follow from the basic attributes of substance, which express some aspect of its essential nature.

Spinoza explicitly identifies substance with God, but obviously this is an unorthodox view in several respects. First, the qualities that describe God's nature are entirely stripped of any anthropomorphic qualities. God is not 'merciful' or 'just' or 'wise', but rather a 'self-caused' or 'infinitely extended' being. God's relation to the world is also profoundly changed. In contrast to a 'transcendent' being, which remains outside the world, Spinoza's God is 'immanent' in the world itself. There is no creation, in the sense of mysteriously bringing the world into existence from nothing – because the world is nothing more than the totality of the finite modes of substance, which must always exist – but only continual change in the configuration of finite modes, which must be explicable in terms of the eternal laws of nature. Spinoza insists that, if God necessarily exists, then surely everything else does as well. Not only does God not choose to create the world, which must necessarily exist, but also everything in the world – from the laws of nature itself to the finite modes of nature – happens in a necessary and determined manner. God is perfectly free, not in the sense that he could have acted otherwise in accordance with his unconstrained will, but in the sense that there are no external impediments to the actions that follow from his nature. Likewise, certain finite modes of nature, that is, human beings, are not free in the sense that God has given them a free will, that is, a power of acting independently of the laws of nature. Rather, they are free to the extent that they are free of external impediments and are able to act in accordance with their own natures. The greatest obstacle to this path is the influence of the passions, but a proper understanding of nature itself, which Spinoza called the "intellectual love of God" (*amor Dei intellectualis*), corrects particular judgements and allows individuals to achieve some degree of blessedness.

For a traditional believer, such views were anathema. Although Spinoza did use the name 'God' to describe substance, there is little in common with the providential God found in the Scriptures. God is not a king, he is not a personal interlocutor and he does not plan or direct the destiny of any part of the world. Indeed, his critics read the famous passage in part IV of the *Ethics*, "*deus sive natura*", in which Spinoza seems to identify God and nature, as tantamount to a profession of pantheism. If God is identical to nature, and nature is composed of infinitely many parts, then there cannot be just one God but infinitely many Gods. But even if we choose not to follow this interpretation, the idea of God as subject to necessity seemed to violate the very independence of God and tie him to blind natural forces. Moreover, the denial of free will and divine purpose seemed to undermine morality itself. If God has created the law, then many would argue that we must have the freedom to either act in accordance with it or reject it, if we are to be meaningfully punished. The idea of an eternal union of the rational mind with nature also did not appeal to those who longed for a more personal sort of immortality.

INTERNAL AND EXTERNAL RELIGION

Spinoza was certainly aware that his views both of religion and of morality clashed with those of most ordinary believers. In the *Treatise* he expresses his idea of God in a more guarded fashion. Some commentators, notably Leo Strauss, have argued that in the *Treatise* Spinoza hides his true, esoteric philosophical view, which was atheistic, behind the exoteric facade of a popular religious view, and that he offers the philosophical reader various clues, such as subtle contradictions, that point him in the right direction (Strauss 1952). What would motivate this method of writing? Certainly, Spinoza had good reason to be fearful that he might be persecuted for his views. After the *Treatise* had been published in Latin and ignited a firestorm of protest, he beseeched his friends in a letter to prevent its translation into the vernacular. It could be that Spinoza adopted this cryptic method as a temporary means to avoid persecution in the hopes that a more enlightened secular society, in which there would be no need to dissimulate, would eventually result. Or it could be that, given his deep pessimism about human nature, it would always be prudent for a philosopher to hide his views from the masses. Either way there is a sharp distinction between the true philosophical atheism and the false popular belief in God. There is just disagreement about whether or not the false belief can be overcome.

However, just as we argued that Spinoza's supposed atheism might be problematic, so too we might question the view that religion is simply false belief for the masses and ought to be either abolished or cautiously endured. Certainly the idea that the *Treatise* contains a hidden esoteric doctrine is doubtful. If Spinoza did systematically attempt to conceal his views, he did not succeed. His most critical contemporary readers – presumably those from whom he would want to hide his views – had little difficulty ascertaining his philosophical views from the text. Although Spinoza was a stringent critic of religion, he never argues that religion should be abolished. And although he believed that the multitude was irrational, he thought that they were neither beyond hope nor that they could become fully enlightened. His strategy in the work was twofold: to distinguish between two kinds of religion, one philosophical and the other imaginative, and then to argue that once we are not confused about the nature and purpose of revealed religion it can be rationally reformed or at least regulated, not only for the good of philosophers but for the multitude as well. Spinoza was neither a medieval nor an Enlightenment philosopher of religion, but something else entirely.

The *Treatise* offers a blueprint for the relation of the two kinds of religion. Before we look a the details of this plan it will be useful to say something more about what distinguishes one kind of religion from the other. The first distinction, as we saw above in our discussion of the two kinds of revelation, is the origin of religious belief. On the one hand, there is knowledge gained by reason on the basis of certain first principles, which are found in nature itself. On the other hand, there is knowledge gained through interactions with the external world, which Spinoza calls the imagination. One leads to direct philosophical knowledge of God, the other to various, and often conflicting, imaginative visions of God mediated by prophets.

The second distinction is between the practical function of these ideas in a person's life. In chapter III of the *Treatise* Spinoza classifies the "worthy objects of desire" into three kinds: "1. To know things through their primary causes. 2. To subjugate the passions; i.e., to acquire the habit of virtue. 3. To live in security and good health". According to Spinoza, reason leads us to the first objective, which is the surest way to the second, and ultimately the third. Since passions are mistaken judgements, when a person acquires rational knowledge they also acquire some ability to subjugate the passions and become virtuous. Since rational individuals understand that they are limited by themselves and better off working together, they tend to form political associations that are marked by cooperation and reasonable compromise rather than conflict and coercion. By definition, the imagination is incapable of achieving the first goal. It is better and most often used to secure the third objective. To achieve this end prophets, who are often proto-political leaders, use certain passions, such as fear and hope, awe and devotion, to modify the actions of the masses. Of course, as most people realize, to live consistently in security and good health also requires that the passions are regulated in certain ways. Prophets cultivate humility to counteract self-aggrandizement and pity to counteract contempt. Thus a complex dynamic develops in a group governed by the imagination in which the passions cause both cohesion and tension among the members. Both forms of religion, then, serve some vision of human flourishing, but whereas rational religion emphasizes what we might call, after A. G. Wernham, 'inner' flourishing first, which leads to positive social interactions as a secondary effect, imaginative religion emphasizes 'external' flourishing in terms of social interactions, which secondarily requires some control – although never proper mastery because that would require reason – of the passions to bolster social stability (Spinoza 1958). Of course, rational religion would be preferable but, in a world governed by the vagaries of fortune, reason is also rare and imaginative religion is more prevalent. The problem is not only to develop the optimal form of each religion but also to determine the best possible relation between them.

We can best understand this ideal relationship if we examine the figures of Moses and Jesus in the *Treatise*. Spinoza has frequently been bitterly criticized by Jewish philosophers, such as the German neo-Kantian Hermann Cohen and his followers, who think that he systematically exalts Jesus and denigrates Moses (Cohen 1980). There is truth in this charge in so far as Jesus is identified with internal religion and Moses with external religion. But it is misleading in so far as it depends on a nineteenth-century German philosophy of history, itself based on longstanding Christian tensions with Judaism, in which the founding religion of Moses would eventually be improved on, and ultimately overcome by, the religion of Christ. Spinoza was not committed to any progressive conception of history and certainly not one in which internal religion would eventually triumph over external religion. To focus on but two key examples, we find important statements of the systematic limitations of reason in the preface to the *Treatise*, in which Spinoza emphasizes the inevitable power of fortune over human affairs, and in the first propositions of part IV of the *Ethics*, in which he states that it is impossible for human beings to avoid the passions and to triumph over the power of nature. A life conducted solely under the guidance of reason may be conceivable but it is not possible for us. Spinoza makes it clear in the *Treatise* that the teachings of Jesus do not annul or supersede the teachings of Moses, but are complementary. If the imagination and the passions are fixtures of human life, then it is important to learn how to regulate them in the context of political and social life. If we are rational creatures and have the power to attain some degree of self-mastery, then we must pursue that end to the best of our ability. Both pursuits overlap, as we have seen, in emphasizing the importance of self-mastery and political life, and in these areas they can, to some extent, inform each other.

The one area where they do not overlap is the first goal – the knowledge of things through first causes – and it is precisely this goal, as we shall see in the next section, that external religion often claims as its own, although it has absolutely no warrant to do so, in order to gain (illegitimate) authority for its political claims. Spinoza often does go relatively easy on Christianity in comparison to Judaism, claiming, for instance, that he does not have the linguistic competence to scrutinize critically the texts of the New Testament as he does the Old, but he squarely places the blame on Christians for their own sectarian strife. Whereas Jesus taught rather than prophesied, using reason to educate, and avoided politics altogether, his disciples violated both boundaries. The disciples were anxious to spread the word of their master and they decided to adopt the philosophical systems of their audiences as the first principle of explanation, whether or not those principles were indeed correct. In this way they mixed various and false philosophical systems with their teachings in order to gain authority. Since each disciple used a different philosophical system to support their beliefs, they produced a situation in which the fundamental terms of the religion had different meanings for different groups, leading to schism and endless conflict. Likewise, early Christians ignored the fundamental lesson of Moses that external religion had to be focused on its practical effects, and instead adopted the proselytizing practices of the disciples as justificatory premises for political life as well. Thus early modern Christians, who knew full well what terrible tragedies followed from religious schism, would be well advised to learn from the example of their Jewish forefathers what the proper relation of church and state should be and avoid justifying political authority on the basis of specious philosophical claims.

RELIGION AND POLITICS

So far we have concentrated on Spinoza's religious doctrines with only some mention of their political implications. But in fact, as the very title of the work indicates, the *Treatise* was from the beginning designed primarily as a treatise about the relation of religion to politics. Spinoza was an important influence in the subsequent Enlightenment, but we have to be careful not to read the views of later thinkers influenced by Spinoza back into his works. On many points Spinoza has a more complex view than is usually attributed to him and that is why careful presentation will allow us a more nuanced appreciation of his legacy.

The first point, worth repeating, is that, because human beings are always subject to the vicissitudes of external events, or what he calls 'fortune', they will always be subject to superstition. So, although a sovereign can justify its authority in secular terms – through, for example, the institution of a social contract – it is not realistic to assume that all or even most people will think of their relation to the state in this way. Indeed, external religion is almost always a central feature of most political life, in that it helps both maintain and legitimate the state. Spinoza does not advocate the neutrality of the state in matters of religion; nor does he propose the constitutional separation of the two. Because the state pursues its own interests – and this means it must seek the best ways to achieve stability within the constraints of human nature – it is not prudent for the state to dispense with religious justifications of authority. The most important question for Spinoza, then, is: who controls the religious justification of political authority?

While the specific form of the relation of church to state will vary and depend on the historical circumstances, it will most often be the case, as Spinoza thought was true in the Netherlands of his time, that state control of the Church – or what is called 'Erastianism' – would be preferable. The central political problem in early modern Europe was the conflict caused by religious schism. Spinoza argued that religious groups stirred the passions of their followers when they claimed that the Bible was not only a guide to living a good life but also a guide to a singular truth. Each side attempted to use the power and authority of the state to enforce their version of the truth and in this way provoked conflict. In the terms of Spinoza's analysis, some particular form of external religion claimed that it was also true internal religion and used this mandate to violate the basic precepts of external religion, that is, to pursue justice and charity. A state-controlled religion, in contrast, makes no claim that it knows the truth, or at least claims this only on the basis of fulfilling the function of an external religion. A state-controlled religion can avoid schism because the truth of a religion is never based on anything other than its ability to instil obedience and ensure political stability and social well-being. The sovereign, rather than the clergy, is in the best position to decide which form of religion fosters that end.

However, unlike Hobbes, who advocated the Erastian idea in monarchical form, Spinoza thinks that the ideal form of the state is democratic. In letter 50, Spinoza remarks that, in contrast to Hobbes, he always preserves natural rights intact. Individuals never completely alienate all or even part of their natural rights to the sovereign but transfer them on the condition that they judge the sovereign able and willing to achieve their ends. The state cannot impose the law without enough individuals who passively obey it and actively support the institutions that enforce it. In the case of religion, this means that the state need not necessarily impose a single religion on the multitude, but rather uses its power to filter the various claims to religious truth on the basis of their compatibility with the well-being of the state.

Spinoza justified religious toleration not on the basis of respect for individual beliefs, but on prudential grounds. It might be tempting for the sovereign to attempt to impose his or her beliefs on the multitude, but on this point Spinoza cites Tacitus, who claimed that the attempt to control ideas produces only rebellion rather than conformity. The state is more powerful when it does not interfere with ideas, which are either indifferent to its success or might provoke rebellion when suppressed. However, because the state is not in principle distinct from religion and has an interest in using religion to help it govern, there are clear limits to toleration. In chapter XIV of the *Treatise*, Spinoza lists the seven dogmas of universal faith – such as the existence of God, the unity and omnipresence of God, God's forgiveness of repentant sinners, and so on – that he deems are necessary to inculcate faith, which he defines as the set of beliefs that lead to obedience. These beliefs are not judged true because of their metaphysical content but in so far as they are useful to the maintenance of the state. When a religious group does not accept one or more of them, intolerance of the group is justified, not because it has false beliefs, but because its beliefs will harm the stability of the state. Of course, although Spinoza thought that the freedom to philosophize should be granted unconditionally by the state, it is not hard to see the weakness of its justification. A democracy may indeed be more fickle than an authoritarian state and find the heretical ideas of a philosopher a danger to its stability.

CONCLUSION

Spinoza's critique of traditional religion was indeed scathing. As many readers pointed out, there is a real danger that the God of the *Ethics* is pantheist and antithetical to any monotheist religion. Although Spinoza speaks of the eternity of mind, it is hardly a doctrine of personal immortality. His attack on free will and commitment to determinism seem to undermine any theory of natural law or the possibility of a moral theory based on personal choice and responsibility. On the other hand, we have seen that, contrary to the popular Enlightenment readings, Spinoza was more interested in reforming religion rather than eradicating it. He did not consider himself an atheist and would have argued against the simple identification of God with nature. His view of freedom was compatibilist and his theory of politics republican. He did not advocate the constitutional separation of church and state, but he did offer a compelling prudential justification of religious toleration. Whatever our verdict on his ideas, there is little question that his work offers us a profound resource for thinking about religion in the modern world.

FURTHER READING

Curley, E. 1988. *Behind the Geometrical Method: A Reading of Spinoza's Ethics*. Princeton, NJ: Princeton University Press.

Garrett, D. 1996. *The Cambridge Companion to Spinoza*. Cambridge: Cambridge University Press.

Gatens, M. & G. Lloyd 1999. *Collective Imaginings: Spinoza, Past and Present*. London: Routledge.

Israel, J. 2001. *Radical Enlightenment: Philosophy and the Making of Modernity, 1650–1750*. Oxford: Oxford University Press.

Mason, R. 1997. *The God of Spinoza: A Philosophical Study*. Cambridge: Cambridge University Press.

Melamed, Y. & M. Rosenthal (eds) (forthcoming). *Spinoza's Theological Political Treatise: A Critical Guide*. Cambridge: Cambridge University Press.

Nadler, S. 1999. *Spinoza: A Life*. Cambridge: Cambridge University Press.

Nadler, S. 2006. *Spinoza's Ethics: An Introduction*. Cambridge: Cambridge University Press.

Ravven, H. & L. Goodman (eds) 2002. *Jewish Themes in Spinoza's Philosophy*. Albany, NY: SUNY Press.

Smith, S. 1996. *Spinoza, Liberalism, and the Question of Jewish Identity*. New Haven, CT: Yale University Press.

Verbeek, T. 2003. *Spinoza's Theologico-Political Treatise: Exploring the Will of God*. Aldershot: Ashgate.

On NATURAL RELIGION/THEOLOGY see also Chs 4, 6, 7, 12, 13, 19, 23; Vol. 4, Chs 8, 12; Vol. 5, Ch. 23. On POLITICS see also Ch. 2. On REVELATION see also Chs 7, 16; Vol. 1, Ch. 14; Vol. 2, Chs 11; Vol. 4, Chs 5, 11; Vol. 5, Chs 8, 23.

12

JOHN LOCKE

Victor Nuovo

John Locke was born in the village of Wrington in Somerset, England, on 29 August 1632 and died on 28 October 1704 at Oates, the country estate of Sir Francis and Lady Damaris Masham in Essex. He was born into a family of minor gentry that had puritan sympathies. His father, an attorney, served briefly as a captain in the parliamentary army during the English Civil War, ending his military activity soon after his regiment suffered defeat in battle. Locke was educated at Westminster School, whose headmaster, Richard Busby (1606–95) was a Royalist who managed to retain his position under the Commonwealth and whose loyalty to the Laudian Church of England and its anti-Calvinist theology remained undiminished.[1] There, Locke received a classical education and became proficient in Latin, Greek and Hebrew.

Locke matriculated at Oxford in November 1652. He was elected to a studentship at Christ Church, a position roughly equivalent to an Oxford college fellowship. Locke took his BA in November 1656 and his MA in June 1658. He remained at Christ Church as tutor until 1667. His earliest writings – reading notes inscribed in commonplace books and an interleaved Bible and four disputations that he never published – reveal a young scholar headed for a clerical career (Long 1959; Harrison & Laslett 1971). In the late 1650s Locke's intellectual interest turned also to medicine, and at about that time he came under the tutelage of Robert Boyle (1627–91) (Stewart 1981). As a member of Boyle's circle, Locke was exposed to more than new medical and natural philosophical knowledge. His early

1. The expression 'Laudian' derives from William Laud (1573–1645), Archbishop of Canterbury during the reign of Charles I. It takes its meaning from his idea of the Church. Laud advocated a national Church, Catholic in polity, liturgy and doctrine, closely allied to the monarchy, and ruled by divine right by an episcopacy that claimed an unbroken succession from the apostolic era. Laudians looked to the Church Fathers for theological guidance, rather than to the medieval scholastics or the Protestant reformers.

commonplace books contain many references to Boyle's writings on theology and the Bible.

Boyle also introduced Locke to a form of life that he seems to have appropriated. This was the character of the Christian virtuoso. The term 'virtuoso' was used to denote an experimental natural philosopher. In a work that Boyle probably had begun at that time, although it was not published until three decades later, he argued that Christianity and experimental natural philosophy were perfect complements. Practice of the latter awakened the mind to the wisdom of God in creation. The performance of experiments whose outcomes were often unexpected disposed the mind and made it docile towards the unforeseen and unexpected content of revelation. Nature and Scripture were, to Boyle's mind, the two fundamental sources of human knowledge. They were to be approached in the same manner, through impartial enquiry. Boyle distinguished docility from mere credulity. The former is driven by curiosity, the latter by desire. Docility is a disposition whereby the mind is attentive to detail and indifferent towards the outcome of its enquiries (Boyle [1691] 2000).

Overall, Locke's theological reading shows a preference for moderate theological positions such as those stated in the works of Richard Hooker (1554–1600), Hugo Grotius (1583–1645), John Hales (1584–1656) and William Chillingworth (1602–44), all of whom envisaged a broad comprehensive church that tolerated diversity of opinion, and that shunned Protestant confessionalism and Roman infallibility. This moderate theological outlook, which prized reason and free agency and Christian universalism, was appropriated by moderate theologians, latitudinarians, who after the Restoration endeavoured to give the Church of England a moderate cast: among these were Simon Patrick (1626–1707), Isaac Barrow (1630–77) and John Tillotson (1630–94), with whose writings Locke was familiar.[2] He regarded Tillotson, who was Archbishop of Canterbury from 1691 until 1694, as his theological counsellor and mentor (De Beer 1976–89: vol. 5, 237).

In the end, Locke made his living neither as a cleric nor as a physician or natural philosopher. His career took a political turn when he entered the household of Anthony Ashley Cooper (1621–83), later the first Earl of Shaftesbury. His fortunes rose and fell with Shaftesbury's political rise and fall. In 1683, like his patron, by then deceased, Locke sought refuge in the Dutch Republic, where he remained until 1689. He returned in the train of William and Mary. Not long after his return to England, Locke published two of his major works: *Two Treatises of Government*

2. 'Latitudinarian' denotes a loosely organized party within the Church of England that was most influential during the seventeenth and eighteenth centuries. Its members, mostly clergy, endeavoured to achieve a broad comprehensive national church by limiting fundamental doctrine to articles having clear biblical authority and which could be stated in a plain historical style, and by permissiveness in liturgical practice. Although Latitudinarians did not regard episcopacy as a divine institution, they favoured its retention for pragmatic reasons.

and *An Essay Concerning Human Understanding* (hereafter *Essay*). The *Epistola de tolerantia* (Letter concerning toleration) was published in the Dutch Republic the same year, seen through the press by Locke's friend, the Dutch Arminian theologian Philipp van Limborch (1693–1712). Locke published his major theological work, *The Reasonableness of Christianity*, in 1695 (in Nuovo 2002: 85–244), and was immediately engaged in controversy concerning the fundamental articles of the Christian religion, that is, the particular doctrines that one must believe to be a Christian. His final major work, which remained unfinished, was a commentary on the epistles of St Paul (Locke 1987).

In May 1703, Locke wrote to his new friend Anthony Collins (1676–1729), and in passing consoled him on the death of his wife by reminding him that he was a Christian and a philosopher. Locke did not elaborate, but it is likely that he intended to suggest that the two were complementary. He doubtless believed that a bare reminder of this was sufficient. Collins had lately entered Locke's inner circle of friends, and there is no doubt that Locke loved him dearly because of his youthfulness, quick wit and brilliant conversation and, most importantly, for what Locke perceived as an affinity of mind expressed in an unexcelled love of truth. No doubt he was also pleased by Collins' willingness to perform minor services for him, such as procuring new works of the learned, mostly theological, and by making sure that their pages were cut and bound according to Locke's specifications. Collins reciprocated. His early letters to Locke express his dazzlement that the great philosopher should consider him his friend and equal in conversation and society (De Beer 1976–89: vol. 7, 776; vol. 8, *passim*).

Although Collins never ceased to venerate Locke, he soon abandoned Christianity for freethinking, as did his friend, John Toland (1670–1722), whom Locke knew but preferred to keep at a distance. Both were profoundly influenced by Locke and this was acknowledged by them. Hence, it may be surmised that there is a tendency in Locke's thought towards deism and freethinking. This tendency may be detected in the key role that natural religion and the law of nature play in Locke's thinking, and in his reputed heterodoxy, in his belief that the human soul is mortal and is conceivably material, and in his hostility towards clerical authority (not always consistent).

As a self-described lover of truth, Locke was committed to following rational enquiry wherever it might lead. Looking back, therefore, from the standpoint of his freethinking heirs, it may appear that Locke set for himself artificial and arbitrary constraints, chief among them an adherence to the Christian religion, whose truth he seems never to have seriously doubted. Writing in 1697 in defence of *The Reasonableness of Christianity*, Locke, albeit anonymously, declared himself a Christian:

> A Christian I am sure I am, because I believe *Jesus* to be the *Messiah*, the King and Saviour promised, and sent by God: And as a Subject of his Kingdom, I take the rule of my Faith, and Life, from his Will

> declar'd and left upon Record in the inspired Writings of the Apostles and Evangelists. (Locke 1697: 344)

He acknowledges that, as a Christian, he has a duty to understand the true sense and meaning of these writings, and to this end he claims the Holy Spirit to be his primary guide, the very same Spirit that inspired the authors of Scripture in the first place. Yet, to Locke's mind, the Holy Spirit always accommodates its communications to human rationality even as it enhances reason's capability and enlarges its scope to include the supernatural. Locke seems to have found Christianity intellectually compelling and satisfying. Understanding why may be the key to his philosophy of religion if not to his entire philosophical programme. Some of his intellectual heirs, most notably William Paley (1743–1805), maintained the connection between Christianity and philosophy. Others did not. Locke's legacy in philosophy of religion is divided.

NATURAL RELIGION

Locke's idea of religion consists of two practical principles: honouring God and obeying the divine law. To honour God involves acknowledging that God exists and is unique, that he is the author of existence, and therefore has a perfect right to require that all creatures obey him and to reward those who do and to punish those who do not. This requirement applies only to rational creatures, that is, to persons who are able to follow a rule. The divine law, which universally prescribes human obligation, is identical to the law of nature, a law, Locke insisted that, although not innate, was discoverable by human reason (Nuovo 2002: 73; *Essay* I.iii.18, I.iv.13; Locke 1975: 78, 92).[3]

Locke believed that this idea of religion was universal and normative. He maintained that God had endowed humankind with sufficient cognitive and volitional capacities to discover its principles and to adhere to them. The main themes of natural religion are developed in his *Essay* and taken together constitute, strictly speaking, a philosophy of religion.

THE EXISTENCE OF GOD

Locke's ontology includes three sorts of beings: God, finite spirits (embodied and disembodied) and bodies. As a prelude to his proof of the existence of God (*Essay* IV.ix.2–3; Locke 1975: 618), Locke modifies this list by restricting it to things

3. Citations of *An Essay Concerning Human Understanding* are by book, chapter and verse, followed by page numbers in Locke (1975).

among these three classes of whose existence we can be certain. He assumes that he and we (his readers) belong to the same class of beings, namely, embodied finite cogitative spirits. We know our own existence by intuition, the existence of bodies through sensation and the existence of God by demonstration, or as Locke embellishes, "by mathematical certainty". Locke's proof has a simplicity, elegance and persuasiveness that has gone unnoticed, which is not to suggest that it succeeds in its intended purpose, although it is surely no less successful than other more celebrated theistic proofs.

Appreciation of the merits of Locke's theistic proof requires that attention be given to his method of argument. According to this method, an argument is a chain of ideas (Owen 1999: 30–61 and *passim*). The method builds on Locke's definition of knowledge as the perception of "the connexion and agreement, or disagreement and repugnancy of any of our ideas" (*Essay* IV.i.2; Locke 1975: 525). It is more akin to a logic of terms than of propositions, although ideas are conjoined into propositions, non-verbal and verbal, that are further connected by means of particles that signify familiar logical relations: negation, conjunction, alternation and so on (*Essay* III.vii.1, IV.v.2; Locke 1975: 471, 574). It is not a formal logic. Agreement, disagreement and other connections are content specific. Unlike formal systems of logic, which, Locke observed, are artificial and are as often employed to promote sophistry as to preserve truth, his natural scheme of logic arises from actual reflections, through observations of "the Actings of our own Minds". These observations reveal the "natural plain order" by which all humankind, even the most untutored, reason about things and draw valid inferences from what they know about them. Locke believed that reasoning of this sort is practised everywhere, by the schooled and unschooled, and that the former are not, for all their schooling, better at it (*Essay* IV.xvi.4; Locke 1975: 670–78, *passim*).

Locke's proof of the existence and attributes of God proceeds as follows. Briefly, he argues that if something exists then there must be something else existing, a being that exists eternally, and this we may properly designate as God. Through a train of ideas, we are supposed to discover a necessary connection between the antecedent and the consequent idea. For the former, he selects himself: a conscious being assuredly finite, one that has a temporal beginning. That I exist is infallibly evident to me because of the indissoluble connection between two ideas – my immediate awareness of my self and, attached to it, the idea of existence – and by the opposition of the former idea with the idea of non-existence (*Essay* IV.ix.3, IV.x.2; Locke 1975: 618, 619). Although it might seem that Locke could just as well have begun his proof with the existence of some physical object, the pen that he held in his hand or the paper on which he was writing, whose actual existence (albeit only its perceived corporeality and not its essence) is immediately known through sensation, his choice of himself is more convenient to his purpose. It leads more directly to the important conclusion that an eternal being, whose existence is necessary if anything else should exist, is, like Locke, a cogitative being and hence a spirit, indeed an infinite spirit.

The sequence of ideas that make up Locke's theistic proof is as follows: I, that is a self or person, exist; my existence has had a beginning; nothing comes from nothing; there is some being that exists eternally. The link that connects the idea of my own existence with that of an eternally existing being is the impossibility, intuitively perceived, that there can be a beginning of existence of finite things *tout simple* unless there also exists an eternally existing being, which is the universal cause of all their beginnings of existence. The argument so stated might be better employed to prove the eternity of the world, a tendency arguably inherent in all theistic proofs, but that was not Locke's intention.

There is a common misconception that Locke's proof fails on account of a fundamental equivocation in it. It is supposed that, knowing nothing about quantification, he unwittingly slid from the argument 'if anything exists, then it must always be the case that something exists' to 'if anything exists, then there must be something that always exists, that exists eternally'.[4] This assessment is more prejudicial than insightful: the result of using a method of logical exposition and appraisal that is not well suited to the peculiarities of Locke's experiential logical method.

The attributes of God are likewise derived according to this method of reasoning and are an expression of Locke's antipathy to any variety of emergentism: "If it be said, there was a time when no Being had any Knowledge, when that eternal Being was void of all Understanding. I reply, that then it was impossible there should ever have been any Knowledge" (*Essay* IV.x.4; Locke 1975: 620). A finite intelligent being will recognize certain powers in itself, for example, intelligence, active power, wisdom and cognition, which, since nothing comes from nothing, must be attributed to the eternally existing source of being without restriction or limitation. Hence, in God these attributes may be properly characterized as infinite. Thus God can be described as a perfect being, the sum of all perfections infinitely and forever realized. So also, God cannot be regarded as material, but as an infinite spirit, for otherwise God would be subject to the limitations and passivity of material bodies. As to the dimensions of God, Locke attributes immensity to the divine being: God fills all eternity and space. Hence, "God's infinite Duration, being accompanied with infinite Knowledge, and infinite Power, he sees all things past and to come; and they are no more distant from his Knowledge … than the present: They all lie under the same view" and at his pleasure (*Essay* II.xv.12; Locke

4. This interpretation may be due to a misreading of Locke's brief statement of the argument: "If therefore we know there is some real Being [i.e. ourselves], and that Non-entity cannot produce any real Being, it is an evident demonstration, *that from Eternity there has been something*; Since what was not from Eternity, had a Beginning; and what had a Beginning, must be produced by something else" (*Essay* IV.x.3; Locke 1975: 620, emphasis added). If the italicized clause were taken to mean 'there has always been something', rather than 'there is something that has always been', then Locke would have been equivocating, but the context shows that he intended the latter. Compare *Essay* IV.x.8 (Locke 1975: 622).

1975: 204). It is clear that the idea of God that Locke has fashioned filled his mind, whenever he thought of it, in a way that no other idea did, so that he could assert without exaggeration that "we more certainly know that there is a GOD, than that there is any thing else without us" (*Essay* II.x.6; Locke 1975: 621).[5] This strong affirmation of God and the self is reminiscent of Descartes and, through him, of Augustine.

Although Locke maintained that this method of proof made it accessible even to uncultivated minds, to untutored day labourers, who if they were to have the time could make use of their cognitive faculties as they found them, he believed that there was a less recondite proof of God, whose wisdom and power are manifest in the "sensible parts of the Universe", and thus ever-present even to those of a less reflective cast of mind (*Essay* IV.x.7, IV.xx.4; Locke 1975: 622, 708).

MORAL RELIGION

Locke maintained that, as with the existence and attributes of God, our knowledge of our moral duty is capable of mathematical demonstration according to his method of proof (*Essay* III.xi.16, IV.iii.18, IV.xii.8; Locke 1975: 516, 548f., 643). Like our knowledge of God, our moral knowledge is not innate; rather, we have a law of nature, which "we being ignorant of may attain to the knowledge of, by the use and due application of our natural Faculties" (*Essay* I.iii.13; Locke 1975: 75). The law of nature is a divine law, and, consistent with the divine nature, is "eternal and immutable"; it is "an eternal law of right", a fitting expression of perfect justice seated in the mind of a perfect legislator, that requires perfect obedience and strict enforcement (*Essay* II.xxviii.8; Locke 1975: 352; *The Reasonableness of Christianity*, Nuovo 2002: 95, 99, 191).

Locke's theory of morality, therefore, may be put under the general category of divine command morality. The idea of morality is a rational idea, hence it would be "brutish", that is, inconsistent with our rational nature, to deny "that God has given a Rule whereby Men should govern themselves" (*Essay* II.xxvii.8; Locke 1975: 352). Both the rule and the obligation to obey it are capable of rational demonstration. As the author of our being, God has the right of a lawgiver over us. The wisdom, justice and goodness of God, proper attributes of a perfectly perfect infinite being whose nature consists of whatever it is better to be than not to be, are proof of God's fitness to will what is best for humankind. With respect to

5. The reader should also consult Locke's argument that there can be one God only, which is presented in a series of letters to van Limborch: see De Beer (1976–89: vol. 6, appendix II, 783–93). Locke's argument is based on the premise that the very idea of God is of a "perfectly perfect" being, the sum of all perfections, of whatever it is better to be than not to be, "the most real of all beings", whose attributes, in particular power and omnipresence, are infinite, which they would not be if there were more than one God.

human motivation, the infinite power of God makes us certain that God is able to apply "Rewards and Punishments, of infinite weight and duration" that extend into a life beyond this one, "for nobody can take us out of his hands" (*Essay* II.28.8; Locke 1975: 549). Finally, the fact that God is omniscient should make us certain that neither our actions nor our motives are hidden, so that God is a perfect judge of all our actions.

Locke's moral theory may be considered voluntarist in the following respects. The moral law itself is not the ground of moral obligation, does not by itself necessitate the will; rather, it is the will and power of God, who commands and enforces it, that obliges humankind. Nor is the mere legislative will of God a sufficient basis of moral obligation, in so far as it is conceived, as Locke must have conceived it, as a pure rational will, that is, as a proper expression of divine wisdom and goodness and not of mere arbitrary sovereign power. An individual's judgement of right or wrong is surely a necessary part of moral obligation, but it is not alone sufficient. The motivation to do justice also involves the individual will, which is determined by desire and aversion, by the pursuit of pleasure and the avoidance of pain. Hence, the will to obey the divine law is finally and properly determined by the prospect of a sure reward or by the threat of an unavoidable punishment, whichever fits, and by the assurance that there is no refuge or escape from the wrath of divine judgement, and finally, God being eternal and omnipotent, by the knowledge that there is nothing to limit the severity and duration of a divine sentence or a divine reward. On the other hand, Locke's moral theory may be considered rationalist in as much as the moral law and its enforcement are fitting expressions of a rational will, and even the will to obey the law involves a measure of rational self-control.

It is noteworthy that Locke offers in outline a rational proof of his theory of punishment in the very chapter of the *Essay* devoted to reason. As an example of rational inference, he sketches out a long argument that proves that human agents are free and self-determining, starting from the idea of divine punishment in another world. The proof consists of the following sequence of ideas: "*Men shall be punished* [in another world], – *God the punisher, – just Punishment, – the Punished guilty – could have done otherwise – freedom – self-determination*" (*Essay* IV.xvii.4; Locke 1975: 673). To elaborate, it is certain that all human wrongdoers will be punished in another world, for God is the punisher and so is not restricted to inflicting only temporal punishments, which may not adequately satisfy the requirement of a supreme justice. Moreover, since God is just, he will punish only those who, if they had chosen, could have refrained from wrongdoing, that is, who were free, self-determining agents.

Locke's reflections on the nature of free human agency are pertinent here. It was his considered opinion that free human agency consists in doing a certain act or refraining from it according to one's choice. Here reason plays a key role. Ordinarily, the power of choice is determined by "the greatest present *uneasiness*" or desire (*Essay* II.xxi.40; Locke 1975: 257). Human agents have their being in the world. They are creatures of desire, schooled by experience and motivated by fear and hope, whose horizons would not extend beyond this world but for the knowledge of the being and attributes of God and for the sure prospect of "*fullness of Joy, and Pleasure for evermore*" and its terrifying negative counterpart. Reason regulates desire by directing the agent to "the pursuit of real Bliss", which is infinitely better than any prospect of temporal good. In order to contemplate this state and compare it with its more immediate prospects, human agents find within themselves the power to suspend immediate desire. It is this power that Locke regards as the epitome of the freedom of finite rational agents (*Essay* II.xxi.41, 51; Locke 1975: 258, 266f.).

A full account of Locke's moral religion must also include his idea of what it is to be a person. It is by being conscious of themselves that individuals are judged to be persons. "*Self* is that conscious thinking thing … which is … conscious of Pleasure and Pain, capable of Happiness or Misery, and so is concern'd for it *self*, as far as that consciousness extends" (*Essay* II.xxvii.17; Locke 1975: 341). However, a person is not only anxious about its well-being for as long as it endures, but is also aware, through its rationality, that its actions have practical value. Hence Locke remarks that the term 'person' is "a Forensick Term", and so is applied properly only "to intelligent Agents capable of Law, and Happiness and Misery" (*Essay* II.xxvii.26; Locke 1975: 346).

THE REASONABLENESS OF REVELATION

Although Locke believed that a religion of nature was realizable everywhere and always, he also acknowledged that powerful forces were ever at work to prevent its realization and to supplant it. Some of these had their source in human nature, specifically in the limitations of human cognitive and active powers, their fallibility and frailty; others were social in origin, in particular, the cunning of priestcraft, which preyed on human weakness and fashioned a near invincible institution that was fed by ignorance and superstition, which were always in great supply. A third element in this unhappy condition was the cowardice of philosophers, who were not ignorant of the truth about God and the foundations of morality and should have taught this truth openly (*The Reasonableness of Christianity*, in Nuovo 2002: 191ff.; "Sacerdos" [The priest], in Nuovo 2002: 17–18). It is noteworthy that Locke did not subscribe to the Christian doctrine of depravity, according to which, as a result of Adam's disobedience, human faculties had become corrupt and incapable of performing their proper functions. He admitted only that Adam's progeny inherited mortality from their progenitor, and that from this condition frailty followed (Nuovo 2002: 92; also "Peccatum originale" [Original sin], in Nuovo 2002: 229).

The effects of these adverse forces, then, are evident in the near universality of polytheism and superstition as well as in the fact, as reported by world travellers, that some societies practised no religion at all. Revealed religion is supposed to disclose a divine remedy for these effects and their causes. Hence, there is a continuity between normative natural religion and revealed religion, and accordingly between reason and revelation. This continuity is epitomized in Locke's assertion that reason is natural revelation, and revelation is reason enlarged.

Reason enlarged is still reason. And Locke is emphatic that supernatural revelation should in no way be regarded as sufficient in itself to do without rational understanding. Anyone who supposes this is an enthusiast and not a lover of truth (*Essay* IV.19.4; Locke 1975: 698).

Reason is enlarged in various ways. First, through revelation, reason acquires factual knowledge about the operation of a special divine providence by which the effects of human frailty and corruption are mitigated and the negative effects of forces adverse to the divine purpose and to human happiness are overcome and finally defeated. It is curious that in *The Reasonableness of Christianity* Locke contends that God did nothing unjust in making humankind mortal as a consequence of Adam's sin, nor should it be supposed that God's intention in this was at all punitive, because a mere mortal existence is better than no existence at all. Yet a central point of the Christian revelation is to show how God intends to restore humankind to its original immortal state (Nuovo 2002: 94). The facts of revelation are not so singular that their meaning can be grasped by considering them by themselves. Revelation also discloses a realm of spirits that transcends and yet encompasses the sensible tangible world. A topical list designed for a theological commonplace book, prepared in 1694, provides a short description of this world. It is a plenitude, at whose apex is God, the best and greatest of beings, who may be three but is most certainly one, beneath whom, in decreasing order of excellence, are serial orders of spirits, and on further descent into the visible world, finite corporeal spirits, other species of animals and varieties of inanimate bodies ("Adversaria theologica" [Theological commonplaces], in Nuovo 2002: 21–3). Revelation is a disclosure of the history of this world, whose main moments, marked by miracles that manifest a divine power capable of achieving its purposes, are also recorded on this list: Adam's Fall and the pre-existence, birth, death and resurrection of the Messiah are most prominent, as are the Mosaic covenant and the gospel. This history includes other noteworthy events: the fall of Angels, the creation of hell, the foretelling of events still to come, including the second coming of the Messiah, now victorious over all his enemies, temporal and spiritual, the resurrection of the dead, the last judgement, and the renewal of paradise, and the restoration of those who pass judgement to a state of eternal bliss. Notwithstanding the supernatural and, from a modern viewpoint, mythological aspects of this history, Locke supposed that when the purpose of revealed religion is properly understood, adherence to it must appear most reasonable, for it is an assured and advantageous way to follow for individuals who desire, as they naturally must, to avoid divine displeasure towards their inevitable moral failures and achieve an invincible reward. In this respect, Locke believed that the

Christian revelation is unique, in as much as it alone among all religions that claim to be founded in revelation offers a mitigation or relaxation of the severity of the moral law.

Revelation, however, requires a warrant, and it is reason's task to provide it. In performing it, reason attends not only to the content of a revelation, but also to the means of its disclosure and propagation. Locke describes two varieties of revelation: original and traditional. An original revelation is the direct infusion of divine knowledge into the minds of those especially chosen to be its bearers, but even this is not self-authenticating. In his discourse on enthusiasm or immediate inspiration, Locke is emphatic that the recipient of an original revelation must first of all be a lover of truth, which is to say, someone who respects the constraints of reason and the practice of rational enquiry and who accepts as true the normative principles of natural religion ("Immediate Inspiration", in Nuovo 2002: 37–41; *A Discourse of Miracles*, in Nuovo 2002: 44–50; see also Locke's chapter on enthusiasm, *Essay* IV.xix; Locke 1975: 697–706). For all the rest, those not among the very few specially chosen, traditional revelation must suffice. They must depend on the testimony of the former, who were purportedly eye- and ear-witnesses of a founding revelation and the inspired authors of documents chosen to record the founders' testimony. Locke was convinced that Christianity is the only purportedly revealed religion that can be counted as true in the fullest sense. He admitted for consideration only two others: Judaism, whose founder was Moses, and Islam, whose founder was Muhammad. He dismissed the latter, because, lacking miracles to confirm it, it is deficient. He argued that the two remaining "mutually confirm each other", but Christianity gains ascendancy because it represents clearly what is only adumbrated in the religion of Moses and his prophetic successors.

WARRANTING CHRISTIANITY

The task of warranting Christianity reduces to the task of warranting the Bible, interpreted from a Christian standpoint. Overall, Locke adopted a strategy devised by Faustus Socinus (1539–1604), the Unitarian heresiarch, and presented by him in a short book that became widely influential, especially among the orthodox (*De Auctoritate Sacrae Scripturae* [Concerning the authority of sacred Scripture]; 1611). In brief, this strategy begins with the certainty that the Christian religion is true and, this being the case, it would be unreasonable to deny the authenticity of the New Testament, which is a first-hand testimony of its founding and its original constitution. The truth of the Christian religion is determined by its content, by the fact that Jesus of Nazareth offered for the first time in human history a clear and uncompromising account of natural religion (Nuovo 2002: 193). If the New Testament is in this respect true, so is the Old Testament, because it is confirmed by the New. To secure a warrant for the Bible, the only task that remains is to clarify its meaning, to authenticate its text and to respond to objections concerning its apparent inconsistencies, the uncertain chronology of events reported in it and the ambiguities arising from the fact that the Bible is written in an alien language and records events in contexts much removed from those of its later interpreters, whose multiple orthodoxies prove the difficulty of the task. Yet, with this strategy, the biblical advocate may proceed with the presumption of truth. Here also the light of reason is essential. Locke supposed that any text is an expression of the mind of its author, and that by means of philological and historical criticism an interpreter may discover the intended meaning expressed in the text. Thus, in *The Reasonableness of Christianity* Locke believed that he discovered the mind of Jesus the Messiah as expressed in his preaching and related actions, and in *A Paraphrase and Notes on the Epistles of St Paul* he explored the mind of St Paul (see the preface to the latter, "An Essay for the Understanding of St Paul's Epistles by Consulting St Paul himself", in Locke 1987: vol. 1, 101–16; Nuovo 2002: 51–66).

THE VARIETIES OF FAITH AND THE PERFECTION OF THE MIND

Locke maintained that religious faith is no different from ordinary states of belief. Although he appealed to the assistance of the Holy Spirit in matters of faith, by this he meant only that the divine spirit operated internally and imperceptibly to enhance ordinary human cognitive capacities and thereby to clarify and sustain judgement. Religious faith, given its object, is accordingly a "Historical Faith" (Nuovo 2002: 166, 268). With respect to content, he distinguished two sorts of Christian faith: saving and consummate. A saving faith consists of just those doctrines whose acceptance sufficed to qualify anyone as a Christian. Basing his opinion on the gospel preaching of Jesus and the Apostles, he concluded that there was only one fundamental positive article of faith: that Jesus is the Messiah, the divine king sent into the world to establish a new covenant. In this respect, Locke was a doctrinal minimalist. However, acceptance of this 'historical' fact involved certain moral obligations: that one repent for all past wrongdoings and endeavour to conform one's life, as much as frailty will permit, to the divine law. All who did this could be assured that they would be judged according to a less rigorous standard than the dictates of the divine law would otherwise require. In addition to this, Locke also believed that it was a duty of all Christians to engage in a continuing study of Scripture. The outcome of this process is an increase of faith, both in its assurance and in its content. The wisdom of God is manifest in the biblical narrative as much as it is in the wonderful contrivances of nature, and all who review that history regularly are sure to enjoy a continual confirmation of their faith. The mind of the Christian progresses to a consummate faith when it appropriates the mind of Christ and of the Apostles as it is expressed in the New Testament.

Locke also expected a further perfection of the mind in the world to come. It became his rational hope, based on a reading of the Bible, that in the world to come all who are saved would receive a new spiritual body, immortal and incorruptible, and with this a set of cognitive faculties whereby the mind would be rendered capable of an "intuitive comprehensive knowledge" of things. Since Locke supposed that these powers would be similar to those that "superior seraphick beings" now have, one may conclude that among things known and enjoyed would be the one true God (*Essay* II.xxiii.13, III.xi.23, IV.ii.1; Locke 1975: 303–4, 520–21, 530–31; Locke 1987: vol. 1, 238; Nuovo 2002: 28–30).

FURTHER READING

Israel, J. 2001. *Radical Enlightenment: Philosophy and the Making of Modernity, 1650–1750.* Oxford: Oxford University Press [esp. chs 11, 24 and 33].

Jolley, N. 2003. "Reason's Dim Candle: Locke's Critique of Enthusiasm". In *The Philosophy of John Locke: New Perspectives*, P. Anstey (ed.), 170–91. London: Routledge.

Marshall, J. 2000. "Locke, Socinianism, 'Socinianism', and Unitarianism". In *English Philosophy in the Age of Locke*, M. Stewart (ed.), 111–82. Oxford: Clarendon Press.

Nuovo, V. 2000. "Locke's Theology". In *English Philosophy in the Age of Locke*, M. Stewart (ed.), 183–215. Oxford: Clarendon Press.

Nuovo, V. 2002. "Introduction". In *John Locke: Writings on Religion*, V. Nuovo (ed.), xv–lvii. Oxford: Clarendon Press.

Nuovo, V. 2003. "Locke's Christology as a Key to Understanding His Philosophy". In *The Philosophy of John Locke: New Perspectives*, P. Anstey (ed.), 129–53. London: Routledge.

Nuovo, V. 2007. "Reflections on Locke's Platonism". In *Platonism at the Origins of Modernity*, S. Hutton & D. Hedley (eds), 207–23. Heidelberg: Springer.

Wolterstorff, N. 1994. "Locke's Philosophy of Religion". In *The Cambridge Companion to Locke*, V. Chappell (ed.), 172–98. Cambridge: Cambridge University Press.

On EXISTENCE OF GOD see also Chs 6, 13, 14, 15, 21; Vol. 1, Chs 18, 19; Vol. 2, Chs 5, 6, 13, 14; Vol. 5, Chs 11, 16. On MORALITY see also Chs 2, 8, 14, 21, 22; Vol. 2, Ch. 12; Vol. 4, Chs 4, 12, 18; Vol. 5, Ch. 6. On NATURAL RELIGION/THEOLOGY see also Chs 4, 6, 7, 11, 13, 19, 23; Vol. 4, Chs 8, 12; Vol. 5, Ch. 23. On REASON see also Chs 8, 16, 21; Vol. 2, Chs 10, 11, 12, 16, 18; Vol. 4, Chs 4, 8.

13

GOTTFRIED WILHELM LEIBNIZ

Jack D. Davidson

Gottfried Wilhelm Leibniz (1646–1716) is best known among non-specialists for his development of the calculus and his incredible thesis that this is the best of all possible worlds. He was born in Hanover two years before the end of the horrific Thirty Years' War. After receiving a doctorate in law, he came to the notice of an influential converted Catholic, through whom he entered the service of the Elector of Mainz, another converted Catholic. Both encouraged one of Leibniz's lifetime passions: working toward Church reunion between Protestants and Catholics and ultimately between the various Protestant dominations. Leibniz's ecumenical work was characterized by good will, tolerance and flexibility. It says something about the cast of Leibniz's mind that he believed that if the differing sides could just agree on a correct metaphysics – his, as it turns out – reconciliation was possible.

In 1672 Leibniz was sent to Paris to present a plan devised to persuade the Sun King that his military ambitions would be manifested more gloriously if directed at Egypt rather than Germany. By the time Leibniz arrived, the political and military situation in Europe had changed enough that the plan was no longer relevant, but the four years Leibniz spent in Paris seem to have been the happiest of his life. There he met some of the most influential thinkers of the day, including Antoine Arnauld, Nicolas Malebranche and the mathematicians Walter Tschirnhaus and Christian Huygens, the latter of whom brought Leibniz up to speed on contemporary mathematical developments. Leibniz had worked out the key principles of calculus by 1673, and determined that integration is the inverse of differentiation by 1675. Leibniz published a paper on the basics of calculus in 1684. Isaac Newton had not published his results yet, and indeed did not publicly claim the invention of calculus until the publication of his *Optics* in 1704. What followed was a nasty dispute concerning priority that continued even after the deaths of the two main participants. The consensus today is that Newton had the fundamentals of calculus by 1666, but that Leibniz came to his ideas independently of Newton.

During this period in Paris, Leibniz took a trip to London to show off his calculating machine, which (when operational) was the most advanced of its time, and met with Hooke, Boyle, Pell and other members of the Royal Society, but not Newton. He also travelled to the Netherlands where he met Spinoza and discussed, among other things, the ontological argument. During Leibniz's stay in Paris, both of his German patrons died. When no position in Paris was offered, he accepted an appointment as a political advisor, historian and librarian to the Duke of Hanover. Leibniz remained in Hanover, serving under a succession of dukes, until his death.

But for trips abroad on diplomatic or historical fact-finding – he was charged with writing a history of the house of his employer – Leibniz spent the rest of his life in Hanover, a sleepy town with a population of 10,000, far from the cultural and intellectual centres of London and Paris. To remain a citizen of letters and to continue contributing to the explosion of learning in his day, Leibniz maintained a voluminous correspondence, much of which was addressed to the leading thinkers of the Continent and England; copies of 15,000 of his letters remain in Hanover today. So extensive was Leibniz's learning by correspondence that by the end of his life he was considered something of an expert on China, although all of his knowledge was gleaned from books, letters and conservations with Jesuit missionaries who had served in China.

Toward the end of Leibniz's life, a long-standing intramural struggle within the Catholic Church involving China reached fever pitch. The debate pitted the Jesuits against pretty much everyone else in the Church: the Dominicans, the Franciscans, the theological faculty of the Sorbonne and much of the Church hierarchy. The so-called Rites Controversy involved two questions: were rites associated with respect for one's ancestors and Confucius essentially religious, or merely social and civil in nature; and did the Chinese language contain a word, and hence the idea, for (a monotheistic and personal) God? At issue was the relation between Christianity and non-Christian thought, especially the thought of an ancient and advanced civilization like China (Mungello 1977; Leibniz 1994; Perkins 2004).

Leibniz was enamoured of the Chinese binary notation in arithmetic – he came up with the idea independently – and with the Chinese language, which he sometimes offers as model for his universal characteristic scheme, the latter a never-completed plan to mechanize reasoning via numerical notation in something like a universal language. Summarizing his unfinished work on the natural theology of the Chinese in a letter to the Jesuit Des Bosses, Leibniz went even beyond the accommodationist position of the Jesuits, writing that: "In … the Chinese doctrines concerning God, spirits, and the human soul … the ancient Chinese more than the philosophers of Greece seem to have come near to truth" (Look & Rutherford 2007: xxvii). In the *Theodicy* and in his correspondence with Des Bosses, Leibniz suggests that, given the bountiful avenues available to God for dispensing grace sufficient for salvation, it is narrow-minded to suppose that a personal knowledge of Christ, at least in this life, was necessary for justification.

In 1716, Leibniz, a general factotum who did mathematics and philosophy in his spare time, who rivalled Leonardo da Vinci in the number and range of original technological ideas, and who far outstripped all of his rivals, including Newton, in making deep and original contributions to more fields of learning than anyone of his age, died alone in Hanover.

LEIBNIZ'S SYSTEM: SELECTED PRINCIPLES AND THESES

Leibniz's philosophical system is complex, sophisticated and often obscure. What follows is no more than a partial sketch of some its core principles and theses.

Leibniz held that because we are imitators of God, our minds are structured such that we can, in principle, understand not only the deep structure of the created universe but also central aspects of God's mind and motivations. Leibniz's belief that God has implanted central innate ideas, of causation, substance, and the self, for example, led to a robust confidence in our ability to do metaphysics, natural theology and philosophical theology.

In various texts, Leibniz talks of two great principles that govern all of our reasoning. First, he held that there is an answer to every why question; to put the point differently, he denied that there are brute facts. This is expressed in the first great principle, the principle of sufficient reason (PSR): the thesis that for any state of affairs there must be a sufficient reason that explains that state of affairs. The principle has consequences for almost every part of his philosophy.

In a short note Leibniz wrote: "I begin as a philosopher, but I end as a theologian. One of my great principles is that nothing happens without a reason. That is a principle of philosophy. Nevertheless, at bottom it is nothing but an affirmation of the divine wisdom, though I do not speak of this at first" (Curley 1972: 58). The claim that God's wisdom is predicated on the PSR is no throwaway line. In the *Discourse on Metaphysics*, commenting on those who, like Descartes and Arnauld, give the wrong answer to the 'Euthyphro dilemma' –Does God command us to do what is morally right because it is morally right, or is it right because God so commands? – Leibniz writes:

> [I]n saying that things are not good by virtue of any rule of goodness but solely by virtue of the will of God, it seems to me that we unknowingly destroy all of God's love and all his glory. For why praise him for what he has done if he would be equally praiseworthy in doing the exact contrary? (Leibniz 1989: 36)

In the *New Essays on Human Understanding* (hereafter *New Essays*), he explains the second great principle:

> Stated generally, the principle of contradiction is: *a proposition cannot be both true and false at once*; and second, that the contradictories or negations of the true and false are not compatible, i.e., that there is nothing intermediate between the true and the false, or better that *it cannot happen that a proposition is neither true nor false.*
>
> (Leibniz 1982: 362, original emphasis)

In the formulation above, Leibniz includes the law of excluded middle –that for any proposition, either it is true or its negation is true – in his expression of the law of contradiction.

Both principles bear on Leibniz's account of truth. In a review of William Kings' *On Evil*, appended to the *Theodicy*, Leibniz writes that "one might say in a sense that these two principles are contained in the definition of the true and false" (1985: 419). According to Leibniz's notorious concept containment theory of truth, a categorical affirmative proposition is true just in case the concept of the predicate is contained in the concept of its subject. This theory appears to entail that all true propositions are analytic, which would have the catastrophic result that all truths are necessary. Leibniz denied that entailment by offering several accounts of contingency. According to the first, states of affairs in the actual world are contingent as long as they are 'possible in their nature', bracketing facts concerning God's attributes. According to the second, a proposition is contingent just in case there is no finite analysis of the predicate concept's containment in the subject concept.

Leibniz held that anything that is physical is in principle divisible. Since he held that a true substance must be a 'true unity', and hence indivisible, the only things that exist, according to his mature metaphysics, are immaterial entities called 'monads'. Since Leibniz also held that substances are by nature active, monads are the source of their own activity: each state is a causal consequence of its preceding state, save for its initial states and any action involving miraculous intervention by God. Indeed, Leibniz held that an action is an action of a substance if and only if that substance was the sole creaturely cause of that action; like Malebranche, Leibniz could make little sense of how created substances could causally interact with each other. It is only because of the pre-established harmony underwritten by God that (i) a particular mind appears to interact with 'its' body, and (ii) bodies appear to interact with other bodies, when there is no genuine interaction in either case.

NATURAL THEOLOGY

Leibniz brought his considerable analytical skills to bear on natural theology. In the *New Essays*, his spokesperson says: "I believe indeed that almost all the methods which have been used to prove the existence of God are sound, and could serve the purpose if they were rendered complete" (Leibniz 1982: 438).

Leibniz defended four arguments for God's existence: the ontological, cosmological and teleological arguments, and the argument from eternal truths. While the argument from design is perhaps the most well-known argument for the existence of God, Leibniz's version is highly idiosyncratic. Instead of the normal instances of order and purpose, for example Paley's watch and the human eye, Leibniz argues that the pre-established harmony could only be orchestrated by God.

Because the presentation in "On the Ultimate Origination of Things" is one of the most elegant expressions of the cosmological argument, I quote it at length:

> Let us suppose that a book on the elements of geometry has always existed, one copy always made from another. It is obvious that although we can explain a present copy of the book from the previous book from which it was copied, this will never lead us to a complete explanation, no matter how many books we go back, since we can always wonder why there have always been books, why these books were written, and why they were written as they were. What is true of these books ... [is true of world states. No matter how] far back we might go into previous states, we will never find in those states a complete explanation [*ratio*] for why, indeed, there is any world at all, and why it is the way it is. (Leibniz 1989: 149)

Unlike most previous versions of the cosmological argument that depend on the impossibility of an infinite regress of causes, Leibniz is willing to grant the possibility that the world is infinite. The argument proceeds as follows. A world, that is, the totality of contingent things, exists (for Leibniz, God is not in any possible world). There must be a sufficient reason for the existence and state of every contingent thing in the world. If the world is eternal, there is a sufficient reason for the existence and state of every contingent thing in the causal activity of some preceding state or entity. However, even if each thing in the world has a reason or explanation, what is left unexplained is why there is a world rather than nothing at all. Since nothing in the world can provide the sufficient reason for the world, the *ratio* must be located in something supramundane. Since the PSR will not be satisfied if the cause of the world is contingent, the ultimate explanation for the world must be some necessary being, and this is God.

Leibniz was proud of what he took to be a significant contribution to the ontological argument. He presented different formulations of the argument, which starts with the premise that, by definition, God is an absolutely perfect being, or the being with all perfections.

Leibniz held that: (i) in the absence of proof to the contrary, the burden of proof is on one who denies that the nature of God is contradictory; (ii) Descartes' form of the argument establishes only the conditional, 'if God is possible, God exists'; and (iii) the possibility of God can be demonstrated. Sometimes, Leibniz used reasoning borrowed from the cosmological argument to prove (iii). The idea is that the created world is possible just in case God is possible, since the existence of the world would violate the PSR were God not possible (and, indeed, actual). The pivotal part of the proof he presented to Spinoza depends on defining a perfection as a simple, absolutely positive property, and the assumption that if 'A perfect being is impossible' is false, it is necessarily false. Leibniz analyses a necessary truth as one that is an identity or is reducible to an identity. For 'A perfect being is impossible' to be necessarily true, there would have to be (at least) two perfections whose incompatibility is an identity or reducible to an identity. Because a property can be incompatible with another property only if one is the negation of the other, positive perfections are, by definition, compatible with all the other perfections. Secondly, since perfections are simple, they lack complexity and so are not reducible to anything more basic. Thus there will never be two positive, simple properties whose impossibility is either an identity nor reducible to an identity (Adams 1994: 135ff.; Blumenfeld 1995: 353ff.).

In addition to the above, Leibniz also offered a proof for God's existence from the reality of the eternal truths: "If there were no eternal substance, there would be no eternal truths; and from this too GOD can be proved, who is the root of possibility, for his mind is the very region of ideas or truths" (Leibniz 1973: 77). Leibniz assumed that logical space exists in the divine mind, including essences: ideas of all possible and necessary truths, including the ideas of possible individuals. The proof presupposes the thesis that there must be something in virtue of which any true proposition is true. Assuming this, there have been three alternative candidates for what there must be in virtue of which eternal truths are true. According to the first, Platonism, necessary truths exist objectively as abstract objects independent of ever being conceived or exemplified. According to the second, necessary truths have no objective, mind-independent reality, but are systems constructed by human thought. Leibniz rejected these first two, arguing instead for a third alternative, according to which necessary truths exist as ideas in the divine mind (Adams 1994: 177ff.).

PHILOSOPHICAL THEOLOGY

Leibniz devoted immense energy to issues in philosophical theology. In what follows, I sketch some of his views on the problems that the doctrines of divine providence and foreknowledge generate for human freedom. In the preface to the *Theodicy*, he writes:

> There are two famous labyrinths where our reason very often goes astray: one concerns the great question of the Free and the Necessary, above all in the production and the origin of Evil; the other consists in the discussion of continuity ... The first perplexes almost all the human race, the other exercises philosophers only. (Leibniz 1985: 53)

For Leibniz, questions concerning divine providence and foreknowledge, divine and human freedom and the problem of evil are inexorably linked; one cannot answer questions regarding any of these issues without a proper analysis of them all.

The question of how divine foreknowledge can be compatible with human freedom is nearly as old as Christianity itself. In the second century, Celsus argued for the falsity of Christianity on the basis that Christ's foreknowledge rendered Judas' betrayal necessary. Origen answered this challenge by claiming that Christ's foreknowledge of Judas' betrayal, while temporally prior, was not causally prior to the act. Commenting on the debate centuries later, Aquinas categorically rejects Origen's solution to this form of theological fatalism, stating that "the things that are going to happen are not themselves the causes of knowledge". This is because "God's knowledge is the cause of things. For God's knowledge stands to all created things as the artist's to his products. But the artist's knowledge is the cause of his products because he works through his intellect" (Aquinas 1964: vol. 4, 31). Aquinas' charge is that Origen's solution violates the doctrine of divine providence: the doctrine that God specifically decreed every thing and state in the created realm. According to the doctrine, God, the ideal artisan, actualizes a world where every determinate detail accords with his perfect plan. For Aquinas and those who follow him, God foreknows *because* he foreordains. Aquinas' emphasis on the causal element of providence greatly exacerbated the problem of human freedom.

The tension between Origen's and Aquinas' different interpretations of providence, foreknowledge and human freedom intensified in the last part of the sixteenth century. Following the crisis of the Protestant Reformation(s), Catholic leaders came together at the Council of Trent (1545–63) to delineate Christian orthodoxy from Protestant heresy. Because issues surrounding the exact understanding of providence, divine foreknowledge, grace and human freedom proved resistant to sharp resolution during the council, Catholic thinkers were there encouraged to continue working on these matters.

A famous proof-text in the late scholastic debate was 1 Samuel 23. While hiding from King Saul in Judah, David was informed that the Philistines were sacking the Hebrew city of Keilah. Through his priest, David asked God if he and his men should go and try to rescue the city. The book of Samuel states, "The Lord answered him, 'Go, attack the Philistines and save Keilah'" (1 Samuel 23:2). Tired and afraid of re-entering Saul's territory, David's men refused to leave their desert hideout. David once more turned to God, who through the ephod answered that if they went, they would defeat the Philistines. David and his men attacked, inflicted heavy losses on the Philistines, and saved Keilah.

The story does not end there. Saul, on learning that his quarry was finally in a walled city, immediately called his army to arms. When David heard that Saul's army was mobilizing, he questioned God once again. He was told that if they remained, the citizens would hand him over to Saul. In light of this knowledge, David and his band of six hundred slipped quietly into the desert. When Saul learned of David's escape, he demobilized and cancelled the Keilah campaign.

Let 'Shlomo' be the name of the Keilahite who would have freely turned David over to Saul, had David remained in Keilah. What God knew, then, was a proposition of this kind: 'If placed in the relevant, fully specified siege conditions, Shlomo would freely turn over David' (call this proposition *S*). Here is the puzzle. *S* is a counterfactual, which means that while *S* is true, the circumstances it described never did nor will occur. What makes it true, and in virtue of what does God know it? This last question strikes most of us as odd. Well, we might say, God knows *S* in virtue of being omniscient. This answer was absolutely unacceptable to medieval and early modern thinkers. Why? Leibniz hints at the reasons in an early letter:

> God either does not decree concerning everything or, if he does decree concerning everything, then he is the author of absolutely everything. Both alternatives involve difficulties. For if God decrees concerning everything and things are in conflict with his decree, he will not be omnipotent. However, if he does not decree concerning everything, it seems to follow that he is not omniscient. For it seems impossible that an omniscient being suspends his judgment about anything.
>
> (Leibniz 2005: 3)

While the first conditional is easy to follow, the second is not. Leibniz, following Aquinas, is emphasizing that the lead doctrine is divine providence, not foreknowledge, which is to say that God foreknows because he foreordains. Indeed, the austere consequence of God's radical independence from the mundane order of causally interacting objects is that all of God's knowledge is self-knowledge.

It is at this point that the Jesuit and Dominican accounts diverge. The Dominican forces were led by Domingo Bañez, better known today as the friend, confessor and spiritual advisor to St Theresa of Avila. Bañez's interpretation of Aquinas held that God knows all necessary truths in virtue of knowing his intelligence, and knows all that will happen in the created realm, including the free choices of created agents, through knowledge of his will. Bañez explained God's knowledge of counterfactuals of creaturely freedom – truths like *S* – in virtue of knowing what he would have done had he created a world in which the counterfactual circumstances were actual.

His Jesuit opponent, Luis de Molina, denounced Bañez to the Inquisition at Castile, arguing that Bañezianism was Lutheranism and Calvinism in Thomist garb, and hence absolutely destructive of human freedom. Bañez returned the favour, charging that Molina's claim that human beings can resist God's grace was Pelagian. Three general models of the causal powers of created substances were available to medieval and early modern philosophers. Occasionalists held that creatures have no causal powers, while deists held that God completes his contribution at creation, and thus that creatures need no divine contribution for action. Most philosophers in this period accepted a position between these two poles, according to which created substances have causal powers, although God must cooperate or concur to bring about the action in question. Molina's theory of freedom – now called 'libertarianism' – holds that an agent is free only when there are no antecedent conditions, including God's general causal contribution to the agent, that are sufficient for the occurrence of that choice.

Molina agreed with Bañez that God knows all necessary truths in virtue of knowing his intelligence, but denied that God knows the free choices of created agents through knowledge of his will, for were that the case the choices known would not be free. Therefore Molina argued that the knowledge God has of the free choices of created agents is outside his control – otherwise they would not be free – and hence are known 'pre-volitionally', that is, (conceptually) prior to and independent of his choice to actualize a particular world. Molina explained God's knowledge of counterfactuals of creaturely freedom – truths like *S* – in virtue of God's pre-volitionally knowing how those agents would have freely chosen had he created a world in which the counterfactual circumstances were actual.

Both theories are problematic. The Dominican position satisfies a robust interpretation of providence. It also explains what makes counterfactuals true and how God knows them, in addition to satisfying the PSR. The cost is that it seems to preclude creaturely freedom and make God the author of sin. The Jesuit position satisfies a robust, libertarian interpretation of freedom. It also explains what makes counterfactuals true. The cost is that it offers a lacuna rather than an explanation of how God knows them, and denies the PSR.

In the next century, the revolutionary but ever prudential Descartes carefully avoided these problems, noting that while it is: "impious to suppose that we could ever do anything which was not already ordained by him ... we can easily get ourselves into great difficulties if we attempt to reconcile this divine preordination with the freedom of our will, or attempt to grasp both things at once" (Descartes 1985: 206). Commenting on this passage, Leibniz replied that:

> Anyone who is convinced that God preordains all things but that he himself is free, and who is shown the conflict between these views but replies only what Descartes recommends, namely, that his mind is finite and cannot grasp such matters, seems to me to be answering the conclusions rather than the argument and to be cutting rather than untying the knot ... There should surely be no contradiction even in the mysteries of faith; much less so in the mysteries of nature. If we wish to stand out as philosophers, we must once again take up the argument ... (Leibniz 1969: 389)

Leibniz believed that part of his calling as a Christian philosopher was "to place reason at the service of faith ... to support and harmonize what the light of nature and the light of reason teach us of God and man", and that an orthodox resolution to these problems was a perfect test case for a sound metaphysics (1985: 123).

Leibniz's *via media* was to side with Molina that the knowledge God has of the free choices of created agents is outside his control, which are hence known 'pre-volitionally'. As we shall see in the next section, this is an important plank in Leibniz's reply to the problem of evil. However, he sides with Bañez in charging that the libertarian account of human freedom Molinism presupposes must be rejected as in violation of a bedrock foundation of a true metaphysics, the PSR. For Leibniz, the only way to satisfy the non-negotiable condition that there be grounds for God's foreknowledge of future free choices – say, Peter's denial of Christ – is that there be antecedent facts about Peter causally sufficient for that choice.

Leibniz, like his contemporaries, held that the complete concept of an individual substance – say Peter – contains propositions concerning every property the substance would have, were it to exist. Unlike his contemporaries, however, Leibniz held that the complete concept of Peter could not have been otherwise, in the sense that had the concept been otherwise, it would not be the complete concept of Peter. This is to say that individual substances, actual or possible, are world-bound. This is not the trivial claim that a non-denying Peter would have a different concept than the one he does; rather, it is the claim that a non-denying Peter is not Peter. This has the consequence that when speaking with metaphysical rigour, there are no counterfactuals. How does God know truths about merely possible and never actual individuals? It is not by the correspondence theory of truth, realistically construed, since the truths described are never actual. By contrast, Leibniz's complete concept theory of substance, and the corresponding complete concept theory of truth, neatly explain God's knowledge thereof. Such knowledge, of course, is necessary for God to providentially choose to actualize the one world that is the best among the infinity of possible worlds.

THEODICY AND PROBLEMS OF EVIL

Leibniz's philosophy is centred on God's creation of the world and his subsequent relation to it. He was keenly sensitive to the fact that various orthodox doctrines, among them providence, divine creation, preservation and concurrence, coupled with the existence of evil, seem to deny God's perfect goodness, holiness, mercy and justice. Such problems and the strategies for justifying God in the face of these problems – he coined the term '*théodicée*' for such enterprises – preoccupied Leibniz early and late in his career. He wrote two book-length studies on such problems, the latter, the *Theodicy*, being the only book he published in his life. His lead reply to these objections, surprisingly enough, was to argue that this is the best possible world. Leibniz's reasoning begins innocently enough with the orthodox view that the perfect being, deciding to diffuse his goodness by creating a world, considers the infinite possible worlds, sees that this world – the possible world now actual – is the best, and so creates it. One might think that not only is the above account orthodox, but that it is required by orthodoxy. After all, God, being omniscient, sees all possible worlds, being omnipotent, can create any of them, and being morally perfect, will choose the best world. Since the PSR is true and this is the world God created, this must be the best of all possible worlds. As is well known, Leibniz's conclusion struck most of his readers, from then to now, as something of a joke, and one in bad taste at that. Before considering that judgement, however, it is worth noting that the above account plays two complementary roles: first as an account of the creation and value of this world, and secondly as an answer to the problem of evil.

There are many versions of the problem of evil. Today it is customary to distinguish the logical problem of evil from the evidential problem of evil. According to the first, the existence of evil – considered chiefly as suffering – is (logically) incompatible with the traditional view of God. For if God is omniscient, he knew all the possibilities for creation, if omnipotent, he could have created any world, and if morally perfect he would have created a world without suffering. But since there is suffering, God does not exist. This argument has lost most of its currency, even among atheists. First, even if sound, it is not an argument for atheism *per se*, but only an argument that a certain conception of God is impossible. More importantly, all a theist needs to do to rebut the argument is to show that it is logically possible for God to have a morally sufficient reason for allowing some evil. Since this is not difficult to show, recent attention has focused on the evidential version of the problem of evil. The advocate of this argument notes that there might well be morally sufficient reasons for God allowing suffering, such as bringing about some greater good, or preventing some worse evil. However, what is incompatible with the traditional view of God's nature is the evidence of pointless suffering, that is, suffering that neither brings about a greater good nor prevents a worse evil. Since our world does contain pointless suffering – consider some of the suffering of non-human animals – God as traditionally conceived does not exist. The problems Leibniz was addressing were closer to the second than the first. For example, one group of opponents Leibniz wrote against were the Socinians; they were theists, but attempted to explain away what they saw as obscurities or contradictions in the Bible. They denied the Incarnation, thought the doctrine of the Trinity incoherent, and believed that the existence of evil showed that God was neither omniscient nor omnipotent.

The following problems are those that most occupied Leibniz. First, it seems that God is implicated in evil by allowing sins that he could have prevented. Secondly, it seems that God is implicated in evil by concurring with, that is, causally contributing to, sinful actions: actions that would not occur had he withdrawn his general concurrence. Thirdly, it seems that God is implicated in evil because he providentially creates just the world he wants, yet this world contains many who will be punished eternally for sins they appear unable to avoid. Fourthly, it seems that God is implicated in evil because the bestowal of salvation is utterly gratuitous, yet those not given grace sufficient for salvation are damned forever (Sleigh 2001).

Leibniz's most general answer to the charge that the nature of the world imputes moral imperfection to God was to argue that, appearances to the contrary, this is the best possible world. Leibniz was sensitive to the criticism that a world just like ours, lacking some token of evil, such as, say, the 2008 cyclone in Myanmar, and whatever follows from the omission of that particular weather pattern, would be a better world than this one. What justified Leibniz's confidence that this kind of objection is mistaken? First, Leibniz believed that it was demonstrable that God, a perfect being, exists. Given that this world exists, we know that God created it. Given that God decided to diffuse and communicate his goodness, there must be a sufficient reason for creating this world. The only reason that would be sufficient for God creating this world is that it is the best of all possible worlds.

Leibniz also had more detailed responses to the critic represented in the last paragraph. First, he pointed out that we lack the perspective to claim that a world like ours but minus Cyclone Nargis, and whatever follows from its omission, would be better than this one. We do not understand the connections between events; why should we think that it is probable, or even certain, that the omission of the relevant antecedent weather patterns would have led to better global results? In this connection, Leibniz would have welcomed recent advances in science that illustrate how a very minute difference in some conditions early on have global consequences for the total system downstream. Leibniz also noted that we tend to focus on what is best for a (very small) part of the world, rather than the world – past, present and future – as a whole. We might be inclined, for example, to say that a world is the best world just in case any token of the world, considered in isolation, is good. Another mistake Leibniz diagnoses is our tendency to assume mistaken standards of world goodness. For example, it is tempting to assume that some anthropocentric standard – say maximizing the happiness of human beings on earth – is what constitutes the best world. Leibniz replied that the proposed standard is too species-centric; why, he asks, should the standard not be expanded to include the happiness of all sentient beings, or perhaps all rational beings, many of which might not be human. If terrestrial human beings constitute merely a small fraction of the beings for whom God considers happiness, any purely anthropocentric standard is mistaken.

Leibniz's positive characterizations of the correct standard of world goodness differ across texts. The candidates seem to be that the best world is one: (i) that maximizes the happiness of rational beings; or (ii) that maximizes the greatest 'quantity of essence'; or (iii) in which the greatest variety of phenomena are governed by the simplest set of laws. Leibniz scholars differ as to which standard, or combination of standards, Leibniz is ultimately committed to, but for our purposes it suffices to note that, in contrast to even a quasi-anthropocentric criterion, at least two of Leibniz's standards are austerely metaphysical. Notice as well that (iii), a standard he offers in many texts, allows Leibniz to offer more details concerning why a world lacking Cyclone Nargis is worse than this one. For the only way God could have prevented the cyclone, without changing the past, would be to change the laws, presumably by rendering them more complex, thus violating (iii). We might, along with Voltaire, insist that saving 130,000 Burmese lives is patently more valuable than a world producing the greatest variety of phenomena consistent with the simplest natural laws. Whether this is so I leave to others. The relevant point is that Leibniz's defence of (iii) does not imply that Leibniz did not care about human misery; he devoted much of his life attempting to eradicate religious and political differences that, among other things, had led to the horror that was the Thirty Years' War. It is rather that, while forward-looking on many fronts, he shared with many of his contemporaries, such as Malebranche, the view that it is unworthy of God to intervene much, if ever, in the created realm. That such views regarding the consequences of divine majesty have lost most of their currency does not make Leibniz misanthropic (Murray 2005).

Leibniz's solutions to various threats to divine perfection underwent revision over his career. A case in point is the privation theodicy associated with Augustine, Aquinas and other scholastics. According to the theory, evil is a lack of being, a lack of reality. Blindness, for example, is a lack of sight proper to a human being. However, since it is a lack of seeing, vision being the positive reality, blindness is only a negation or privation, and thus there is nothing for God to be responsible for. Early on Leibniz remarked that this is "as though someone were a cause of the number three and wanted to deny that he was a cause of its oddness" (Leibniz 2005: 23). Yet by the end of his life, he endorsed a version of the theodicy he earlier thought to be a wretched subterfuge. The story of that attitudinal shift is still poorly understood. Three other justifications are endorsed throughout most of his career. One justification was the claim that the source of sin was contained in the divine intellect, and not the divine will. The main idea is that when God creates or actualizes a world, that world contains many of its features independent of God's will or antecedent desire. These features include the free choices of human beings, were they actual. This relates to Leibniz's claim that God decrees the good features of the world, and merely permits the evil. This in turn is understood as a modified version of the greater good justification, according to which God is justified in permitting evil only if permitting that evil is necessary for God in discharging his moral obligation to himself. Failing to create the best of all possible worlds – in which sin plays a necessary role – would have been a failure of his obligation to himself to communicate his goodness by creating the best of all possible worlds.

The most perplexing justification of God's perfections is Leibniz's claim that individuals are world-bound; for example, any counterpart in another possible world that fails to betray Jesus is not Judas. Put negatively, Judas cannot complain that he lacks the grace to resist betrayal, since without the betrayal, he would not be Judas. Put positively, this is the best possible world because it is the only world that contains Jesus Christ.

LEIBNIZ'S SINCERITY

Bertrand Russell's monumental *A Critical Exposition of the Philosophy of Leibniz*, first published in 1900, helped launch Leibniz's stature as a philosopher of the first order in the English-language world. In the preface to the second edition (1937), Russell writes that Leibniz:

> had a good philosophy which (after Arnauld's criticisms) he kept to himself, and a bad philosophy which he published with a view to fame and money. In this he showed his usual acumen: his bad philosophy was admired for its bad qualities, and his good philosophy, which was known only to the editors of MSS., was regarded by them as worthless and left unpublished … I think it probable that as he grew older he forgot the good philosophy which he kept to himself, and remembered only the vulgarized version by which he had won the admiration of Princes and (even more) of Princesses. (1937: x)

There is powerful evidence against Russell's dissimulation hypothesis, according to which Leibniz had two distinct philosophies, one private and the other public. First, Leibniz's private philosophy, the mass of writings that were unpublished in Leibniz's day, are of a piece with the public writings (much of this material was not available to Russell); it turns out that there is no recognizable private philosophy as such that differs significantly from his published work.

Secondly, during his happy but too brief years in Paris, Leibniz worked to put off returning to Hanover, an intellectual backwater. By the late 1690s he began complaining to correspondents of the cost of his intellectual isolation. Despite his manifest unhappiness, he later declined offers for the head librarianships of the Vatican and later of Paris because he was unwilling to convert to Catholicism (Ross 1984: 6). Despite his admiration for and friendship with many influential Catholics, it is hard to deny that his Lutheranism, his chosen expression of Christianity, mattered to him.

Thirdly, in important exchanges – with Arnauld in 1686–87, and with Locke's philosophy in the early 1700s in the *New Essays* (intended for publication) – Leibniz does not shrink from defending core (and often wildly idiosyncratic) doctrines that his interlocutor disagreed with, sometimes with passion (think Arnauld). This is hardly the behaviour of a thinker with a crypto-philosophy.

Fourthly, removing God from Leibniz's philosophy does not just strain his metaphysics; rather, without God, there is no system. Works viewed today as central, if somewhat cryptic, expressions of his metaphysics – the so-called *Discourse on Metaphysics* and *Monadology* – do not simply include God: they are explications of God and his creation.

FURTHER READING

Antognazza, M. 2007. *Leibniz on the Trinity and the Incarnation: Reason and Revelation in the Seventeenth Century*, G. Parks (trans.). New Haven, CT: Yale University Press.
Broad, C. 1975. *Leibniz: An Introduction*. Cambridge: Cambridge University Press.
Brown, S. 1984. *Leibniz*. Brighton: Harvester.
Cover, J. & D. Rutherford (eds) 2005. *Leibniz: Nature and Freedom*. New York: Oxford University Press.
Jolley, N. 2005. *Leibniz*. London: Routledge.
Mates, B. 1986. *The Philosophy of Leibniz*. New York: Oxford University Press.
Mercer, C. 2000. *Leibniz's Metaphysics: Its Origins and Development*. Cambridge: Cambridge University Press.
Rutherford, D. 1995. *Leibniz and the Rational Order of Nature*. Cambridge: Cambridge University Press.
Savile, A. 2000. *Leibniz and the Monadology*. London: Routledge.
Sleigh, R., Jr 1990. *Leibniz and Arnauld: A Commentary on their Correspondence*. New Haven, CT: Yale University Press.
Wilson, C. 1989. *Leibniz's Metaphysics: A Historical and Comparative Study*. Princeton, NJ: Princeton University Press.

On EVIL/PROBLEM OF EVIL see also Chs 18, 19; Vol. 1, Chs 18, 19; Vol. 2, Ch. 16; Vol. 4, Chs 12, 18; Vol. 5, Chs 19, 22, 23. On EXISTENCE OF GOD see also Chs 6, 12, 14, 15, 21; Vol. 1, Chs 18, 19; Vol. 2, Chs 5, 6, 13, 14; Vol. 5, Chs 11, 16. On FOREKNOWLEDGE see also Vol. 2, Chs 2, 6. On NATURAL RELIGION/THEOLOGY see also Chs 4, 6, 7, 11, 12, 19, 23; Vol. 4, Chs 8, 12; Vol. 5, Ch. 23. On TRUTH see also Chs 3, 8; Vol. 1, Ch. 13; Vol. 2, Ch. 17; Vol. 4, Chs 8, 18; Vol. 5, Ch. 4.

14

GEORGE BERKELEY

Roomet Jakapi

George Berkeley (1685–1753), Irish philosopher and Anglican cleric, was born in County Kilkenny. He studied at Kilkenny College and Trinity College, Dublin, graduating from Trinity College in 1704. A few years later, in 1707, he received his MA and was elected a fellow. He was ordained a priest in 1710.

Berkeley's first major work, *An Essay Towards A New Theory of Vision* (hereafter *New Theory of Vision*), appeared in 1709. The book is a significant contribution to the study of visual perception. Berkeley's views in metaphysics and epistemology are famously advanced in *A Treatise Concerning The Principles of Human Knowledge* (hereafter *Principles*; 1710) and *Three Dialogues between Hylas and Philonous* (hereafter *Three Dialogues*; 1713). The discourse *Passive Obedience* (1712) offers a theoretical account of moral and political issues.

Between 1713 and 1720, Berkeley spent time in London and travelled on the Continent. In 1721 he received the degree Doctor of Divinity and published *De motu* (Of motion), a tract on natural philosophy. He was appointed Dean of Derry in 1724. He married Anne Forster in 1728, and from 1729 to 1731 he lived with his family on Rhode Island. Berkeley wanted to found a college in Bermuda but did not receive the financial support he was promised and thus returned to London. After the years in America he published another influential work, *Alciphron, or the Minute Philosopher* (hereafter *Alciphron*; 1732). He also published *The Theory of Vision, Vindicated and Explained* (1733), and a critique of the calculus, *The Analyst* (1734), followed by *A Defence of Free-Thinking in Mathematics* (1735). In 1734 Berkeley became Bishop of Cloyne. He wrote on economics in *The Querist* (1735–7), and his last book, *Siris: A Chain of Philosophical Reflections and Inquiries* (1744), provides a broad philosophical account of the world, starting from the virtues of tar-water and ending with the Holy Trinity. Berkeley died and is buried in Oxford.

Berkeley is best known for his idealist metaphysics and empiricist epistemology. His contribution to the philosophy of religion can be divided into three branches: arguments for the existence of God, discussions on the theological foundations of morality and, finally, accounts of the meaningfulness of religious language.

ARGUMENTS FOR THE EXISTENCE OF GOD

Berkeley produced three (more or less distinct) arguments for the existence of God.[1] Two of these are to be found in his widely read works, the *Principles* and *Three Dialogues*. As both arguments involve specific premises derived from his metaphysical system, it is first necessary to get an overview of the system.

In Berkeley's ontology, two kinds of entities – minds (spirits) and (their) ideas – exist. Minds are substances, perceiving and acting beings. Ideas are ontologically dependent on minds; they exist only in as much as they are perceived by minds. Ideas exist *in* minds but they are nonetheless distinct from minds: they are not properties, attributes or modifications of the mind.

Minds are spiritual substances and these are the only substances there are. The words 'mind', 'spirit' and 'substance' refer in effect to one and the same thing. There are no material substances in Berkeley's world. Bodies such as trees and mountains are collections of ideas as perceived by spirits. Different bodies are composed of different collections of ideas, that is, different combinations of smell, figure, taste, motion, colour and other ideas of sense. There are no external, material bodies or qualities to produce or cause those ideas in the mind. Nor are the ideas of reflection or those "formed by help of memory and imagination" produced by matter (*Principles* §§1, 25). Both the so-called primary and secondary qualities of bodies are nothing but ideas perceived by minds (§§9–15).

The mind or spirit is a simple, non-composite substance: "as it perceives ideas, it is called the *understanding*, and as it produces or otherwise operates about them, it is called the *will*" (§27). Perception as such is a passive reception of ideas. Yet the mind is essentially active in as much as it "operates about" ideas. The active, "thinking things" are the only causes. Ideas are entirely passive, causally inert. We, human beings or minds, have some causal power over the ideas of imagination. Also, we are able to act, to move our fingers, for example, and thus cause some changes in the "realm" of sensible ideas (see Fleming 2006).

In Berkeley's view, there is one eternal and infinite mind, spirit or substance – God – who has created a system of finite spirits or substances such as angels and human minds (souls). The status of animal minds remains somewhat unclear. According to Berkeley, animals perceive and, thus, are not mere collections of ideas, but it seems that he would not allow that animals have minds in the sense of spiritual substances.

1. For the view that Berkeley did not offer three different arguments but rather employed a single strategy of inference in different contexts, see Jesseph (2005).

God has also created bodies, or "sensible objects", "sensible things", "real things", but these are not external, material bodies as explained above. God regularly produces certain collections of sensible ideas in human minds in accordance with the laws of nature, which are established by his will. The bodily or sensible world is in human minds in so far as it is perceived by them, but it is also in God's mind (understanding) since he knows all things eternally and also knows the ideas he actually produces in us.

The first argument for the existence of God is set out in sections 25–33 of the *Principles*. It begins with the observation that "all our ideas, sensations, or the things which we perceive, by whatsoever names they may be distinguished", are passive. Ideas, including those of extension, figure, motion, rest, solidity and number, exist only in the mind and are transparent to the mind. No power, agency or activity is to be found in them. Nor can they represent (by resemblance) "any active being" (*Principles* §25). For, according to Berkeley, "an idea can be like nothing but another idea" (§8). Hence the familiar supposition that the ideas of sense are caused by extension, figure and motion is false (§25).

Furthermore, we perceive "a continual succession of ideas" and there must be some cause of those ideas. The cause must be a substance since ideas cannot cause anything. As there is no material substance, the cause must be a spiritual substance (§26). I know my mind is active in as much as I can "excite ideas in my mind at pleasure, and vary and shift the scene as oft as I think fit. It is no more than willing, and straightaway this or that idea arises in my fancy" (§28). However, "the ideas actually perceived by sense have not a like dependence on my will. When in broad day-light I open my eyes, it is not in my power to choose whether I shall see or no, or to determine what particular objects shall present themselves to my view". In other words, the ideas of sense are typically not "creatures of my will". So, they must be produced by "some other will or spirit" (§29). The ideas perceived by the senses are "more strong, lively, and distinct" than those formed by the imagination. They are more stable, orderly and coherent, produced "in a regular train or series, the admirable connexion whereof sufficiently testifies the wisdom and benevolence of its Author" (§30). These ideas, then, must be produced "by the will of another and more powerful spirit" (§33).

Thus, Berkeley first eliminates material substance and *external* bodies and qualities. His argument starts from the premise that ideas of sense are "visibly inactive", causally passive. He then asks what is the cause of the perceived "continuous succession" of these ideas, and concludes it to be a spiritual substance much more powerful than we are. Most of these ideas are independent of human will and, therefore, must be produced by God's will. The last move in the argument, from the ideas of sense as contradistinguished with those of the imagination, to the goodness, wisdom and power of God, is done by a reference to the "admirable" design of the sensible world.

The second argument, found in the second of the *Three Dialogues*, starts with the familiar premise that "sensible things cannot exist otherwise than in a mind or spirit" (*Works* 2: 212). This time, however, the argument runs in a different direction; namely, towards God's intellect. The sensible things, or the ideas I perceive by my senses, "depend not on my thought", that is, they arise in my mind independently of my will: "it being not in my power to determine at pleasure, what particular ideas I shall be affected with upon opening my eyes or ears" (*ibid.*: vol. 2, 214). From this it follows that sensible things, though perceived by me, *exist* independently of my mind: they "have an existence distinct from being perceived by me" (*ibid.*: vol. 2, 212). But to exist independently of my mind is to be perceived by some other mind. There is, therefore, "some other mind wherein they exist", and by whom they are perceived. The whole sensible world is perceived by "an infinite, omnipresent spirit, who contains and supports it". God perceives, or rather "knows and comprehends" the created world (*ibid.*). The sensible things actually perceived by me exist in the mind of God. So do they exist "during the intervals between the times of my perceiving them", as Berkeley explains in the third dialogue (*ibid.*: vol. 2, 230ff.).

The existence of the divine mind or perceiver follows from the fact that the sensible things are ontologically independent of human minds. The ontological independence (distinct existence) of the sensible things is inferred from their causal independence of human minds (see Ayers 1996: xxxi–xxxiii). How or in what sense the temporal sensible things or ideas exist in or are perceived by God's infinite mind is not made clear. Berkeley considers it sufficient to assert that "these ideas or things by me perceived, either themselves or their archetypes, exist" in God's mind (*Works* 2: 214). The things I perceive by my senses "are known by the understanding, and produced by the will, of an infinite spirit" (*ibid.*: vol. 2, 215).

Berkeley's third argument is foreshadowed in the *New Theory of Vision* and stated in an elaborate form in dialogue IV of *Alciphron*. The complex argument of *Alciphron* starts with a reformulation of the traditional argument from design, but then it turns into the specifically Berkeleyan 'divine language' argument.

Berkeley relies on the general premise "that the being of things imperceptible to sense may be collected from effects and signs, or sensible tokens" (*Alciphron* IV.4). Thus, for example, one can infer from motions perceived by sense the existence of "a mover or cause", and from "reasonable motions (or such as appear calculated for a reasonable end)" one can conclude the existence of "a rational cause, soul or spirit" (*ibid.*). The motions in question are sensible effects or signs, and the cause responsible for the production of these effects is inferred from them by reason.

Whereas human bodies are "actuated" by the souls to which they belong, most natural motions in the world, including the motions of heavenly bodies as well as the inner motions of animal and vegetable bodies, are independent of human will. The "natural productions and effects" follow from the same universal laws of motion, which hold always and everywhere. The "animals and vegetables", "the elements and heavenly bodies", appear to be wisely interrelated and organized, so that "they may be collected to be parts of one whole, conspiring to one and the same end, and fulfilling the same design". The wonderful design of the natural world manifests the infinite power and wisdom of a rational designer, "one and the same Agent, Spirit, or Mind" (IV.5).

Furthermore, in Berkeley's view, the existence of God is known to me as certainly and obviously as the existence of human persons distinct from me: persons as "individual thinking things", "invisible thinking principles", souls or spirits. I infer the existence of another human soul from certain "visible signs and tokens", such as the appearance and motions of the body that it "actuates". Likewise, I conclude from the signs, tokens and effects in nature which are independent of human will that they are brought forth by the Infinite Spirit (*ibid.*).

The presence and existence of another person is most evident when the person speaks to me. In a similar manner, Berkeley thinks that the most compelling evidence of the existence of God is provided by the fact that God speaks to human beings (IV.6). He does so "by the intervention and use of arbitrary, outward, sensible signs" which have "no resemblance or necessary connexion with the things they stand for and suggest". Such a use of signs is constitutive of any language, whether natural or artificial, human or divine. In a natural human language, words (spoken or written) are the sensible signs (sounds and characters) that are "arbitrarily" made to stand for certain things (IV.7). The language God speaks to us is the Visual Language. It is formed by visual appearances in our minds (ideas of sight, visible ideas) that "suggest" or "signify" (certain qualities of) tangible things. According to Berkeley's novel theory of visual perception put forth in the *New Theory of Vision*, the proper and immediate objects of sight are only light and colours. The "distance, magnitude, and situation" of (external) tangible objects cannot be seen immediately but only by the mediation of those immediate objects of vision (*New Theory of Vision* §§1, 2). "There is no resemblance between ideas of sight and things tangible", Berkeley says (§117). Nor is there a "necessary connection" between them. Visual objects are "arbitrary" signs that "suggest" tactile objects, just as words in a natural language "suggest" the things they signify. Thus "the proper objects of vision constitute a universal language of the Author of Nature" (§147). Similarly, in *Alciphron*, Berkeley states that "the proper objects of sight are light and colors, with their several shades and degrees; all which, being infinitely diversified and combined, form a language wonderfully adapted to suggest and exhibit to us the distances, figures, situations, dimensions, and various qualities of tangible objects" (*Alciphron* IV.10). God has "arbitrarily" connected these two distinct kinds of objects. He constantly speaks to our eyes, informing us about the tangible objects and directing our actions towards them. We learn this language gradually, from early childhood, so that our knowledge of "the connection between the signs and things signified" becomes habitual (IV.11).

Although the latter argument, unlike the two former ones, is consistent with the existence of external material things or bodies, it nonetheless suggests that visual appearances are produced directly by the will of God, not by such bodies.

For Berkeley, "this optic language" is, in fact, "equivalent to a constant creation" (IV.14).

GOD AND MORALITY

Berkeley's general stance on morality, both on the theoretical and the practical plane, was that it ought not to, and in effect cannot, be separated from religion. His ideas and arguments in the field reflect a deep and growing worry that such a pretended separation of ethics from religion has already taken place in the minds of several freethinking dissenters. Developments in this direction, he thought, would have disastrous consequences for society in general. He clearly followed a conservative line of thought according to which religion is a pillar of all civil society. Thus, in *A Discourse Addressed to Magistrates and Men in Authority* (1738), he declares that "obedience to all civil power is rooted in the religious fear of God" (*Works* 6: 208) and "without a religious principle men can never be fit materials for any society" (*ibid.*: vol. 6, 210). He also asserts in the same tract that religious notions ought to be "early imbibed" in people's minds, "before their grounds and reasons are apprehended or understood" (*ibid.*: vol. 6, 203). These notions or "prejudices", he holds, have a particularly good and strong influence on the moral and social behaviour of people throughout their lives. Prejudices differ from other opinions in that they are accepted on trust, not "acquired by reasoning". Some prejudices, above all "the prevailing notions of order, virtue, duty, and Providence", are *true* and very *useful* (*ibid.*: vol. 6, 202ff., 211). As most people will never be able to examine those "salutary notions" and find out their truth by reasoning, they ought simply to assent to them, and think and act in accordance with them.

Berkeley's passionate opposition to ethical egoism, sensual hedonism, relativism and secularism is vividly expressed in dialogues I–III of *Alciphron*. The work aims to defend the Christian religion against those he calls "free-thinkers", "deists" or "minute philosophers". Berkeley's targets, although not mentioned in the text by name, are such non-conformist thinkers as Anthony Collins, Bernard Mandeville, John Toland and several others. He takes the starting-point of the moral discourses of his freethinking enemies to be the view that "every wise man looks upon himself, or his own bodily existence in this present world, as the centre and ultimate end of all his actions and regards" (*Alciphron* I.9). The proper aim of one's actions, according to the view, is to gain and enjoy sensual pleasures, that is, the "natural good things", the "real objects" of one's "appetites, passions, and senses".

The freethinkers want to "bring us down to the maxims and way of thinking of the most uneducated and barbarous nations", Berkeley warns, "and even to degrade human-kind to a level with the brute beasts" whose happiness consists in nothing else but bodily pleasures. Furthermore, according to their godless "system", "there is no Providence, no spirit, no future state, no moral duty" (I.13). In response to this barbaric way of thinking, Berkeley contends that the faculty of reason is as natural to human beings as are the senses, passions and appetites. People entertain "many different and inconsistent" opinions concerning God and moral duty, but some opinions, notions and tenets may well be true and demonstrable by reason (I.14–15). What reason tells us is that the "general well-being" or happiness of humankind is a greater good than the "private happiness" of an individual, or of a certain group of people. The happiness of an individual is dependent on the happiness of others. A truly wise rational agent, then, pursues the greater good or end, the general well-being of humankind, by following certain moral principles, which, Berkeley thinks, have a "necessary connexion" with that end (I.16).

The pursuit of merely personal interest, which in the freethinkers' opinion consists in sensual pleasure, leads to several vices such as "drunkenness" and "gaming". Those, however, are not necessarily bad, or, at least, so Mandeville had argued in his *Fable of the Bees* ([1714] 1988). In dialogue II of *Alciphron*, Berkeley objects to Mandeville's idea that private vices are public benefits in as much as they circulate money and promote industry, and thus contribute to the public good. Healthy people with numerous offspring, Berkeley says, will in the long run consume much more and contribute more to the well-being of the nation than "fashionable rakes" who die young in sickness, misery and loneliness. The latter are very poor in "the art of computing" pleasures, as they do not consider different kinds of pleasure or the long-term consequences of their actions. Berkeley suggests a hierarchy of pleasures: the highest and most lasting are the pleasures of reason, then those of imagination and, lastly, the fleeting pleasures of sense that we have in common with animals. The happiness of a human being necessarily includes the higher pleasures and cannot be found without considering the happiness of other people.

It is by means of the faculty of reason that we judge whether an action is morally right or wrong, just or unjust, Berkeley explains in dialogue III. Contrary to the positions of the 3rd Earl of Shaftesbury and Francis Hutcheson, Berkeley rejects the "moral or interior sense", a specific faculty allegedly responsible for the perception of the "beauty of virtue" or of the "moral beauty" of our actions. There is no moral sense analogous to sight and other senses. Even the beauty of visible objects, consisting "in a certain symmetry or proportion pleasing to the eye", is properly perceived "by reason through the means of sight". In moral matters, reason, not the falsely supposed interior sense, is our guide.

On the whole, Berkeley maintains in *Alciphron* that morality cannot do without the notions of divine providence, freedom of the will, immortality of the soul, a future state of rewards and punishments, and duties prescribed by God. Morality is a branch of natural religion.

The eschatological dimension of Berkeley's ethics is manifest in the discourse *Passive Obedience*, originally delivered as three sermons. When addressing the issue of considering the consequences of our moral actions, he makes it clear that the ultimate end of human actions is *eternal* happiness, not any "temporal advantage". Only God, "a sovereign omniscient Spirit", "can make us for ever happy, or for ever miserable" (*Passive Obedience* §6). The only way to the bliss in heaven is obedience to God's laws, which can be found out both by reasoning and by reading the Scriptures. These laws are instituted by God's will and are, thus, binding on his rational creatures.

The human being has a body and a mind, and thus belongs to both the *natural* and the *moral* world. God governs and directs the natural world by means of physical laws such as "the universal law of gravitation" (§27). In a similar way, God governs the moral world by means of moral laws of nature such as 'Thou shalt not forswear thyself', 'Thou shalt not commit adultery' and 'Thou shalt not steal'. To the list of God-given moral rules or laws Berkeley adds, "Thou shalt not resist the supreme power" (§15). A principal difference between these two kinds of law is that the moral laws "imply a duty" (which presupposes human free will) whereas the physical laws do not (§33). Both kinds of law are immutable and universal, that is, they apply always and everywhere. The laws will apply even in situations where God's direct intervention, and a suspension of a relevant law, might well prevent much damage and suffering. "The Author of nature", Berkeley explains, "acts according to certain fixed laws, which He will not transgress upon the account of accidental evils arising from them" (§27). The evils or sufferings in question will be compensated in the afterlife (§42).

The end of morality set by God is the general or universal well-being of all human beings, not "the private good of this or that man, nation, or age" (§7). Berkeley discusses two alternative ways ("methods") of how God could possibly direct humanity to the realization of that end. God could, first, oblige "every one upon each particular occasion to consult the public good, and always to do that which to him shall seem, in the present time and circumstances, most to conduce to it", or, secondly, enjoin "the observation of some determinate, established laws, which, if universally practiced, have, from the nature of things, an essential fitness to procure the well-being of mankind" (§8). Berkeley argues against the first possibility, claiming that, for a finite being, it is impossible to "calculate" all the consequences of a particular action. It is "far more easy to judge with certainty, whether such or such an action be a transgression of this or that precept". Furthermore, if there were no rules to direct our actions, there would be no "sure standard" of morality, and this would ultimately lead to chaos (§§9–10). Thus, Berkeley concludes, God as a wise being has chosen the second method, namely, governing with the help of determinate universal laws. The view Berkeley takes here has often been misconstrued as a form of rule-utilitarianism (see Häyry & Häyry 1994). On that reading, he introduces two alternative utilitarian strategies, two ways of how *human beings* could possibly try to achieve happiness, and then rejects the act-based approach and adopts the rule-based approach. It is clear, however, that Berkeley explains what methods *God* uses to govern the moral world. The only choice human beings as free agents have is that between obeying God's laws and transgressing them. Berkeley does not point out whether God could have possibly established some other laws instead of the above ones.

The moral laws of nature are such that "if they be all of them, at all times, in all places, and by all men observed, they will necessarily promote the well-being of mankind, so far as it is attainable by human actions". This necessary connection between the "constant observation" of the God-given moral rules and the "universal well-being" of humankind, Berkeley claims, is evident to anyone who takes "an impartial survey of the general frame and circumstances of human nature" (*Passive Obedience* §15). Moral principles that are not established by God's will are not laws. They are not binding on us; nor have they such a necessary tendency to promote the well-being of humanity.

RELIGIOUS LANGUAGE

Berkeley's reflections on religious language are to be seen as an apologetic response to such freethinkers as Toland and Collins, who had questioned the significance of some religious notions. At the same time, Berkeley opposed the views of such divines as William King and Peter Browne, who, he thought, tended towards agnosticism. *Alciphron* contains two discussions on religious language, one pertaining to the terms signifying the attributes of God, the other concerning terms and propositions that express the Christian mysteries.

In dialogue IV, sections 17–21, Berkeley explains that, and how, we can have a direct and proper notion of God's attributes. He does so by introducing the scholastic "doctrine ... of analogical perfections in God, or our knowing God by analogy" (*Alciphron* IV.21). He appeals to Aquinas, Suárez and "other Schoolmen" to show that such words as 'knowledge', 'wisdom' and 'goodness', when spoken of God, are to be taken in their "proper sense" or "proper formal meaning", but proportionately to God's infinite nature. Berkeley subscribes to the "analogy of proportionality", according to which "the perfections which exist in the creature exist also in God, but in the creature and in God they exist in the mode proper to each" (Winnett 1974: 149). The terms in question, Berkeley says, are borrowed from perfections in creatures, and then attributed to God, excluding from their signification "everything that belongs to the imperfect manner wherein" the attributes are found in the creatures. God is literally wise and good but in an infinite degree (cf. Aquinas, *Summa theologiae* q. 13. a. 2, 3). Berkeley distinguishes between 'metaphorical' and 'proper' analogy. In the first case, we attribute "human passions and parts [e.g. anger or an eye] to God". As "those parts and passions, taken in their proper signification ..., include imperfection", they can be only metaphorically attributed to God. In the second case, we attribute such perfections as knowledge or goodness to God "proportionally" as explained above (*Alciphron* IV.21).

In dialogue VII, Berkeley gives an interesting account of the meaningfulness of terms and propositions concerning such Christian mysteries as God's grace, the Holy Trinity, original sin, and the rewards and punishments in the afterlife. In response to the freethinkers' contention that such terms and propositions do not stand for (clear and distinct) ideas and thus are meaningless, Berkeley offers a novel theory to explain their "use" and "significance". The view he attributes to freethinkers is derived from but does not coincide with Locke's theory of signification:

> Words are signs: they do or should stand for ideas, which so far as they suggest they are significant. But words that suggest no ideas are insignificant. He who annexeth a clear idea to every word he makes use of speaks sense; but where such ideas are wanting, the speaker utters nonsense. (*Alciphron* VII.2)

According to this view, every meaningful, categorematic term (in a proposition) must "suggest" or stand for a distinct idea. Terms that do not meet the criterion are meaningless, and so are propositions containing them. Furthermore, according to the position, the only proper function or "use" of words is "to raise those ideas in the hearer which are in the mind of the speaker; and if they fail this end they serve to no purpose" (VII.2). Propositions containing an idealess term (or terms) cannot be understood and should not be assented to. Allegedly, such propositions include propositions expressing the Christian mysteries, for instance, those about God's grace. There is no clear and distinct idea corresponding to the term 'grace' and, therefore, one "cannot assent to any proposition concerning it, nor, consequently, have any faith about it" (VII.4).

Berkeley replies, first, by expanding the range of the functions of language: "[T]here may be another use of words besides that of marking and suggesting distinct ideas, to wit, the influencing our conduct and actions, which may be done either by forming rules for us to act by, or by raising certain passions, dispositions, and emotions in our minds" (VII.5). Words can be used, then, for various purposes and, in some cases, words are meaningfully used without "suggesting" clear and distinct ideas. A proposition containing a term that does not stand for a distinct idea may well be "useful and significant". There is yet another group of significant words, those denoting the mind or spirit and its operations, which do not stand for (distinct) ideas because the mind as "an active principle" cannot be represented by passive ideas (VII.5).

The term 'grace' in its religious contexts is as "useful and significant" as are the terms 'number' and 'force' in their relevant practical and theoretical contexts, Berkeley states. True, we cannot form a single, distinct idea of grace, "separate or abstracted from God the author, from man the subject, and from virtue and piety its effects" (VII.7). But neither are there any single, distinct ideas signified by the terms 'number' and 'force'. Berkeley says: "I can't abstract the idea of number from the numerical names and characters, and all particular numerable things" (VII.5) or to conceive "force abstracted from body, motion, and outward sensible effects" (VII.6). There is no doubt, however, that the "numerical names and characters" can be meaningfully used and that they are very useful both in practice and speculation (VII.5, 11–12). As to force, the notion itself is very controversial, Berkeley points out, referring to the contemporary debates on the nature of force among prominent natural philosophers and mathematicians such as Gottfried Wilhelm Leibniz, Evangelista Torricelli and others. It is not even clear "whether force is spiritual or corporeal; whether it remains after action; how it is transmitted from one body to another", and so on (VII.6). A distinct idea of force is not easier to form than that of grace (*ibid.*). The term is nevertheless very useful in natural philosophy: "there are very evident propositions or theorems relating to force, which contain useful truths" (VII.7).

In Berkeley's view, 'grace' is on a par with 'force'. Both notions are surrounded by theoretical controversies. We cannot form a distinct idea of either the one or the other. "Ought we not", Berkeley asks:

> by a parity of reason, to conclude there may be possibly diverse true and useful propositions concerning the one as well as the other? And grace may … be an object of our faith, and influence our life and actions, as a principle destructive of evil habits and productive of good ones …? (VII.7)

In other words, the Christian belief in grace, which implies assent to certain propositions containing the term 'grace', is quite sensible. The propositions can be understood (to some extent) without entertaining a single, distinct idea of grace. They are useful in the sense that they produce good effects on those who assent to them.

On the whole, the freethinkers' criterion of meaningfulness is inadequate. Words have other – practical and theoretical – uses or functions besides the communication of distinct ideas. Some terms (in propositions) may be meaningful without "suggesting" distinct ideas. It is important to notice that Berkeley does *not* identify the meaning of such terms as 'force' and 'grace', and of the relevant propositions, with the other uses or functions of language or with good effects resulting from certain uses of language. He is not saying, for example, that the meaning of 'grace' is constituted by the fact that propositions containing the term, if assented to, tend to produce good habits. Nor is he saying that 'force', in the propositions of natural philosophy, does not stand for anything. Rather, his view seems to be that the meaning or content of these terms (in propositions) can be grasped indirectly by comprehending the meaning of certain related terms. Thus, in relation to force, we do have ideas of bodies, motions, "outward sensible effects"; we learn the meaning of 'force' from relevant contexts. Likewise, in relation to grace, we do comprehend the meaning of 'God', 'man', 'virtue', 'piety': we know the author, the subject and the effects of grace. We also know it is a supernatural "power or motive", and so on.

Propositions regarding the Christian mysteries are special in that they concern supernatural realities of which human beings cannot have proper understanding: they are above human reason. For Berkeley, this does not mean, however, that they are utterly incomprehensible or non-cognitive as some commentators would have it (see Berman 1981). He held the mysteries to be divine truths or doctrines revealed by God in the Bible and, thus, regarded the relevant biblical and theological propositions expressing the mysteries as true and meaningful propositions. The talk of mysteries, he holds, can be understood to some extent, and this understanding partly explains the good effects faith has on believers. He says, for example, that the belief in the Holy Trinity produces "love, hope, gratitude, and obedience". The belief is possible without having "any abstract or distinct ideas of trinity, substance, or personality" since one is capable of grasping the revealed truth that "the Father, the Son, and the Holy Ghost, are God, and that there is but one God" and that the three divine persons are one's "Creator, Redeemer, and Sanctifier", respectively (*Alciphron* VII.8). The comprehension of the meaning of these terms and of the relations involved explains the influence that the belief in the Trinity has on one's mind, life and actions.

In a similar way, Berkeley holds, one cannot have an idea of original sin "in abstract, or of the manner of its transmission", yet the belief in it may produce in one's mind a "salutary sense" of one's unworthiness and of the goodness of one's Redeemer. From these emotional effects "may follow good habits, and from them good actions" (VII.10). It is implied here that the believer does understand that human beings are guilty by nature and do not deserve the redemption offered by Christ. Finally, the belief in post-mortem rewards and punishments may cause a person to refrain from an evil action "for reasons which all men can comprehend" (VII.10). The person understands that the action may lead to dreadful punishments in the afterlife that are inconceivable in this life.

It could be said that Berkeley's most significant contributions to the field nowadays called 'the philosophy of religion' are his divine language argument for the existence of God, his account of the meaningfulness of terms and propositions concerning the Christian mysteries and his case made against the separation of morality from religion.

FURTHER READING

Berman, D. 1994. *George Berkeley: Idealism and the Man*. Oxford: Oxford University Press.

Botterill, G. 2007. "God and First Person in Berkeley". *Philosophy* **82**: 87–114.

Clark, S. 2005. "Berkeley on Religion". In *The Cambridge Companion to Berkeley*, K. Winkler (ed.), 369–404. Cambridge: Cambridge University Press.

Hedenius, I. 1936. *Sensationalism and Theology in Berkeley's Philosophy*. Uppsala: Almqvist & Wiksells.

Hooker, M. 1982. "Berkeley's Argument from Design". In *Berkeley: Critical and Interpretive Essays*, C. Turbayne (ed.), 261–70. Minneapolis, MN: University of Minnesota Press.

Kline, D. 1993. "Berkeley's Divine Language Argument". In *George Berkeley: "Alciphron, or the Minute Philosopher" in Focus*, D. Berman (ed.), 185–99. London: Routledge.

Sillem, E. 1957. *George Berkeley and the Proofs for the Existence of God*. London: Longmans, Green.

On EXISTENCE OF GOD see also Chs 6, 12, 13, 15, 21; Vol. 1, Chs 18, 19; Vol. 2, Chs 5, 6, 13, 14; Vol. 5, Chs 11, 16. On MORALITY see also Chs 2, 8, 12, 21, 22; Vol. 2, Ch. 12; Vol. 4, Chs 4, 12, 18; Vol. 5, Ch. 6. On LANGUAGE see also Vol. 2, Chs 4, 11, 12; Vol. 4, Chs 3, 8; Vol. 5, Chs 13, 20.

15

VOLTAIRE

David Williams

François-Marie Arouet de Voltaire (1694–1778) was the author of a wide range of moral, philosophical and political essays and treatises. After experiencing early success as a dramatist, he was exiled from Paris following a quarrel with an aristocrat, and in 1726 he went to England, where the impact made on him by English empirical science and philosophy in the two years he spent in London would be deep and long-lasting. In the early 1730s his reputation as a freethinker grew rapidly, and in 1734, in the wake of various controversies and accusations of religious non-conformity, he took refuge in Cirey in Alsace-Lorraine where he worked with Madame Du Châtelet, one of the leading female scientists of her day, on a translation of Isaac Newton's *Principia*. In 1750 he accepted Frederick II's invitation to join the royal court at Potsdam. Moving from Prussia to Geneva in 1755, he soon offended the Genevan authorities, and by 1759 he had settled in Ferney, where he remained until his triumphant return to Paris in the last weeks of his life. In the 1760s Voltaire rose to new heights of fame as a result of his militant engagement with the forces of religious dogmatism and intolerance; his personal involvement in a series of sensational causes-célèbres, in which the authority of the state, the Church and the courts was openly challenged, attracted international attention. A remarkably prolific writer working in many different genres, he lead the 'party of humanity' at a time of great danger for French dissident philosophers, sustaining and inspiring their mission of reform and progress. After his death, Voltaire's intellectual legacy was ensured with the publication between 1784 and 1789 of the great seventy-volume Kehl edition of his complete works, directed by Pierre Beaumarchais. He was not the most profound thinker of his generation, but he was arguably one of the most influential.

Voltaire's pronouncements on religion provoked sharp controversy during his lifetime and have continued to do so for more than two centuries, often to the detriment of objective commentary. Today Voltaire still survives more as an iconic defender of victims of persecution and intolerance than as a religious philosopher *per se*. His historic mission to 'crush the infamous' made his name a household word throughout eighteenth-century Europe, and cemented his reputation as a star of the Enlightenment, especially after the sensational trial and execution in Toulouse in 1762 of Jean Calas (Pomeau 1994a: 131–59). It was the Calas case, highlighting the vulnerable position of the Protestant minority in France, which moved Voltaire to write the *Traité sur la tolérance à l'occasion de la mort de Jean Calas* (Treatise on tolerance on the occasion of Jean Calas' death), one of his most memorable essays on religious intolerance and fanaticism, whose themes still resonate strongly.

The long aftermath of this and other public confrontations with the ecclesiastical and judicial authorities in *ancien-régime* France has to some extent overshadowed Voltaire's other, less high-profile contributions to theological debate. It is still much easier to determine what the public Voltaire was against than to identify any coherent philosophy relating to fundamental matters of belief belonging to the private Voltaire, a problem further compounded by the fact that Voltaire himself often denied the value and purpose of 'systems', particularly those designed to prove, or disprove, the existence of God. Distaste for systems did not, however, prevent him from engaging with them. In fact, he wrote prolifically on the subject of religion, and the rich mosaic of his views is spread across a large corpus of essays and treatises, extending also to his poetry, theatre, historical writings, letters and short stories.[1] For all his professed contempt for metaphysical systems, his interest in religion remained obstinately at the centre of his intellectual preoccupations.

Voltaire's criticism of modern religious doctrines, and particularly those of the Roman magisterium, is rooted in sixteenth- and seventeenth-century traditions of French scepticism and freethinking (Pomeau 1956: 30–34). As far as religious philosophy and metaphysics are concerned, the works of Pierre Bayle and Gottfried Wilhelm Leibniz stand out as seminal sources of intellectual inspiration, but among the earliest formative influences the most important were English rather than French or German. He first learned about English deism from Lord Bolingbroke, whom he met in Paris in 1719 (D71), and it was through Bolingbroke also that he first heard the names of John Locke, Isaac Newton, Samuel Clarke and other English proponents of a worldview that in eighteenth-century Paris still went against the grain of the orthodoxies of Descartes and Malebranche. Voltaire was born into, and grew up in, a rich, intellectual environment in which deism, providentialism, rationalism, scientific materialism and Christianity engendered vigorous debate. His early education was greatly influenced by tutors such as the Abbé Gédoyn and the Abbé Châteauneuf, through whom he was admitted to

1. References to Voltaire's works are to the Voltaire Foundation's *Œuvres complètes de Voltaire* (hereafter *OCV*; 1968–). In the case of works not yet published in that edition, references are to the *Œuvres complètes de Voltaire* (hereafter M; 1877–82). References to Voltaire's letters are to the second, definitive edition edited by Theodore Besterman (hereafter D; 1968–77). Quotations are given in English translation, translated by the author.

the freethinking circle of Ninon de Lenclos (Pomeau 1985: 32–6), and his anti-metaphysical inclinations were soon apparent when he committed himself publicly to deism and natural religion in 1722 in the *Epître à Julie* (Epistle to Julia), later to become the *Epître à Uranie* (Epistle to Uranus; M 10:479), composed in response to Louis Racine's Jansenist poem *La Grâce* (Grace).

Voltaire's deism took shape in fact well before his departure in 1726 for England, a country where he could "learn to think" (D299), and his antipathy towards Christian revelationist doctrine was well known to contemporaries in Paris in the early 1720s. By the 1740s, anti-Christian writings were being falsely attributed to him as a matter of course, and he was widely associated with Spinozism (James 1984: 66–87). Schooled by Jesuits at the Collège Louis le Grand at a time when the social, political and economic repercussions of Louis XIV's 1685 revocation of the Edict of Nantes were still being felt, the young Voltaire was absorbing the lessons of Baconian and Lockean empiricism, together with the principles of Newtonian physics and cosmology. The new epistemological horizons opened up by late seventeenth-century English philosophical, scientific and theological debate were still unfolding in the early decades of the eighteenth century, exposing Voltaire not only to English science but also to the exegetical techniques of biblical criticism that he discovered in the works of English religious controversialists, early deists and 'enemies of priestcraft' such as John Toland, Anthony Collins, Matthew Tindal and Thomas Woolston, as well as those of the later generation of deists led by Thomas Chubb, Conyers Middleton, Peter Annet and, of course, Bolingbroke himself (Torrey 1930: 12–198; Besterman 1967: 23–41).

Voltaire spent almost two years in London between 1726 and 1728, and the first fruits of the London experience were the *Letters Concerning the English Nation*, first published in 1733, and adapted for French readers in 1734 as the *Lettres philosophiques* (Philosophical letters). The original collection of twenty-four 'letters' on a wide variety of topics contains no fewer than seven devoted to English religious sects and institutions, four to Newtonian science, another to Bacon, another to Locke and in the French version Voltaire added a twenty-fifth letter on Pascal, the so-called *Anti-Pascal*. The *Lettres philosophiques*, offering succinct, informative and provocative accounts of anglican latitudinarianism, Socinianism, natural religion, freedom of thought and conscience, all with a subversive subtext on the beneficial, stabilizing effects of English (as opposed to French) religious life on the civil order, proved to be political and religious dynamite in France, and the work was ritually burned in Paris by the public executioner in 1734.

The publication of this incandescent text in France marked the start of Voltaire's reputation as a dangerous dissident and unbeliever, and from 1734 onwards he would find it advisable to conceal his personal religious position behind a mask of irony and delicate inference. An exception is the 1734 *Traité de métaphysique* (Treatise on metaphysics), where his reservations about revealed religion and the nature and purpose of God are openly expressed, and where his admiration for Locke, Clarke, Collins, 3rd Earl of Shaftesbury and Mandeville is explicitly acknowledged. In chapter 2 of this treatise Voltaire addresses with unusual frankness the "difficulties regarding God's existence" (*OCV* 14:429–39). Subsequent chapters explore the proposition of God's existence further, together with its ethical and metaphysical implications. This is a work in which Voltaire's personal beliefs crystallize unambiguously, and in it he articulates a position from which he never moved: acceptance of the existence of God presented difficulties, but there were absurdities in the contrary position (M 22:201). Deism, believing in the existence of God on the testimony of reason but rejecting all aspects of revealed, incarnational religion, offered the only tenable position. In the *Traité de métaphysique*, Voltaire said what he thought, but this bold treatise would never appear in print in his lifetime: "I sought to tell the truth too much" (D1035). Other texts, composed with the general reading public and the censors much more in mind, are more circumspect. For example, in *La Métaphysique de Newton, ou parallèle des sentiments de Newton et de Leibniz* (Newton's metaphysics, or parallels between the views of Newton and Leibniz), composed in 1736–7 and eventually forming the first part of the 1738 *Eléments de la philosophie de Newton* (Elements of Newton's philosophy), the sparse 'truths' of his own deistic convictions are so carefully inferred as to be almost undetectable behind the towering figure of Newton himself. The reader is informed neutrally that Newton believed in the existence of an infinite, omnipotent being, the divine creator of nature and of humanity and, less convincingly for Voltaire, a being still intimately involved in human affairs and human destiny. Gravitation, materiality, the mathematically ordered movement of the planets, the space–time continuum and humanity itself, in short the whole intricate mechanism of the natural universe, all required for Newton the continuing presence of a divine, benevolent intelligence, without whose presence virtue and morality were meaningless:

> Newton was deeply convinced of the existence of a God, and by this word he meant not just an infinite being, an omnipotent creator, but a master who relates to the beings he has created; for without this relationship, recognition of God is just a sterile idea which leaves the human race with no morality or virtue. (*OCV* 15:195)

In the nine chapters of the *Eléments*, Voltaire's meditations on the questions of God's existence and nature, natural religion, cosmology, causation theory, the immortality of the soul, monads, pre-established harmony, materiality and gravitation take their inspiration from Newtonian science rather than Newtonian theology, about which he remained relatively reticent.

Voltaire returned to France in 1728 converted to Newtonianism, and with his own brand of deism reinforced. This was not comfortable ideological territory to occupy, deism being synonymous in early eighteenth-century French orthodox circles with atheism. For this reason he found it tactically more prudent to describe himself as a theist, particularly after 1752 (Pomeau 1956: 428 n.3). In the entry "Théiste" in the 1764 *Dictionnaire philosophique* (Philosophical dictionary) he defined theism thus:

> The theist is a man firmly persuaded of the existence of a Supreme Being, as good as he is powerful, who has created all living, sentient and thinking beings and who has assured the future of their species, who punishes crimes without being cruel, and rewards virtuous actions. The theist does not understand how God punishes, how he pardons, for he is not rash enough to flatter himself that he understands how God acts, but he knows that God does act, and that he is just. (*OCV* 36:545–6)

In *Sur le théisme* (On theism), first published in 1742 under the title *Du Déisme*, he had stated more provocatively that theism was "common sense not yet informed by revelation", as compared to the "common sense perverted by superstition" of orthodox religious systems (*OCV* 28B:19). The reason theists did not shed blood for their beliefs was because they were philosophers, and while philosophers can be guilty of error they were never guilty of plotting against each other. The more emollient tone of the 1764 dictionary entry on theism helps to occlude any residual traces of the dangerously controversial deism and *philosophie* of the 1742 pamphlet as Voltaire's public challenge to doctrinaire authoritarianism intensified, and the need to distance himself from atheistic materialism, "that most pernicious monster" (*OCV* 39:391), increased. Voltaire's stance against atheism, with which deists were often charged, was partly tactical and partly a matter of principled abhorrence of the atheist position. In the self-interrogation over the proposition of God's existence that he had conducted in the *Traité de métaphysique*, atheistically tinged hesitations can be detected, but it is difficult to find echoes of those hesitations in subsequent writings. In act III, scene 1 of his 1759 play *Socrate*, Socrates affirms the existence of a God who is "incomprehensible, incommunicable, eternal, just and omnipotent", but begs to be spared further "metaphysical subtleties" (M 5:388–9). In the same scene he warns his judges to take care "never to turn religion into metaphysics; its essence is morality" (M 5:389). Similarly, the entry "Dieu, dieux" (God, gods) in the 1741 *L'Opinion en alphabète* (The A to Z of opinions) expands on God's existence in a similarly circumspect but affirmative way: "We are certain of a very small number of things. There is something, therefore there is something eternal, for nothing comes of nothing. That is a sure truth on which our minds can rest" (M 18:358).

The argumentation of *La Métaphysique de Newton* and the *Eléments* is predicated unambiguously on God's existence, with no concessions made to the merits of the atheistic alternative. Whether the earlier 1734 hesitations were ever really resolved at a private level remains an open question; as far as the textual evidence is concerned, Voltaire never again openly questioned the existence of God, and never again treated atheism sympathetically, his objections being not only philosophical but also social and political. In the entry "Athée, athéisme" (Atheist, atheism) in the *Dictionnaire philosophique*, for example, Voltaire insists that it is in the interests of all people that there should exist a divinity who punishes what human justice cannot prevent (*OCV* 35:375–92). Metaphysics and theology were open to argument, but the need for God as a bastion of the civil order was always self-evident to him. Repudiating both the God of the Catholic Church and the godless universe of the atheists, the Voltaire of the 1760s always justified the existence of "a God of punishments and rewards". This was "the God of all wise men", and it is in this light that the celebrated, brutally pragmatic statement in the 1769 *Epître à l'auteur des Trois Imposteurs* (Epistle to the author of the three imposters), "If God did not exist, we would have to invent him" (M 10:403), takes on meaning: a frankly expedient view to be re-stated subsequently in correspondence (D 16168, 16752). The public role of Voltaire's God in the later stages of his thought was thus primarily to inspire fear of punishment in the next world and to reinforce justice in this one. Voltaire detested the tyranny of priests and the dangerous absurdities of their teachings, but he did not believe that the moral and political order could be sustained in a society bereft of religious faith. In this pragmatic context he appeared to return to the Newtonian assurance of the moral nature of God's 'relation' to humanity.

Whereas in the *Traité de métaphysique* he had taken the view that those who needed religion in order to become "honest men" were to be pitied (*OCV* 14:481), in the 1760s and 1770s he accepted that neither institutional religion nor atheism could promote social cohesion and stability, and that a simple belief in a judgemental God could serve as a powerful restraint on forces that might otherwise lead to social breakdown. Without such a God human beings would succumb to the bleak horror of their natural condition and natural inclinations. In the 1775 *Histoire de Jenni, ou l'athée et le sage* (Jenni's story, or the atheist and the wise man) he located this 'pure religion' at a point between the two poles of the world of confusion and horror offered by priests and atheists, describing it as "the little zone of virtue". Over the years Voltaire's 'public' God changed from 'a plausible hypothesis' into 'an axiom', an instrument of social control and a necessary restraint on the excesses not only of the people but also of their rulers: "So belief in a God who rewards good actions, punishes bad ones and forgives trivial faults is the most useful belief for the human race to have; it is the only brake we have on the powerful" (M 21:574). This goes some way to explaining his otherwise surprising decision in 1759–60, in his capacity as lord of the manor and seigneurial dispenser of justice in his estates in the Gex, to commission the building of a church in the gardens of his château in Ferney. For religious and political reasons the dechristianization of the serfs of the Gex was never part of his mission: "Where there is nothing, the king loses his rights, and God also" (D 15566). Morality and public order depended on communal belief in a God of rewards and punishments, and if churchgoing in Ferney bemused his Parisian friends, for Voltaire the maintenance of the people's faith in that God through public example was an integral part of his civic responsibilities as their *châtelain*. All who govern know that it is necessary to put God into people's mouths "to serve as a bit and a bridle" (D 16684). Social and political considerations aside, however, in terms of personal belief the evidence of his writings point to a sincere acceptance of the bare bones of the proposition of God's existence, "the adoration of a Supreme Being, divorced from all superstition" (D 7139) that went beyond mere questions of sociopolitical pragmatism.

Voltaire's position as a public enemy of the Church became particularly confrontational after the clandestine circulation of a scandalous pamphlet, composed around 1749, which would eventually be published, again not in Voltaire's lifetime, as the *Sermon des cinquante* (A sermon to the fifty; hereafter *Sermon*). The parodic blasphemies contained in this contentious pamphlet placed Voltaire at real risk of arrest and imprisonment, and understandably he took elaborate steps to secure his anonymity, although few contemporaries were fooled. The *Sermon* is the first major Voltairean text to mount a direct, prolonged assault on the doctrines of revelation, and consists of a 'prayer' followed by a 'sermon' preached by a Voltairean persona in the guise of one of the fifty "educated, pious and reasonable people" assembled in an imagined Silesian setting. The text is an affirmation of theistic principles and of the virtues of natural religion, anchored to a closely argued critical commentary on the Old and New Testaments, and offering a foretaste of the themes of the 1752 *Poème sur la loi naturelle* (Poem on natural law): "In a word, no artifice, no fraud, no imposture" (M 21:451). The Bible, the fountainhead of revelationist doctrine and as such a target for Voltaire's unrelenting animosity, is turned against itself to undermine the basic foundations of Judaeo-Christian belief.

In this muscular polemic Voltaire accuses first the Jews and then the Christians of betrayal and distortion of the true nature of God, perpetuated through textual corruption and extravagant doctrinal accretions of which the Christian doctrine of the Trinity was a particularly flagrant example: "The Trinity was thought up, and to make people believe in it the gospels were falsified" (M 24:451). To promote the simple, humane virtues of a natural, doctrinally pared-down religion, the blood-soaked atrocities and horrors of the Old Testament are dramatically evoked, together with a corrosive attack on the central articles of the Christian faith, with particular reference to the Incarnation, the Trinity and the dual nature of Jesus (M 24:449–54). Emphasis on the historical Jesus, a secularized and humanized construct, is a familiar feature of Voltairean religious discourse: "Born an Israelite, he always lived as an Israelite" (*OCV* 56C:224). And in a long sequence of twelve chapters in *Dieu et les hommes* (God and humanity), Jesus emerges as a "rustic Socrates" and as an ally of theism (*OCV* 69(1):410–78). This signalled the acceleration of a process of reassessment in which Voltaire's views on Jesus would gradually lose their earlier satirical edge and make way for a more 'socratic', human figure (Pomeau 1956: 376–90). The reorientation of emphasis is completed in the sixteen 'doubts' listed in the 1777 *Histoire de l'établissement du christianisme* (History of the foundation of Christianity) relating to rabbinical and gospel accounts of Jesus' life, accompanied by a shocking desacralization of Old and New Testament narratives.

The *Sermon* presents a "good and just" God, belief in which involved an act of faith, certainly, but one derived from the enlightened mind liberated from its chains. Such a belief would enable a blasphemous modern Christianity to return to "holy, natural religion" (M 24:453–4) and to a God revealed only in reason and in the laws of the cosmos. Voltaire always rejected the dark, pessimistic mysticism of the Jansenist view of God, nature and humanity, and he never qualified the almost visceral hostility to Jansenism that he had first expressed in the *Anti-Pascal*. Nature, not canonical authority, was the authentic source of revelation, and nature always triggered in Voltaire a heightened spiritual awareness, as a number of contemporaries testified: Lord Brougham's report of the Comte de Latour's description of Voltaire's euphoria as the sun set over the Jura mountains is perhaps the best-known account (Brougham 1845: vol. 1, 141–2). Voltaire acknowledged God as the Great Architect whose original design was still apparent in the workings of the cosmic machine. God was the Prime Mover, but "everything else is hidden in the night" (D 16958). That crucial *caveat* has enabled some to align Voltaire's position with that of an agnostic, or even a closet atheist (Besterman 1967: 41).

January 1768 saw the appearance of two major professions of theism, the first being the *Dîner du comte de Boulainvilliers* (Dinner with Count Boulainvilliers), where Voltaire defined his religious philosophy in hardnosed terms set within a framework of ironic denunciation of Christian orthodoxies, and linking religious belief once more to moral purpose: "love enlightened by wisdom, supported by love of the Eternal Being, the rewarder of virtue and avenger of crime ... Preach God and morality, and I tell you that there will be more virtue and more happiness on earth" (*OCV* 63A:343, 397). The second was *La Profession de foi des théistes* (The theist profession of faith), published a few months later in June, and addressed probably to Frederick II. Here Voltaire compared the fanatical excesses of Catholicism and the absurdities of its tenets with the moral virtues and rational elegance of theism, to which cause Jesus himself was again recruited as "an adorer of God who preached virtue, and an enemy of the Pharisees, a just man, a theist" (M 17.71).

In this interesting text Voltaire also attacked the "ridiculous fables" and the socially and politically divisive exclusivity of Judaism, with its worship of "a local god" (M 27.28). Judaism is presented, alongside Christianity, as the antithesis of the universality, rationality and humanitarian essence of theism, illustrating once again how central critical exegesis of the Old and New Testaments and mockery of ecclesiastical authority are to Voltairean theological discourse (Cotoni 1984: 306–65; Schwarzbach 1971: 95–260). In the *Sermon des cinquante* too, the "absurdities" and "abominations" of the Jews to be found in Old Testament narratives are catalogued in great detail, and Voltaire would return frequently in later years to the inhumanity of early Jewish societies with increasing hostility, leading some modern scholars to accuse him of anti-Semitism (Hertzberg 1968: 280–92; Badir 1974: 199–214). The issue of Voltaire's anti-Semitism is still hotly debated, but difficult to pin down. In "Des Juifs" (On the Jews; M 19:511–41) and "Circoncision" (Circumcision; *OCV* 35:600–613), for example, the Old Testament is certainly used to cast the Jews in an unfavourable historical light in long, quasi-anthropological explorations of the roots of Judaism in the barbarous practices of earlier ancient peoples. Conversely, however, in the 1761 *Sermon du rabbin Akib* (Rabbi Akib's sermon) Voltaire rehearsed his arguments against religious intolerance precisely in a context of protest against persecution by the Inquisition of Jews, as well as Muslims and Christian heretics, in contemporary Lisbon (M 24:281–4). In many texts, moreover, Judaism is treated primarily as a political rather than religious phenomenon, the covert issue being power and the forging of a national identity. Elsewhere, as in *Dieu et les hommes*, Voltaire praised the contribution of Jewish scholars to current theological debate (see sections 14–30, *OCV* 69(1):334–409), and in *Un Chrétien contre six juifs* (A Christian against six Jews) the attack on Jewish "superstitions" entailed little criticism of modern Jewish culture. Much of Voltaire's treatment of ancient Judaism was abrasively satirical, but no more so than his attacks on modern Catholic Christianity, which, in his view, had adapted and absorbed the worst aspects of ancient Jewish mythology (Schwarzbach 1998: 27–91; Sutcliffe 1998: 107–26).

A remarkably wide-ranging comparative analysis of the interlocking histories not only of Christianity and Judaism but also of the links of both to Islam is to be found in the 1766 *Examen important de milord Bolingbroke* (Lord Bolingbroke's important inquiry). Voltaire made a major contribution to contemporary European knowledge of Islamic culture and belief (Badir 1974: 147–82), but his attitude towards Islam, as with Judaism, was often deeply ambivalent. On the one hand, he rejected widely held assumptions of Christian superiority over Islam, but on the other, as with Judaism, analysis of Islamic doctrines was often simply a device to upbraid Christianity obliquely. In the article "Alcoran ou plutôt le Koran" (Al Koran, or rather the Koran) in the 1771 *Questions sur l'Encyclopédie* (Questions on the encyclopedia), Muhammad's teachings are praised (M 17:104–5) and their binding spiritual and political power, enabling Islam to draw many, otherwise disparate, nations together, is contrasted with the more somber history of a Christianity stained with the blood of the casualties of fanatical sectarianism. Elsewhere, however, Voltaire is less generous towards Islam. In his tragedy *Le Fanatisme, ou Mahomet le prophète* (Fanaticism, or the Prophet Muhammad), first performed in 1742, the portrayal of Muhammad perpetuates the stereotypical image of the Prophet as a pitiless tyrant and an imposter, and of Islam as a religion imposed by the sword. Voltaire's hostility to Islam in this flamboyant piece of theatre was reaffirmed in 1748 in *De l'Alcoran ou de Mahomet* (On the Koran or Muhammad). Animosity still resonates in the first section of "Alcoran ou plutôt le Koran", where the Prophet is denounced as a charlatan and the Koran as a collection of absurdities, but the rest of the entry reflects the emergence of a much more sympathetic view accompanied by a marked softening of tone. Voltaire's knowledge of Islam drew mainly on Jean Gagnier's *Vie de Mahomet* (Life of Muhammad) of 1732 and George Sale's 1734 English translation of the Koran (the latter also containing an informative "Preliminary Discourse", translated into French in 1751), as well as translations of other Islamic texts by André du Ryer and Ludovico Marracci. Although he could not read Arabic, between 1730 and 1740 he engaged nevertheless in a serious study of Islamic theology, paying particular attention to Islamic debates on free will in which he saw distinct parallels with Christian, and especially Jansenist, doctrines of divine grace and pre-determinism. Echoes of the impact of Islam on his reflections on providence, optimism and free will can be seen, for example, in *Du Fanatisme* (On fanaticism), "Déisme, théisme", the *Essai sur les moeurs* (Essay on customs), the *Catéchisme d'un honnête homme* (An honest man's catechism), the *Examen important de milord Bolingbroke*, the *Défense de mon oncle* (Defense of my uncle) and the *Lettre civile et honnête* (A civil and honest letter), as well as in philosophical stories such as *Zadig, ou la destinée* (Zadig or destiny), *L'Ingénu* (The simple man) and the *Histoire des voyages de Scarmentado* (Story of Scarmentado's travels).

The issues to which Voltaire most frequently returned, often in an Islamic context, were free will and providence, their implications succinctly elucidated for the general reader by the Angel Jesrad in *Zadig, ou la destinée*, and most memorably of all in *Candide, ou l'optimisme* (Candide, or optimism). Providentialist theory had been widely disseminated in vulgarized form in England by Alexander Pope, whom Voltaire greatly admired (D 303), and whose 1733 *Essay on Man* he had translated in 1737–8 as the *Discours en vers sur l'homme* (Discourse in verse on man). English providentialism had made a considerable impact on French theological and philosophical circles in the early years of the eighteenth century through works such as William Derham's *Astro-Theology* of 1715, translated into French in 1732 by Noel-Antoine Pluche. Although Voltaire had flirted tentatively with aspects of Leibnizian optimism in the 1730s and 1740s, he was never entirely convinced by the Leibnizian rationalization of the problem of evil. In the 1750s those doubts would harden and would lead him eventually to discard all attempts to reconcile evil with the notion of a necessarily benevolent God. "God", he wrote in his *Notebooks*, "is the eternal Geometrician, but Geometricians do not love" (*OCV* 81:420).

The debate over the dispensations of divine providence had come to a head in France in the late-seventeenth-century exchange of views between Pierre Bayle and William King (Brooks 1964: 15–19). In the entries "Pauliciens" and "Rorarius" in the 1697 *Dictionnaire historique et critique* (Historical and critical dictionary), and also in the *Réponse aux questions d'un provincial* (Reply to a provincial's questions) of 1701–3, Bayle had concluded that reason-based systems were incapable of resolving the paradox arising from the coexistence of evil and the assumption of divine justice and vindication, and that the appeal to Scripture on the issue was unconvincing. In 1702 King countered Bayle's doubts in *De origine male* (On the origin of evil), arguing the case for the necessary existence of evil as an indispensable component of the general good. The debate was refuelled in 1710 with the publication of Leibniz's essays on theodicy, first published in French as the *Essais de Théodicée sur la bonté de Dieu, la liberté de l'homme et l'origine du mal* (Essay on theodicy concerning God's benevolence, human freedom and the origin of evil). The term 'theodicy', first coined by Leibniz in 1697, refers to attempts to defend the principle of God's goodness in permitting the existence of evil (Brooks 1964: 11–19). The *Theodicy*, a substantial, scientifically sophisticated treatise, addressed the two key issues raised in the Bayle–King exchange: first, the problem of free will, a concept seemingly incompatible with belief in an omnipotent and omniscient God, but indispensable if human beings are to bear moral responsibility for their actions; secondly, the question of God's benevolence, given the admission of evil into creation.

Responding to Bayle's points, Leibniz sought in parts 2 and 3 of the *Theodicy* to demonstrate that in creating the world, God, an infinitely wise and benevolent 'First Cause of Things', could out of logical necessity only have created the best world possible, having reviewed through time and space all the potential models and 'compossibles'. The world as we know it thus came into existence as an *optimum* of logic and rationality, a *plenum* subsuming evil as a regrettable, but necessary, part of the natural order, everything in creation existing within balanced optimal parameters within which evil was not denied but rationally accounted for as an integral link in a Great Chain of Being (Barber 1955: 83–9). The purpose of the *Theodicy* was to show that evil was not willed by God, but it was permitted, and that permission did not compromise God's goodness. For Leibniz, human beings lived in the best of all possible worlds, although that did not imply acceptance of Dr Pangloss' insistence that everything was good and that evil did not exist, the satirical spin that Voltaire would later put on Leibnizianism in *Candide*. In the 1730s another German philosopher, Christian-Friedrich Wolff, would harness Leibnizian optimism and monadology theory to a rigorous, mathematically based demonstration of the truths of the Christian faith in a series of treatises on ontology, logic and cosmology, satirized in *Candide* as "cosmolonigologie". Wolff's reinterpretation of the *Theodicy* was still very much in the air in France throughout the 1750s (*ibid.*: 123–40). At a time when Christian solutions relating to original sin and predestination were facing serious challenges, the Leibniz–Bayle dialogue had become central to Voltaire's religious thinking at a very early stage, as is clear from the *Anti-Pascal*, where he had defended an 'optimistic' worldview using arguments drawn from the *Theodicy*. Voltaire's initial reactions to Leibniz were not, in fact, always negative; the Leibnizian concept of evil coincided closely to the views expressed in "Puissance, Toute-puissance" (Power, omnipotence) in the *Dictionnaire philosophique* for example, but early signs of resistance to Leibniz can be detected in *La Métaphysique de Newton* where the theory of the *plenum* is rejected, and where the flaws in Leibnizian science are exposed mercilessly to the test of Newtonian physico-theological lines of reasoning. The evidence of the correspondence during the years spent at Cirey with Madame Du Châtelet (a prominent Leibnizian), and especially of the letters written in March 1739, suggests that Voltaire's interest in Leibniz and theodicy would be intense and sustained (Vaillot 1988: 76–8).

After Madame Du Châtelet's death in 1749, Voltaire's view of Leibnizianism would become increasingly hostile, and in the 1750s he became convinced that Leibnizian optimism was a system whose crushing fatalism paralysed the human will to act, removing all potential for change and progress. On All Saints Day 1755, the Lisbon earthquake occurred, and with that cataclysmic event Voltaire's break with optimism was marked in 1756 with the publication of the *Poème sur le désastre de Lisbonne*. In this bleak, emotive poem the rejection of what he now called "a cruel philosophy hiding behind a consoling name" (D 6738) was uncompromising, and heralded the darker themes of *Candide* itself, in which the deficiencies of Leibnizian–Wolffian optimism would be mocked in the immortal Panglossian catchphrase, "All is for the best in the best of all possible worlds". All philosophical attempts to vindicate the notion of a just God were finally buried for Voltaire in the ruins of Lisbon (Besterman 1962: 24–41), and would be replaced in *Candide* with a much bleaker interpretation of the human condition in which evil was an endemic, universal and inexplicable reality, a condition to which human beings alone could give meaning. With *Candide*, Voltaire came very close to the acceptance of a godless universe, and modern commentators continue to argue about the existential implications of the tale's enigmatic conclusion where responsibility for the cultivation of "the garden" in a dangerous and uncertain world seems to fall exclusively on frail human shoulders.

After 1760 Voltaire would devote himself to mapping out the new, more sobering metaphysical landscape of Candide's garden. Events such as the Lisbon disaster, the Calas trial and the horrors he witnessed during the Seven Years' War no doubt darkened his mind and contributed to the gradual relocation of God to the periphery of an absurd (almost in the Camusian sense) universe, a view that characterizes his theological perspective in the last two decades of his life. In a 'diatribe' written six years before his death, *Il faut prendre un parti, ou le principe d'action* (You must take sides, or the action principle), he reviewed for the last time his thoughts on materiality, cosmic dynamics, intelligent design, the soul, free will, determinism, evil and theodicy. In a prefatory commentary set out in the form of a conversation between an atheist, a Manichean, a pagan, a Jew, a Muslim, a theist and a 'citizen', Voltaire uses the secular voice of the latter to acknowledge the ultimate futility of the quest for answers: "I will console myself with the feeling that my ignorance is unshakeable, that what knowledge I am allowed to have is certainly useless to me, and that the Great Being will not punish me for having wanted to find the answer and not succeeding" (M 28:520–21).

Voltaire died on 30 May 1778, technically a Catholic, but the formal profession of faith made to his confessor, Abbé Gaultier ("a nice old imbecile"), to avoid the indignities reserved for the body of a heretic, was carefully crafted, and he avoided taking communion (Pomeau 1994b: 328–33). As he struggled to outmanoeuvre Gaultier's final assaults with the viaticum, the prayer for the dying, and the other rites of a public, Church-approved death, his final request was to be allowed simply to die in peace. Fighting his last duel with the Church he detested, the death scene recalls words written eight years earlier in the *Entretiens chinois* (Chinese conversations), which neatly encapsulate the essence of his personal religious philosophy: "To obey the rules of dying here you cannot die without oil; elsewhere you have to hold a cow's tail. Leave the oil and the tail aside, and serve the Master of the Universe" (M 27:34).

FURTHER READING

Florida, R. 1974. *Voltaire and the Socinians*, Studies on Voltaire and the Eighteenth Century 112. Oxford: Voltaire Foundation.

Gargett, G. 1980. *Voltaire and Protestantism*, Studies on Voltaire and the Eighteenth Century 188. Oxford: Voltaire Foundation.

James, E. 1978. "Voltaire and the Nature of the Soul". *French Studies* **32**: 20–33.

Langdon, D. 1985. "On the Meanings of the Conclusion of *Candide*". *Studies on Voltaire and the Eighteenth Century* **238**: 397–432.

Mason, H. 1963. *Pierre Bayle and Voltaire*. Oxford: Oxford University Press.

Tichoux, A. 1988. "Sur les origines de l'*Anti-Pascal* de Voltaire". *Studies on Voltaire and the Eighteenth Century* **256**: 21–47.

On ATHEISM see also Vol. 4, Chs 2, 10, 20; Vol. 5, Chs 6, 17. On EXISTENCE OF GOD see also Chs 6, 12, 13, 14, 21; Vol. 1, Chs 18, 19; Vol. 2, Chs 5, 6, 13, 14; Vol. 5, Chs 11, 16. On FREE WILL see also Ch. 9; Vol. 1, Ch. 18; Vol. 2, Chs 2, 7, 9, 19; Vol. 5, Ch. 22. On ISLAM see also Vol. 2, Ch. 10. On JUDAISM see also Vol. 1, Chs 9, 10; Vol. 2, Ch. 8; Vol. 5, Chs 8, 15. On PROVIDENCE see also Vol. 2, Ch. 16. On SCRIPTURE see also Chs 3, 4; Vol. 1, Chs 9, 13, 17; Vol. 2, Ch. 19; Vol. 4, Ch. 3; Vol. 5, Ch. 12.

16

THE DEISTS

Peter Byrne

In many current textbooks in theology and philosophy of religion, 'deism' is used to refer to belief in a first cause who made the world but no longer exercises any providential control over it (that is, a deist believes in a first cause that is utterly non-providential). The labels 'deist' and 'deism' were much used in eighteenth-century European and American thought to refer to an active, albeit loose, intellectual movement. Belief in an absentee God was not the uniting, or even a prominent, factor among thinkers in this movement. The characteristic mark of deism is well brought out in Samuel Johnson's definition of 'deism' in his *A Dictionary of the English Language* of 1755: "The opinion of those that acknowledge God, without the reception of any revealed religion".

Deism, so defined, turns around two notions of vital importance in the history of Western religious thought: revelation and reason. The deists, in various ways, attacked the ideas of revelation and revealed religion. The more moderate taught that revelation, while it is possible in principle and perhaps exemplified in the case of Christianity, can provide no surety for any religious truths that go beyond those that reason can discover. The more extreme taught that there is no such thing as genuine revelation. The notion that a God who is worthy of worship will seek to publish religious, saving truths via a revelation is absurd. Deists maintained that all religious truths are discoverable by the unaided human reason (even if, perhaps, some of these rational religious truths have been revealed as well). Reason is omni-competent in religion. As a consequence, they held that genuine religious truths are ahistorical, and this in two ways. First, they do not depend on historical figures like prophets, or historical traditions of testimony, to be known about. Secondly, they do not deal in any historical events (such as the resurrection of one of these prophets). Religious truth is universal and rational. Another way of putting this last point is that religious truth is contained wholly within natural religion. So, the deists can be recharacterized as those thinkers who rejected (or severely limited) revealed religion in favour of natural religion.

But who were the deists? Given our definition of deism, many philosophers of ancient paganism can be classed as deists, and deism is as old as the history of philosophy. This is so because, in its broadest sense, deism is that stance in the epistemology of religious belief that holds that there are substantive religious truths that philosophy can deliver and that also holds that philosophy is not dependent for its knowledge of these truths on an established religion, with its myths, sacred documents and cult. So, in the broadest sense, anyone is a deist who holds that: knowledge of divinity is attainable; philosophy can provide that knowledge; philosophy is free to criticize and even reject established, traditional religious cults. Thus we may count the Stoics as deists in this sense, although of course this labelling of them is anachronistic. Deism of the eighteenth century is part of an attempt to recapture the independence of rational, philosophical thought on religion and morals from the control exercised over it for so many centuries by the Christian churches. The spirit of this attempt is captured well in the subtitle of the first volume of Peter Gay's study of the Enlightenment: *The Rise of Modern Paganism* (1967). Deism was part of an attempt to restore the independence of philosophy from established religion that was characteristic of pagan Greece and Rome. It was no accident that Socrates figures as a hero in numerous deistic works. Here was a philosopher put to death for criticizing popular religion.

The first account of deists that uses that term is reckoned to be by Pierre Viret in *Instruction Chrétienne* (Christian teaching; 1564). Viret's treatment of deism is important for eighteenth-century thought because it was fully summarized in the *Dictionnaire historique et critique* (Critical and historical dictionary) by Pierre Bayle (which appeared in instalments from 1696 onwards). Viret was an anxious defender of the faith. What he notes in his treatment of the deists is the rise of Renaissance humanist thinkers who poured scorn on the Christian Scriptures while contending that God was knowable via the philosophical intellect. The materials for 'the rise of modern paganism' can indeed be found in the inheritance of Renaissance humanism. In particular, we find a new confidence in non-revealed sources of thinking about God going hand in hand with a naturalistic approach to extant religious beliefs and cults. On the latter point, it is notable that the Renaissance saw the birth of independent historical investigation into the formation and reliability of the Jewish and Christian Scriptures. The writings of Isaac de la Peyrére (1596–1676) are important in this regard.

The term 'deist' as a self-applied and other-applied description becomes widespread with the emergence of a series of British religious thinkers from the 1690s onwards. Among the most important of these are: Peter Annet (1693–1769), Charles Blount (1654–93), Henry St John Bolingbroke (1678–1751), Thomas Chubb (1679–1747), Conyers Middleton (1683–1750), Thomas Morgan (*d.* 1743), Matthew Tindal (*c.*1657–1733), John Toland (1670–1722) and Thomas Woolston (1670–1733). These and other British thinkers popularized the mix of ideas set out thus far. Deistic ideas rapidly spread to the European continent, where notable deistic thinkers included Voltaire and Reimarus. Strong elements of deism can also be found in the writings of Gotthold Lessing, Jean-Jacques Rousseau and Immanuel Kant. Deism played a prominent part in the intellectual and public life of the infant American republic. The most important American deists are Ethan Allen (1738–89), Benjamin Franklin (1706–90), Philip Freneau (1752–1832), Thomas Jefferson (1743–1826) and Thomas Paine (1737–1809).

Thus far we have defined deism as the view that all religious truths are discoverable by reason. It is a matter of some debate how far all those we now classify as deists shared a common set of religious tenets going beyond this simple affirmation. There are at least three reasons for the non-uniformity of religious philosophy among those whom we call deists. One is that the label 'deist' has stuck to those thinkers who were criticized as deistic by orthodox theologians in eighteenth-century debate. Defenders of Christianity threw around the label in much the same way 'communist' was thrown around in the West during the cold war. What traditionalists were interested in was identifying those thinkers who had the temerity to attack, explicitly or implicitly, Christian Truth. Thus, in one of the most thorough counter-blasts to British deism, John Leland (1754) treats of such thinkers as Thomas Hobbes and David Hume, as well as thinkers we would now call deists. Moreover, he recognizes no clear distinction between deism and atheism. Another reason why there is non-uniformity in the views of deists is that it was essential to their approach to religious philosophy to defend the freedom of the individual thinker to develop his or her own views. They were notable champions of freethinking who were not going to be constrained by any notions of orthodoxy. A third reason for variety picks up on Leland's treatment of deism: many thinkers classed as deistic were engaged in strategies of concealment. Thus Anthony Collins (an important contributor to debates on the rational basis of Christianity, on liberty of thought and on the freedom of the will[1]) has been treated as a deist, when in fact there are strong reasons for thinking he was an early English atheist. There was very good reason to keep atheism under wraps in eighteenth-century Britain. Persecution for religious heresy was real. A number of British deists were successfully prosecuted for their 'blasphemous' views. Those deists who were not closet atheists disagreed about the precise content of the set of rational truths about God that they could oppose to the falsities of revealed religion. A contemporary commentator, Samuel Clarke, distinguished four species of deist: (i) those who asserted the existence of a creator but denied any form of divine government of the world; (ii) those who believed in a creator and divine governor but who denied this governor was a moral being, and therefore denied a moral providence to the world; (iii) those who believed in a creator, a governor, and who also held that this being was a moral being, exercising a moral providence over all things, but denied an immortal soul, thinking that providence was played

1. His main works include *A Discourse of Free-Thinking* (1713), *A Philosophical Enquiry into Human Liberty* (1717) and *A Discourse of the Grounds and Reasons of the Christian Religion* (1724).

out wholly in this life; and (iv) those who asserted a moral creator and governor and who accepted that moral providence was continued in a personal immortality for human beings (Clarke 1711: 15–27). Despite this variety, it is possible to find an account of the essence of rational, natural religion that is common to many deists. Thus Blount in his *The Oracles of Reason* of 1695 lists the following: (i) there is an infinite, eternal God; (ii) he governs the world by providence; (iii) our duty is to worship and obey him; (iv) worship consists in prayer and praise to him; (v) obedience to God consists in following the rules of reason and virtue; (vi) the expectation of rewards and punishments after this life is grounded on God's providence; and (vii) if we err from these rules we can repent and expect mercy (1695: 197–8). The anonymous author of *Deism Fairly Stated and Vindicated* of 1746 (presumed to be Peter Annet) has a very similar list of the fundamental precepts of the deists: (i) there is a God; (ii) eternal happiness comes from contemplating God and following truth; (iii) truth is founded on the nature of things; (iv) God created us for our happiness; (v) happiness for human beings comes about through conformity to truth and reason; (vi) sincerity and repentance for failings in pursuit of truth will be acceptable to God; and (vii) to aspire to imitate God so far as is possible is the only end of true religion (Annet 1746: 10–12).

These lists are similar in part because of the influence of earlier attempts to find the articles of a simple universal faith that all people of good conscience can discover. Notable precursors are Lord Herbert of Cherbury's common notions of religion (see below) and the articles of a universal faith set out by Spinoza in the *Tractatus Theologico-Politicus*, chapter 14. Such lists arise from a major stimulus to deistic thought; namely, a reaction against the religious strife of seventeenth-century Europe that took the form of searching for an uncontroversial minimum to saving faith that all could agree on. In the hands of a paradigmatic representative of British deism such as Tindal, deism acquires a simple emphasis on three notions: God, soul/immortality, and morality. That is to say, the core of natural religion comes to be the belief that reason can demonstrate the existence and nature of a benevolent God, together with some doctrine of a future life in which human happiness can be completed. These two notions are then joined to a belief that there is a natural (that is, a non-revealed, universal, rational) moral law. This law is sufficient to guide human beings in how to behave, and God requires nothing more than acknowledgement of his existence and the following of the law to reward human beings with the happiness that will be the outcome of his benevolence. Given these three notions, there simply is no need of a revealed path to God or a system of faith and worship based on such a revelation. Deism becomes, in consequence, a religious outlook that has no place for a sacramental system or people to run such a system. Priests and priestcraft are condemned. Most importantly, deists rejected the need for a Redeemer to mediate between God and humanity. The highest status they could give to Jesus was that of noble religious thinker who republished the religion of nature in the face of the persecution of the priestly class of his time and place.

It is notable from the lists provided by Annet and Blount that the God of these deists is, in at least one fundamental respect, a providential creator and not a *deus abscondus*. Both affirm that God has an interest in human happiness and indeed that God will be the source of human happiness. Both lists seem to envisage an everlasting life in which divinely granted human happiness will be delivered, although not all deists did believe in immortality. Both authors are notable for the attacks they make on miracles. Such rejection of divine intervention in the world and human history is based on a number of grounds, but not on the claim that God lost interest in his creation after some initial act of world fashioning. Deists had to attack miracles in general because miracles were used by the orthodox as evidence for the reliability and truth of revelation, and the deists took a dim view of revelation. Miracles could be criticized on the ground that it is morally arbitrary of God to intervene at some points in human history and not others; or on the ground that a perfect God will create a world that is perfect in its providential government and thus in no need of later adjustment by the divine creator.

KEY FIGURES IN BRITISH DEISM

Some meat can be put on the bare bones sketched so far by a brief examination of a few selected thinkers.

Lord Herbert of Cherbury (1583–1648)

Edward, Lord Herbert of Cherbury is in some ways an odd 'deist' to begin with. Although frequently referred to in these terms, it is arguable that he was not a true deist. The first reason for not considering him a deist is that he does not think that true religion arises out of reason (strictly considered). Moreover, he allows some role to revelation in religious life. Finally, the label 'deist' tends to obscure his connections to Renaissance humanism and Platonism.

Herbert is, however, a major source of deistic ideas and establishes themes that are central to many eighteenth-century deists. One of these themes is that there is a simple religion that all people can grasp at any time, at any place. This religion is summed up by Herbert in the five Common Notions (or Catholic Articles) of Religion. They are to be found throughout his religious writings and comprise: (i) there is one supreme deity; (ii) he is to be worshipped; (iii) virtue and piety are the chief parts of worship; (iv) we ought to repent of our sins; (v) rewards and punishments for virtue/vice in this life will be completed in a life to come (Herbert [1624] 1937: 291ff.).[2] In his main philosophical work, *De veritate* (Concerning

2. The list also occurs in Herbert's *De religione Gentilium* (Concerning the religion of the Gentiles; 1663) and *De religione Laici* (Concerning the religion of the laity; 1645).

truth), these common notions are declared to be the product of 'natural instinct'. This, one of four faculties responsible for human cognition (the other three are inner sense, outer sense and discursive reason), is the reservoir of innate principles placed in the human mind by God. Innate principles equal 'common notions' and we have them in all areas of human enquiry. One of the aims of Herbert's epistemology is to answer the radical, Pyrrhonian scepticism that had reared its ugly head in the Renaissance. The mind has to make inferences from its ideas via the use of discursive reason. It can be assured that it does so in the direction of truth because it is guided by the common notions, which in turn have a divine authority. In religion, as elsewhere, the sceptic feeds doubt by dwelling on the fact of human disagreement. The common notions of religion trump religious disagreement by pointing to an alleged universal theology shared by the human race. In this, and in other aspects of his writing, Herbert introduces one of the great themes of later deistic religious philosophy: the concern with religious certainty. In the face of competing claims to revelation, or conflicting interpretations of the same revelation, we must fall back on a core of simple religious principles that, somehow, can be seen to be free of the corruption of human transmission down the centuries because they are immediately evident to the human mind.

Two other significant themes in later deistic writing are also prominent in Herbert: the concept of God and the concept of human nature. Herbert's God is very much the God of traditional philosophical theology. His justice, however, has become a benevolent concern for human welfare. This God has no wrath in the face of human sin that he needs to vent by punishing a scapegoat. He will certainly not create some human beings foreseeing or foreordaining that they will have no chance of salvation because they have been born in the wrong place or the wrong time. Herbert's conception of human nature is such as to rule out the Fall. He rejects the story of an inherited sin that puts us all in a state of guilt, which guilt then has to confront divine justice. Thus Herbert's religious philosophy has no need of a Redeemer in history to set the divine–human relation to rights. In all of this he is absolutely typical of the later deists.

Unlike those of the deists proper, Herbert's works do not openly criticize or ridicule Christianity, its scriptures and its theology. However, while he avowedly puts forward the five Common Notions of Religion as tests for judging which, if any, revelation is true, he also hints that knowledge of them is sufficient for salvation. In reality, therefore, he leaves no room for Christ as the mediator between God and humanity, and he gives Christian revelation no essential place in a salvation history of the human race. Indeed, he has a universal, ahistorical picture of divine–human relationships that is typical of deism.

Herbert's writings contain many strictures on, and warnings about, the unreliability and uncertainty attaching to tradition-based forms of so-called revelation. He makes it plain that it is inappropriate for a God worthy of worship to pass down religious truths from one person to another. In this he is, once again, typical of deists proper. But unlike them he has a positive place for a form of revelation within divine providence. In *De veritate* he genuinely welcomes personal communication from God to the pious individual. Herbert's God, when approached in prayer by the pure-hearted, will give individuals direct guidance as to how they should live their particular lives. In this, and in his marked Neoplatonism, he is quite unlike the eighteenth-century deists.

John Toland (1670–1722)

John Toland is most famous for his development of the epistemological side of deism in *Christianity not Mysterious* (1696). This work exhibits both the preoccupation with religious certainty within British deism and its marked tendency to rely on Locke's Way of Ideas to articulate discussion of that problem. Toland relies on Locke's epistemological vocabulary while departing from the map of reason and faith Locke sets out in book IV of the *Essay Concerning Human Understanding* (hereafter *Essay*). Locke distinguishes propositions according to, contrary to and above reason. While rejecting propositions contrary to reason, he contends that there are truths above reason passed down to us in a reliable revelation. Toland denies this. Religious truth is confined to truths according to reason. Toland holds that "reason is the only foundation of all certitude, and that nothing revealed, whether as to its nature or existence, is more exempted from its disquisitions than the ordinary phenomena of nature" (1696: 6). Reason, in the form of the testimony of our own ideas, is the only basis for assenting to any propositions proposed to us. The distinction between reason and faith is thereby abolished. Worthwhile faith becomes "a most firm persuasion based upon substantial reasons" (*ibid.*: 138).

The upshot of Toland's rejection of truths that are above reason is the rejection of all mysteries in religion. And while, of course, this is not explicitly stated, a further consequence must be the denial of Christian doctrines such as the Incarnation and the Trinity. Although Toland does not present himself as an attacker of Christian dogma, he has most surely undermined it. Moreover, on his account, revelation ceases to be a ground of assent to any propositions whatsoever. Toland distinguishes between revelation as a means of information and as a ground of assent. A truth that reason can in principle vouch for may be such that a given individual comes to first learn of it only through reading some 'sacred' text. But that it is in this text cannot be the reason for regarding it as true. Once such a truth has come to my notice I must be capable of inspecting it, understanding it and judging it to be true by the use of my reason. Toland sees a major advantage in this severe religious rationalism: by confining religious truth to what reason can demonstrate, human beings are thereby liberated intellectually and practically. If people are bound to take religious dogmas on trust, then they are forced to accept the authority of established faiths and their institutions. Thus they will be obliged to continue in that religion in which they were first educated.

In his *Letters to Serena* of 1704, Toland outlines a history of religions that is shared by many deists. According to this history, natural religion was once lived.

Established religions of the present, such as Christianity, are remnants of this original religion, although mightily overlain by centuries of superstition and other products of priestcraft. Many deists took it for granted that established, institutional religions such as they saw around them could exist only in societies with wealth, property and organized systems of power. Thus in its original state, humankind must have known of no institutional religion. Free of its corruptions, human beings would have worshipped God in a wholly rational way. Toland gives the core of this view in *Letters to Serena* via some particularly weak verse:

> Natural religion was easy first and plain,
> Tales made it mystery, offerings made it gain;
> Sacrifices and shows were at length prepared,
> The priests ate roast meat and the people starved. (1704: 130)

This underlying picture of early human beings as plain-living philosophers has, perhaps, little to recommend it. But the deists' preferred history of religions gave them a powerful motive to advocate an irreverent, critical examination of the history of actual religions. Deism was, in this way, an important stimulus to the historical-critical study of religion.

Matthew Tindal (c.1657–1733)

Tindal, and in particular his 1730 study *Christianity as Old as the Creation*, justly receives much attention in studies of British deism. As with Toland's *Christianity not Mysterious*, it does not openly declare Christianity *per se* to be false or corrupt. It contains a lengthy argument for the conclusion that the true religion is coterminous with the religion of nature. This consists of a set of timeless, universally knowable truths about God coupled with equally timeless and universal truths of obligation.

Tindal's highly repetitive arguments for his main conclusion display reflections on the three significant themes in deistic religious philosophy: divine nature, human nature and religious certainty. His account of the divine nature is paramount among these. He follows the standard notion of God as an all-perfect being, but deduces specifically deistic conclusions from it. Perfection leads to immutability. Divine immutability entails that God could never have given one law for humanity at a given time and place and another law for humanity at a different time and place. God's law for us must be universal and timeless. Not only is this a direct blow against the Christian idea of an Old Covenant for the Jews and a New Covenant from Jesus, but it is also a positive argument for the claim that natural religion equals true religion. From divine perfection follows divine justice. Like Herbert, Tindal interprets divine justice as an unwavering concern for human happiness. Divine perfection also entails that God needs nothing for himself and is the acme of disinterestedness. Thus we get this conclusion: "It unavoidably follows, nothing can be a part of the divine law, but what tends to promote the common interest, and mutual happiness of his rational creatures; and everything that does so, must be a part of it" (1730: 12). Justice in God also entails that he would not have vital requirements for human living that only some people, at some times and places, could be aware of. Divine justice as well as divine immutability therefore entail that God will only treat with human beings via a general and not a special revelation. Thus natural religion must be sufficient for the guidance of life. The theme of religious certainty enters in at this point. It would be contrary to the aims of a just, disinterested, happiness-distributing God to wrap up his law for us in terms that made it hard to discover or interpret. This God would want to make the divine requirements for living plain, simple and easily discoverable. They will largely consist in the standard moral obligations that conscience discloses to us.

Tindal's perfect God wants to establish relations with humanity in furtherance of human well-being. Tindal adds in the common Enlightenment conception of human nature as uniform across history and geography to produce a deduction that only the universal, timeless, simple religion of reason contains the divine law. This deduction is worth quoting at length:

> From these premises, I think, we may boldly draw this conclusion, that if religion consists in the practice of those duties, that result from the relation we stand in to God and man, our religion must always be the same. If God is unchangeable, our duty to him must be so too; if human nature continues the same, and men at all times stand in the same relation to one another, the duties which result from thence too, must always be the same: and consequently our duty to both God and man must, from the beginning of the world to the end, remain unalterable; be always alike plain and perspicuous; neither changed in whole, or part: which demonstrates that no person, if he comes from God, can teach us any other religion, or give us any precepts, but what are founded upon these relations. (*Ibid.*: 17)

Tindal's main contentions show why, in the terms of his book's subtitle ("The Gospel, a Republication of the Religion of Nature"), if the Christian gospel is true it will be a republication of the religion of nature. Jesus can be no more than a noble individual who attempted to restore natural religion to its original purity.

THE COURSE AND LEGACY OF DEISM

Deism provoked a huge debate in Britain on the origins and rational status of Christianity in the first half of the eighteenth century. Deistic ideas were, however, still very much alive in French and German thought until the end of the century.

As indicated above, deism played a major role in the religious and political thought of the Thirteen Colonies/United States. In its transatlantic setting, deism survived as an active force into the start of the nineteenth century (see Paine's *The Age of Reason* of 1794).

Commentators are apt to write of 'the demise of deism' by the start of the nineteenth century. There was something inherently unstable about deism. It was both pessimistic and optimistic by turns. It was negative about revelation and tradition as sources of reliable religious ideas. But it was wildly optimistic about the ability of reason to discern God's existence and nature plus the universal laws of morality. Eighteenth-century critics, notably Joseph Butler in his *The Analogy of Religion*, were not slow to point out the instability of this mix. Butler's argument is that there are problems in natural religion analogous to those the deists find in revealed religion. Hume and Kant were, of course, to explore more thoroughly the problems in supposing that reason can demonstrate the existence and nature of a perfect divine being. The core metaphysical, rationalist optimism of deism was not to survive.

Nonetheless there is something misleading in the notion of the demise of deism. Many of deism's key contentions against the authority and plausibility of what passes for revelation became the permanent possession of later religious sceptics. It is impossible to imagine the work of early English atheists, such as the poet Shelley or the philosopher Jeremy Bentham, without the deistic inheritance behind them. Deism 'softened up' Christianity. In this respect it is very much alive today. I illustrate this point with a selection of three deistic themes that are still with us: miracles, religious diversity and pluralism, and the relation between faith and history.

Miracles

Contemporary philosophers of religion are apt to assume that scepticism about miracles and miracle narrations began with section 10 of Hume's *Enquiry Concerning Human Understanding* (hereafter *Enquiry*). Even if they know that Hume's discussion has many parallels to Locke's in book 4 of the *Essay*, they will not realize that it is possible to find most of Hume's main points in British deists well before the publication of the *Enquiry*. As noted already, deists attack miracles because miracle narrations were the main plank in the 'external evidences' used to warrant Christianity as a reliable revelation. Across a range of deistic texts we find a comprehensive treatment of the general and detailed issues concerning rational assent to miracle stories. Their assault on belief in miracles sparked enormous interest and is well worth studying today. Notable in this regard is that deists such as Thomas Chubb have an answer to Locke's claim that miracle stories may be antecedently plausible if we view them in the light of the assumption that there is a God willing and able to intervene in nature in support of some revelation (*Essay* IV.xvi.13). Then, urges Locke, the fact that they relate events contrary to the normal course of nature is no argument against their prior probability. As Locke puts it: "For where such supernatural events are suitable to ends aimed at by him, who has the power to change the course of nature, there, under such circumstances, they may be the fitter to procure belief, by how much more they are beyond or contrary to ordinary observations". Chubb's response is that the miracle stories Christian thinkers wish to support are unlikely candidates for instances of divine intervention in the world, because no just, perfect God would want to attest by their means a revelation so limited in scope as Christianity. The whole story of a God able and willing to intervene in history so as to place his stamp on some revelation is antecedently unlikely in the light of divine justice, and therefore miracle narrations continue to have low prior probability (Chubb 1741: 42–3).

Religious diversity and pluralism

The deists wrote at a time when it was possible for educated Westerners to be aware that Christianity was but one religion among others. Their strong sense of divine justice allies them with today's religious pluralists, in so far as the deists take it that religious truth cannot be exclusive to Christianity. Their main argument remains important in present-day debates: it would be manifestly unjust, and therefore impossible, for God to confine essential, saving truths to a specific revealed religion. For God would foresee that many members of the human race would have no chance to grasp these truths, because they lived before the founding of this religion or were too far geographically and culturally removed from it.

Faith and history

The deists have a major responsibility for creating awareness of how a religion, such as Christianity, claims to have saving faith and at the same time makes that faith dependent on propositions about historical events and on the historical transmission of its beliefs. Something as important as religious truth, the deists argue, should be certain and certainty demands that religious truths be based on evidence and grounds available in the present. Claims about events in ancient history lack certainty. In addition, the historical transmission of beliefs is productive of error and therefore doubt. This theme is one aspect of deistic rationalism and is found running through thinkers such as Tindal, Morgan, Blount and others. The relationship between faith and history is, of course, famously treated by later writers such as Lessing and Kierkegaard. But the deists played a large part in articulating this important set of questions. Moreover, one aspect of their response to these issues stands as an enduring legacy to liberal religious thought in the Western world. This is the response that separates from religion proper claims about the remote past and claims that depend on historical traditions. The separation is achieved by locating religion proper largely in moral awareness and action. The significant trend of identifying religion with a moral message, cutting it free from both recondite history and abstruse claims of religious metaphysics, has one of its main roots in deism. Moral interpreters of religion from Kant to the present day owe a debt to the British deists' concern to identify a plain and simple natural religion whose behavioural manifestation consists only in fulfilling our obligations to our fellows.

FURTHER READING

Betts, C. 1984. *Early Deism in France*. The Hague: Martinus Nijhoff.

Byrne, P. 1989. *Natural Religion and the Nature of Religion*. London: Routledge.

Harrison, P. 1990. *"Religion" and the Religions in the English Enlightenment*. Cambridge: Cambridge University Press.

Herrick, J. 1997. *The Radical Rhetoric of the English Deists*. Columbia, SC: University of South Carolina Press.

O'Higgens, J. 1970. *Anthony Collins: The Man and His Works*. The Hague: Martinus Nijhoff.

Stephen, L. 1881. *English Thought in the Eighteenth Century*, vol. 1. London: Smith & Elder.

Sullivan, R. 1982. *John Toland and the Deist Controversy*. Cambridge, MA: Harvard University Press.

Walter, K. 1992. *The American Deists*. Lawrence, KS: University of Kansas Press.

Waring E. 1967. *Deism and Natural Religion: A Source Book*. New York: Ungar.

On HUMANISM see also Ch. 5; Vol. 2, Ch. 19; Vol. 5, Ch. 6. On REASON see also Chs 8, 12, 21; Vol. 2, Chs 10, 11, 12, 16, 18; Vol. 4, Chs 4, 8. On REVELATION see also Chs 7, 11; Vol. 1, Ch. 14; Vol. 2, Chs 11; Vol. 4, Chs 5, 11; Vol. 5, Chs 8, 23.

17

JONATHAN EDWARDS

Sang Hyun Lee

Jonathan Edwards was born in East Windsor, Connecticut, on 5 October 1703, the son and grandson of Puritan ministers. He studied at the College of New Haven (now Yale) and tutored there before accepting the pastorate in Northampton, Massachusetts, first as assistant to his distinguished maternal grandfather, Solomon Stoddard, then for twenty-three years as his successor until he was dismissed by his congregation in 1750 over the issue of who should be admitted to the Lord's Supper. Edwards then served a mission church in Stockbridge, Massachusetts, ministering to Native Americans and also accomplishing much important writing, until called to the presidency of the College of New Jersey (now Princeton), where he died from smallpox inoculation within three weeks of his arrival, on 22 March 1758.

The resurgence of interest in scholarly studies of Edwards since Perry Miller's 1949 intellectual biography has been nothing less than remarkable. The three hundredth anniversary of Edwards' birth was celebrated at an international conference at the Library of Congress in Washington, DC. All of the twenty-six volumes of the monumental critical edition of Edwards' works by Yale University Press have now been published. The materials not included in the Yale edition are now available electronically from the Jonathan Edwards Center at Yale.

Edwards is certainly the greatest philosopher-theologian of colonial America. In the minds of some, he is perhaps one of the giants to be ranked with the greatest minds of Western Christianity, such as Augustine, Aquinas, Luther and Calvin. The greatness of Edwards, like many of his predecessors, is that he attempted to restate in a highly original way the historic tradition of the Christian faith in a lively conversation with the intellectual trends of his day.

DISPOSITIONAL ONTOLOGY

When Edwards began studying philosophy as a college student, the traditional Western conception of reality as consisting of substances and forms was becoming problematic. The empiricist epistemology of John Locke made it senseless to speak about the unperceivable substance hidden behind qualities. The influential Newtonian science thought of reality more in terms of motions and laws of motions than in terms of fixed forms and substances. The young Edwards took the challenge head-on in his early notes on scientific and philosophical matters, and began to think about reality as a dynamic and relational system of law-like habits rather than as a system of substances and forms.

Edwards began by asking the question: what is an atom? He used the answer that was prevalent in his day. An atom is a body "that cannot be made less" or "whose parts cannot by any finite power whatsoever, be separated from one another" (1980: 212, 208). Edwards moved on from this definition to reason that an atom defined as impenetrability, indivisibility or solidity can only be an activity of 'resisting' against annihilation by any finite power. Edwards then contends that such 'resistance' can only be the very activity of the infinite being itself, namely, God. An entity, Edwards concludes, is "the Deity acting in that particular manner in those parts of space where he thinks fit", that is, according to such "laws" that God had previously established (*ibid.*: 215).

An entity, then, is an act of God: his act of resisting annihilation. But there is more. God causes resistance according to previously established laws. These laws then govern the manner of God's act of resisting annihilation. And these laws are abiding realities and thus constitute the relative and yet permanence of entity.

When laws pertain to the being and actions of perceiving beings, Edwards calls them 'habits', and "all habits are nothing but a law that such actions upon such occasions should be exerted" (1994: 358). Here Edwards has redefined Aristotle's *habitus* as a dynamic and relational conception. Habits are ontologically abiding 'general laws' and not mere customs or the ways something happens or is done. Habits as general laws actively govern the way something is and acts. Like the great nineteenth-century American thinker, Charles Sanders Peirce (*see* Vol. 4, Ch. 17), and unlike David Hume, Edwards gave habit a realist definition (Murphey 1961: 157–63). For Edwards and Peirce, habits have an ontological reality apart from their manifestations in actual events and actions.

That to which a habit is a disposition is now a *real* possibility and not a *mere* possibility. It is now certain that a type of action not only may but will occur whenever a certain type of occasion arises. So Edwards, like Peirce, considered habits and general laws as possessing a kind of reality now even when they are exerted in actual events. For both of them, the real is more than the actual.

If habits and laws are dynamic and also ontologically abiding principles, they could then function as the principles of structure and permanence of the created reality. So, Edwards says that "it is laws that constitute all permanent being in created things, both corporeal and spiritual" (1980: 391). The actual being of an entity is the direct activity of God. But what gives an entity a real although relative permanence is the law that God abides by as he causes existence.

Here, then, is a dispositional conception of the world. The created world abides as a system of permanently fixed general laws or tendencies that God has established and according to which he causes actual existences (resistances) in time and space. The world exists abidingly in the mode of virtuality or real possibility that is a midpoint between pure potentiality and full actuality. And, as God causes the actual existences according to the general laws, the world is constantly being moved from the mode of virtuality to full actuality. On the one hand, Edwards has conceived of the world in a way that is logically as far removed as possible from the deistic position. Without God's direct involvement, the actual world simply would not exist. On the other hand, Edwards' position is not a simple occasionalism, as has been thought by some (e.g. Crisp 2003). Edwards' view is an occasionalism only in the sense that God moves the world from virtuality to actuality every moment through an immediate exercise of his power. But this is not an unqualified occasionalist position, since the world has an abiding reality as a system of laws and habits that God's immediate causal actions abide by.

BEAUTY AND RELATIONAL ONTOLOGY

Laws and habits constitute the structure and relative but real permanence of the created world. If this is the case, being is inherently relational. Habits are "laws that such actions upon such occasions should be exerted" (Edwards 1994: 357). Laws and habits are then 'general laws' that govern the actual exercises of entities. They are relations of relations. Therefore, relations, for Edwards, are constitutive of the way, or of what, a being is. What is more, habits and laws are the ways according to which God causes resistances (existences). Relations of entity, therefore, constitute the existence of an entity as well. Then, being can be incremental through the actualization of relations.

To say that each law is established by God means that it is established in a manner fitting to the law that governs God's own actions. According to Edwards, since the law of God's being is true beauty or excellence, each finite law and thus finite being is created to relate to each other in a manner fitting to the law of the whole of the true beauty of God. The relationality of an entity has three dimensions: relations within itself (self-identity, self-love or the self valuing what it values), relations with other entities and relations with the whole. The first two dimensions of relationality are meant to be harmonious with the third dimension, the fitness to the beauty of God. So Edwards says, "the world was made to have all parts of it nicely hanging together and sweetly harmonious and corresponding" (1994: 198). In other words, each entity is intended by God to be an image or type of the law of God's beauty.

This is not to say that every entity, and every relation, in the world is in fact harmoniously related to God. Some individual harmonies have to be omitted in order for the whole viewed as a whole to be beautiful (1980: 334). Edwards does not develop this point into a theodicy, but the direction of his theodicy, if he cared to develop one, is at least hinted here.

What is beauty? The common denominator for all forms of beauty, according to Edwards, is similarity or proportion. Simple beauty is an agreement or similarity found in a small number of relations, while complex beauty is a proportion of a large number of relationships taken as a whole. A complex nexus of relations can be odious if the relationships as a whole do not constitute a proportion. If a complex nexus of relations make up a proportion, such a proportion is a higher proportion and a higher beauty than simple beauty.

Secondary beauty is agreement and proportion found in relations among material things, and is an image of the primary beauty, which is the consent or love between perceiving beings. True beauty is a proportion or consent that is harmonious with and does consent to the proportion or beauty of the whole. A consent that consents to a confined or limited aspect of reality is a confined or false beauty. God's beauty, which is the beauty of the whole that governs the system of being, is the most complex beauty and the most universal consent or love. God's beauty is true beauty. This means that God's beauty is a kind of proportion, since proportion is the common denominator of all beauties. But the proportion of God's beauty that has its singular meaning is the proportion of the most complex nexus of relations considered as a whole. In the singularity of the proportion of God's beauty lies the transcendence of God's beauty, while in the fact that such a high beauty as God's is also a kind of proportion lies the continuity of God's beauty with the most mundane form of beauty in the world.

As Roland Delattre pointed out in his seminal work on Edwards' concept of beauty, beauty is an objective reality and indeed a principle of being (1968: 22–3). As we have seen, God's immediate action according to the pre-established laws constitutes every actual being. Now beauty is the content of the law. God's pre-established laws and God's immediate act of causing actual existence are not mutually exclusive. The principle of beauty of the laws and God's immediate action therefore constitute the actual being of an entity. As Edwards stated in an early note in his philosophical writings, "For being, if we examine narrowly, is nothing else but proportion" (1980: 336).

Delattre (1968: 25) also noted that primary beauty (i.e. consent or love between perceiving beings), for Edwards, is not just a beautified reality but a dynamic, beautifying principle. Every time a perceiving being's habit is exercised beautifully and in a manner harmonious with the true beauty of God not only their actuality as a perceiving being but also the beauty of their action and relations is again actualized and thus increased. Although the sanctified person's exercise of their habit is what is increasing actuality and beauty, ultimately it is God himself who is enlarging his internal beauty in time and space through the knowledge and action of the sanctified human being. Thus, a sanctified person through his or her knowledge and action can participate in God's own enlargement of his being and beauty.

Ultimately, the creativity of beauty is grounded in the creativity of the true beauty of the law or disposition of God. According to Edwards, God brought about the world in order to repeat in time and space God's own internal beauty. Thus, he writes, "the beauties of nature are really emanations or shadows of the excellences of the Son of God" (1994: 279). For him, God is the creative reality and power of beauty. (We shall return to the topic of God's creation of the world at a later point.)

IMAGINATION, KNOWLEDGE AND THE SENSE OF THE HEART

Edwards accepted Locke's empiricist contention that any and all doctrines whereby the validity of knowledge is based on an authority extraneous to the actual sense-experience of the world should be rejected. Edwards also agreed with Locke that the fundamental materials from which knowledge is to be derived are the 'simple ideas' received through the five external sense organs and also through reflection or introspection about the internal acts of the mind. Edwards writes, "there never can be any idea, thought or act of the mind unless the mind first received some ideas of sensation, or some other way equivalent, wherein the mind is wholly passive in receiving them" (1980: 390).

But Edwards certainly must have noticed that, on the issue of how simple ideas become related in the mind, Locke was at best ambiguous. Locke speaks of the mind's capacity to 'intuit' or 'notice' certain connections among simple ideas and also about the mind's 'combining' and 'comparing' of those ideas (*An Essay Concerning Human Understanding* [hereafter *Essay*] II.xiv.1). Locke, however, does not offer a systematic account of how the mind's relating activities occur.

In a chapter entitled "Of the Association of Ideas" in the *Essay*, Locke does discuss how the mind acquires 'habits' of associating and 'uniting' certain ideas with others. But he considers such habitual associations and unions of ideas only as a kind of 'madness' and as the source of 'unnatural connections' among ideas (*Essay* II.xxxiii.5–6). Here was an opportunity to develop a dispositional conception of the mind's combinatory activities. But the rationalist side of Locke would not allow him to consider a propensive and non-intellectual activity of habitual association as playing a legitimate role in cognitive processes.

The Cambridge Platonists, especially the 3rd Earl of Shaftesbury and Ralph Cudworth, both of whom Edwards read very early in his life, saw the mind as active in cognitive processes. The mind for them was a 'forming' power that can grasp the organic wholes out of particulars. But these thinkers were still working with the old notion of innate ideas that are applied to sense-data. Cudworth spoke of the mind's creative activity in cognitive processes as one of applying to sense-data "intelligible ideas exerted from the mind itself, that is, by something native and domestic to it" (quoted in Willey 1957: 157). These Cambridge men certainly inspired Edwards in developing a conception of the mind's active contribution to cognitive processes, but Edwards was too Lockean to be satisfied with the notion of the mind's applying its own innate ideas to the ideas of sensation.

How to mediate between sensation and the mind's activity without compromising the empiricist principle that knowledge should be derived only from the simple ideas of sensation was the challenge that Edwards faced. Edwards' answer is that the mind's imaginative activity responds to the ideas of sensation by ordering those ideas in the mind in the way they themselves are disposed to be related.

Edwards nowhere announces or elaborates a theory of the imagination. In fact, he uses the word 'imagination' in a narrow sense of having in mind ideas of physical things when the mind is not perceiving them. But if we piece together Edwards' statements about the mind's ordering activity, we can reconstruct a theory that is implicitly at work in his epistemology. Edwards' theory in fact anticipates the theories of later thinkers such as Addison, Kant and Coleridge, and deserves greater attention than it has received thus far.

First of all, the mind's imaginative or ordering activity is the function of the habit of the mind. As Edwards says:

> The mind perceives that some of its ideas agree in a manner very different from all its other ideas. The mind therefore is determined to rank those ideas together in its thoughts; and all new ideas it receives with the like agreement, it naturally and habitually and at once places to the same rank and order. (1980: 361)

The habit of mind will also 'excite' the absent but similar ideas and hold them together with the others in the mind's view.

It is important for Edwards that the mind is capable of having several ideas together so that it can perceive the relations between these ideas. Edwards was not working with the Aristotelian notion of abstracting universals from composite ideas. For him, ideas of sensation are simple and nothing can be abstracted.

It is not that the imagination imposes relations on sense ideas. Edwards has a relational ontology that enables him to see the simple ideas of sensation as coming into the mind with inherent dispositions to be related in certain ways. The imagination responds to the relational tendencies of the ideas themselves and makes them explicit in the mind's view. It is important, then, that the direction of the mind's habit corresponds to the relational dispositions of the simple ideas so that the imagination can order sense ideas in the way the ideas themselves are disposed to be related. We shall return to this matter shortly.

The imagination is also creative in the sense that it can order ideas in a relational context that is wider than what is immediately given in sensation. All things, according to Edwards, were created by God to be 'images or shadows' of God's beauty. The ideal knowledge of objects, therefore, requires a perception of them in their relation to other objects and ultimately to God as revealed in Christ and the history of redemption.

Is the direction of the mind's habit, in virtue of which it can 'recognize' and respond correctly to similar ideas as related, innate or acquired? The human mind, according to Edwards, is born with the general ability or direction of the mind's habit to recognize and order ideas according to the rules of contiguity in space and time, cause and effect, and similarity or agreement (1980: 391). By implication, sense ideas come into the mind with the tendency to be related according to the above three rules. Now, similarity or agreement, for Edwards, is the common denominator of all forms of beauty. The beauty of love between persons, however, is an agreement of a higher order. Edwards calls it 'consent'. And consent is a more complex beauty, while agreement among things is simple beauty. God's beauty is the infinitely highest form of consent. Can the mind's general ability to recognize similar ideas be developed in such a way that it can become the specific habit to recognize the divine beauty? Before the Fall, Adam and Eve possessed the 'supernatural' principle that enabled them to recognize the divine beauty, which after the Fall has been withdrawn from human beings (1970: 381–3).

According to Edwards, the Holy Spirit will dwell in an elect person and function 'in the manner of' a new disposition of the person, thereby enabling him or her to recognize the divine form of beauty revealed in the 'divine things', such as the events in Christ's earthly life (2002b: 197). The Holy Spirit acts as a specific form of the sanctified person's innate general disposition to order resembling ideas together. This specific form of the human disposition cannot be acquired through experience. At this point, for Edwards, theology and philosophy merge into one.

It is important to note that Edwards identifies the habit of mind with "a sense of beauty" or "the sense of the heart" (1959: 206). Sense organs are instruments through which information from outside the mind is passively received. How, then, can the imaginative activity of the mind's habit be a sensation? How can the habit of mind be a 'sense'? The imaginative activity of the mind's habit, for Edwards, is a sensation because only through this ordering activity can the relations among known objects in the world be received into the mind and become knowable by the mind. In this sense, then, the habit of mind is like other senses.

According to Edwards, the imagination, affections and the understanding converge in an integrated event of an immediate sensation. Edwards' view, therefore, must be seen as an anticipation of the later-eighteenth- and the early-nineteenth-century English Romanticism that attempted to bring together the Cambridge Platonists' moral and aesthetic sense and dynamic view of the mind, the empiricist stress on sensation and the association of ideas, and the increasing recognition of the importance of feeling.

Edwards thought of the imagination as a synthesizing power that not only holds together various ideas in the mind but also discerns their integrated and coalesced unity of relational meaning constituting a whole and not just an aggregate. The sanctified person's perception of God's beauty, therefore, is a "simple idea" (1959: 205). God's majesty and grace are experienced by the sanctified person in a simple idea of their "sweet conjunction" of what can be expressed in words only as a "sweet, and gentle, and holy majesty" and also as a "high, and great, and holy gentleness" (1998: 793).

It would be a mistake to think of Edwards' 'sense of the heart' as a 'sixth sense' unrelated with other aspects of the mind. Edwards' 'sense of the heart' refers to the imaginative power of the mind, the habit of the mind. In sensing beauty, the mind does not transcend or 'go beyond' sense ideas. Their relational meaning is apprehended through the function of the imagination, but the sense ideas remain what they are as the materials for knowledge. Edwards describes his experience of God's beauty in nature as follows: "God's excellency, his wisdom, his purity and love seemed to appear in everything: in the sun, moon and stars; in the clouds and blue sky; in the grass, flowers, trees; in the water and all nature" (1998: 794). Nothing in the earthly creation is transcended or left behind. The knowledge of God, for Edwards, is not a 'mystical' form of knowledge in the sense of a knowledge that moves away from the concrete temporal and spatial world.

Further, Edwards' religious epistemology is not a 'mystical' kind of epistemology in the sense of providing an esoteric knowledge unrelated to other forms of knowledge and other functions of the human self. The ideal apprehension of things, for Edwards, is a 'sensible knowledge', in which the knower is affected by the beauty of the known object. There is a constructive commerce between the ideal knowledge of things, 'sensible knowledge', on the one hand, and the 'mere notional understanding', on the other (2000: 459). The latter can provide the former with materials for knowledge, while the former facilitates the latter.

THE TRINITY AND THE END FOR WHICH GOD CREATED THE WORLD

Edwards' replacement of substance metaphysics with a dispositional ontology naturally led to a reformulation of the traditional Western conception of God as an absolutely immutable substance. God, for Edwards, is no longer the changeless 'pure form' as in scholastic theology but the dynamic being whose "essence is to incline to communicate himself" (1994: 277–8). Edwards does preserve the traditional conception of God as fully actual, however. But God's actuality, for Edwards, is no longer static but inherently disposed to self-enlargement. The logic behind the dynamic nature of God is the logic of dispositional ontology. An entity is essentially a disposition. And when this disposition is exercised, this entity is actual. But although an entity be actual, it remains essentially a disposition and therefore disposed to further exercises. An entity is inherently disposed to repeat its actuality through the further exercises of its disposition. God as the sovereign disposition is also disposed to repeat his actuality through the further exercises of his dispositional essence.

In his doctrine of the Trinity, Edwards uses both his dispositional ontology and the personal analogy (the self, understanding, the affections and will) as well as the social analogy of the Trinity as a 'society'. God is essentially the all-sufficient disposition to know and love the true beauty (i.e. God himself). The First Person or the Father is "deity in its direct existence". God's "direct existence" can only be the very first exercise of the divine disposition to know and love the true beauty. In the Father the deity is actual in a "most absolute", "prime" and "unoriginated manner" (2002b: 131). In the Father, of course, actuality and disposition coincide because God's "direct existence" is both God's actuality and the abiding divine disposition, as the divine disposition cannot be thought of as prior to the Father (Lee 1988: 188).

The Father as the divine disposition now exercises himself in his reflexive knowledge of himself and thereby repeats his actuality in an intellectual way. This intellectual exercise of the Father's disposition is an "infinite exercise … that is completely equal to such an inclination in perfection" (1994: 272). In other words, the intellectual repetition of God's actuality is intellectually fulfilled to an infinite perfection. Thus the Second Person of the Trinity is God's repetition of himself plus an infinite increase of this repetition.

Edwards refers to the Holy Spirit both as the love between the Father and the Son and as the Father's Love of his Idea of himself. The Holy Spirit is the affectional repetition of the Father's (or the Father's and the Son's) actuality plus its infinite increase. So the Father, the Son and the Holy Spirit, for Edwards, constitute the full and complete exercise of the divine disposition and thus the full and complete actuality of God's being.

This fullness of actuality, however, is true for the immanent Trinity, that is, for God *ad intra* or God as God is within his internal being. The *ad intra* and *ad extra* distinction Edwards makes between the being of God as God is in himself and the being of God as God is repeated, increased or self-communicated in time and space, protects the prior actuality of God so that God's being does not have to be seen, as in process thought, as still in process of being actualized. For Edwards, God as God *ad intra* is fully actual.

God remains essentially a disposition, however. God is inherently disposed to repeat his prior actuality through further exercises of the divine disposition. God, whose dispositional essence is fully exercised *ad intra*, "delights in the exercise of his perfection, delights in all kinds of its exercise" (2000: 97). "All kinds of its exercise" refers to God's exercise of the divine disposition *ad extra*, that is, in time and space. So the divine dispositional essence, which is inherently disposed to further exercises, moved God to created the world "as though he were not in his most complete and glorious state without it" (1989: 215).

Now God's exercise of his original dispositional essence would result in more actuality of the divine being. Since God *ad intra* is fully actual, the additional exercise of the divine disposition could not be the self-realization of God *ad intra*. Rather, the divine disposition's exercises *ad extra* in creating the world brings about "an increase, repetition or multiplication" of God's prior internal actuality (1989: 203). God's creation of the world is an act of 'self-communication', 'self-enlargement' and 'self-extension'. The idea of 'repetition' here is important because Edwards preserves God's prior actuality by asserting that God's self-enlargement *ad extra* is not God's act of self-realization of God as God but an act of becoming again what God already is from eternity. The *ad extra/ad intra* distinction also enables Edwards to assert that God is fully actual and always in a process of self-extending. In short, Edwards attempted to adhere to the traditional concept of God's prior actuality and to view God as genuinely involved in time and space.

It should be noted that Edwards mixes in his conception of God's creation of the world both teleological and emanationistic language. Edwards' use of such terms as 'flowing forth' and 'diffusion' remind one of the Neoplatonic conception of emanation. Edwards, however, also says that in creating the world God 'aims at' and 'seeks' something. The fact is that God's creation of the world, according to Edwards, is both like 'emanation' and also teleological. God's creation of the world is like emanation or 'overflowing' because it is an act of God's 'self-enlargement', in which God's exercise of his disposition brings about more divine actuality outside God in time and space. The creation is an ontological increase and thus is in a sense similar to emanation. But, at the same time, God's creation of the world, for Edwards, is a purposive act, the goal of which is the repetition in time and space of God's prior actuality. Plotinus attempted to protect God's perfection by not conceiving it as a teleological act, because he thought seeking something admits of a lack. But by conceiving God's self-enlargement in time and space as an act of repeating in time and space God's prior fullness, Edwards was able to see God's creation of the world as a genuinely purposive activity, and one that imbues the created world with ultimate meaning and purpose.

Edwards points out that the process of God's self-extension in time and space will require "an eternal duration", and "the time will never come when it can be said it has already arrived at this infinite height" (1989: 256). This is so because what has to be repeated in time is the infinite fullness of God's internal actuality. The eschaton will be the time when the elect are all gathered in the Church. But history will continue in the new heaven and the earth, and the process of the divine beauty's self-extension will go on in heaven for an everlasting time. In this way the distinction between God and the world will never be annulled.

The end for which God created perceiving human beings, according to Edwards, is subservient to the 'chief end' of God's creation. By knowing and loving God's beauty, sanctified persons repeat in a limited but real way and thereby promote God's own end in creation and participate in what God himself is doing in history.

Edwards, in his doctrine of the will, is a compatibilist, and thus what God the Holy Spirit does by indwelling in the sanctified person "in the manner of a new disposition" is also that person's own voluntary action. In and through the saints' knowledge and love of God, God himself emanates and re-emanates his own glory. The non-perceiving physical universe is also intended to be the "image and shadow" of the divine beauty. It is in and through the saints' knowledge and love of non-sentient beings as the "images and shadows" of the divine beauty that the physical universe achieves the actuality of what it is ultimately meant to be: the image of God's beauty.

Edwards' theological ethics logically follows from his discussion of God's end in creation. It was not an accident that Edwards completed his "Dissertation Concerning the Nature of True Virtue" immediately after he completed, in February 1755, the "Dissertation Concerning the End for Which God Created the World". Without a love for God ("benevolence to Being-in-general"), there cannot be true virtue. An interesting aspect of Edwards' ethics is that he recognized the legitimacy and value of 'common morality' (e.g. the sense of duty and justice), which is based on the sense of 'secondary beauty'. So Edwards recognized the utility of the natural human 'moral sense' espoused by such British moralists as Francis Hutcheson. But according to Edwards, although such morality may be useful, it falls short of true virtue. Without a love of God and therefore of all beings in relation to God, one does not love the true beauty that God is and loves. Only with "a benevolent propensity of heart to Being in general" (1989: 547) can one truly value what God valued in creating the world: the repetition in time and space of the true beauty of God himself.

FURTHER READING

Anderson, W. 1980. "Editor's Introduction". *The Works of Jonathan Edwards, vol. 6: Scientific and Philosophical Writings*, W. Anderson (ed.), 52–136. New Haven, CT: Yale University Press.

Daniel, S. 1994. *The Philosophy of Jonathan Edwards: A Study in Divine Semiotics*. Bloomington, IN: Indiana University Press.

Guelzo, A. 1989. *Edwards on the Will: A Century of American Theological Debate*. Middletown, CT: Wesleyan University Press.

Helm, P. & O. Crisp, (eds) 2003. *Jonathan Edwards: Philosophical Theologian*. Aldershot: Ashgate.

Kuklick, B. 1985. *Churchmen and Philosophers: From Jonathan Edwards to John Dewey*. New Haven, CT: Yale University Press.

Lee, S. 1988. *The Philosophical Theology of Jonathan Edwards*. Princeton, NJ: Princeton University Press.

Lee, S. (ed.) 2005. *The Princeton Companion to Jonathan Edwards*. Princeton, NJ: Princeton University Press.

Pauw, A. 2002. *The Supreme Harmony of All: The Trinitarian Theology of Jonathan Edwards*. Grand Rapids, MI: Eerdmans.

Smith, J. 1992. *Jonathan Edwards: Puritan, Preacher, Philosopher*. London: Geoffrey Chapman.

Stein, S. 2006. *The Cambridge Companion to Jonathan Edwards*. Cambridge: Cambridge University Press.

Zakai, A. 2003. *Jonathan Edwards's Philosophy of History*. Princeton, NJ: Princeton University Press.

On BEAUTY see also Vol. 5, Ch. 16. On SCIENCE see also Vol. 2, Ch. 12; Vol. 4, Chs 7, 11, 12, 15, 17, 19; Vol. 5, Chs 4, 19. On THE TRINITY see also Chs 3, 9; Vol. 1, Chs 14, 17, 20; Vol. 2, Chs 2, 8, 15; Vol. 4, Ch. 4; Vol. 5, Chs 12, 23.

18

THOMAS REID

Ryan Nichols

Thomas Reid (1710–96) is a philosopher of the Scottish Enlightenment renowned for his contributions to epistemology, philosophy of mind and our understanding of the nature of human freedom, and for being the progenitor of the 'common sense' school of philosophy. He received a Master of Arts degree from Marischal College, and matriculated there again for a divinity degree. He was licensed to preach by the presbytery of Kincardine O'Neil in 1731, and became an ordained minister to New Machar, Aberdeenshire, in 1737. Following his ministerial work, he was invited on to the faculty of King's College, Aberdeen, as a regent in 1751. This began an illustrious academic career that would lead to his appointment as Professor of Moral Philosophy at the University of Glasgow in 1764, succeeding Adam Smith in that duty. He was elected a Fellow of the Royal Society of Edinburgh in 1783, and served multiple terms as Vice-Rector of the University of Glasgow. He died on 7 October 1796.

Reid is best known for a legacy of common-sense philosophy transmitted by students and aficionados such as Dugald Stewart and James Beattie, even though that legacy should not be taken reliably to represent Reid's considered views. Reid's influence was keenly felt in the pedagogies of early American universities and in the structure of interpretations of early modern philosophers. In contemporary Anglo-American philosophy, Reid's reputation has risen sharply on the strength of his theories of perception, knowledge, action and free will.

Concerning Reid's philosophy of religion, his principal influences were Samuel Clark, Joseph Butler and his teachers and colleagues in Aberdeen, including George Turnbull (see Stewart 2004). Reid was an active participant in the Aberdeen Philosophical Society, whose members concurred that David Hume posed a great threat to the integrity of Christian doctrine. Reid, like Butler, crafted analogical arguments on behalf of the faith, and he states, without much novelty, a design argument and a cosmological argument for God's existence. Reid's prescient, long-lasting contribution to the history of philosophy of religion concerns the way he shifts his emphasis as apologist from proving God's existence on to the task of showing that it is rational for one to believe in God's existence. As a testament to this, leading defenders of Christian belief within the Anglo-American philosophical tradition frequently pay homage to Reid's trailblazing effort to focus on and articulate the conditions under which religious belief is made rational.

Before discussing Reid's views in the philosophy of religion, we must raise an interpretive puzzle. From his published work, he appears to enjoy placid confidence in his religious belief and to be free from concerns to defend it against attack. His published work in philosophy of religion is scarce. What there is he scatters through his three major works, which are the *An Inquiry into the Human Mind on the Principles of Common Sense* (hereafter *IHM*; 1764), *Essays on the Intellectual Powers of Man* (hereafter *EIP*; 1785), and the *Essays on the Active Powers of Man* (hereafter *EAP*; 1788). In these works Reid infrequently discusses venerable issues in the philosophy of religion, such as proofs for God's existence or the problem of evil.

In his lectures and unpublished work, however, he vigorously attacks Hume, atheists and their arguments with surprising vitriol. The fact that Reid does not thoroughly address canonical issues in philosophy of religion in the context of his published work, despite the personal and professional importance of his religious commitments, is a conundrum. The principal source for Reid's philosophy of religion outside his published works is a set of student notes – a total of three transcripts – from Reid's lectures on natural theology at Glasgow in the years 1763–80.[1]

To understand the puzzling nature of this divide in Reid's scholarly corpus, consider Reid's relationship to Hume. Reid confesses that his philosophy of mind and theory of perception are but a response to Hume's theories (Reid 2002b: 210–11). He does not say this for effect; his published discussions of issues about the mind typically proceed by identifying where Hume (or others who propagate the Way of Ideas) went wrong. Hume's *A Treatise on Human Nature* (hereafter *Treatise*) was published in 1739–40, and Hume's *Philosophical Essays Concerning Human Understanding* (later titled *An Enquiry Concerning Human Understanding*; hereafter *Enquiry*) was published in 1748. These texts, especially the *Treatise* but also the *Enquiry*, were available to Reid as he crafted a theory of the mind.

Both these works include varied and forceful attacks on religious belief. Indeed, this feature of Hume's *Treatise* and *Enquiry* would have been much more apparent to Reid than it is to readers of Hume today. However, despite Reid's frequent explicit and implicit reference to these texts, and despite the fact that

1. Note that none of these lectures are in Reid's hand, even though a collection of one set of these student notes has been published as *Thomas Reid's "Lectures on Natural Theology"* (hereafter *LNT* or *Lectures*; 1981). I shall refer to Reid's lectures on natural theology and *Thomas Reid's "Lectures on Natural Theology"* because these notes – two unpublished, one published – are reliable indicators of what Reid believed. However, because Reid is not their author, they should not be taken as definitive.

they both appeared long before Reid's first major work, Reid almost never isolates and discusses Hume's anti-religious arguments. Furthermore, Hume's *Dialogues Concerning Natural Religion* (hereafter *Dialogues*) was published in 1779 while Reid was lecturing on natural theology and long before Reid would publish his two sets of *Essays*. But this book had little discernible influence on Reid's thinking. Why does Reid assiduously respond to Hume's work on the mind and human nature but neglect Hume's principal arguments in the philosophy of religion?

There is no single, persuasive answer to this question, although there are several converging considerations. One response is that Hume's work in the philosophy of religion was not, in Reid's opinion, deserving of a response. Dale Tuggy represents this camp. He says that Reid "dismissed" Hume's *Dialogues* "as old news, a mere rerun of Hobbes' and Bolingbroke's watery theism". Tuggy adds that Reid "apparently considered it too off-track, too wrong-headed to demand his full attention" (2004: 290). However, Tuggy presents no textual evidence for this contention other than to observe that other common-sense philosophers also did not immediately respond to Hume's *Dialogues*. A second response is that Reid was aware that he lacked interesting, novel arguments with which to rebut Hume's criticisms. This could be because either (i) Reid did not highly appraise his counter-arguments, or (ii) Reid believed that the counter-arguments already circulating in the milieu were satisfactory. Reason (ii) is unsatisfactory because the first common-sense response to Hume's philosophy of religion was presented by Reid's student, Dugald Stewart, in 1828; (i) may lie closer to the truth.

Thirdly, Elmer Duncan (Reid 1981: xx–xxiii) believes the role of the intellectual climate of the day inhibited Reid from feeling a compulsion to respond. Atheism was not culturally tolerated at this time and place, and no theory was capable of replacing theism's account of the origin of humanity and the world. So Reid could take the challenges presented by Hume as intellectual curiosities, but not as serious threats to the cogency of his faith. However, if this interpretation were correct, and theism implies anti-scepticism, then Reid would have had the same reason to be lackadaisical in responding to Hume's scepticism, which he was not. Besides, this is *David Hume* – Reid's nemesis, countryman and correspondent – who is presenting challenges to arguments for God's existence and to the rationality of religious belief. Despite the courteous customs of eighteenth-century British publishing, these connections provide Reid with considerable impetus to publish responses to Hume.

Fourthly, we must recalibrate our expectations for a philosophy of religion as we approach Reid's corpus. When we read an eighteenth-century philosopher writing on religion, we naturally expect to read proofs or disproofs for God's existence. Unusually for his time, Reid expends virtually no effort in all his published work either in an attempt to prove God's existence or to refute disproofs of God's existence. In part this may be because he believed his philosophical talents lay in other areas. In part this is because he sought to change the debate in philosophy of religion from dispute about *proofs for God's existence* to a discussion of the *epistemology of religious belief.* Alvin Plantinga's methods in philosophy of religion very closely parallel Reid's. Neither philosopher purports to offer proofs of God's existence that would convert an unbeliever. Both philosophers primarily focus on questions *de jure* over questions *de facto*. These methodological predilections would explain why Reid constructs an analogical case for the rationality of religious belief, but offers only scaffolding for a philosophy of religion. I do not minimize the dearth of detailed discussion about God and belief in God in Reid's corpus. However, by treating philosophy of religion debates in his published works as epistemological problems, he deals with them in his own prescient way.

THE ROLE OF GOD IN REID'S PHILOSOPHY

The methodological interest of Reid's approach to the philosophy of religion lies in the way he shifts discussion from arguments for and against God's existence to arguments about the status of belief in God's existence. Contrast Reid's approach with that of Leibniz. For Leibniz, God's existence lies at the centre of a rich, metaphysical system. As such, Leibniz's system is invested in the defence and proof of God's existence and a number of metaphysical theses that he believes are corollaries to a commitment to the existence of God. Were we to remove God from Leibniz's system, the resulting collection of propositions would fail to cohere well and would be implausible.

Prima facie, Reid's philosophical system seems to bear a similar relationship to God as Leibniz's bears to God. Reid mentions God under various names on every other page, after all. However, if one removes God from Reid's system, it does not fall apart in the way Leibniz's does. This is owing to the fact that Reid's system is not pervaded by propositions that are entailed by or inferred from propositions about God or God's knowledge, being or goodness (see Wolterstorff [2004: 80] comparing Aquinas and Reid).

This issue has been developed under the aegis of the following question: is a commitment to God detachable from Reid's philosophical system, and if so, to what extent? A 'yes' answer means that the references to God in Reid's work are merely a heartfelt expression of his religious feeling, and that propositions about God do not bear important logical relationships to other important propositions for Reid. As is implied, we may respond to the question by assessing the quantity of detachability.

Contemporary historians of philosophy often endorse a 'yes' answer. One interpretation indicates that Reid uses God in his "commonsense realism" as a mere means to "an anti-skeptical philosophy that people could live by, whose truth ultimately rested on a conviction of God's veracity" (Popkin 1965: 68). In other words, God was not important philosophically for Reid as much as Reid's use of God in the development of his common-sense system was important for the dissemination of Reid's work to religious believers. With reference to God in the vanguard of Reid's philosophical system, the preponderance of Reid's theistic readership was able easily to be led to anti-sceptical conclusions. This suggests that God is strongly detachable from Reid's system since Reid's use of God is conceived as a matter of marketing to an audience. Another proposal concurs with the previous thought that God serves as a last resort to fend off scepticism, but adds that this is not a coy strategy for Reid to get an audience for his work. Instead, this is Reid's sincere belief. In other words, Reid held that the "only defense against the skeptical outcome of his nativism ... is his belief that God would not deceive us" (Daniels 1989: 117). This suggests that God is not detachable from Reid's system but that God should be. A third proposal stands in apparent contrast to these views. Consider Reid's frequent appeals to the goodness of the creator in crafting senses for us that are not systematically misleading. Keith Lehrer invites "the modern reader to substitute the principle of natural selection for Reid's principle of divine benevolence. By so doing, one will obtain a thoroughly modern doctrine" (Lehrer 1989: 66; see also Lehrer & Warner 2000; De Bary 2002). This implies that God can be detached from Reid's system, and that doing so creates a defensible position, whether or not Reid would have been happy with the result.

One way to focus the dispute is to identify the reasons Reid offers for the truth and justification of the first principles of contingent truth (see De Bary 2002: ch. 5). Through the first principles, Reid identifies what he considers to be the common-sense foundations for proper reasoning about philosophical problems. The principles affirm processes of human reasoning, for example 'human memory is reliable', and also assert statements such as 'the objects of immediate perception are mind-independent'. Either their truth and justification depend on propositions about God, or they do not. If they do, then Reid's appeal to God is not detachable from (this part of) his philosophical system. God would then occupy a role in Reid's system similar to the role given God by Descartes: as guarantor of the foundations of knowledge. If they do not, then God is detachable in this way.

Although the evidence is mixed, it points to the thesis that the truth and justification of the first principles do not depend on propositions about God and that, therefore, God is at least weakly detachable from Reid's system. On behalf of this conclusion, consider that Reid objects to Descartes casting God as guarantor of truth (*EIP* 481).[2] In addition, unlike Descartes, Reid is a fallibilist about foundations for knowledge. In other words, Reid does not believe that his first principles are necessarily true or unrevisable, and he does not believe his justification for them makes them incorrigible or certain. To what degree one can detach God from Reid's system in part resolves into questions about the extent to which Reid is a progenitor of the contemporary movement known as 'reformed epistemology'.

---

2. References to *Essays on the Intellectual Powers of Man* are page numbers in Reid (2002a), unless stated otherwise.

RATIONALITY AND BELIEF IN GOD

The most promising means of developing Reid's account of the rationality of belief in God is by comparing and contrasting his account with 'reformed epistemology'. This term refers to a methodology in the theory of knowledge that employs theological presuppositions concerning our relation to God to epistemological problems in order to establish the limits of knowledge. Its central tenets include an opposition to strong forms of foundationalism, a belief that our reasoning faculties, in addition to our wills, are tainted by original sin, and a concomitant belief that this renders our reasoning faculties incapable of achieving proof of God's existence.

Strong foundationalism is a theory about the structure of empirical knowledge according to which a necessary condition on basic beliefs is that they be certain and produced by reasoning faculties. Strong foundationalism prohibits beliefs such as 'There is a tree before me' from qualifying as basic. Reformed epistemologists typically argue that strong foundationalism is false for two main reasons. First, foundational principles are typically incapable of non-circular proof or non-circular justification. Secondly, its criteria for foundational beliefs are self-referentially false. The affinities between these platforms of reformed epistemology and Reid's views about the Way of Ideas are strong and have been noted (Wolterstorff 1983).

Reid offers a like-minded critique of what he took to be Humean foundationalism. Reid is a fallibilist about the foundations of empirical knowledge. For example, the last of the dozen first principles Reid lists is that "in the phaenomena of nature, what is to be, will probably be like to what has been in similar circumstances" (*EIP* 489). For Hume, this by no means qualifies as a foundational principle because one can mount an argument to the effect that this principle is unproven and unprovable. Reid's criticism, like the first criticism I have identified with reformed epistemology, is that foundational beliefs do not require proof of their own. He says:

> There are ways by which the evidence of first principles may be more apparent when they are brought into dispute; but they require to be handled in a way peculiar to themselves. Their evidence is not demonstrative, but intuitive. They require not proof, but to be placed in the proper point of view. (*EIP* 42)

Reid echoes this point throughout his discussion of first principles (see *EIP* §6.4).

Reid does not state the second criticism, but he does foreshadow it. He argues against Hume that if a faculty such as perception is taken to be unreliable, then we *ipso facto* have reason to believe that the faculty of reason is also unreliable. To express this point Reid employs a theological idiom, and identifies what we call the strong foundationalist with a description he thinks is more forthright: scepticism. He says:

> Reason, says the sceptic, is the only judge of truth, and you ought to throw off every opinion and every belief that is not grounded on reason. Why, Sir, should I believe the faculty of reason more than that of perception; they came both out of the same shop, and were made by the same artist; and if he puts one piece of false ware into my hands, what should hinder him from putting another?
>
> (*IHM* 169;[3] see *EIP* 463)

He argues that just as perception and memory sometimes err because of "disorders of the body", so reason is subject to the same problems (*EIP* 244–5).

Following these criticisms, reformed epistemologists mount a case on behalf of a theocentric theory of knowledge. Plantinga says that he endorses "Reidian foundationalism" (1993: 183). The key point linking these criticisms with a theocentric reply lies in the nature of the justification relation, that is, the relationship between a belief and the facts that make the belief likely to be true. Reid and the reformed epistemologist concur that reason is unnecessary and insufficient for the justification of all beliefs. This interpretation of Reid places him within the externalist camp. The reformed epistemologist then contends that the source of justification for our beliefs lies, not in reason, but in the formation of the beliefs in accordance with God's design plan for us.

One can harvest from Reid's corpus a similar theory on which design by God contributes to the justification of our beliefs. The passage cited above, among others, points in this direction. But Reid is notoriously vague about the implications and significance of his theism on his epistemology, a point that the previous sections illustrate. Furthermore, Reid denies a key corollary of reformed epistemology regarding the justification of belief in God's existence. For Reid, this belief is not justified merely by being formed by a properly functioning human mind, but rather its justification apparently follows from a consideration of arguments on behalf of the proposition that God exists. In fact, this is the interpretation of the leading reformed epistemologist and Reid scholar Nicholas Wolterstorff (1983: 60).

Theological propositions make no appearance within Reid's first principles of contingent or necessary truths. Reid also does not require God to vouchsafe his principles. He displays the nuance of his epistemology and its independence from theology in the following passage, where he asks, in relation to the reliability of our senses:

> Shall we say, then, that this belief is the inspiration of the Almighty? I think this may be said in good sense; for I take it to be the immediate

3. References to *An Inquiry into the Human Mind on the Principles of Common Sense* are page numbers in Reid (1997).

> effect of our constitution, which is the work of the Almighty. But, if inspiration be understood to imply a persuasion of its coming from God, our belief of the objects of sense is not inspiration; for a man would believe his senses though he had no notion of a Deity. He who is persuaded that he is the workmanship of God, and that it is part of his constitution to believe his senses, may think that a good reason to confirm his belief. But he had the belief before he would give this or any other reason for it. (*EIP* 231–2, cited in Helm 2004b: 113–14)

The precise implications of this pregnant passage are not easy to determine. However, this passage expresses Reid's desire to minimize God's role in justifying our perceptual beliefs. Reid does not hold that the belief that God has created our constitutions provides a "good reason" to believe our perceptual beliefs. Instead, our knowledge of the objects of our perceptual beliefs is independent of our knowledge of God's existence and goodness, and probably independent of the fact of God's existence and goodness. In this way Reid's view contrasts with Plantinga's proper function theory of warrant since, for Plantinga, if we do not believe in God we have an undefeated defeater for our perceptual beliefs.

According to Reid, belief in God is not a first principle; it possesses very few of the traits he attributes to first principles. It is not absurd not to believe in God (*EIP* 463), belief in a perfect being does not have "the consent of ages and nations" (*EIP* 464), and it is not a belief that is held independently of education and acculturation (*EIP* 467). Furthermore, he contends that reason is the final judge regarding what parts of allegedly revealed religion are genuinely revealed (*LNT* 1–2). Reid is not a reformed epistemologist *per se*. And yet we can see in his discussion of rationality and belief in God that he prefigures many of the issues that would become dear to those who are.

ARGUMENTS FOR GOD'S EXISTENCE

Reformed epistemologists decry attempts to prove God's existence since authors of such arguments must place undue confidence in human reason. Reid, though, is sanguine about the prospects of natural theology. He offers a design argument and a cosmological argument for God's existence. However, as Wolterstorff says, "Though God is central in Reid's thought, Reid's arguments for God existence [*sic*] and nature are entirely peripheral. They occur along the way, incidentally, tucked into discussions of other topics, never formulated with rigor" (2004: 96). (Arguments *against* God's existence were equally ineffectual in the modulation of Reid's theistic belief.)

Reid's cosmological argument derives from Clarke's argument, as Tuggy (2004: 308 n.19) has demonstrated. The closest Reid comes to discussing the cosmological argument in his published work is in the *Essays on the Intellectual Powers of*

Man in the context of his discussion and defence of the principle "That whatever begins to exist, must have a cause which produced it" (*EIP* 497).

Reid defends this principle against a barrage of attacks by Hume. Reid argues that if Hume's scepticism about causation were allowed to undermine our justification for this principle, then a host of inferences about everyday causal attributions would at once be rendered unjustified (*EIP* 497–8). He contends that this causal principle stands as an *a priori* justified, necessary truth, and cannot be proved from experience (*EIP* 498). Reid pinpoints the source of Hume's attack on this principle as arising from faulty commitments to ideas, as well as from Hume's claims that whatever we can conceive is possible and that causation is merely constant conjunction (*EIP* 503).

This defence sets the stage for a formal presentation of a cosmological argument, but Reid refrains from presenting the argument in *Essays on the Intellectual Powers of Man*. He loosely describes a version of the argument in his lectures on natural theology. No extant copy of these lectures is in Reid's hand; what we have are student copies of Reid's lectures.

The structure of Reid's reasoning from his causal first principle to the conclusion that God exists is obscure (*LNT* 66–7). Reid says that every being must be either contingent or necessary. "We call that *contingent* which either might or might not be and that *necessary* which must be. Whatever either might or might not be depends on the will of some agent with power to bring it to pass or not" (*LNT* 66). He then argues that to suggest that the "Supreme Being" exists contingently "evidently would be absurd" (*LNT* 66). He does not here discuss the unintelligibility of a one-directional infinite series of contingent causes or of a circular series of contingent causes. Since this discussion occurs in the context of an analysis of the attributes of God, Reid is not attempting to prove that God exists to a non-believer.

The most intriguing, and problematic, feature of the fledgling argument Reid mentions concerns the way he employs his unique theory of agency and active power in the construction of his argument. Reid's theory of agency asserts that all causes are agent-causes and that there is no mere event causation (*EAP* 1.6, 527a; see Tuggy 2000: 5). He holds that any physical event can be properly explained only by appeal to a personal cause upstream in the causal sequence. This account of causation makes the final conceptual move in the argument – from the establishment of a first cause to proving that the first cause is God – easier for Reid than it is for others. Indeed, perhaps this step becomes too easy for Reid. Although he develops his account of agent causation independently of his cosmological argument, so that there is no overt begging of the question, Reid's theory of agent causation is infused with his theistic outlook in such a way that his use of it in this context raises legitimate methodological questions.

In the context of this discussion of God's necessary existence, Reid concludes not only that God exists, but that God is perfect, or, in his words, that God has "Every Attribute which can make a Being the Object of our adoration and esteem"

(1766 lecture notes, p. 78; quoted in Tuggy 2004: 292). This is used to prove, contrary to Hume's suggestion in the *Dialogues*, that there can be but one God.

The design argument is of more importance to Reid (*EIP* 508–9). He believes it is a first principle of necessary truth "that design, and intelligence in the cause, may be inferred, with certainty, from marks or signs of it in the effect" (*EIP* 503). This takes the form of the following universally generalized necessary truth:

> Necessarily, of effect *E* and person *P*, if *E* exhibits marks of design then *P* is entitled to infer that *E*'s cause *C* is an intelligent agent.

This is an unusual principle to denominate as a necessary "metaphysical" truth (*EIP* 503) since it is an epistemic thesis about what it is permissible for one to infer.

Reid labours to show that this is a necessary first principle. His case is weighted to show that it is a first principle, and not to show that it is necessarily true. Among considerations for its status as a first principle is that it is "too universal to be the effect of reasoning", by which he means that people – the learned and the vulgar – accept it even though they have not inferred it from other principles (*EIP* 504). Also, the principle is got "neither by reasoning nor by experience; and therefore, if it be a true principle, it must be a first principle" (*EIP* 508). He cites Cicero and John Tillotson, and recognizes that they do not prove the principle but they do place it in the appropriate context (*EIP* 505–8). Consistent with other first principles, it is not capable of proof, which is the point of designating it as a *first* principle.

A special feature of Reid's argument is his defence of the first premise. He argues that the inference rule used to conclude that certain effects are caused by intelligent agents is applicable to the problem of other minds. In effect, Reid argues that the first principle and a commitment to other minds stand or fall together such that "the man who maintains, that there is no force in the argument from final causes [the design argument], must, if he will be consistent, see no evidence of the existence of any intelligent being but himself" (*EIP* 512; Tuggy 2000: 296). Reid also delves into this comparison in a manuscript from the Edinburgh University Library (published in Stewart 2004). A commitment to the existence of other minds makes its way into Reid's first principles of contingent truths (*EIP* 484), which implies that Reid believes that the existence of other minds cannot be proven by reason. When taken together with Reid's analysis of the nature of first principles, he can be interpreted as foreshadowing the epistemological parity argument found in Plantinga's *God and Other Minds* (1967).

The first necessary principle serves as an opening premise in the argument, to which Reid adds some empirical data. The second premise says, "That there are in fact the clearest marks of design and wisdom in the works of Nature" (*EIP* 509). Reid voices this principle in stronger terms in his logic lectures in which he says (transcribed in the hand of another), "No man can ever conclude from Experience, that any the least effect, that appears to have the least design in it, can be without a designing Cause" (Stewart 2004: 156). Reid chooses as an example "the true system of the sun, moon, and planets". Since it "has been discovered, no man, however atheistically disposed, has pretended to shew how a better could be contrived" (*EIP* 509). Given Reid's knowledge both of the elliptical (not circular) orbits of planets in our solar system, and of the controversies that this 'lack of perfection' created within the Catholic Church, Reid's confidence is surprising.

From these two premises Reid draws a conclusion to this argument. He says, "the conclusion is, that the works of Nature are the effects of a wise and intelligent cause" (*EIP* 510). Hume's epistemic objection to the inference from the premises to the conclusion weighs most heavily on Reid's mind. Hume contends that the argument is not cogent on the grounds that this is the only universe of which we are aware. One cannot justifiably engage in effect-to-cause reasoning from the observations of a single case to an intelligent cause. Reid replies that Hume's objection is beholden to a false assumption regarding the conditions under which such an inference to an intelligent cause is justified. Hume's objection, he says, "is built on the supposition, that our inferring design from the strongest marks of it, is entirely owing to our past experience of having always found these two things conjoined" (*EIP* 511). But if Hume's criticism does pose a problem for the design inference, it also undermines our belief in other minds. This is because Reid also does not witness the intelligence of another person bringing about some effect (*EIP* 511).

Reid's beliefs about God's attributes follow from his endorsement of the design and cosmological arguments, and from revealed religion. He says that we can infer God's attributes from three sources: (i) "the appearance of such attributes in the operations of Nature we may collect that they exist in the Deity"; (ii) from God's necessary existence; and (iii) from God's unlimited perfections" (*LNT* 62–3). Hume objects to (ii) and (iii) as being potential sources of knowledge of God since, if God is not to be a fiction, all knowledge of him must be knowledge of matters of fact. This type of knowledge allows inferences only from experience (*LNT* 63).

THE PROBLEM OF EVIL

Reid's concern with the philosophical problem of evil would seem to be substantial not only because it was known from antiquity as generating problems for belief in a perfect deity, but also because in his lengthy service as a minister he no doubt had a rich store of experiences colouring his reflections about pain and suffering. More personally, only one of Reid's six children survived him. He had probably employed his keen philosophical mind to examine the issue from all sides. Yet he writes little about it. At the end of *Lectures*, in what he labels "Lect. 84th", he addresses the problem of evil in less than two thousand words.

Reid distinguishes three forms of evil: "1. the evils of imperfection, 2. Evil which they call natural Evil, 3. Moral *evil*" (*LNT* 101). The first form of evil refers to the fact that God's creatures, animal and vegetable, could have been given greater degrees of perfection, but were not. The second form, of more concern, is "suffering & pain which we see endured by beings in the Universe". The third form refers to the "violation of the laws of Virtue by moral & reasonable agents" (*LNT* 101).

Reid makes several brief points about the problem of natural evil. First, he offers a form of the soul-making theodicy by saying that "it is by natural evil that men are trained unto wisdom & prudence in their conduct". He admits that "we are not competent judges & cannot possibly determine" whether these virtues could have been achieved in humankind without the natural evil (and the degree of natural evil) we witness in our world (*LNT* 101).

This is his central reply to the problem of natural evil. The response has two components: an appeal to the soul-making form of a greater good theodicy, and a corollary reference to the inefficacy of the human mind to penetrate God's decision-making. The second feature of his response has special interest given characteristics of his theory of knowledge. By this remark I refer to its nascent externalism about justification and its emphasis on human fallibility in our formation of a wide variety of beliefs.

Reid's response to natural evil in the *Lectures*, although compact in presentation, contains an internal tension. Reid concomitantly juxtaposes his affirmation of our ignorance of why natural evils are necessary for the cultivation of human virtue with some forceful epistemological claims of his own. These include that "from the present constitution of things we see they [natural evils] are necessary to our acquiring any prudence or wisdom" and that "as far as we perceive they are necessary consequences of good general laws" (*LNT* 101–2). Reid presents these comments as answering the problem, but he does not explain his caveats and does not attempt to justify the necessities to which he refers. His use of perceptual language in his appraisal of his knowledge of these apparent necessary truths is significant since it calls to mind his own direct theory of perception and the non-inferential knowledge it produces.

The cornerstone in Reid's response to the third form of evil – moral evil – is human freedom. Reid does not revisit his theory of human freedom and agency in the *Lectures*. In *Essays on the Active Powers of Man*, he offers a robust theory of freedom, which is often thought to resemble contemporary forms of agent-causal libertarian freedom (see Rowe 1991; Yaffe 2004). There he says, "By the Liberty of a Moral Agent, I understand, a power over the determination of his own Will. If, in any action, he had power to will what he did, or not to will it, in that action he is free" (*EAP* 599a–b). Reid believes human agents are mental substances that cause events in the physical world freely and often. He applies this theory of freedom to moral evil in order to conclude that "all moral evil then is not properly the doing of God but of men, who by abusing their power are liable to misery & are then justly punished for their misconduct" (*LNT* 103).

CONCLUSION

Reid's philosophy of religion is underdeveloped and does not favourably compare in breadth and depth to the work of most of his contemporaries. The role God plays in Reid's philosophical system is easily overestimated, given his frequent mention of God. He endorses views about the rationality of religious belief that resonate with contemporary trends in defences of Christian doctrine, even though he cannot be classified as a reformed epistemologist. He states without development a design and a cosmological argument. His enduring contribution to philosophy of religion lies in his methodology, and not in any argument for God's existence.

FURTHER READING

Cuneo, T. & R. Van Woudenberg (eds) 2004. *The Cambridge Companion to Thomas Reid*. Cambridge: Cambridge University Press.

De Bary, P. 2002. *Thomas Reid and Scepticism: His Reliabilist Response*. London: Routledge.

Gallie, R. 1998. *Thomas Reid: Ethics, Aesthetics, and the Anatomy of the Self*. Dordrecht: Kluwer.

Lehrer, K. & B. Warner 2000. "Reid, God and Epistemology". *American Catholic Philosophical Quarterly* **74**: 357–72.

Nichols, R. 2008. "Natural Philosophy and Its Limits in the Scottish Enlightenment". *The Monist* **90**: 233–50.

O'Connor, T. 1994. "Thomas Reid on Free Agency". *Journal of the History of Philosophy* **32**: 605–22.

Wolterstorff, N. 2001. *Thomas Reid and the Story of Epistemology*. Cambridge: Cambridge University Press.

On COMMON-SENSE see also Vol. 4, Ch. 17. On EPISTEMOLOGY see also Vol. 5, Ch. 22. On EVIL/PROBLEM OF EVIL see also Chs 13, 19; Vol. 1, Chs 18, 19; Vol. 2, Ch. 16; Vol. 4, Chs 12, 18; Vol. 5, Chs 19, 22, 23. On RATIONALISM see also Chs 20, 22; Vol. 5, Ch. 22.

19

DAVID HUME

Paul Draper

David Hume's (1711–76) interest in the relationship of religious belief to reason began no later than his early teens and lasted his entire life. Many scholars situate this interest in the broader context of Hume's evidentialism, his empiricism and his scepticism. There is no doubt that his evidentialism, his belief that "A wise man … proportions his belief to the evidence" ([1748] 1975: 110), together with his empiricism, his view that "experience [is] our only guide in reasoning concerning matters of fact" (*ibid.*: 110), are the guiding principles of his religious epistemology. It is doubtful, however, that his scepticism plays an equally important role, although it obviously plays some role. Although Hume did hold that reasoning is not the cause of most religious belief, trying to understand that position in terms of his more radical sceptical views about the limitations of reason is apt to mislead for two reasons.

First, Hume notoriously wore many hats (sceptic, naturalist, logician, historian, etc.), and the hat he wore when he focused his attention on religion was rarely that of the radical philosophical sceptic. This is obvious in his work on the anthropology, history, sociology and psychology of religion, but it is no less true when he was engaged in what we would today call the philosophy of religion. For example, his critique of the design argument is, as we shall see, based on principles of inductive logic explained in Hume's *Treatise on Human Nature* (cf. Barker 1983). Thus, that critique assumes that some inductive reasoning is good and some bad, and so is not based on any general scepticism about induction. Further, even if Hume was a causal sceptic, which is debatable, he did not base his critiques either of belief in miracles or of the cosmological and design arguments on such scepticism, and his "physical arguments" for the mortality of the soul appear to presuppose causal realism.

Secondly, Hume was quite clear that religious beliefs are not the sort of beliefs that are irresistible in spite of the failure of reason to support them. The psychological and sociological factors that cause most religious beliefs (e.g. terror) are not inevitably present nor are they inevitably efficacious when they are present. Indeed, in Hume's opinion, reason can play a crucial role in helping one to avoid the beliefs those factors tend to produce, and such avoidance has no negative practical consequences, either for the individual or for society. Hume himself rejected the Calvinist beliefs of his upbringing at a very early age, and probably for intellectual reasons, as indicated by his remark that "he never had entertained any belief in religion since he began to read Locke and Clarke" (Boswell [1777] 1947: 76). Further, if Hume was ever *tempted* by deism, the sole source of that temptation was philosophical reasoning.

THE DESIGN ARGUMENT

Hume is often credited with refuting the design argument, or at least one popular version of it. Yet much has also been written about whether Hume himself believed that the design argument succeeds. All that seems clear is that Hume had serious doubts about the argument and that on occasion at least he questioned those doubts. This ambivalence can be seen in a letter he wrote (to Gilbert Elliot) dated 10 March 1751, in which he described the doubts he had as a teenager about the design argument as a product of a "restless Imagination" engaged in a "perpetual struggle … against Inclination, *perhaps* against Reason" (Greig 1932: 154, emphasis added). Here I shall focus on the reasons for his doubts about the design argument and not on his doubts about those doubts.

In part II of Hume's *Dialogues Concerning Natural Religion* (hereafter *Dialogues*), the character Philo points out that, according to his interlocutor Cleanthes, "order, arrangement, or the adjustment of final causes is not, of itself, any proof of design; but only so far as it has been experienced to proceed from that principle" (Hume [1779] 1998b: 48). In other words, Cleanthes' design argument is what Hume calls an "argument from experience". It is based on the fact that some ordered systems (e.g. watches) are known by observation to have been intelligently designed. When some members of one class are *known by observation* to be members of another class, Hume says that there is a "union" between the two classes. Using Hume's terminology, Cleanthes' argument can be formulated as follows:

> There is a union between the class of ordered systems and the class of objects that were produced by one or more intelligent beings.
> The (observable) universe is an ordered system.
> So, The (observable) universe was produced by one or more intelligent beings.

More generally, arguments from experience have the following form:

> There is a union between class *A* and class *B*.
> *k* is a member of class *A*.
> So, *k* is a member of class *B*.

Hume recognizes that arguments from experience with true premises support their conclusions to varying degrees. None, of course, are deductively valid, but some confer (in the absence of opposing evidence) practical certainty on their conclusions (Hume calls these "proofs"), some make their conclusions probable but not certain and some provide little or no support for their conclusions.

By a "species of philosophical probability", Hume means a good reason for holding that an argument from experience whose premises are known to be true fails to amount to a proof. According to Hume, there are three such reasons: "imperfect experience", "contrary causes" and "a third arising from ANALOGY" (Hume [1739] 1888: 142). The first two of these have to do with what Hume calls the "strength of the union" between *A* and *B*. By "imperfect experience", Hume means an insufficient number of what I shall call 'confirming cases': members of *A* that are known by observation to be members of *B*. The fewer the number of confirming cases, the weaker the union between *A* and *B*. By "contrary causes", or what could be called 'disconfirming cases', Hume means members of *A* that are known by observation *not* to be members of *B*. The greater the number of contrary causes, the weaker the union and hence the weaker the argument from experience. The third reason that an argument from experience can fail to be a proof has nothing to do with the strength of the union on which the argument is based. Rather, it has to do with the strength of the analogy between *k* and the confirming cases: the members of *A* that are known by observation to be members of *B*. Hume says that, "An experiment loses its force, when transferr'd to instances, which are not exactly resembling" (Hume [1739] 1888: 142).

Although Hume (strangely) mentions only the first two species of probability in *An Enquiry Concerning Human Understanding*, Philo explicitly appeals to the third species when he attacks the design argument in part II:

> What I chiefly scruple in this subject, said Philo, is not so much, that all religious arguments are by Cleanthes reduced to experience, as that they appear not to be even the most certain and irrefragable of that inferior kind. That a stone will fall, that fire will burn, that the earth has solidity, we have observed a thousand and a thousand times; and when any new instance of this nature is presented, we draw without hesitation the accustomed inference. The exact similarity of the cases gives us a perfect assurance of a similar event; and a stronger evidence is never desired nor sought after. But wherever you depart, in the least, from the similarity of the cases, you diminish proportionably the evidence; and may at last bring it to a very weak *analogy*, which is confessedly liable to error and uncertainty.
>
> (Hume [1779] 1998b: 46, original emphasis)

In this passage, Philo first points out that, while arguments from experience can be so strong that they provide a "perfect assurance" of their conclusions, this requires an "exact similarity of cases". When this similarity is not exact, the argument does not amount to a proof of its conclusion, and in general the more dissimilar the cases, the lower the degree of probability conferred by the argument on its conclusion.

Applying this to the design argument, Philo claims that the universe, even if it is ordered, bears little resemblance to human-made ordered systems. In other words, he challenges the strength of the analogy between the universe and the only ordered systems that are known by observation to be members of the class of objects that were produced by intelligent beings:

> If we see a house, Cleanthes, we conclude, with the greatest certainty, that it had an architect or builder; because this is precisely that species of effect, which we have experienced to proceed from that species of cause. But surely you will not affirm, that the universe bears such a resemblance to a house, that we can with the same certainty infer a similar cause, or that the analogy is here entire and perfect. The dissimilitude is so striking, that the utmost you can here pretend to is a guess, a conjecture, a presumption concerning a similar cause; and how that pretension will be received in the world, I leave you to consider. (*Ibid.*)

The point in this passage is clear. When we see a house for the first time, without having observed its causal history, the (observed) "union" between ordered systems and objects that were intelligently designed makes it certain that the house was intelligently designed, not just because of the strength of that union – that is, not just because many members of the class of ordered systems have been observed to be intelligently designed (and so confirm the union) and none have been observed not to have been intelligently designed – but also because of the strength of the analogy between the house in question and the ordered systems that confirm the union, which include after all other houses and most likely other houses that are extremely similar to the house in question in size, shape, organization of parts and so on. (Of course, there will always be *some* differences, but these are relatively minor in this case.) The (observable) universe, however, bears numerous striking dissimilarities to every ordered system that confirms the union in Cleanthes' design argument. Philo does not deny that the universe is a member of the class of ordered systems, but he emphasizes that it is not "*precisely* that species of effect" that we have experienced to result from intelligence. In other words, it is Hume's third "species of philosophical probability" that plays the crucial role in Philo's critique.

Philo makes two claims about the significance of these dissimilarities, the second stronger than the first. First, he claims that, because of these dissimilarities and contrary to what Cleanthes explicitly claims when he first states his argument (*ibid.*: 45), the design argument is not a proof of its conclusion: as far as arguments from experience go, it is not "the most certain and irrefragable of that inferior kind". In order to conclude that:

> an orderly universe *must* arise from some thought and art [i.e. in order to have a *proof* of an intelligent cause], ... it were requisite, that we had experience of the origin of worlds [because then the analogy between our universe and the ordered systems that confirm the union would be strong]; and it is not sufficient surely, that we have seen ships and cities arise from human art and contrivance. (*Ibid.*: 51–2, emphasis added)

Secondly, Philo claims that, because of these dissimilarities, the premises of Cleanthes' argument do not even make its conclusion probable. At best, they confer a very low degree of probability on that conclusion, only enough to justify a "guess" or "conjecture" about the origin of the universe.

Cleanthes initially concedes the first claim, but challenges the second. Comparing his inference to the inference that some house results from intelligence, he says: "[my] inference, I allow, is not altogether so certain, because of the dissimilarity which you remark; but does it, therefore, deserve the name only of presumption or conjecture?" (*ibid.*: 47). This response is reasonable, especially since Cleanthes accounts for two of the most striking dissimilarities between the universe and human-made ordered systems in a very simple and natural way: he claims that the great size and complexity of the universe show that the author of nature has much more power and much more knowledge than the intelligent beings that produce clocks and houses (*ibid.*: 45). Two additional replies to Philo can be found in part III of the *Dialogues*. First, Cleanthes tries to strengthen the crucial analogy by focusing on natural ordered systems within the universe (like the human eye) instead of on the universe as a whole. Secondly, he takes back his initial concession to Philo, claiming that, even though the design argument violates the "principles of logic" (because of the weakness of the crucial analogy), it is nevertheless an "irregular" *proof* of its conclusion (*ibid.*: 57). There is no doubt that Philo is correct in claiming that Cleanthes' argument is weakened by the dissimilarities in question; but it is hard to prove exactly how much it is weakened. As Hume recognized, there are no rules that we can apply here to settle the matter, and our intuitions may pull us (or at least some of us) in opposite directions, especially if we both (i) revise Cleanthes' argument by substituting 'the human eye' for 'the (observable) universe' and (ii) imagine ourselves living in the *pre-Darwinian* world of eighteenth-century Britain. Perhaps this is why the design argument continued to be popular in the English-speaking world long after the *Dialogues* were published.

THE PROBLEM OF EVIL

Another influential point made by Hume about the design argument is that, even if it succeeds, it does not establish any conclusion of *practical* religious significance. In other words, its conclusion implies nothing about how one should act. In part V of the *Dialogues*, Philo points out that nothing in the argument proves that the designer is a single deity as opposed to many, perfect as opposed to flawed, alive as opposed to dead, and so on. Indeed, even if Ockham's razor favours a single intelligent designer, the analogy with human artifacts and their human designers favours multiple deities, and highly anthropomorphic ones at that. Cleanthes responds that establishing an intelligent cause of natural order is a sufficient foundation for religion, especially since Philo fails to establish any of the more specific design hypotheses he proposes. This sets the stage for a discussion of the problem of evil in part X and especially in part XI, where Philo attempts to show both that (i) the design argument cannot establish the moral attributes of the deity, and (ii) an argument from evil can establish that the cause or causes of the universe, if there are any, are less likely to be benevolent (or malevolent) than to be indifferent to our well-being. Together, (i) and (ii) prove that, even if Cleanthes' design argument is sound, it fails to provide a sufficient foundation for a natural religion of *practical* significance. For in the absence of special revelation, we have no good reason to worship or praise or even petition a deity that is completely indifferent to our well-being.

In part X, Philo defends what contemporary philosophers of religion call a 'logical argument from evil' because it attempts to show that the existence of evil (or some other known fact about evil) is logically incompatible with the existence of an omnipotent, omniscient and perfectly good creator. At the end of part X, Philo backs off this argument, "allow[ing, if only for the sake of argument], that pain or misery in man is *compatible* with infinite power and goodness in the Deity, even in [Cleanthes'] sense of these attributes" (Hume [1779] 1998b: 103, original emphasis). Philo's argument in part XI is what today would be called an 'evidential argument from evil', because it tries to establish that one or more facts about evil bear some significant negative evidential relation to theism other than the relation of logical incompatibility. Specifically, he claims that the hypothesis that the cause or causes of the universe are indifferent to our well-being explains the "strange mixture of good and ill which appears in life" better than the "common" hypothesis that the cause or causes of the universe are benevolent.

At first glance, this claim appears to be false because, while indifference is compatible with allowing or causing both pleasure and pain, it is also compatible with allowing or causing pleasure but no pain or pain but no pleasure. Philo points out, however, that the operations of nature are generally "carried on by an opposition of principles, of hot and cold, moist and dry, light and heavy" (*ibid.*: 113). Thus, given this background knowledge, a mixture of pleasure and pain would be expected on Philo's 'hypothesis of indifference'. On theism, however, this background knowledge does not lead one to expect such a mixture, because pleasure and pain have obvious moral significance that those other opposed "principles" do not. In other words, on theism but not on the hypothesis of indifference, there is not just a difference but a *relevant* difference between pleasure and pain on the one hand and these other opposites in nature on the other, a difference that gives one reason to expect pleasure to exist without pain, or at least without as much pain as we find in life. So Philo's position that the hypothesis of indifference does indeed account for the mixture of pleasure and pain in the world better than theism does is a plausible one. Further, neither the theistic hypothesis nor the hypothesis of indifference seems, at least to Philo, to be more probable than the other prior to considering the good and evil in the world, and the mixture of virtue and vice in the world just adds to the evidence against theism. Philo concludes that the hypothesis of indifference is more probable than theism all things considered, and this implies that theism is probably false.

This argument, although underdeveloped by contemporary standards, is nevertheless superior to many contemporary arguments from evil in two respects. First, it employs an evidence statement that mentions both pleasure and pain instead of just pain. Hume, unlike many contemporary philosophers, recognized that, if the question is not one of logical incompatibility, then it is at best dialectically deficient to argue that the suffering in the world is evidence against theism without at least addressing the issue of whether the pleasure in the world is equally strong evidence for theism. Secondly, instead of just claiming that theism fails to explain the pattern of good and evil in the world, the argument claims that theism does not explain that pattern as well as some plausible alternative hypothesis. Hume's insight here is that the debate over how much evil theism needs to explain in order to avoid disconfirmation cannot be resolved without comparing theism to its plausible alternatives. Again, much ink has been wasted by contemporary philosophers because they failed to follow Hume's lead on this.

PHILO'S REVERSAL

Given how powerful Philo's criticisms of the design argument are, Philo's infamous 'reversal' in part XII of the *Dialogues*, where he appears to defend the design argument, has long puzzled commentators. Finding a solution to this puzzle is, perhaps, more urgent for those who assume that Philo always speaks for Hume; but the problem of how to interpret Philo's apparent change of heart obviously remains even for those who recognize that the views expressed by each of the three main characters in the *Dialogues* include some that Hume accepted and others that he rejected.

A variety of explanations for Philo's reversal have been proposed. One of the most plausible is based on the idea that Philo's alliance with Cleanthes in part XII is deceptive in the same way that his earlier alliance with Demea is deceptive.

Throughout the first eleven parts of the *Dialogues*, Philo appears to side with Demea in defending the view that God's nature, far from resembling our own, is mysterious and incomprehensible. Demea fails to realize, however, that the purpose of Philo's alliance is to expose the absurdity or vacuity of common religious belief and practice. Cleanthes recognizes what Philo is up to all along, while much to his chagrin Demea finally catches on at the end of part XI and for that reason makes up some excuse to "leave the company" (Hume [1779] 1998b: 115). It is perhaps not surprising, then, that with Demea gone, Philo now pretends to form an alliance with Cleanthes. He truthfully claims to believe that *a* design argument is sound, but leaves unstated the fact that the conclusion of this argument is not identical to the conclusion of Cleanthes' design argument. Cleanthes' argument concludes that the universe was intelligently designed. Philo, however, consistent with his earlier doubts about the strength of the analogy on which Cleanthes' design argument is based, concludes that "*the cause or causes of order in the universe probably bear some remote analogy to human intelligence*" (*ibid.*: 129, original emphasis). This is a much more modest conclusion than Cleanthes' for two reasons. First, it is restricted to the cause or causes, not of the universe as a whole, but only of the order within the universe. Secondly, Philo's conclusion differs from Cleanthes' because only a *remote analogy* to human intelligence is asserted.

Taken together, these two differences are of great significance. To see why, notice that the specific sort of order we find in the "productions of human contrivance", which Cleanthes describes as "a curious adapting of means to ends" (*ibid.*: 45), is most obviously present in nature in living organisms and their parts. Indeed, it is arguable that biological systems are the only clear examples of 'mechanical order' in nature. This suggests an argument for the surprising conclusion that Darwin actually vindicated the conclusion of Philo's design argument. For both biological systems and human-made machines are produced by a process of imperfect replication and selection. In the case of machines, the process is one of trial and error, a combination of replication with non-random variation and conscious selection. For example, human designers do not create complex flying machines (or complex machines of any sort) like the Sopwith Camel from scratch. Rather, they start with primitive planes such as the one built by the Wright brothers. Then they replicate that plane with variations they think might improve performance, preserving what works in future generations and discarding what does not. Thus, one way that the causes of mechanical order in the living world could bear an analogy to the causes of machines and yet not involve conscious intentions is by involving replication with *random* variation and *non-conscious* selection. Such a process will be much slower than the process by which the airplane has evolved, but it will be analogous. Therefore, Darwin's theory shows that the natural causes of biological order really are analogous, *remotely*, to the causes of machines, just as Hume, in this instance speaking through Philo, had concluded. This also demonstrates that Philo's design argument, even if it is sound, is most definitely not a "sufficient foundation for religion".

MIRACLES

The focus of the *Dialogues* is, of course, natural religion, which Hume clearly took very seriously, at least in its *a posteriori* form. In his opinion, if there is any "true religion", it is justified by *a posteriori* philosophical reasoning such as the design argument and not by *a priori* reasoning or revelation. Revealed religion is, for Hume, "false religion" and thus in almost all cases either "superstition" or "enthusiasm". Hume recognized, however, that attempts had been made to base popular revealed religions like Christianity on reason and in particular on the *a posteriori* grounds of miracle reports, especially the reports found in the Bible. Accordingly, Hume took up the issue of whether these reports can be trusted in his famous essay, "Of Miracles" ([1748] 1975: §X). This essay has had enormous influence, especially on contemporary philosophy of religion.

The essay is divided into two parts. In the second part, Hume gives various reasons for thinking that the testimony we have concerning miracles is of relatively low quality. At least some of the claims he makes in defence of this position are no doubt correct. For example, he points out that many of the miracle reports we have are made by advocates for a religion in an effort to recruit new members, adding that otherwise honest people will sometimes lie "for the sake of promoting so holy a cause" (*ibid.*: 118). No one would deny that this makes those reports less credible than they would otherwise be. Hume also mentions that apparently incompatible religions all report miracles, which at least *tends* to undermine the credibility of all such reports. Arguments like these, however, were well known before Hume wrote his essay. In addition, they are ultimately historical in nature, and Hume makes no effort to engage in the sort of detailed historical examination of actual miracle reports that would be required to show that not a single miracle has ever been supported by testimony of high quality.

Hume's reasoning in the first part of the essay is, however, more original, more interesting and more philosophical. There he tries to show that only testimony of the highest *conceivable* quality could justify a belief in miracles (with the clear implication being that no actual testimony about miracles comes even close to meeting this standard). Hume's approach to this issue is based on some of the same philosophical principles that he employed in his discussion of the design argument. For example, just as there is no *a priori* connection between order and intelligence, so too there is no *a priori* connection between testimony and its veracity. Thus, just as the design argument must be an argument from experience, an argument from testimony for the occurrence of a miracle must be an argument from experience. This means that believing that some miracle *M* occurred on the basis of testimony of a certain sort is justified only if there is (i) a sufficiently strong union *U* between the class of instances of testimony of that sort and the class of instances of true testimony, and (ii) a sufficiently strong analogy between the testimony that *M* occurred and some of the instances of testimony that confirm *U*.

But how do we judge whether the crucial union and analogy are 'sufficiently strong' to justify believing that *M* occurred? One factor that must be taken into account is the strength of any arguments from experience against the occurrence of *M*. By the very definition of a miracle, however, there must be an argument from experience against *M*'s occurrence that amounts to a full proof in the sense of 'proof' explained earlier (in the section "The Design Argument"). Suppose, for example, that *M* is Fred's stepping out of a boat at sea and then walking around (unaided by technology) on the surface of the water. If the occurrence of this event really is a miracle, then it must violate an established law of nature. For Hume, this implies that there is at least one exceptionally strong argument from experience against the occurrence of such events. For example, such an argument might be based on the union between the class of human beings that step *onto* a body of (liquid) water and the class of human beings that step *into* that body of water. This union is supported by a very large number of confirming cases and weakened by no "contrary causes". Further, unlike the cases that confirm the union between water and non-solid substances, which for Hume's "Indian prince" are restricted to southern climates, the cases that confirm the union here are extremely diverse and thus no doubt include many cases that are closely analogous to Fred's case. Thus, at least one argument from experience in support of the claim that *M* did not occur amounts to a proof.

Of course, even proofs can vary in strength. While no proof will have fewer contrary causes than another (because no proof will have any contrary causes), one proof might have more confirming cases than another or a slightly stronger analogy (since a *perfect* similarity of *distinct* cases is impossible). Thus, Hume admits that it is *possible* to reasonably believe in the occurrence of a miracle on the basis of testimony, although he adds that even then confident belief would be impossible since the evidence provided by the weaker proof must still be "deducted" from the evidence provided by the stronger. He concludes that no one can reasonably believe in the occurrence of a miracle on the basis of testimony unless the falsity of that testimony would be "more miraculous" than the miracle reported. Clearly this is a standard that no actual miracle report has ever met.

Philosophers still debate the merits of this argument. While most would agree that Hume's method of weighing competing arguments from experience against each other is seriously flawed, many remain convinced that the core of Hume's argument can be reconstructed with success (e.g. Fogelin 2003). Others maintain that no such reconstruction is possible (e.g. Earman 2000).

THE COSMOLOGICAL ARGUMENT

Hume was as dismissive of what he took to be *a priori* arguments in natural religion as he was of miracle reports. He briefly discusses a version of the cosmological argument – the argument from contingent objects – in part IX of the

Dialogues, where Cleanthes speaks for Hume in raising various objections to the argument. The argument, defended by the character Demea, is based on the principle that every contingent thing must have a prior cause. Therefore, there is either an infinite succession of prior contingent causes or else an ultimate or first cause that exists necessarily. The former alternative is unsatisfactory because the whole eternal chain of causes would itself constitute a contingent thing and so would itself demand a cause. Therefore, the second alternative must be the true one. All contingent things must depend for their existence on some entity that exists necessarily, and this entity Demea (optimistically) calls a "Deity."

Cleanthes raises three objections. First, he objects to the whole idea of an *a priori* argument for God's existence. Since we can clearly conceive the non-existence of any being, no being can exist necessarily. Thus, God's existence is a matter of fact, from which it follows that it can be established only by experience. Secondly, if we allow for the possibility of some unknown qualities by virtue of which a deity exists necessarily, then why not allow for the possibility of unknown qualities by virtue of which the universe exists necessarily? Finally, Cleanthes rejects the causal principle on which the argument is based. If each (temporal) 'part' of an infinitely old universe is caused by an earlier part, then no additional cause or explanation is required of the whole, for the whole has no separate reality over and above its parts.

While contemporary philosophers do not agree with Cleanthes' 'conceivability criterion' for what is possible in the broadly logical sense, Cleanthes' second and third objections are still taken seriously today. This is one of the reasons that the so-called '*kalām* cosmological argument', which is based on the more plausible causal principle that whatever begins to exist has a cause of its existence, is currently more widely discussed than the argument from contingent objects, in spite of the fact that the *kalām* argument depends on the premise that the universe had a beginning, which is more questionable than the premise that the universe is contingent.

THE MORTALITY OF THE SOUL

Hume's posthumous publications include, in addition to the *Dialogues*, an essay called "Of the Immortality of the Soul", which was first published in 1777. The essay has three parts.

In the first part, Hume challenges metaphysical arguments for the immortality of the soul. Such arguments, he says, are all based on the assumption that thought cannot be a quality or an effect of a material substance and so must inhere in an immaterial soul that was not produced by the material world. Hume claims that one can neither know *a priori* nor decide by abstract reasoning whether or not, as a matter of *fact*, thought can inhere in or be the effect of matter. He adds that, even if an eternal spiritual substance does permeate the universe, it does not follow that souls are immortal. For just as human bodies are among the forms that matter temporarily takes, so too human souls may be among the forms that spirit takes, forms that are replaced at death by other forms in which those souls have no interest. Indeed, the fact that human beings sometimes lose their memories or even their consciousness prior to death supports this view.

In the second part of the essay, Hume addresses moral arguments for the immortality of the soul, especially arguments based on the assumption that God's justice demands a heaven and a hell. He rejects such arguments partly because nothing human beings do merits *everlasting* reward or punishment. Further, he affirms a consequentialist theory of punishment, and then asserts that no proper end or purpose can be served by punishment "after the whole scene is closed" (Hume [1777] 1998a: 93). His discussion here is of limited significance, both because it presupposes traditional Christian ideas about the afterlife and also because it focuses almost entirely on God's justice, ignoring the issue of whether or not God's benevolence implies an afterlife. Hume does, however, make one interesting point that applies to God's moral goodness generally. He says that "it is very dangerous to affirm, that [God] must always do what to us seems best. In how many instances would this reasoning fail us with regard to the present world" (*ibid.*: 92). Hume's point is this. If God does exist, then we can infer from God's goodness that God has good reasons for allowing the various horrific evils we find in the world. We do not, however, know what these reasons are. Thus, it could very well be the case that God also has good reasons unknown to us to allow our annihilation, and so we cannot correctly infer from God's goodness that we will be rescued from the grave.

Finally, Hume examines what he calls "physical arguments", that is, arguments based on the "analogy of nature". He maintains that these arguments strongly support the mortality of the soul. For example, he points out that weakness of the body in infancy, in sickness and in old age is typically accompanied by weakness of the mind. Indeed, even "Sleep, a very small effect on the body, is attended with a temporary extinction: at least, a great confusion in the soul" (*ibid.*: 95). This is strong evidence that, in the absence of supernatural assistance of some sort, the complete dissolution of the body in death is accompanied by the complete dissolution and thus permanent extinction of the soul.

CONCLUSION

Any history of the philosophy of religion will examine the philosophical contributions of theologians, atheologians and philosophers of religion. Hume belongs in the third group and is arguably the most influential member of that group in the entire history of philosophy. Unlike all too many contemporary thinkers who claim to be philosophers of religion, he is fully entitled to membership in that group because he had no use for apologetics, whether theistic or atheistic, religious or anti-religious. Greatly influenced by Newton, his philosophical enquiries about religion were 'experimental' in the sense that he genuinely tested his positions by argument and was willing to let his beliefs follow the arguments, no matter where they led. The importance of this contrast between Hume on the one hand and theologians and atheologians on the other cannot be overemphasized. By seeking justification for their religious beliefs, theologians and atheologians inevitably bias their enquiries and so fail to achieve their goal. Hume sought truth rather than justification, which made it possible for him to obtain the latter even if he, like all of us to one degree or another, fell short of the former.[1]

FURTHER READING

Butler, R. 1960. "Natural Belief and the Enigma of Hume". *Archiv fur Geschichte der Philosophie* **42:** 73–100.

Draper, P. 1991. "Hume's Reproduction Parody of the Design Argument". *History of Philosophy Quarterly* **8**: 135–48.

Gaskin, J. 1988. *Hume's Philosophy of Religion*, 2nd edn. Atlantic Highlands, NJ: Humanities Press.

Hurlbutt, R. 1965. *Hume, Newton, and the Design Argument*. Lincoln, NE: University of Nebraska Press.

Mossner, E. 1954. *The Life of David Hume*. Austin, TX: University of Texas Press.

O'Connor, D. 2001. *Hume on Religion*. New York: Routledge.

Owen, D. 1987. "Hume versus Price on Miracles and Prior Probabilities". *Philosophical Quarterly* **37**: 187–202.

Pike, N. 1970. "Hume on the Argument from Design". In David Hume, *Dialogues Concerning Natural Religion*, N. Pike (ed.), 127–38. Indianapolis, IN: Bobbs-Merrill.

Smith, N. 1947. "Introduction". In David Hume, *Dialogues Concerning Natural Religion*, N. Smith (ed.), 1–75. New York: Thomas Nelson.

Swinburne, R. 1970. *The Concept of Miracle*. London: Macmillan.

Tweyman, S. 1986. *Skepticism and Belief in Hume's Dialogues Concerning Natural Religion*. Dordrecht: Martinus Nijhoff.

Yandell, K. 1990. *Hume's "Inexplicable Mystery": His Views on Religion*. Philadelphia, PA: Temple University Press.

On EVIL/PROBLEM OF EVIL see also Chs 13, 18; Vol. 1, Chs 18, 19; Vol. 2, Ch. 16; Vol. 4, Chs 12, 18; Vol. 5, Chs 19, 22, 23. On IMMORTALITY OF THE SOUL see also Ch. 10; Vol. 1, Chs 2, 4; Vol. 2, Chs 12, 16. On NATURAL RELIGION/THEOLOGY see also Chs 4, 6, 7, 11, 12, 13, 23; Vol. 4, Chs 8, 12; Vol. 5, Ch. 23.

1. I am grateful to C. Mickey Lorkowski and David O'Connor for helpful comments on a preliminary draft of this chapter.

20

DENIS DIDEROT

David Adams

Any attempt to assess the attitude Denis Diderot (1713–84) took towards religion has to cope with the fact that the eighteenth-century *philosophes*, of whom Diderot was among the most prominent, are still rather controversial figures. To some commentators, both in their own time and in ours, their influence was a negative and baleful one. One of Diderot's contemporaries described him as a man "blind to the principles of religion and morality" (Chaudon 1759: 95), a comment echoed frequently during his lifetime (Trousson 1997) and even into our own day. Hence, the online *Catholic Encyclopedia* asserts that in the *Encyclopédie*:

> Reason gradually freed itself from the superstition of the past and claimed absolute independence. Ancient, or rather Christian, conceptions of God and the world were not even deemed worthy of the serious consideration of a 'thinker' ... soon the possibility of miracles and revelation was denied, while mysteries were regarded as absurd. Thus, in the place of traditional beliefs, new ideas were introduced, tending to rationalism, materialism, naturalism, and deism.
>
> (*Catholic Encylopedia* n.d.)

The persistence of these views (which certainly characterize much of what we now mean by 'the Enlightenment'; see Israel 2006b) has coloured to a considerable extent the way in which Diderot's attitude to religion has been perceived even by those with no theological axe to grind. His atheistic reputation has, conversely, helped to propel him into the ranks of those who are eulogized for leading the campaign against superstition and obscurantist religious dogma of all kinds. In his recent survey of modern intellectual trends, Francis Wheen hails the *Encyclopédie* as the very summa of Enlightenment thinking:

> 'Enlightenment' had two meanings, both evident in the *Encyclopédie*: the discovery of truth and its diffusion ... The Enlightenment had

> many critics, but its illuminating influence and achievements were apparent in the history of the next two centuries – the waning of absolutism and superstition, the rise of secular democracy, the understanding of the natural world. (2004: 6)

At a time when, for reasons that the *philosophes* would have readily recognized, secular and spiritual forces are once again at odds in Western civilization, the invocation of Diderot's name as a standard-bearer against religious intolerance points to his perceived importance as an enemy of anti-rationalism, and a champion of reason and rational enquiry. The question therefore arises of knowing to what extent this reputation is justified, and whether he can indeed be properly regarded as one of the founders of the Enlightenment campaign against religion in general, and against Christianity in particular.

EARLY EXPOSURE TO RELIGION

In one sense, it is quite understandable that Diderot's relationship to religion and to the Catholic Church should figure so prominently in assessments of his importance over two centuries and more. He was, after all, born into a deeply religious family, with which he retained close links all his life. His uncle was canon of the local cathedral in the eastern French town of Langres, where Diderot was born in 1713 (Hanna 1964). His younger brother, Didier-Pierre, became a priest with strong Jansenist leanings, which created deep hostility between the two men throughout their lives; his younger sister Angélique became a nun, and died insane in a convent in 1748. Diderot himself was educated by Jesuits at the college in Langres, where he showed outstanding brilliance in all his studies, receiving the tonsure in 1726, before proceeding to embark in 1729 on a theology degree at the Sorbonne. We know that he obtained his master's degree in 1732, and in 1735 a full degree in theology, which entitled him to an ecclesiastical benefice. But at some point thereafter he abandoned formal study, and with it the idea of becoming a priest; for a decade or more he seems to have led a bohemian life, educating himself in a number of disciplines, and earning a precarious living as a private tutor and a reviewer for journals.

The importance of these (unfortunately incomplete) biographical details is twofold. In the first place, we know that he was raised in an unusually pious home environment, surrounded as he was by close family members with strong connections to orthodox religious practices and beliefs; he was therefore exposed during his formative years to the teachings and practices of the Catholic Church, both at home and in his schooling. In the second place, we know that until he was on the verge of manhood, Diderot actively pursued a theological education, and showed every sign of wanting to enter the Church as his brother and sister did.

When we ask why he took this decision, we have to be careful to respect the historical and personal context in which his ideas developed. This is, first, because it is difficult to separate those views from his ideas on other intellectual questions, and secondly because they did not follow a simple sequential pattern that allows us to trace a clear 'evolution' in his thinking. Unlike Descartes, Rousseau or Kant, for example, Diderot is not a systematic thinker concerned to work out an all-encompassing explanatory account of what or how we know. His work exhibits, rather, a tendency to recur to the same theological questions (such as the nature and existence of God, the problem of theodicy, and the relationship between God and the individual) in relation to other concerns; that is, he sees them as problems to be considered in the context of other philosophical enquiries, such as the nature of matter, or what science can tell us about the physical world. He returns to them at intervals throughout his career, and examines them anew in the light of his changing perspectives on other questions. It is with this approach in mind that we need to examine Diderot's ideas on religion.

DIDEROT'S IDEAS ON RELIGION BEFORE 1760

As we do so, we shall need to bear in mind three major considerations. The first is that strict censorship existed in France under the *ancien régime*, and all new works had to be submitted for approval by (usually) specialist censors appointed by the authorities. Books of all kinds might incur the wrath of the censors for any number of reasons; in particular, the Catholic Church exercised a narrow and intolerant censorship, and was forever watching for signs of heresy or atheism (McManners 1998). Works that elicited little adverse comment in Great Britain at the time, such as Voltaire's *Letters Concerning the English Nation* (1733), were severely condemned and sentenced to be destroyed by the ecclesiastical authorities when they were published in France. Even novels such as Marmontel's *Bélisaire* (1767), which preached toleration and made no direct attack on Christianity, sooner or later fell foul of the authorities, despite having been approved officially when first published (Renwick 1974).

The second point to be borne in mind is that Diderot himself fell victim to this climate of hostility to the dissemination of new ideas, and his career can, in this respect, be divided into two parts. Prior to 1749, he was uninhibited in expressing his theological (and other) views in print, in a way that brought him considerable notoriety. But in that year his frankness earned him a sentence of three months in the prison at Vincennes, which he hated and which he remembered all his life. So keen was the memory of his incarceration, indeed, that he took care for the remainder of his career either to disguise his more subversive views, as in the *Encyclopédie* (which he edited between 1751 and 1772), or to refrain from publishing them at all during his lifetime. Hence, many of his most original and significant works did not see the light of day until long after his death, and the reassessment of his reputation in a variety of fields is consequently far from complete even today.

The third point concerns the larger theological context within which he was writing. As Jonathan Israel (2001) has argued, controversially but cogently, what we call the Enlightenment was in many respects an attempt to come to terms with, or to absorb, the impact of the doctrines of Spinoza. That is to say, many of the ideas that we associate with the period are a response to, or derive from, the doctrine that God and Nature are one. Diderot was as affected by this intellectual climate as any of his contemporaries, and we shall see that much of his work can be better understood in the context of the momentous changes in outlook occasioned by the work of Spinoza.

Although we have little information on the development of Diderot's ideas during the early 1730s, the appearance of his first works in the mid-1740s showed that he had moved a considerable distance from the orthodoxy to which he had subscribed as a young man. The earliest of his writings to bear any trace of his own views on God is his translation of Shaftesbury's *Essay Concerning Virtue and Merit* of 1745. Arguing that the universe displays an organic, and perhaps even divine, unity (a doctrine that Spinoza would certainly have recognized as deriving from his own), Diderot maintains that virtue is independent of belief (silently resurrecting Pierre Bayle's contention to this effect in the *Pensées sur la comète* [Miscellaneous thoughts occasioned by the comet] in 1682; see Hazard 1935: vol. 2, 212–15) and that atheism is preferable to fanatical religion, especially if fanaticism leads the believer to commit murderous acts in the hope of obtaining salvation. At this stage in his career, however, Diderot's focus (or more accurately, that of Shaftesbury, whose work he largely adopts; Venturi 1939: 49–50) is less on religious belief than on the question of knowing on what basis moral judgements can properly be made. His preference is for a utilitarian definition of morality, which will benefit society as a whole, and for a practical assessment of beauty, according to which a thing is beautiful if it fulfils its natural functions perfectly.[1] In such a perspective, the notion of doctrinal religious moral prohibitions is largely dispensed with; in this way, without wholly abandoning any system of formal belief, Diderot is no longer committed to the view that God is necessary either to explain our existence or to impart moral values. Indeed, he argues that by behaving virtuously and loving our fellow human beings, we achieve a god-like status here on earth, with no need for doctrinal complexities to guide us.

Much of this deistic and anti-fanatical outlook is retained in his *Pensées philosophiques* (Philosophical thoughts; hereafter *Pensées*; 1746), a work that provoked responses and rejoinders for decades afterwards (Morin 1975). While many of the arguments he deployed were commonplace in atheistic and deistic writings

1. This view was quite compatible with orthodoxy; the pious Charles Bonnet (1770) made the same point.

by that time, the *Pensées* struck a chord by its pithy and lapidary style, and for the ambiguity of its views on religion. It is true that in its own time the work was widely attacked for its alleged atheism and incredulity; yet one need not take so narrow a view of its significance. Depending on which sections one selects, it is equally possible to see in it a lingering attachment to Christianity (LXI) alongside a rejection of miracles (LIII) and of the authority of Scripture (LX). But it can also be read as a defence of scepticism (XXVIII) alongside an acceptance of materialist arguments deriving from Lucretian atomism (XXI), and a belief that God's handiwork is attested by the whole of Nature (XX). While the final section reiterates a defence of 'natural religion', this concept seems to consist of little beyond an inner conviction of the existence of an all-powerful God; this entity seems to be the source of our moral sense and, to judge from hints in the text, enjoins us to be tolerant, virtuous and humanitarian, but is not otherwise defined. Indeed, the *Pensées* as a whole leave one with the impression that Diderot is conducting a debate with himself as much as with his adversaries, in an attempt to clarify and fix his own religious beliefs. He seems nonetheless to have quite quickly come to the view that all revealed religions are little more than deformed versions of 'natural religion' set out in the *Pensées*, and that Christianity was in this sense not distinct from other creeds. These ideas are set out in a short tract, *De la Suffisance de la religion naturelle* (Of the sufficiency of natural religion), which dates from about 1746, although it did not appear until 1770. This growing alienation from Christianity did not, however, presage a wholesale adoption of deism on Diderot's part, because the next work in which he expressed religious ideas, *La Promenade du sceptique* (The sceptic's walk; hereafter *Promenade*; written in 1747 and published only in 1830) is a rather confusing *tour d'horizon* encompassing deism, atheism and a kind of bastardized Spinozism that gives prominence to, but cannot quite accept, Spinoza's belief that God and nature are one, and sees primarily the logical difficulties of this position without wholly rejecting it. The *Promenade*, an often ponderous allegory in itself, is perhaps best regarded as evidence of Diderot's continuing vacillation in his religious views, and of his increasing failure to identify any creed to which he could adhere wholeheartedly. He seems to waver between a materialism that would identify creator and creation, and a lingering belief in their separateness, without at any point declaring unambiguously any clear position. As Israel points out in *Enlightenment Contested* (2006a: 818–21), *De la Suffisance*, *Les Pensées philosophiques*, and *La Promenade du sceptique* all testify to the wider battle being waged in France at the time between Newtonian–Voltairian deism and an atheistic monism derived from Spinoza, although Diderot was not yet firmly in either camp.

Hence (though the matter cannot be decided conclusively on the rather confusing evidence of the text), there is some basis for stating that by the late 1740s Diderot was fast losing any lingering belief in any form of organized religion, and that even deism was now less appealing to him than it had been. Instead, he now began gradually to explore the consequences of a more mechanistic, materialist explanation of the universe. His ambition to arrive at such a view accounts for much of what we find in his next work, the *Lettre sur les aveugles* (Letter on the blind; hereafter *Letter*) of 1749.

The *Letter* is the first work by Diderot in which we find clear evidence of his tendency to blend fact and fiction seamlessly. The chief character is Nicholas Saunderson, who was, as Diderot says, professor of mathematics at Cambridge, although he exaggerates somewhat in making him wholly atheistic (Diderot 2000: 215–20). Saunderson's blindness is intended as a riposte to those who claim to see God in nature. Raging at God for having made him blind, Saunderson explains his imperfection by reference to the (metaphorically) blind workings of chance: atoms combine fortuitously to create beings who have a greater or lesser degree of completeness, which determines whether or not they can survive in a meaningless universe. On his deathbed he tells a visiting minister of religion, "If you wish me to believe in God, Mr Holmes, you must make me touch him" (Israel 2001: 710). Contemporary accounts state that Saunderson was no great enthusiast for religion, but was prepared to receive the sacraments on his deathbed, although he was prevented from doing so by the delirium that overcame him at the end. This scene thus offers a good example of Diderot's characteristic tendency throughout his career to blend fact and fiction.

But while such a view, ascribed to Saunderson, was no doubt controversial, it is really incidental to Diderot's polemical purposes in the *Letter.* In the first place, he wants to emphasize that our view of the world depends on our senses, or lack of them: taking Locke's *An Essay Concerning Human Understanding* (1690) as his starting-point, Diderot asks what difference the absence of one sense would make to our behaviour. The blind have no sense of moral outrage at nudity, but condemn theft unreservedly. Hence, while we may all have some innate, perhaps God-given, sense of moral values, those values are not necessarily shared by everyone, and may vary from one individual to another for reasons beyond our control.

At the same time, Diderot uses blindness in a more fundamentally epistemological way. Saunderson performs calculations by using a system of pins pushed into holes in a board, with different arrangements of pins standing for different numbers. His system enables him to converse about mathematics with the sighted, and Diderot draws from this the conclusion that perception is essentially mathematical, and that mathematics is the universal language of communication; that is, it functions as the common point of contact between all the senses, however many or few an individual may possess. Knowledge is therefore essentially mathematical, and if there is any God, he is imperfect, as his laws demonstrate, and of no significance in explaining creation. Indeed, the logical perfection of mathematics gives more certain knowledge than the study of natural laws, with their unpredictable eccentricities, can offer. If it is possible to see a progression up to 1749 in Diderot's thinking, it lies in his gradual estrangement from orthodox belief of any kind, and a rejection of the central doctrines of Christianity. A quasi-Lucretian atomism explains creation, and the theologically neutral power of mathematics provides the key to understanding the properties of material things (Hobart 1995: 153–82).

The controversial *Letter* was Diderot's last word on religion in a book entirely of his own devising for some years to come. This was partly because by that time he was fully occupied with the task of co-editing the *Encyclopédie* in collaboration with the mathematician D'Alembert, and partly because his imprisonment in Vincennes had taught him to beware of offending the authorities with his writings. Nonetheless, among the hundreds of articles that he contributed to the *Encyclopédie*, in addition to editing it, there were many that, if properly read and understood, give clues to the development of his ideas at this time (Proust 1962).

THE *ENCYCLOPÉDIE* (1751–72)

Because of its massive size (it eventually ran to thirty-three folio volumes, published between 1751 and 1772, with an index that appeared in 1780), the *Encyclopédie* could conceal many subversive or 'philosophical' views in the most obscure or unlikely places. Hence, articles dealing with God or with Christianity could be impeccably orthodox, but readers seeking stronger fare could find it in articles to which they were guided by the cross-references placed at the end of many entries. It was thus possible to derive a much less reassuring impression of the work if one read articles by Diderot such as "Agnus Scythicus" (1751), which warned of the dangers of accepting uncorroborated reports of apparently miraculous happenings (Werner 1971: 79–92), or "Philosophy of the Chinese" (1753), which defended the (allegedly) deistic doctrines accepted in China.[2] The impression that individual readers gained of the work, therefore, depended on which articles they read, and which cross-references they took the trouble to follow up.

While the vigorously anti-Christian, and even atheistic, tone of the *Letter* is toned down in the *Encyclopédie*, Diderot used the work repeatedly over many years to question the traditions and basis of Christianity, and indeed of all systematic religions. Partly for this reason, and partly because it shared some characteristics of other 'philosophical' works of the time that were banned, the *Encyclopédie* was denounced by the Paris Parlement in January 1759, and its official *privilège* was withdrawn a few weeks later.

Yet it took some time for this unfavourable impression of the *Encyclopédie* to crystallize clearly in the minds of the authorities. This was in part because many articles were entirely orthodox, and also because its approach to religious questions

2. Israel (2006a: 640–43) notes that Chinese philosophy was often linked with Spinozism, and had been since the time of Bayle.

was not as confrontational as they had come to expect from Diderot. This modulation of his approach can readily be explained not only by the strategy of the work as a whole, and by its concentration on the inadequacies of ecclesiastical tradition rather than on overt mockery of the sacred, but also by his own doubts and uncertainties about religion, which resurfaced in the 1750s after apparently being conquered by 1749.

THE "PRAYER" (1754)

A few years ago, the manuscript of a short "Prière" (Prayer) in Diderot's own hand came to light in a copy of his *Pensées sur l'interprétation de la nature* (Thoughts on the interpretation of nature) published in 1754 (see Diderot 2004). Although the "Prayer" was previously known from a later printed version included in an unreliable 1773 edition of Diderot's works, there was no proof of its authenticity until this autograph copy turned up. While there can never be any guarantee that Diderot is not playing games with his readers, the fact that only one copy is known in manuscript does lend it an air of intimacy and even secrecy, suggesting that we should take it seriously. It casts a clear light on his religious uncertainties at this time, and although Diderot does not require belief in God to make him love virtue, he does hope for reward in the afterlife. Echoing the arguments that Pascal uses in his *Pensées* (Thoughts; 1670) to persuade the sceptic to believe, Diderot will act as though God were able to look into his soul, and as though he were standing before his Maker.

The "Prayer" is not irrefutable evidence that Diderot now believes in God; but it does at least tell us that he is willing to lead his life as though he believes, and to model his conduct on virtue, without railing against the inequities of fate; this is a position at some remove from the blatant, even mocking, atheism of the *Letter*. The 1754 manuscript is all the more significant for an understanding of Diderot's complex attitude towards religion in that it dates from a time when we have little other firm evidence of his religious views, and what we do have is by no means consistent. On the one hand, we have the articles that he contributed to the *Encyclopédie*. On the other, we also have his more personal writings, especially his two plays *Le Fils naturel* (The natural son) of 1757, and *Le Père de famille* (The father of a family) of 1758. These texts, like the "Prayer", bespeak a willingness to believe in God, who is sometimes identified with Providence, but there is again a marked absence of any categorically Christian or doctrinal belief. When Diderot refers to the deity in his plays, it is usually as 'le Ciel' (heaven), rather than as any recognizably doctrinal concept. The will of heaven is made known to us through the voice of conscience, and the innate love of virtue evident in most human beings, to which we can conform if we choose to do so; indeed, in the case of any individual fit to be a member of a civilized society, the voice of conscience will not be silenced unless he or she does behave virtuously.

DIDEROT'S IDEAS ON RELIGION AFTER 1760

Yet this simplistic piety, devoid of doctrinal trappings and of any overtly religious content, could not really satisfy Diderot for long, and did not take him significantly beyond a position he had reached some years earlier. Even in *The Father of a Family*, the unfeeling, censorious Commandeur shows that conscience will not necessarily inflect the conduct even of men of distinction. A parallel dichotomy can be found in Diderot's near-contemporary novel *La Religieuse* (The nun); this was begun in 1760, and he worked intermittently on it for the next twenty years or more (May 1954), although it was not published until 1796, a dozen years after his death.

The Nun depicts the forcible incarceration in a convent of a young woman, Suzanne Simonin, who is illegitimate and abandoned by her family. Like his two plays, Diderot's novel allows some space for belief in human goodness: Suzanne herself is largely innocent (although not wholly so by the end of the narrative), and she encounters examples of self-sacrifice and true piety among the nuns and among those in the outside world who try to help her. Indeed, she even makes reference to Christ as her Saviour, and reads her Bible; yet the novel, like the plays, is much more strongly inclined towards deism, to a belief in God free of any doctrinal content.

But at the same time, like *The Father of a Family*, the novel demonstrates that individuals exist who remain impervious to the promptings of conscience, and who behave with brutal cruelty towards those who oppose their will. This point is made more emphatically in the novel than in the play, because it is illustrated by characters (such as the mother superior in the convent at Longchamp) who are supposedly imbued with the spirit of religion, so that the moral basis of Christianity as a religion of charity is largely undermined.

This point of view is developed further in *Le Neveu de Rameau* (Rameau's nephew), a work that, like *The Nun*, was not published for many years after Diderot's death,[3] although it absorbed much of his creative energy during the 1760s. *Rameau's Nephew* pits two speakers, 'He' and 'I', against each other in a dialogue that encompasses, *inter alia*, the education of children, the history of music and the disreputable conduct of some of the leading figures of contemporary Parisian society. This latter consideration may explain why Diderot carefully shielded the text from even his closest friends, for fear of provoking the ire of powerful adversaries, but this was not the only reason for his silence. In *Rameau's Nephew*, Diderot effectively undermines the basis of any religious belief: individuals such as Rameau have no moral sense, and no conventional understanding

3. The first edition of *Rameau's Nephew* was Goethe's German translation of 1805; the first correct French edition appeared only in 1823, and a bowdlerized English translation was published in 1878.

of virtue, and therefore no desire to seek God. Nor does it contain any optimistic doctrine of human improvement, such as we might expect to find from the pen of a man who had edited the *Encyclopédie* with its strong emphasis on technological progress and its belief in the power of reason to improve the lot of mankind. All the conventional arguments that Rameau's interlocutor deploys to convince him that good is better than evil are fruitless, and they cannot even agree on what constitutes vice and virtue.

While neither speaker can be said to emerge clearly victorious from the encounter, it is apparent that Diderot (who to some extent represents 'I') now harbours strong doubts that virtue is either innate or that it will necessarily guide all people. If the cruel mother superior depicted in *The Nun* did at least have some semblance of religious belief to guide her, Rameau almost revels in his admission that he is an unprincipled wastrel, who flaunts his lack of moral sense, to the outrage of his interlocutor. He remains deaf to all entreaties to mend his ways, blaming his misconduct on his "paternal molecule", which we might nowadays call his genetic inheritance. By the time he was writing *Rameau's Nephew*, therefore, Diderot had moved very far indeed from the belief in some form of deity that can be discerned in the "Prayer" of 1754, and seemed to have at least stood on the threshold of a godless, amoral world where traditional pieties were the object of mockery and scorn.

The key to this altered perspective is provided by his renewed interest in materialism (Lange 1879), a term best understood in his case as a belief that matter is organized in accordance with natural laws over which we have no control. Hence, nature can produce, for complex reasons beyond our full understanding, what we take to be anomalies. This view had of course been adumbrated in the *Letter* in 1749, where Saunderson asked what offence he had committed against God to deserve his blindness. The question had remained unanswered in his terms, but it is clear from the *Letter* as a whole that it is the operation of imperfect natural laws that explains Saunderson's condition (Chouillet 1977: 107–8). This (unintentionally?) echoes Leibniz's doctrine, in his *Essais de Théodicée sur la bonté de Dieu, la liberté de l'homme et l'origine du mal* (Theodicy essay on the benevolence of God, the free will of man and the origin of evil), published in 1710, that God operates in the best way possible, rather than the best possible way. There is in fact some evidence that Diderot knew Leibniz's work, if only at second-hand, in the late 1740s. Be that as it may, Diderot took the matter no further at that time,[4] and, as we have seen, became more closely attached to some form of religious belief during the years leading up to the composition of *Rameau's Nephew.* He now revisits the question of how the laws of nature operate, but this time examines

4. His view was reiterated in his letter to the dramatist Paul Landois on 29 June 1756 (see Diderot 1975– : vol. 9, 258).

more the moral consequences to which they can lead, rather then the sensorial anomalies discussed in the *Letter.*

However, although Rameau is still judged by his interlocutor on the basis of moral norms derived from traditional Christian teaching, *Rameau's Nephew* makes no mention at any point of the role of God in determining the laws of nature or moral conduct. The conventional judgements uttered by his interlocutor may enable Rameau to be condemned by 'right-thinking' members of society, but their views have no effect on him, and provide no means of rectifying his conduct or values. In such circumstances, Diderot appears to have reached an impasse in his system of belief: God is absent, nature can produce individuals who are morally bankrupt, and no remedy is to be found.

A similar outlook informs the *Rêve de d'Alembert* (D'Alembert's dream; hereafter *Dream*), written in 1769 but not published until 1830. This discretion in delaying publication is as understandable now as it was in earlier cases: in the *Dream*, Diderot advocates a wholly materialist interpretation of creation, in which matter is transformed from living to dead to living, in an endless cycle that presupposes that sensitivity is inherent in matter itself, and is merely quiescent in what we take to be 'dead'. Diderot thus comes close to stating a belief in the identity of God with God's creation, since there is now no need for any divine intervention to explain the workings of nature; the process is more all-embracing than in the *Letter*, and the *Dream* is notable in particular for its exploration of the sexual consequences of materialism, which are, unsurprisingly, divorced from any moral considerations of the kind that customarily inflect human relationships in Western, Christian societies.

Indeed, his *Supplément au voyage de Bougainville* (Supplement to Bougainville's voyage; hereafter *Supplement*), which was written in 1772 but published only in 1796, takes these sexual investigations further, and establishes, with a gleefully Voltairian irony and an undisguised mockery of Church teaching, that marriage, fidelity and continence are contrary to human nature, and that primitive societies (such as that of Tahiti in which the work is set) are more 'advanced' than those of Europe: they know nothing of God, the Bible or the Church, and are not impeded in living their lives 'naturally' and, of course, happily. This atheistic joy in innocently indulging human appetites was both an echo of the primitivism extolled by figures such as Jean-Jacques Rousseau, and a riposte to it since, while Diderot deplored, as Rousseau did, the depredations of European civilization and its deformation of our natural tendencies, he located happiness in human society, not in the misanthropic solitude of the sage of Geneva (Mason & Wokler 1992: xv–xxi).

The marked hostility to Christianity shown in the *Supplement* echoes that of another work written at the same time, *Les Eleuthéromanes* (Those zealous for freedom), published in 1796. This is a violent diatribe, in the name of nature, against the domination exerted by the Church and the monarchy; Diderot has his 'child of nature' proclaim:

"La nature n'a fait ni serviteur ni maître;
Je ne veux ni donner ni recevoir de lois":
Et ses mains ourdiroient les entrailles du prêtre,
Au défaut d'un cordon pour étrangler les rois.
["Nature has created neither servant nor master;
I do not wish to make or be subject to laws";
And his hands would plait the guts of the priest,
For want of a rope with which to strangle kings.]
(Diderot 1875: vol. 9, 15–16, my translation)[5]

Such bloodthirsty ferocity might easily have become moral nihilism of the kind that Joseph de Maistre, among others, was to accuse the *philosophes* of fomenting (Berlin 2002: 131–54). Yet Diderot did not long remain in this mood, for his novel *Jacques le fataliste et son maître* (James the fatalist and his master; hereafter *Jacques*; written 1770–82, and published in 1796) offers a more humane perspective on human life than these macabre outpourings. Ecclesiastical figures are shown as corrupt, venal or absurd, but the focus of the novel is its sympathy for the plight of the underdog, and a conviction that charity alone can save us from the perils of selfishness, jealousy and hatred. The novel makes much of Jacques' alleged fatalism, which he attributes to Spinoza, but it would be difficult to show that its inspiration is genuinely Spinozist. For one thing, Jacques' fatalism is a vacillating belief, which is ultimately devoid of significance, since he continues to act as though he were free. For another, the equation of God with nature, which was so distinctive a feature of Spinoza's thinking, does not feature here. Finally, the novel does explore (echoing to some extent the *Supplement*) a physiological determinism that accounts for universal features of human behaviour such as the force of the sexual impulse, and the tendency of to break off relationships unpredictably as individuals seek new partners; at the same time, like earlier works by Diderot, it advocates goodness to others and forgiveness as essential ingredients of human happiness.

By the time he wrote *Jacques*, therefore, Diderot had come to adopt a perspective in which religion had no place, and in which the positive capacities and qualities of human beings were foregrounded in his view of individual conduct and in his moral thinking. His journey to this point was not an easy one, and was fraught with self-questioning and reversals of earlier views; yet there seems little doubt that by the time he died in 1784 he had evolved a position in which his earlier alternations between belief and atheism had been replaced by a confidence in humanity that typified much of the more positive thinking of the Enlightenment in Europe as a whole.

5. The last two lines are often erroneously attributed to Jean Meslier (1664–1729), a recalcitrant priest whose *Testament* was published by Voltaire, in a heavily doctored edition, in 1764.

FURTHER READING

Furbank, P. 1992. *Diderot: A Critical Biography*. London: Secker & Warburg.
Hoyt, N. & T. Cassirer 1965. *Encyclopedia, Selections: Diderot, D'Alembert, and a Society of Men of Letters*. New York: Bobbs-Merrill.
Mason, J. 1982. *The Irresistible Diderot*. London: Quartet.
Wilson, A. 1972. *Diderot*. New York: Oxford University Press.

On NATURE/NATURALISM see also Chs 21, 22; Vol. 4, Chs 5, 10; Vol. 5, Ch. 4. On RATIONALISM see also Chs 18, 22; Vol. 5, Ch. 22. On VIRTUE see also Ch. 21; Vol. 1, Chs 2, 11, 14, 15.

21

IMMANUEL KANT

Eckart Förster

The philosophy of Immanuel Kant (1724–1804) covers a wide range of topics, yet questions concerning God and religion were of central importance to his thought throughout his life. His mother was a pietist, and from early on instilled in Kant a sense for the beauty and harmony in nature, in which she encouraged her son to see the traces of God's wisdom. Kant never lost his affinity for this way of looking at the world in general, and for the physico-theological argument for God's existence in particular, although his philosophical convictions imposed serious limitations on what could be known about God.

In one of his earliest publications, a Latin dissertation titled *Principiorum primorum cognitionis metaphysicae nova dilucidatio* (A new elucidation of the first principles of metaphysical cognition; 1755), Kant attempted to prove God's existence. His argument there proceeds from the concept of possibility and can be summarized as follows. To judge that something is possible is to say that the concepts or representations related in the judgement do not contradict each other but are compatible. This may be called the formal condition of possibility. But there is also a material condition. For in all comparisons, what is to be compared must be given beforehand. If there is nothing to be compared, there can be no comparison and hence no possibility. This means that, for Kant, nothing can be conceived as possible unless whatever is real in every possible representation or concept exists. And, he maintains, it must exist with absolute necessity, because in its absence nothing at all would be possible. Thus possibility itself would be impossible, which cannot be thought without self-contradiction.

Moreover, Kant claims, all the realities that make up the material for all possible representations must be thought of as united in a single infinite being. For if they were distributed among several existing things, any of them would have its existence limited in certain ways, as is the case with all finite things. But absolute necessity does not belong to such privations in the way it must belong to the realities in question: the manner and degree of such limitations would be contingent. To exist necessarily, therefore, the realities in question must exist without any limitations whatsoever. That is to say, they must constitute a single, infinite being. This being we may call 'God', who is thus the absolutely necessary principle of all possibility. But it is also the ground of the unity of our experience of these realities. For our experience of the world is single and all-embracing which, Kant maintains, would be unthinkable unless all things are "maintained, in mutual relations, by their common ground [*principio*], namely the divine intellect" (1.413).[1]

> [T]hat there is anything at all which can be thought, from which, through combination, limitation, and determination, there subsequently results the notion of any conceivable things – this would be unintelligible unless whatever is real in a notion existed in God, the source of all reality. (1.395–6)

A few years later, in *The One Possible Basis for a Demonstration of the Existence of God* (1763), Kant revised this argument. Realities may oppose each other and cancel each other out, like a force operating in one direction and an equally strong force in the opposite direction. The result would be a privation, or a void, which cannot be part of God's existence. Thus God cannot contain the realities themselves, but only the ground of all realities. But even this revised argument could not satisfy Kant for long. Eventually he realized that he, as well as all thinkers before him who believed they could prove God's existence by philosophical methods, had confused the necessity of thought with the necessity of things. As he put it in 1781 in his *Critique of Pure Reason*:

> A concept is always possible if it does not contradict itself. That is the logical mark of possibility … Yet it may nonetheless be an empty concept, if the objective reality of the synthesis through which the concept is generated has not been established in particular; but as was shown above, this always rests on principles of possible experience and not on principles of analysis (the law of contradiction). This is a warning not to infer immediately from the possibility of concepts (logical possibility) to the possibility of things (real possibility). (A596)

In other words, logical necessity is not the same as necessary existence; nor is logical possibility the same as real or objective possibility. Consequently, in the *Critique of Pure Reason*, Kant sets out to show that theoretical proofs of God's existence are *in principle* impossible because it is not possible by theoretical means

1. All references in the text are to the volume and page numbers of Kant (1900–). These appear as marginal numbers in all standard translations of Kant's works. Numbers preceded by the letter A refer to the first edition of Kant's *Critique of Pure Reason*. The translations I have used (and occasionally modified) are those in Kant (1992–).

to show the 'real possibility' of God, that is, to show that the concept of God is not an empty concept. In addition, Kant explains in detail how the three traditional proofs of God's existence – the 'ontological', the 'cosmological' and the 'physico-theological' arguments – fall short of their intended goal. The ontological proof infers the existence of God from the concept of God as a most perfect being, alleging that a perfect being cannot lack anything the possession of which would make it more perfect, hence it cannot lack existence. But 'existence' denotes a spatiotemporal position, Kant argues, not a predicate or a perfection: there is no contradiction involved in thinking that the being itself, with all its predicates, does not exist. The cosmological argument, by contrast, asserts that everything contingent must have a cause for its existence, which again must have a cause until one assumes an uncaused and therefore necessary first being. But this argument, by itself, does not tell us anything about the properties of this allegedly necessary being. It does not, for example, establish that this being has any moral qualities. Its identification with, for example, the Christian God must remain entirely unwarranted unless the argument falls back on the ontological argument with its claim that only the most perfect being is a necessary being. Both arguments thus collapse together. This leaves the physico-theological argument. It infers God's existence from the "purposiveness and harmonious adaptation of so much in nature", which seems to presuppose an intelligent author as its cause: "This proof always deserves to be mentioned with respect. It is the oldest, the clearest, and the most accordant with the common reason of mankind. It enlivens the study of nature, just as it itself derives its existence from this study and through it receives ever renewed force" (A623). But this line of reasoning, drawing as it does on an analogy with human art, could at best establish an architect of the world, a Demiurge who gives a particular form to a substance not of his own making. It does not establish the existence of an all-sufficient primordial being who created the world itself. In order to reach its goal, therefore, the argument would have to proceed from the contingency of the purposive objects of nature to the idea of a necessary cause, and from there to the identification of that cause with the all-perfect being. In other words, it would have to fall back on the two previously mentioned arguments and, since they have been shown to fail, the physico-theological argument cannot succeed either.

It is important to realize that in the *Critique of Pure Reason* Kant does not claim to have demonstrated the non-existence of God, but only to have shown that theoretical reason must remain agnostic with regard to God's existence. All existential claims are synthetic and thus go beyond what is thought in a concept; consequently, the truth-value of such claims cannot be decided without recourse to experience. This qualification is crucial, because by limiting theoretical knowledge to possible experience, Kant opens a space for moral enquiry, and with it for objects that are non-empirical and are thus not objects of possible experience.

This may be illustrated with the help of an example. According to theoretical reason, every event has an antecedent cause. Within its domain, the realm of possible experience, causal determinism therefore rules supremely, and freedom, which is a spontaneous cause without antecedent determination, could not occur. But by limiting the principle of determinism to possible experience, Kant can argue that freedom is at least not impossible, for its origin does not lie in the empirical world but rather in what he calls the supersensible or intelligible realm. On the other hand, practical reason is certain of the reality of a moral law. This law manifests itself first and foremost in our realization that certain actions that did happen ought not to have happened. This cannot be explained by reference to antecedent natural causes: "However many natural grounds or sensible stimuli there may be that impel me to *will*, they cannot produce the '*ought*' but only a willing that is yet far from necessary but rather always conditioned" (A548). But if I ought to have willed and acted differently, Kant claims, I must have been free to do so; hence the moral law presupposes the reality of freedom.

So, by curtailing theoretical reason in this way, the *Critique of Pure Reason* at the same time provides room for genuine moral philosophy, and it is only in the latter context, according to Kant, that philosophy can speak of God with authority. To understand this we must realize that the lesson we learned from Kant with respect to modality – that real possibility must be distinguished from merely logical possibility – also applies to practical reason: if the concepts of practical reason are not empty concepts, their real possibility must be demonstrable. Their "possibility and practical reality", however, consists in their achievability or "realizability" (*Ausführbarkeit*) (5.457). In other words, what ought to be done must be doable: an end that is prescribed must be achievable, or we are dealing with empty concepts. Now, if the ends of pure practical reason were such that they are inevitably prescribed yet not achievable without God's cooperation, Kant argues, then God's existence would have to be a necessary postulate of pure practical reason. ("By a postulate of pure practical reason, I understand a *theoretical* proposition, though one not demonstrable as such, insofar as it is attached inseparably to an *a priori* unconditionally valid *practical* law" [5.122].)

This argument is developed most prominently in Kant's *Critique of Practical Reason* (1788), where it takes the following form. If freedom is possible, it must be autonomous. For freedom does not mean randomness or arbitrariness. Even a free will is law-governed. However, a will can only be subject to law and remain free at the same time if the law to which it is subject has been authored by itself. The only such law is the moral law. It is not just a law of prohibition, however, but a law that requires its realization in the physical world:

> This law is to furnish the sensible world, as a *sensible nature* (in what concerns rational beings), with the form of a world of the understanding, that is, of a *supersensible* nature, though without infringing upon the mechanism of the former ... For, the moral law in fact transfers us, in idea, into a nature in which pure reason, if it were accompanied with suitable physical powers, would produce the highest good,

> and it determines our will to confer on the sensible world the form of a whole of rational beings. (5.43)

Consequently, such a highest good – the ultimate end of our morality – must be possible in the sensible world, or the moral law would prescribe something unachievable: "If, therefore, the highest good is impossible according to practical rules, then the moral law, which commands us to promote it, must be fantastic and directed to empty imaginary ends and must therefore in itself be false" (5.114).

This last claim of Kant's has been challenged even by the best and most faithful of his commentators (e.g. Beck 1960: 242–5), who argue that the relevance of the moral law cannot depend on whether the highest good is possible or not. So let us look at Kant's claim more closely.

The concept of the highest good, Kant tells us, "contains an ambiguity that, if not attended to, can occasion needless disputes" (5.110). The 'highest' can either mean the 'supreme' (*supremum*) in the sense that it is not subordinate to a higher condition; or it can mean the 'complete' (*consummatum*) in the sense that it is "that whole which is not part of a still greater whole of the same kind (*perfectissimum*)" (5.110). Now virtue is undoubtedly the highest condition of all that can be practically desirable: it is the supreme good. But this does not mean that it is also the entire and perfect good for a human being who, in virtue of being finite and physical, also has needs and desires:

> [F]or this, *happiness* is also required, and that not merely in the partial eyes of a person who makes himself an end but even in the judgment of an impartial reason, which regards a person in the world generally as an end in itself. For, to need happiness, and to be also worthy of it, and yet not to participate in it cannot be consistent with the perfect volition of a rational being that would at the same time have all the power, even if we think of such a being only for the sake of the experiment. [For] virtue and happiness together constitute possession of the highest good for one person,[2] and happiness distributed in exact proportion to morality (as the worth of a person and his worthiness to be happy). (5.110)

As Kant points out, and as will readily be admitted, experience does not show that virtuous actions will meet with corresponding happiness; it seems, rather, often to suggest the opposite. Nor does it follow from the definitions of these terms that virtue implies happiness, or happiness virtue. Their proportional relation is neither an empirical truth nor an analytic one. Is the highest good impossible,

2. That Kant's argument here concerns that which 'one person' must rationally desire will become important later.

then? Must it be said that the moral law is "directed to empty imaginary ends and therefore in itself false" (5.114) because its ultimate object is unachievable?

This is where God enters as a necessary 'postulate' of pure practical reason. To begin with, even theoretical reason has to draw a distinction between the sensible and the supersensible world. Given this distinction, it is not impossible that a causality other than natural causality produces the required connection in this world between virtue and happiness:

> [I]t is not impossible that the morality of disposition should have a connection, and indeed a necessary connection, as cause with happiness as effect in the sensible world; but this relation is indirect, mediated by an intelligible Author of nature. This connection, however, can occur only contingently in a system of nature which is merely the object of the senses and as such is not sufficient to the highest good. (5.115)

The highest good, then, would be possible if there was a being that both knows our moral worth and is causally efficacious over nature. That is to say, pure practical reason must postulate God's existence as the sole condition of the real possibility of the highest good.

Thus Kant's argument. How well does it stand up to philosophical scrutiny? If, in the concept of the highest good, we must distinguish between the 'supreme' good (virtue) and the 'complete' good (happiness proportional to virtue), then it seems we must also distinguish between their respective 'real' possibilities, that is, their respective achievabilities. For the supreme good not to be an empty concept, it must be possible to realize moral ends in the physical world, because it is towards other beings in this world (and ourselves) that we have moral duties. For the complete good not to be an empty concept, it must be possible that virtue and happiness correspond proportionally.

In the *Critique of Practical Reason*, Kant does not clearly distinguish these two arguments but rather unites them in a single antinomy: if the highest good is not realizable, then the moral law itself must be inherently false. But this is not convincing. Let us call the argument that a virtuous disposition (moral ends) is realizable in nature the realizability argument (*R*), and the argument that there can be a proportional correspondence between virtue and happiness the proportionality argument (*P*). Then *R* must be valid if the moral law is not to be 'false', for a law that cannot be applied and hence regulates nothing is not a law. But whether or not *R* is valid is independent of the validity of *P*. The validity of *R* depends solely on whether I can realize ends in a deterministic world; it does not depend on whether there can be a proportional happiness resulting from it. Even if I knew that *P* was invalid, the moral law would retain its binding force as long as I knew that *R* was valid. Only *R* is required for the 'supreme' good; *P* is required only for the 'complete' good. Unfortunately, Kant blurs this distinction when he claims that the moral law would itself be 'false' if the highest good was unrealizable.

The shortcomings afflicting Kant's position in the *Critique of Practical Reason* are overcome in his third Critique, the *Critique of the Power of Judgment* (1790). By this time, investigations into the nature of beauty, more precisely, into the nature of natural beauty, had led Kant to the discovery of a hitherto unknown *a priori* principle, a principle indigenous to the power of judgement. It reveals to us:

> a technique of nature, which makes it possible to represent it as a system in accordance with laws the principle of which we do not encounter anywhere in our entire faculty of understanding, namely that of a purposiveness with respect to the use of the power of judgment in regard to appearances, so that this must be judged as belonging not merely to nature in its purposeless mechanism but rather also to the analogy with art. Thus it actually expands not our cognition of natural objects, but our concept of nature, namely as a mere mechanism, into the concept of nature as art. (5.246)

This principle of the power of judgement states that nature exhibits a formal purposiveness relative to our faculties. As such, it "mediates" between the concepts of nature and the concept of freedom and "makes possible the transition" from the legislation of the one to that of the other (5.196). Hence we have *a priori* reason to regard the realization of moral ends in nature as possible; the moral law is not void and inherently 'false'.

There is, then, no reason to postulate God's existence for the objective validity of the supreme good. Is there a reason to hang on to the thought of a perfect or complete good and to postulate God's existence for its possibility? This question also receives a remarkable new answer in the *Critique of the Power of Judgment*, this time in connection with Kant's discussion of teleology in nature. In our experience of the world, Kant now argues, we come across objects that we cannot regard mechanically as mere aggregates of their parts, but have to view as internally organized and purposive: living organisms. They in turn stand in essential relations to the elements of their environment (water, air, light, food, mates, etc.), without which they could not exist and propagate themselves. In other words, once we assume natural purposes, we must also assume the means for the realization of their ends. These, in turn, must be regarded as purposive even though their modes of operation may be entirely mechanical. That is, once we admit natural purposes we cannot but extend our teleological reflections to nature as a whole: "This concept leads reason into an order of things entirely different from that of a mere mechanism of nature, which will here no longer satisfy us" (5.377).

If things in nature stand in relation to other things as means to ends, and the latter in turn may be means to yet other ends, the question arises whether this natural chain terminates in a being that is not a means to other natural ends?

This can only be the human being, since it alone can set purposes for itself and use all other objects of nature as means to its own ends. Endowed with the ability to create ends of their own choosing, human beings assign and arrange things in such a way as to further their own happiness, and from this point of view, humanity may be said to be the ultimate end of *nature*. But we only need to ask why human beings should exist on earth in the first place in order to realize that nothing in nature has an unconditional worth or is a *final* end ("A *final end* is that end which needs no other as the condition of its possibility" [5.434]).

Only if a human being is regarded not merely as a natural being but also as a being capable of freedom and autonomy, and hence author of, and subject to, the moral law, is a human being an end in itself and hence must never be treated as a mere means to other ends. We can give to ourselves an absolute, not merely relative, worth through the principle on which we base our actions and become potential members in a moral world as a kingdom of ends. In this way, our existence can be viewed not only as an end of nature but as the final end of *creation*: "we recognize the human being as the end of creation only as a moral being" (5.444).

We can now reconnect with our discussion of the highest good as the perfect good. It may now be regarded not only as the perfect harmony of virtue and nature, but as the final end of creation. "For if creation has a final end at all, we cannot conceive of it except as having to correspond to the final end of morality (which alone makes possible the concept of an end)" (5.453). But *if* we conceive of an end of creation in the above sense, moral relations must be a condition of its realization just as much as the laws of physical nature are a condition of its realization. In other words, there must be consequences attached to violations of the moral law, just as there are consequences attached to violations of nature's laws. For a law whose transgressions had no consequences would not be a law constitutive of the final end of creation. Consequently, Kant points out, the question arises where the executive authority with respect to the law of morality is to be sought. It is this question, then, that obliges us to go beyond the physical world and to seek an intelligent supreme principle with respect to the relation of nature to the moral side of our being. For if the world be not altogether devoid of a final end, Kant claims, any bad man dwelling in a world subject to moral laws and being part of creation, must "sacrifice his subjective end (of happiness), as the sole condition under which his existence can be congruent with the final end" (5.443). If this is so, then there is but a short argument to the assumption of the *Critique of Practical Reason* that such an omnipotent moral being would also not permit that a virtuous creature who is both in need of happiness and also worthy of it might nevertheless not partake of it (5.110).

We can thus summarize Kant's position with regard to God's existence as found in his *Critique of the Power of Judgment*. We are determined *a priori* by reason to further the highest good in the world as far as is possible for us. But the fact that we have set this concept of a highest good before us *a priori* is not enough.

Only virtue as the *supreme* good is entirely within our control. For the objective reality (real possibility) of the concept of a *complete* good it is further required that creation should have a final end.

> For the objective theoretical reality of the concept of the final end of rational beings in the world it is requisite not merely that we have a final end that is set before us *a priori*, but also that the existence of creation, i.e., the world itself, has a final end – which, if it could be proven *a priori*, would add objective reality to the subjective reality of the final end. (5.453)

This would amount to a "moral proof of the existence of God", as the heading of §87 of the *Critique of the Power of Judgment* states. But such a proof has obvious limitations, which Kant spells out in §88. From the seemingly purposive structure of nature and the moral autonomy of the human being we infer the assumption of a final end of creation, and from there the concept, not just of a creator of the world, but of a moral author of the world, a God. But the concept of an end is a concept that derives its meaning from the context of human agency. When we apply it to God, we transfer it, by means of an analogy, to a being we do not know independently. The concept of an end of creation, therefore, can be a concept for reflective judgement only, not for determinate judgement:

> For we cannot presume to understand that just because the principles of morally practical reason are essentially different from those of technically practical reason in us, they must also be so in the supreme cause of the world if it is assumed to be an intelligence, and that it needs a special and different kind of causality for the final end than for mere ends of nature; hence we cannot presume that in our final end we have not merely a *moral ground* for assuming a final end of creation (as an effect) but also for assuming a *moral being* as the original ground of creation. But we may well say that *given the constitution of our faculty of reason*, we could not even make comprehensible the kind of purposiveness related *to the moral law* and its object that exists in this final end without an author and ruler of the world who is at the same time a moral legislator. (5.455; cf. 464 n.)

There is, however, another complication. If we view the highest good as the end of creation, all connotations of *individual* happiness must recede into the background. The final end of creation is not the individual moral being but can only be humanity in mutual ethical relationships. To realize the end of creation, humanity's ethical efforts must ultimately coincide to create such a state. Kant addresses this topic in a work published three years later in 1793, *Religion Within the Boundaries of Mere Reason*. Not surprisingly, instead of our duty to promote the highest good, Kant now emphasizes our duty to promote "the highest good as a social (*gemeinschaftliches*) good" which is a duty "not of human beings toward human beings but of the human race toward itself" (6.97).

Initially, it must seem impossible that an ethical commonwealth is achievable as a collective human effort. As early as 1784, in a brilliant essay called "Ideas for a Universal History From a Cosmopolitan Point of View", Kant had argued that the human being is inflicted by nature with "an unsocial sociability", that is, the need to enter into social relationships while at the same time being antagonistic and driving towards isolation: "he expects opposition on all sides because, in knowing himself, he knows that he, on his own part, is inclined to oppose others" (8.21). This social antagonism, Kant had argued, is what awakens the individual's powers and talents "in order to achieve a rank among his fellows whom he cannot tolerate but from whom he cannot withdraw" (8.21). It is nature's way to ensure the development of all our different capacities and talents, and thus to force a development from barbarism to culture and civilization, and from there to, eventually, a "civic union of the human race" (8.29). Yet this very nature of ours is what seems to make impossible the highest good in the sense of the supreme good, if it is understood as a social or *gemeinschaftliches* good.

In *Religion Within the Boundaries of Mere Reason*, the social unsociability of the members of society is called, in analogy with the Hobbesian state of nature, the ethical state of nature. Even agents with the best of intentions find themselves surrounded by envy and greed, social rivalry and power struggles. By being a member of society we are in an equivalent state to the Hobbesian state of nature, namely in a state of danger and unpredictability in which our moral disposition is under continuous attack from temptations to violate it. "[I]t suffices that they are there, that they surround him, and that they are human beings, and they will mutually corrupt one another's moral disposition and make one another evil" (6.94). If the highest good is to be possible as a social good, then, it can come about only through a union of *all* individuals, who must jointly leave the ethical state of nature in order to form a "universal republic based on laws of virtue".

Such an ethical commonwealth would have to have a different "principle of unification" (*Vereinigungsprinzip*), as Kant calls it, than the civil state from which it is to emerge, and consequently also a different form and constitution. For a civil state to be possible, statutory laws are required that bind its members together externally. These are enforced by three different powers (legislation, executive and jurisdiction) that of necessity are divided among three different departments within the state. By contrast, an ethical union, which has virtue as its binding principle, must be based on a legislation that is "purely internal" (6.100). What matters here is not only the legality of actions, as in a civil state, but the dispositions or *Gesinnungen* from which the actions spring. But these are inner states and hence not accessible to others, sometimes not even to the agent himself. There must therefore be a power, outside humanity, that knows the intentions and dispositions of the agents and combines the three powers of a state within itself. To constitute an ethical commonwealth, therefore, there must be, in Kant's words, an omniscient being that is an omnipotent and holy legislator, a benevolent ruler and preserver of the human race, and an administrator of his own holy laws, that is, a righteous judge. The idea of such a divine being, Kant points out, is contained analytically "in the concept of a people regarded as a[n ethical] community" (6.140).

We must thus distinguish three distinct elements with regard to the highest good as the final end of creation: a subjective condition of its possibility (changed dispositions of its members); an objective condition of its possibility (the threefold power of legislation, execution and jurisdiction united in one omniscient being); and an objective consequence (mutual happiness).

> Since by himself the human being cannot realize the idea of the highest good inseparably bound up with the pure moral disposition, either with respect to the happiness which is part of that good or with respect to the union of the human beings necessary to the fulfillment of the end, and yet there is also in him the duty to promote the idea, he finds himself driven to believe in the cooperation or the management of a moral ruler of the world, through which alone this end is possible. (6.139)

A closer look at this solution, however, reveals that it is ultimately untenable. First consider "with respect to happiness". In an ethical commonwealth, morality and happiness are inevitably in harmony. Since in such a commonwealth the actions of all individuals are guided by the principles of one's own perfection and the happiness of others, they would themselves be the authors of their own enduring happiness and that of others. As Kant had already stated in the first *Critique*, in a moral world, "freedom, partly moved and partly restricted by moral laws, would itself be the cause of the general happiness, and rational beings, under the guidance of such principles, would themselves be the authors of their own enduring welfare and at the same time that of others" (A809). God would not be required to bring about such perfect harmony. However, we do not all act virtuously; on the contrary, as members of a civil society, we "mutually corrupt one another's moral disposition and make one another evil". The efforts of an individual have little effect with respect to the highest good unless everyone else strives towards the same goal. Therefore, secondly, God is required "with respect to the union of the human beings necessary to the fulfillment of the end". This, however, cannot be maintained either. For God cannot make us morally good without changing moral autonomy into heteronomy for which one would deserve no moral credit, and hence no happiness either. He can *demand* that we be moral, but he cannot make us so. The idea that God might alter our moral dispositions is incompatible with Kant's fundamental moral assumption.

Thus, not even God can bring about an ethical commonwealth: neither with respect to the happiness nor with respect to the union of the human beings necessary to the fulfilment of this end. It must therefore remain philosophically undecidable whether the highest good is possible or not, or whether there is a final end of creation.

In Kant's final analysis, practical reason must share the philosophical agnosticism to which theoretical reason was committed in the *Critique of Pure Reason*. The question of whether God exists as a substance outside our thoughts cannot be decided philosophically, neither theoretically nor practically. At the end of his career, Kant was convinced that philosophy can only examine its own principles through which it constitutes itself as theoretical and practical reason. And such examination reveals, among other things, that we constitute ourselves as free rational agents through the moral law. As a rational agent I ought to act in accordance with principles from which, if everyone acted according to them, the highest good as a social good would inevitably result. The thought of such a highest good entails, for the reasons stated, the thought of a highest being in which the powers of jurisdiction, execution and legislation are united. As Kant puts it in his last, unfinished work, the so-called *Opus postumum*: "Reason inevitably creates objects for itself. Hence everything that thinks has a God" (21.83). But this is only an ideal of self-constituting practical reason. In the execution of our duties, God's existence outside the human reason can remain undecided and undecidable. "Est deus in nobis", Kant quotes Ovid approvingly. Ethics and religion coincide: "Religion is conscientiousness (*mihi hoc religioni*). The holiness of the acceptance and the truthfulness of what man must confess to himself. Confess to yourself. To have religion, the concept of God is not required (still less the postulate: 'There is a God')" (21.81).

FURTHER READING

Beck, L. 1960. *A Commentary on Kant's "Critique of Practical Reason"*. Chicago, IL: University of Chicago Press.

Bohatec, J. 1966. *Die Religionsphilosophie Kants in der "Religion innerhalb der Grenzen der bloßen Vernunft"*. Hildesheim: Georg Olms.

Förster, E. 2000. *Kant's Final Synthesis*. Cambridge, MA: Harvard University Press.

Henrich, D. 1960. *Der ontologische Gottesbeweis*. Tübingen: Mohr.

Marty, F. & F. Ricken (eds) 1992. *Kant über Religion*. Stuttgart: W. Kohlhammer.

Wood, A. 1970. *Kant's Moral Religion*. Ithaca, NY: Cornell University Press.

On EXISTENCE OF GOD see also Chs 6, 12, 13, 14, 15; Vol. 1, Chs 18, 19; Vol. 2, Chs 5, 6, 13, 14; Vol. 5, Chs 11, 16. On MORALITY see also Chs 2, 8, 12, 14, 22; Vol. 2, Ch. 12; Vol. 4, Chs 4, 12, 18; Vol. 5, Ch. 6. On NATURE/NATURALISM see also Chs 20, 22; Vol. 4, Chs 5, 10; Vol. 5, Ch. 4. On REASON see also Chs 8, 12, 16; Vol. 2, Chs 10, 11, 12, 16, 18; Vol. 4, Chs 4, 8. On VIRTUE see also Ch. 20; Vol. 1, Chs 2, 11, 14, 15.

22

GOTTHOLD EPHRAIM LESSING

David Bell

The thought of Gotthold Ephraim Lessing (1729–81) is characterized from the outset by a fearless and radical independence that led him to resist the lure and comfort of systems that claimed the prerogative of knowing the truth. He once wrote, with characteristic tongue in cheek, but at the same time pinpointing one of the essential features of his way of thinking, that if he was satisfied with what he had written he tore it up, but if he was not satisfied he put it into print, for his thinking was for his own enlightenment (Lessing 1886–1924: vol. 16, 293–4). This critical openness is the hallmark of his innovative approach to literary criticism, drama and aesthetics, which has rightly earned him a place as a seminal figure in German literary history, but throughout his life he was also deeply engaged with philosophical, theological and religious issues and his contribution in this sphere is no less significant.

His father was an orthodox and scholarly Lutheran pastor in Kamenz, Saxony, and his upbringing there, combined with his schooling in Saint Afra, Meissen, ensured that he had a thorough grounding in theology and church history. This marked the start of his lifelong interest in these disciplines, which in the last decade of his life, following his appointment in 1770 as librarian to the Duke of Brunswick-Lüneburg in Wolfenbüttel (a post formerly held by Leibniz), came to dominate his work. It was in this capacity that he became involved in very public controversy, provoked by his publication of fragments from the work of the radical deist Hermann Samuel Reimarus, a daring enterprise that sent shockwaves through the world of Protestant theology. Similarly, his provocative defence of the reviled Spinoza unleashed a debate that raged after his death and brought that philosopher's significance for the Enlightenment into a new light.

At the height of the Reimarus debate, Lessing protested, "I am an amateur of theology, not a theologian. I have taken no oath on any particular system. I am not obliged to speak any language other than my own" (Lessing 2005: 122).[1] His self-characterization should not disguise the reality of his erudition and extensive theological knowledge, but it is a pointer to the fact that the significance of his contribution to the philosophy of religion lies above all in his groundbreaking re-evaluation of the concept of religious truth and the relationship between reason, revealed religion and historical truth. His works, which demonstrate a willingness to adopt different perspectives in a way that was confusing to contemporaries and which has ever since led to much debate about the unity and consistency of his thinking, are essentially a heuristic device to get ever closer to the truth.[2] Lessing does believe that there is an ultimate truth, but rejects the idea that the human mind could ever grasp the totality of that truth, as memorably summed up in *A Rejoinder* (1778):

> Not the truth which someone possesses or believes he possesses, but the honest effort he has made to get at the truth, constitutes a human being's worth. For it is not through possession of truth, but through its pursuit, that his powers are enlarged, and it is in this alone that his ever-growing perfection lies. Possession makes us inactive, lazy, and proud.
>
> If God held fast in his right hand the whole of truth and in his left hand only the ever-active quest for truth, albeit with the proviso that I should constantly and eternally err, and said to me: 'Choose!', I would humbly fall upon his left hand and say: 'Father, give! For pure truth is for you alone!'. (Lessing 2005: 98)

1. Where possible, quotations from Lessing's works are translations by H. B. Nisbet in Lessing (2005). All other translations are my own.
2. There have been widely divergent interpretations on the question of the unity of Lessing's thought and where his ultimate 'loyalties' lie. An overview is provided by Wessell (1977: 16–37). The early interpretation by Loofs (1913) locates Lessing firmly in rationalistic or Enlightenment thinking, seeing Lessing's positive appraisal of Christianity as a mere exoteric cloak; more recently Allison (1966) provides a convincing appraisal of his relation to Enlightenment thought. Early attempts to redress the balance away from Lessing's rationalism can be found, for example, in Koch (1928). Thielicke (1957) addresses the apparent tensions between Lessing's rationalism and positive view of religion in a way that effectively 'Christianizes' Lessing. Pons (1964) offers a more balanced assessment of the tensions between Lessing's rationalism and attitude to Christianity, noting his dissatisfaction with both. Wessell (1977: esp. 37–46) puts forward an interpretation founded on the idea that Lessing takes up contradictory positions in order to uncover truth, in a fashion analogous to a Kuhnian paradigm shift. The relationship between reason and history is the focus in Bollacher (1978). Chadwick's introduction to his edition (Lessing 1956) offers a nuanced assessment of the relation between reason and revelation. Nisbet's edition (Lessing 2005, the most complete available in English) contextualizes Lessing's oeuvre concisely and thoroughly.

The corollary of this reasoning is that any position he takes up or defends has a provisional quality and its value lies in the extent to which it guides him on the path to "ever-growing perfection". It is this conviction that Lessing brings to bear on his response to the competing claims of religion and philosophy, faith and reason to hold the key to truth and certain knowledge.

THE DEVELOPMENT OF LESSING'S THOUGHT IN THE 1750S AND 1760S

From his earliest years it is clear that his position towards the orthodoxy he grew up with was marked by a critical independence. "The Christian religion is not something which one should accept simply on trust from one's parents" (Lessing 1985–2003: vol. 11/1, 26), he wrote to his father in 1749, explaining that what counts is not blind acceptance, but a belief founded on rational conviction and expressed in moral actions. In saying this he is at the same time not only asserting his open-minded independence, but also reflecting the progressive ideas of Enlightenment rationalism, with which he aligns himself from his student days. While broadly embracing the rationalism of Leibniz, his frame of reference extends much wider, from the rational theology of the English deists to the scepticism of Pierre Bayle[3] and the radical undercurrent inspired by Spinoza.[4] His views on the relative validity and truth-value of different perspectives and doctrines predisposed him not only to tolerance of opposing viewpoints but also to a willingness to defend the persecuted, which was to manifest itself most strongly in his engagement with the thought of Spinoza, but also in his first forays into theological debate.

His earliest work on theological matters, although unpublished in his lifetime, was his incomplete essay of 1750, *Thoughts on the Moravians*, which mounts a defence of the brethren against attacks from the orthodox establishment. In a manner that was to become a characteristic theme throughout his life he argues that the only valid criterion for evaluating religious belief is its power to inspire moral action. This ethical pragmatism is matched by his sceptical attitude towards all dogmatism in theology and philosophy. Moreover, his view of Christ as an inspired teacher and his argument that contemporary orthodoxy had lost the simplicity and ethical purity of authentic Christianity clearly show him at this early stage to be sympathetic to a rationalistic deistic position that holds natural religion to be essentially a practical moral doctrine, which positive religion has corrupted over time through the accretion of dogma and mystery. This rationalist approach is evident again in his first published theological works, a series of vindications of figures in church history accused of heresy (the *Vindications*). In the first of these, the *Vindication of Hieronymus Cardanus* (1754), his defence of

3. See Allison (1966: 1–49); Nisbet (1978).
4. For an analysis of the role of Spinoza as a profound radical impetus behind the Enlightenment, see Israel (2001).

the Renaissance philosopher accused of atheism in his comparison of Christianity, Islam, Judaism and paganism is that Cardanus is a sincere Christian because he neglects powerful arguments in support of Islam, which Lessing presents as being most consistent with reason and natural religion in that it does not demand irrational belief in revelations and mysteries as necessary for salvation. The vindication of Cardanus, while erudite and sincere, is, however, an indirect means for Lessing to engage with an issue that goes far beyond the question of Cardanus' alleged heresy: it raises what was to become a key theme in his work – the question of the validity of the historical 'proofs' of Christianity and the need to subject these to rational scrutiny.

In the years 1752–5 Lessing collaborated closely with Moses Mendelssohn in Berlin, and debated intensely with him over the philosophy of not only Leibniz and Wolff, but also Spinoza, who was central to the *Philosophical Dialogues* published by Mendelssohn in 1755 (Mendelssohn 1997: 96–104). This confluence of ideas is discernible in the 1753 fragment *The Christianity of Reason* (Lessing 2005: 25–9). A rationalistic Leibnizian framework is clearly in evidence, but, as hinted at by the title, what Lessing is striving for is not so much a way to make Christian doctrine *conform* to reason, to justify a rational Christian theology, but an approach that will be able to extract by rational deduction a truth that can ultimately be grasped by reason alone. Specifically, Lessing applies a Spinozistic conception of the world as the result of an *immanent* and *necessary* causality, which he describes as the thought of God. Lessing uses the notion of the Trinity to illustrate this deductive process, anticipating and providing the groundwork for an approach to the relationship between reason and revelation that was to come to the fore in his final completed work, *The Education of the Human Race* (1781).

Lessing's philosophy of religion in these early years, then, is formed around the twin bases of his grounding in orthodox theology and his embracing of progressive rationalism. To these he added his independence and sceptical attitude to dogmatism, his recognition of the imperative to subject all evidence, particularly textual historical evidence, to sound rational criticism, and his willingness to entertain diverse positions, including those of the reviled and excoriated, as a means of uncovering truth. The later 1750s were, in terms of his output, devoted more to literary matters, but in the early 1760s, while in the service of the Prussian General von Tauentzien in Breslau, he once more turns to his theological interests, producing a number of fragments that reflect the development already identified. *On the Reality of Things Outside God* clearly points to a monism that excludes a transcendental God: "However I try to explain the reality of things outside God, I have to confess that I can form no conception of it" (Lessing 2005: 30), while *Spinoza only put Leibniz on the Track of Pre-established Harmony* (*ibid.*: 32–4), a response to Mendelssohn's 1761 revision of his *Philosophical Dialogues*, argues that Spinoza goes much further in his consistent monism, which he implicitly supports, and which Leibniz's pre-established harmony was specifically designed to circumvent. *On the Manner of the Propagation and Dissemination of the*

Christian Religion and *On the Origin of Revealed Religion* show Lessing following through consistently on the rationalistic line, but coloured by an explicit rejection of the transcendence of God, in accordance with Spinoza's monism. The first of these two fragments argues that the spread of Christianity can be explained entirely through natural causes and requires no supernatural intervention. The second reflects the deistic view of revealed religion as essentially a corruption of the purity of natural religion; the usefulness of each religion, however, is preserved in the extent to which it contains the 'inner truth' of natural religion as modified in particular historical circumstances. To this extent all revealed religions are "equally true and equally false" and "The best revealed or positive religion is that which contains the fewest conventional additions to natural religion" (2005: 36). This position is the clearest statement in Lessing's work of a consistent deistic position that appears to reject outright the claim of Christianity – or any other revealed religion – to be of divine origin. Nevertheless, even in *On the Manner of the Propagation and Dissemination of the Christian Religion*, Lessing warns against concluding that this could lead to conclusions 'disadvantageous' to religion (1886–1924: vol. 14, 331–2). This may well be seen as a disingenuous sop to the orthodox, but it perhaps also anticipates a new tendency in Lessing's thinking in the 1770s, which is marked by a radical reappraisal of his approach to orthodoxy and revelation, paving the way for the development of the most innovative and influential aspects of his philosophy of religion.

THE 1770S: LESSING IN WOLFENBÜTTEL AND THE REIMARUS CONTROVERSY

By the time Lessing was appointed librarian in Wolfenbüttel in 1770 he already enjoyed an established reputation as writer and critic, and although he completed his powerful tragedy *Emilia Galotti* in these years, most of his energies were devoted to theological and philosophical research in the unique opportunities afforded in the ducal library. His best-known dramatic work, *Nathan the Wise*, also arose, of course, from his engagement in the religious controversy over Reimarus which he unleashed and which was to dominate the decade. He soon found material that enabled him to continue in the spirit of the *Vindications*, with essays on Berengar of Tours, Andreas Wissowatius and Adam Neuser, but it was his study of Leibniz, given new impetus by the recent publication of the *New Essays on Human Understanding* (1765), that enabled him to develop the approach adumbrated in the *Vindications* in a new and creative way. The new direction is indicated in a letter to Mendelssohn as early as 9 January 1771, where he expresses his anxiety, "That in throwing away certain prejudices, I have thrown away a little too much with them, which I shall have to retrieve" (1985–2003: vol. 11/2, 144). His concern is that he has been too hasty in dismissing certain notions as false without taking full account of how different positions, even apparently contradictory ones, may in fact contain an element of truth from a certain perspective. This approach is given a further boost by the fact that he believed this to be at the heart of Leibniz's way of thinking and harmonizing tendencies. This is best illustrated by his essay *Leibniz on Eternal Punishment* (1773), where he explains that Leibniz was willing to defend the orthodox doctrine of eternal torment because it was closer to the truth than the opposite standpoint, its outright denial, which was the position of his Socinian opponent Ernst Soner. Lessing is inspired by Leibniz's willingness to entertain and examine all opinion in order to discover that sense in which it may be accepted as true, setting aside his own set of beliefs and provisionally accepting ones he did not explicitly hold in order to progress along the path to truth. Lessing endorses this approach and then applies it to critique the approach of the liberal rationalist theologians, or 'neologists', such as J. A. Eberhard, who had attacked Leibniz's defence as inconsistent and the doctrine of eternal punishment as inhuman and contrary to reason. Lessing, however, identifies in the orthodox doctrine the rational truth that "nothing in the world is isolated, nothing is without consequences, and nothing is without eternal consequences" (2005: 52) and is therefore unwilling to discard the orthodox doctrine outright on account of its practical heuristic value in uncovering a truth that is entirely consistent with reason.

Lessing's position caused a stir and some confusion among contemporaries, for he appeared to be defending orthodoxy. His brother Karl could not understand how he could apparently turn his back on his literary career and fall back into the orthodox camp. What Lessing was doing, as he reveals in a letter to Karl on 2 February 1774, was seeking to demolish what he saw as the untenable and dangerous position of the liberal theologians, who "under the pretext of making us reasonable Christians" turn us into "unreasonable philosophers". This is why he is not yet willing, in his search for the "pure water", to abandon the "impure water" of orthodoxy, if the alternative is to bathe the baby in the "filth" of liberal rational theology (1985–2003: vol. 11/2, 615). There is, then, a clear tactical dimension in his approach, but behind this onslaught on neology that was misunderstood by contemporaries there is already an indication of a radicalism that takes him beyond the methodology of Leibniz, which he supports, but which is actually conceived by Leibniz as a means of bolstering Christianity, whatever his private opinions about the 'truth' of eternal punishment might be. In the same letter to his brother, Lessing concedes, "We are one in our conviction that our old religious system is false", and his interpretation of the notion of eternal punishment does away altogether with the idea of the supernatural. Again we see Lessing moving in the direction of Spinoza's more rigorous naturalism. However, this revision of his attitude to orthodoxy marks the beginning of the articulation of his radical analysis of the validity of historical arguments for the truth of a revealed religion and his subtle new approach to the relationship between reason and revelation, which sought to re-evaluate the function of revealed religion in human progress towards greater understanding of the truth.

It was, of course, in the context of the Reimarus controversy[5] that Lessing came to formulate his most individual and significant contribution to theology. During his time in Hamburg prior to his move to Wolfenbüttel, Lessing had become acquainted with the family of Reimarus and acquired the manuscript of the latter's *Apology or Defense of the Rational Worshippers of God*, which constituted, as Lessing later described it, "nothing less than a full-scale onslaught on the Christian religion" (Lessing 2005: 96), which denounced the latter as an irrational fabrication by zealots. Lessing, encouraged by exemption from censorship, published a series of anonymous fragments from the manuscript (*Fragments*). The first, in 1774, *On the Toleration of Deists*, attracted little attention and he proceeded in 1777 to publish a further five, more radical fragments concerning, among other things, absurdities in the idea of universal revelation and inconsistencies in the biblical accounts of the Israelites' crossing of the Red Sea and, more provocatively, in the resurrection narratives. A sixth fragment, *On the Aims of Jesus and His Disciples*, appeared in 1778. At bottom, Lessing's motive was a continuation of the campaign he had already launched against the neologists, which sought to reappraise the nature of the truth that was to be found in revealed religion. He concedes that the author of the *Fragments* is correct when he demonstrates that the Bible cannot be literally true and that attempts to found a religion on a flawed historical basis alone are therefore untenable, but he is unwilling to accept that Christianity should therefore simply be dismissed. Not only has it proved useful and beneficial in empirical reality, but it has also served to enable human beings to *progress* in their quest for rational truth. In the 1777 publication Lessing adds his own "Counter-propositions", which make clear the distinctiveness of his position. The arguments in the *Fragments* should have no effect on the Christian for whom the 'truth' of Christianity is a fact: "In short, the letter is not the spirit, and the Bible is not religion. Consequently, objections to the letter, and to the Bible, need not also be objections to the spirit and to religion" (Lessing 2005: 63). This defence of Christianity was designed, in opposition to the pernicious woolly-mindedness of liberal theology, to provoke a reassessment of what constitutes truth and a re-evaluation of the role of revealed religion in humanity's moral and rational evolution. What resulted, however, was an outraged response from the orthodox establishment. Lessing's counter-arguments did not refute Reimarus directly; they merely asserted that his case affected only the 'letter' and not the 'spirit' of Christianity, but in so doing took away the argument that the truth of Christianity had a secure basis in historical evidence. Initial theological responses came from Johann Daniel Schumann in Hanover and Johann Heinrich Ress in Wolfenbüttel, aiming to answer Reimarus. But it was Johann Melchior Goeze, senior pastor of St. Catharine's Church in Hamburg and a leading conserva-

5. For an account of the controversy, see A. Schilson's commentary in Lessing (1985–2003: vols 8, 9).

tive Lutheran theologian, who became Lessing's principal antagonist, precisely because he perceived that from his perspective as shepherd to his flock Lessing's argument was more pernicious than that of Reimarus in that it could dupe the faithful into accepting that the historical authority of the Bible was not essential. In the essay *On the Proof of the Spirit and the Power* (actually a response to Schumann's defence of the traditional historical proofs of miracles and prophecy) Lessing had already drawn a distinction between "contingent truths of history" and "necessary truths of reason" and argued that the former, indeed *any* empirical evidence, cannot legitimately be used to demonstrate the latter, which include the essentially rational, 'inner truth' of Christianity, as they are of an entirely different category (*ibid.*: 85ff.).

Goeze's polemic with Lessing became increasingly heated and the pastor increasingly perplexed by his opponent's true position, not least because of his predilection for metaphor, exemplified in the *Parable*, which described a strange but beautiful palace and how an apparent fire provoked those who argued over its design and origin to try to rescue the plans, not the edifice itself; the fire, however, was merely the northern lights. Nevertheless, in his attempt to pin Lessing down, he cited ten statements from the "Counter-propositions", provoking Lessing to respond in the *Axioms*, which arguably contain the core of his theological position that the truth of Christianity is essentially independent of Scripture: "*Thus, however much we may depend on these writings, it is impossible for the whole truth of the Christian religion to be based on them*" (Lessing 2005: 130), and further: "*The religion is not true because the evangelists and apostles taught it; on the contrary, they taught it because it is true*" (*ibid.*: 138). With his *New Hypothesis on the Evangelists as Merely Human Historians* (although it remained incomplete and unpublished in his lifetime) Lessing argued that the Gospels all depended on an original Aramaic Gospel and interpreted them as historical and literary documents in their own context. In this respect he clearly owes much to the method of Spinoza in his *Theologico-Political Treatise*. Although the detail of Lessing's hypothesis may have proved inaccurate, this is commonly held to be highly influential in the theological debates over the historical status of the Gospels that were to follow. Meanwhile, the dispute with Goeze became increasingly bitter, with Lessing producing a series of eleven *Anti-Goeze* pamphlets that added little of substance to the main issues. Increasingly frustrated and outmanoeuvred, Goeze finally demanded of Lessing that he explain what he understood by 'the Christian religion', to which he mischievously replied in his *Necessary Answer to a Very Unnecessary Question* (Lessing 2005: 172–7) with the statement that it was defined by various creeds from the early Christian period. He remained silent as to what he really believed. What is clear, however, is that he cannot accept the orthodox case that the historicity of the Gospels demonstrates the truth of Christianity and dictates the acceptance of certain beliefs and dogmas. The truth of Christianity is encapsulated rather in what he describes as *The Religion of Christ*, which is that which Christ himself "recognized and practiced as a human being" and which, unlike the "Christian religion", is contained in the Gospels "in the most clear and distinct language" (*ibid.*: 178–9). This message, too, is at the core of the drama *Nathan the Wise*, which Lessing wrote in 1779 when he was forbidden to engage in any further polemics with Goeze.

Set in Jerusalem during the crusades, the play is not merely a *plea* for tolerance of all religions, specifically Judaism, Christianity and Islam; instead it shows that tolerance is a rational imperative, since all three of these revealed religions have a claim to be based on historical evidence, which means, in Lessing's terms, that all are equally false, while all are equally true in that they contain an identical 'inner truth'. The celebrated parable of the rings, told by the Jew Nathan, when challenged by Saladin to give the reason for his remaining true to his faith, draws on the familiar tale by Boccaccio, which suggests that it is not yet possible to distinguish which of the three rings, handed down by the head of the family to the favourite son, is the true one. Lessing goes considerably further, however, when a judge brought in to arbitrate argues that *all* three rings must be false, and the original ring lost, since the bearers clearly do not display the quality that the ring confers, namely to make the bearer beloved before God and human beings. The claims of the ring-bearers – and revealed religions – to be 'true' can therefore be entertained only if they can demonstrate the power of the ring through their actions. All three religions have the potential to do this because they are united in their common humanity, a message that is reinforced dramatically by the play's denouement showing the protagonists representing the religions to be related, by blood or adoption, in one family. This eloquent conclusion to the Reimarus controversy has meant, of course, a wider dissemination of Lessing's thinking on religious truth and tolerance. In many ways it still clearly aligns Lessing with Enlightenment deism, but, as has already been suggested, from the early 1770s, although he certainly rejects the orthodox position, he finds the radical deistic response equally inadequate to account for the benefits and progress that revealed religion can be argued to have produced. This focus on the practical dimension is evident in *Nathan the Wise*, but it is in Lessing's final completed work, *The Education of the Human Race*, that he applies his analysis of different categories of truth to an interpretation of the role of revelation in human history in terms of it demonstrating a dynamic evolution of reason itself, in a way that arguably anticipates Hegel.

ENDGAME: *THE EDUCATION OF THE HUMAN RACE* AND THE SPINOZA CONTROVERSY

The first fifty-three of the one hundred paragraphs that constitute *The Education of the Human Race* had already been published by Lessing (although he did not acknowledge that he was the author) as part of his response to Reimarus in 1777, in order to counter the argument that revealed religions were corruptions of an original natural religion; instead, they are seen as representing progressive stages in the evolution of humanity towards maturity and in the incremental increase in rational understanding. In the preface he summarizes the spirit in which the work should be approached:

> Why should we not see in all the positive religions simply the process whereby human understanding in all places can alone develop, and will develop further still, instead of reacting with either mockery or anger to one of them? If nothing in the best of worlds deserves this scorn, this indignation on our part, why should religions alone deserve it? (Lessing 2005: 218)

The basis of the essay is an analogy between education and revelation, which implies that the latter is a means whereby human understanding is developed in a progressive sense. The origin of the analogy can be traced back to the Church Fathers, but Lessing's concept is far more radical in that it anticipates, in theory at least, the ultimate superfluity of revelation. Lessing presents Judaism and Christianity as successive stages in the 'education' of humanity, that is, in the evolution of its religious consciousness. Recalling Spinoza, he argues that revelation reflects the culture and condition of the people who receive it, but it is clear that Lessing also envisages a progression to a higher level of rational insight. Thus he traces the evolution of the Hebrews' understanding of the concept of the one God as something not merely accepted on trust as a revelation, but something that their reason now came fully to understand. The Old Testament is therefore compared to an elementary primer, which is then superseded by a more advanced textbook, namely the New Testament, whose essential truth, as taught by Christ (introduced not as the redeemer or Son of God, but as a human being and teacher) was the idea of the immortality of the soul. There is, then, an inner esoteric rational truth contained within the exoteric revelation and the usefulness of revealed religion lies in the impetus it gives to human beings to uncover and comprehend that truth fully. There is a symbiosis of revelation and reason, whereby the former guides our reason, which in turn illuminates that revelation (§36; Lessing 2005: 226). It is in this sense that successive revelations become superfluous, albeit not for all individuals at the same time, and this prompts Lessing, when he seems to be on the point of declaring that the New Testament is about to be superseded, to pause and reconsider whether there is not some rational truth to be discovered in other revealed doctrines, very much in the manner he had earlier identified in his essay on Leibniz and eternal punishment. He briefly considers the doctrines of the Trinity,[6] original sin and justification through Christ, with a view to uncovering this process that shows "the development of revealed truths into truths of reason"

6. The argument recalls *The Christianity of Reason*; see Nisbet (1999).

(§76; Lessing 2005: 236). His assertion in the following paragraph – that revelation has therefore guided humanity to a conception of God that human reason would "never" have attained alone – appears in conflict with the statement of principle in §4 that revelation "gives the human race nothing which human reason, left to itself, could not also arrive at" (Lessing 2005: 218). This apparent contradiction has provoked major disagreement among commentators, and there is no clear and unassailable resolution. Part of the answer, at least, seems to lie in the *context* of each statement: §4 states as a matter of principle Lessing's conviction that rational certainty derives from the nature of the mind itself, whereas §77, perhaps with something of a rhetorical flourish, refers to the empirical occasion that stimulates the recognition of this rational truth. The implication of Lessing's approach to Judaism and Christianity remains, however, crystal clear: that this process will continue until such time as a "new, eternal gospel" will come about, where people will do good for its own sake, because it is right and rational (§§85–6; Lessing 2005: 237–8).

Lessing's case operates, then, on different levels. On the one hand, it justifies and vindicates the pragmatic value of revealed religion, not only in a practical moral sense, but also in terms of its role as a stimulant to the mind's never-ending progression towards truth. On the other hand, it suggests that ultimately revelation is dispensable, or at least that a time can be envisaged where it will no longer be required. Furthermore, it has already been shown that Lessing held no brief for belief in the supernatural and this must be extended to his interpretation of revelation here. Although he writes of divine revelation, it is clearly not conceived as supernatural intervention by a transcendent creator: instead it appears that 'revelation' itself is a wholly *natural* process, which conceives, in a Spinozistic fashion, of a divinity that is immanent in nature. The implication of the essay is therefore a justification of a monistic philosophy. Goeze was perhaps right in fearing that the reasonable Christian might be misled by Lessing into accepting a position that ultimately did away with revelation and the notion of a transcendent God altogether. Nevertheless, Lessing does make it clear that the New Testament is far from exhausted as a primer, and the road to perfection is unending. The final parts of the essay stress the provisionality of the position he is taking, and he even speculates that this process can be fulfilled only if we embrace the notion of metempsychosis. The quest in search of that eternal gospel of humanity is also something that is to be found in his Masonic dialogues, *Ernst and Falk* (1778–80; Lessing 2005: 184–216), which draw a parallel between freemasonry and the Church; the institutions are the exoteric shell, but true freemasonry promotes that brotherhood of humanity proclaimed in *Nathan the Wise*, just as the inner truth of all religions binds them as one.

Although *The Education of the Human Race*, as Lessing's last completed work, retains a provisional and speculative element, it is legitimately viewed as "the culmination and the keystone of Lessing's philosophy of religion", where "all of the various aspects of his thought … find their decisive expression" (Allison 1966:

147–8). Nevertheless, despite this apparent finality, Lessing's religious thought was to provoke renewed controversy from beyond the grave. In 1785 Friedrich Heinrich Jacobi published his record of a conversation he had with Lessing in July and August 1780, just months before his death.[7] He astounded the public by claiming that Lessing had professed himself to be a Spinozist who embraced the monistic 'One and All' of the philosopher whom Jacobi held to be the epitome of his thesis that all rationalistic systems necessarily end in atheism. Various points of connection with Spinoza have been identified but it clearly makes no sense to take Lessing's assertion, "There is no other philosophy than that of Spinoza" (Lessing 2005: 244) at its literal face value; he was, after all, hostile to the very idea that a single system could lay claim to possess the whole truth. There is no reason to doubt the veracity of Jacobi's account and his record of the conversation testifies to the detailed knowledge both men had of this neglected philosopher. Concrete evidence of Lessing's knowledge and reading of Spinoza is hard to establish (see Bell 1984: 27–37); there is no evidence that he consciously aligned himself with the radical undercurrent of Spinozistic and naturalistic thinking of fringe figures such as Friedrich Wilhelm Stosch that Jonathan Israel (2001) identifies as one of the hidden motors of the Enlightenment. Nevertheless, a number of conclusions are indicated by the conversations with Jacobi. It is clear from his remark "I have no more use for the orthodox concepts of the deity" (Lessing 2005: 243) that he has dispensed entirely with any notion of a transcendent creator outside nature and he shows himself to be entirely in accord with the monism of Spinoza in a way that tallies with his arguments in *The Education of the Human Race* and elsewhere. Further, in accordance with this naturalistic approach, he is relaxed about embracing Spinoza's determinism, shocking Jacobi by stating, "I see that you would like to have a free will. I have no desire for a free will" (*ibid*.: 246), a view that distinguishes him from Leibniz and mainstream Enlightenment and aligns him with the radical Enlightenment inspired by Spinoza.

It seems highly improbable that Lessing was suddenly embracing new views in his conversations with Jacobi. He no doubt took some pleasure in toying with Jacobi's sensibilities, just as he had deliberately confused Goeze, but his statements about Spinoza are, once again, reminders as to his drive to discover truth wherever he could find it. This may well be the most significant element in his legacy in the history of the philosophy of religion. The debate over Lessing's Spinozism and atheism that was provoked by Jacobi's revelations provided a profound impetus to a proper understanding of Spinoza's work and Lessing's pioneering role in that respect is brought to light. In theology, although his specific propositions about the genealogy of the Gospels may be flawed, he paved the way for the development of this approach to historical studies of the Scriptures in the nineteenth

7. Lessing (2005: 241–56); the conversations were included in Jacobi's *On the Doctrine of Spinoza in Letters to Mr Moses Mendelssohn* (1785). For accounts of the Spinoza controversy, see: Scholz (1916); Bell (1984: 71–96); Vallée (1988).

century. In broader and more profound terms, his mediating interpretation of the roles of reason and revelation, which relies on postulating a progressive rational insight into the truths that religion contains, breaks new and fruitful ground. It hammers home the inadequacy of both the orthodox reliance on the historical evidence as proof and the radical deist dismissal of religion on account of that flawed evidence. In his re-evaluation of the importance of the historical evidence he steers a new path, whose influence is discernible in Fichte and Kierkegaard, and perhaps most of all in Hegel and in the concept of religion as a manifestation of the evolution of human consciousness.

FURTHER READING

Allison, H. 1966. *Lessing and the Enlightenment: His Philosophy of Religion in Relation to Eighteenth-Century Thought*. Ann Arbor, MI: University of Michigan Press.

Fischer, B. & T. Fox (eds) 2005. *A Companion to the Works of Lessing*. Rochester: Camden House.

Lessing, G. 1955. *Nathan the Wise*, B. Morgan (trans.). New York: Ungar.

Lessing, G. 1956. *Theological Writings*, H. Chadwick (ed. & trans.). London: Black.

Lessing, G. 2005. *Philosophical and Theological Writings*, H. B. Nisbet (ed. & trans.). Cambridge: Cambridge University Press.

Pons, G. 1964. *Gotthold Ephraim Lessing et le Christianisme*. Paris: Didier.

Vallée, G. (ed.) 1988. *The Spinoza Conversations between Lessing and Jacobi: Text with Excerpts from the Ensuing Controversy*, G. Vallée, J. Lawson & C. Chapple (trans.). Lanham, MD: University Press of America.

Wessell, L. 1977. *G. E. Lessing's Theology: A Reinterpretation*. The Hague: Mouton.

Yasukata, T. 2002. *Lessing's Philosophy of Religion and the German Enlightenment: Lessing on Christianity and Reason*. Oxford: Oxford University Press.

On MORALITY see also Chs 2, 8, 12, 14, 21; Vol. 2, Ch. 12; Vol. 4, Chs 4, 12, 18; Vol. 5, Ch. 6. On NATURE/NATURALISM see also Chs 20, 21; Vol. 4, Chs 5, 10; Vol. 5, Ch. 4. On RATIONALISM see also Chs 18, 20; Vol. 5, Ch. 22. On REVEALED RELIGION see also Vol. 4, Ch. 12; Vol. 5, Ch. 23.

23

WILLIAM PALEY

Roger White

William Paley was a clergyman, philosopher, and religious apologist, best known for his classic presentation of the argument from design. Born in July 1743 in Peterborough, England, Paley trained for the Anglican priesthood at Christ's College, Cambridge. He was later appointed fellow and tutor at Christ's College and lectured in various philosophical subjects, most significantly in moral theory. He rose gradually through the ranks of the Anglican Church, eventually becoming Archdeacon of Carlisle, and sub-dean at Lincoln Cathedral. His latitudinarian views and insistence on basing Christian belief and ethics on reason raised suspicion in some quarters. This may have prevented him from higher appointments in the Church. He died on 25 May 1805.

Paley's major work consists of four books. His Cambridge lectures on ethics were published as *The Principles of Moral and Political Philosophy* (hereafter *Principles*; [1785] 2002). The book does not delve deeply into foundational questions, but is intended rather as a practical guide. *Principles* presents a simple utilitarian view rooted in a theological understanding, suggesting that "what promotes the general happiness is required by the will of God" (*ibid.*: 47). Accordingly, Paley defines *virtue* as "the doing of good to mankind, in obedience to the will of God, and for the sake of everlasting happiness" (*ibid.*: 25). Like other utilitarian thinkers, Paley rejects the idea that we are blessed with a moral sense, arguing that our intuitive moral judgements are more a reflection of our arbitrary prejudices than of moral truth. In some respects the book is progressive for its time, with strong condemnations of social injustices such as slavery. But for the most part, in contrast to thinkers such as Jeremy Bentham, Paley's work was conservative, using utilitarian theory to defend the status quo. While not particularly original, *Principles* has been credited with the dissemination of utilitarian thought in England. But it has had no lasting influence.

In *Horae Paulinae* ([1790] 1860a), Paley sought to defend the biblical account of the life of the apostle Paul as found in the Acts of the Apostles and in Paul's Epistles. In *A View of the Evidences of Christianity* (hereafter *Evidences*; [1794]

1860b), he extends the defence to the Gospel accounts of Jesus, engaging in particular with Edward Gibbon's *History of the Decline and Fall of the Roman Empire* ([1776] 2000). These works were successful in their day, and Paley's *Evidences* was required reading at Cambridge for many years. But they are of little philosophical interest.

The work for which Paley is remembered is his *Natural Theology: Or Evidence of the Existence and Attributes of the Deity, Collected from the Appearances of Nature* ([1802] 2006). As the subtitle suggests, Paley presents an argument for the existence of God as understood by traditional Christian theology, taking as his premises facts about the natural world. Through the influence of this work Paley's name has become strongly associated with the term 'natural theology'. But Paley was following in a tradition of apologists looking to the natural world for knowledge of God. Paley's work was to some degree derivative of earlier works such as John Ray's *The Wisdom of God Manifested in the Works of the Creation* ([1691] 1977).

While not especially original, *Natural Theology* was enormously successful. It is perhaps Paley's engaging prose, skilful rhetoric and imaginative use of analogies that made it supersede similar apologetic works in influence. Like his *Evidences*, *Natural Theology* became required reading at Cambridge and Oxford. And its central arguments were widely accepted in the scientific community for many years. Paley's most famous admirer was Charles Darwin, who, as it happens, later occupied Paley's room in Christ's College. Darwin recalls in his autobiography ([1893] 2000) that he found Paley's books the few stimulating works that he was required to read. Darwin was deeply impressed by Paley's arguments, and they appear to have inspired Darwin to develop his own revolutionary ideas. Ironically, the most significant impact of *Natural Theology* was to inspire the theory that many take to have decisively undone Paley's system.

Paley's influence among philosophers has waned. His descriptions of the natural world are outdated, and his general theorizing has been thoroughly eclipsed by Darwin. Yet the opening chapter of *Natural Theology* containing the famous watch analogy has become a classic and continues to be a staple of introductory philosophy of religion classes and anthologies. The larger work is rarely read in detail today although it contains interesting arguments that repay close reading. It is not without reason that great thinkers like Darwin were impressed by it in their day.

NATURAL THEOLOGY

In *Natural Theology*, Paley presents a version of the argument from design for the existence of God. Unlike some theistic arguments it is an empirically based argument taking as its premises the observed features of the natural world. While not attempting to give a watertight *proof* of God's existence, Paley's argument is very ambitious. He seeks to show that it is overwhelmingly probable, given what we observe from nature, that the world was created by a wise, powerful and good God.

The overall structure of *Natural Theology* is as follows. Paley begins with the central argument that there are features of the natural world providing overwhelming evidence of the work of one or more designers. A number of objections are then addressed. In each case Paley argues that a parallel objection would lead to an absurdly sceptical position with respect to an obvious artefact such as a watch. Paley then devotes twenty chapters to a detailed examination of cases from nature that he takes to support his argument. Most of these are taken from the anatomy of living things, but a chapter each is given also to chemistry and astronomy. As Paley himself notes, part of his strategy here is that if a few scientific details of his account turn out to be mistaken, his overall argument should be unaffected, so vast is the evidence speaking of design. Up until this point Paley has been making a case that *some* kind of intelligent agent, or agents, are responsible for various features of the world. Lastly, Paley argues that there is one such agent with the attributes of the God of traditional theism. As one might expect, Paley's more ambitious conclusion is found less convincing even by Paley's admirers. His basic argument for design is what has been most influential and significant.

Paley famously begins by asking us to compare the reactions we might have to stumbling upon a *stone* and a *watch* when crossing a heath. We might be content to suppose that the stone had always existed, with no explanation to be given for its present form. Not so with the watch. We are rationally compelled to conclude that an intelligent agent contrived the watch. What is it about the watch but not the stone that compels this response? The watch, unlike the stone, is composed of a multitude of parts that work together to perform a function. Not only are many parts required in order for the watch to keep regular time, but also the parts must be of a very specific shape and arranged in a particular way. Small changes in shape or arrangement of the parts destroy the function of the watch. For convenience let us call this feature that Paley takes to be a clear mark of contrivance *complex functional organization* (this is not Paley's term). Now the works of nature, Paley continues, display this same feature only to a far greater degree. Paley illustrates this fact with a detailed examination of the *eye*, among numerous other cases. If we find in nature the same features so obviously telling of design in the case of the watch, Paley concludes, we ought also to be sure that the eye and such like are the work of a designer, albeit one of much greater power and wisdom.

To be clear on the nature of Paley's argument it is important to distinguish it from another famous presentation of the argument from design, namely that considered by David Hume in his *Dialogues Concerning Natural Religion* (hereafter *Dialogues*; [1779] 1993). There is a common misconception that Paley presented essentially the same argument as Hume, and that Hume effectively demolished the argument.[1] This is not the case. Although Hume's *Dialogues* had not yet become influential, Paley was well aware of them. And while he makes only brief reference

1. See, for example, Le Mahieu (1976); Ferre (1962).

to Hume's *Dialogues*, Paley appears at various points to have Hume's work in mind. Although Paley's argument may have weaknesses of its own, it is largely unaffected by Hume's brilliant critique.

In the *Dialogues*, Hume has the character Cleanthes draw a comparison between the world and machines (such as watches) that are known to have been made by human beings. Cleanthes suggests that by the 'rules of analogy' we must conclude that the world and its machine-like parts are likewise the products of a designer. The rules of analogy are what are later summarized as "similar causes prove similar effects, and similar effects similar causes" (Hume [1779] 1993: 49). While in later chapters Paley does make similar appeals to bolster his case, it is clear that his main argument is quite different. With a few simplifications we might summarize the two arguments as follows:

Hume

H1. The world and its parts resemble machines such as a watch.
H2. Watches and such machines are known to have been designed.
H3. From similar effects we should infer similar causes.
Therefore, we should conclude that the world is the product of design.

Paley

P1. The world and its parts display complex functional organization.
P2. From complex functional organization we should infer the work of a designer, unless there is a serious rival hypothesis that can adequately account for it.
P3. There is no serious rival hypothesis that can adequately account for the complex functional organization found in nature.
Therefore, we should conclude that the world is the product of design.[2]

Paley does not appeal to our knowledge that watches are designed or to any principle of analogical reasoning. His discussion of the watch plays a role only in supporting P2. According to Paley, even someone who had never seen a piece of machinery even remotely like a watch could rationally judge that the watch had a designer. It is not that when we examine the watch we notice similarities to other familiar machines that we know to be designed, and infer from like effects to like causes. According to Paley we can tell immediately from the structure of the watch – from its delicate arrangement of parts working together to keep regular time – that it was designed. Paley uses the watch example in an attempt to elicit our natural

2. The interpretation of Paley's argument is a matter of some dispute. For rather different reconstructions see: Nuovo (1992); Sober (1993); Oppy (2006).

response that this is a reasonable inference. We are then asked to apply this same thinking to the eye and other natural objects.

Although he does not state it explicitly in these terms, Paley's argument might best be understood as an inference to the best explanation. The functional complexity we find in the watch, the eye and other pieces of machinery cries out for explanation. The obvious and most compelling explanation is that they were designed for the purpose of performing a function. Only a better rival explanation could shake our rational confidence that they were designed.

The difference between Hume's and Paley's arguments is important for assessing their force. Hume famously launches a barrage of powerful objections to the design argument that he has set up. These are largely irrelevant to Paley's argument. For example, Hume argues that the strength of an analogical inference crucially depends on the degree of similarity of effects. If objects *A* and *B* are all but identical then we can with confidence conclude that they were produced in similar ways. But the strength of such an inference diminishes dramatically as there are differences between the objects. Furthermore, if *A* also resembles *C* in important respects, this may present a rival hypothesis concerning the origin of *A*. Much of Hume's demolition of his design argument consists in showing weaknesses in the analogy between the natural world and human artefacts, and noting that the world resembles not only man-made machines, but in some respects plants and animals also.

Such objections have no bearing on Paley's argument. Paley's evidences of design are taken not from the world as a whole but largely from the anatomy of animals. Animals themselves do, of course, resemble animals (as they do machines). But the overall resemblance to man-made machines as opposed to other things is not important to Paley's argument. What matters for Paley's argument is just that his cases display what we have called complex functional organization. And this is not in dispute.

Of course, in avoiding Hume's objections Paley's argument takes on the burden of insisting on P2: that complex functional organization is by itself evidence for design (unmediated by analogical reasoning). A crucial question in the evaluation of Paley's argument is whether he is correct in supposing this. Hume and others explicitly deny it. According to Hume, there is no way that one can rationally discriminate among rival hypotheses concerning the cause of an object when considering the object by itself. It is only on the basis of experience with similar cases that we can form any expectation concerning the cause of a particular object. Paley takes P2 to be a matter of common sense, the case of the watch being merely an illustration of its application.

The case of the watch plays a further rhetorical role for Paley. He considers a range of objections to the design argument and seeks to show that each would lead to an implausibly sceptical position if applied to the inference about the watch. The strategy here is to show that the various objections 'prove too much'. The general form of the response is:

> If this objection to the argument from design were cogent it should apply with equal force to the case of the watch, leading us to conclude that we cannot rationally infer that the watch has a designer. But this is absurd. We can rationally infer that the watch was designed (without having seen or heard of them having been designed, or of anything similar having been designed). So this objection must be mistaken, and we should be no more moved by it in the case of the argument from design.

Paley applies this strategy to a number of objections. We have never seen an eye being designed and made, nor do we have any idea how that might have been done. But it would not diminish our confidence in the slightest that a watch was designed if we were entirely ignorant of manufacturing processes. There are many parts of animals that appear to serve no purpose, or indeed that function rather poorly. But the same might be true of the watch without casting any doubt on its having been designed. We sometimes hear the alleged evidences of design in nature dismissed on the grounds that matter had to be arranged in some manner or other, and it might just as well have been arranged in the way that we find it as any other. Paley invites us to consider someone responding in the same manner on finding a watch and hence being sceptical about its having been designed. Surely, Paley suggests, this would be absurd.

One difference between the cases of the watch and the eye is that we know that eyes develop by a hereditary mechanism from the organism's parents. Advances in our understanding of these mechanisms should allow us to give a detailed explanation of how each eye came to have its particular features. Does this understanding obviate the need to invoke the work of a designer? Paley asks us to imagine that we find that a watch contains an intricate automated factory capable of manufacturing new watches resembling itself. Far from decreasing the force of the evidence for design, this would only increase our amazement at the skill and ingenuity of the watchmaker. Nor would it diminish the need to invoke a designer if we supposed that there was no first watch, but that each watch was manufactured by a predecessor. According to Paley, no matter how much we might understand the mechanisms by which each watch was produced, we would be no closer to accounting for the crucial feature: that the parts are arranged in a manner allowing them to keep regular time. Only the work of intelligence can account for that.

Might there be other ways of explaining complex functional organization of parts without appeal to intelligence? Paley considers a number of suggestions. First, perhaps there is a 'principle of order' by which matter arranges itself into complex living structures. Paley has little patience for this suggestion. Once again we are asked to imagine the parts of a watch spontaneously forming themselves and joining together to form a fully functioning watch. What understanding has been gained by applying the words 'principle of order' if we are not implicitly invoking the work of an intelligent agent? Paley complains that we have no example or analogy by which we might understand what this proposal amounts to. Furthermore, we do not find order universally in nature, as we might expect to if there were an unguided general tendency for nature to produce order. Much of nature is irregular and unordered, like the forms of rocks and mountains and coastal boundaries. That order is found only where necessary – as in the functioning parts of organisms– speaks of the work of an agent with foresight.

Secondly, Paley considers some evolutionary ideas that we now associate with Jean-Baptiste Lamarck. (It is doubtful that Paley had read Lamarck's work, but similar ideas were known at the time.) The idea here is that small heritable changes occur in the anatomy of animals as a result of repeated activity. Over generations these changes accumulate to produce new useful anatomical structures. Paley complains that apart from there being no observations to support this hypothesis, it clearly cannot account for all, or even most, of the appearances of design in nature. Tendons and ligaments cannot develop by repeated attempted use, Paley argues, as they are no use at all until they are in place. Similarly, an animal without vision or even a conception of sight is incapable of striving to see and thereby gradually developing eyes.

The most intriguing possibility that Paley considers comes close to Darwin's theory of natural selection. According to this proposal, over an infinite length of time all possible structural forms might arise by chance. Without the guidance of a designer, matter randomly cycles through endless combinations eventually producing all the complex organisms that we observe and many more. The species of organisms we see are relicts of this infinite variety. Many have died out. Only those capable of survival and reproduction remain with us. Paley once again asks us to consider whether we would take someone seriously who proposed such an explanation for the existence of watches, telescopes, knitting machines and steam engines. He objects further that the hypothesis does not fit well with what we observe. Were organisms arising by chance over an infinite span of time we should expect to find a far greater variety of creatures, as there are surely many more possible creatures capable of living and reproducing. Further, suggests Paley, we should not expect plants and animals to be arranged in natural categories of genera and species.

It is intriguing that in his classic presentation of the argument from design Paley should come so close to entertaining the theory that poses the largest threat to his case. (The suggestion was not original with Paley. It dates back to Lucretius, who was probably following Epicurus.) Darwin's theory has the resources to answer each of Paley's objections. In Darwin's system organisms develop from a common ancestor by small random changes. The organisms eliminated in the process are not merely those that *cannot* survive and reproduce at all, but all those who lose in the fierce competition for survival. An infinite span of time is not required for this process to produce a variety of plants and animals. It would appear that a limited variety of creatures clustered in groups of similarity is just what we should expect from Darwin's process. And the story cannot be so readily applied to watches and steam engines. These do not reproduce, and nor do their functions increase their capacity for survival.

Finally, having established to his satisfaction that intelligent agency is responsible for the wonders of nature, Paley extends his argument to the conclusion that this agent is the God of traditional theology. His arguments in this regard can seem somewhat half-hearted, depending on an attenuated conception of God. According to Paley, traditional attributes such as *omniscience*, *omnipotence* and *infinity* are to be understood as superlatives expressing only that God's powers are so far beyond ours that they are at the limits of what we can grasp. Thus understood, Paley takes the extraordinary details of nature that he has described to provide ample support for these attributes. In defence of the *unity* of the designer, Paley appeals to the uniformity of natural laws. If the world were ultimately the work of a committee of agents, Paley argues, we should not expect to find the same regular behaviour displayed throughout nature. Paley devotes the longest chapter to a defence of the *goodness* of the designer. But little insight into the problem of evil emerges. Paley takes divine goodness to be established by two facts: that the vast majority of cases of obvious contrivance in nature are clearly beneficial; and that pleasure is given to creatures beyond what is required for other purposes.

CONTEMPORARY RELEVANCE

While Darwin is widely held to have delivered the death blow to Paley's arguments, structurally similar arguments from design continue to be discussed by philosophers and occasionally by scientists today. Contemporary debates over new versions of the argument from design closely parallel those in Paley's work. For example, our universe is said to be 'fine-tuned' for life. Numerous physical constants such as force strengths and particle masses must lie within very narrow intervals in order to create a stable environment and materials for life to develop. While we do not have the structural complexity of organisms in this case, we have a multitude of contingent factors requiring mutual adjustment to bring about an end. Some argue that the best explanation for this fortuitous arrangement is the foresight and intention of God or some intelligent being (see Swinburne 2004). Indeed, the parallels to Paley's work go further, as many of the responses to the fine-tuning design argument are similar to those that Paley anticipates. Some suggest that we should not be surprised to find that the universe's fundamental constants take life-permitting values, as they had to take some values and they could just as well take their actual values as any. Others suggest that perhaps it is not unlikely that without the aid of a designer the universe should meet the conditions for life to evolve. For there might be some more basic laws that constrain the constants to take life-permitting values. (To some degree this parallels the suggestion of 'principles of order'.) Still others suggest that our universe may be the latest in an infinite sequence of universes (or one of many simultaneously existing universes). These vary randomly, eventually cycling through all possible combinations of physical constants including those permitting life to evolve. We only get to observe a universe that is capable of sustaining life. And at least one physicist has resorted to a quasi-Darwinian model of replicating universes to account for the data alleged to support design.[3]

Paley dismissed talk of 'principles of order' as a mere empty use of words. But ideas in this vein are now taken seriously among some scientists in the growing field of complexity studies. Research is conducted on systems in which a kind of ordered complexity arises spontaneously from a simple set of laws and initial conditions. Some researchers, such as Stuart Kauffman (1993), suggest that these results may provide insight into the origins of life and its subsequent evolution in ways that supplement the basic Darwinian account.

While not taken seriously by most scientists, critics continue to attack the standard neo-Darwinian account of evolution on grounds similar to Paley's. The closest contemporary heirs to Paley's project are the recent proponents of 'intelligent design theory' such as Michael Behe (1996). Behe notoriously argues that there are molecular machines within cells displaying 'irreducible complexity' that standard Darwinian mechanisms have great difficulty accounting for. Following Paley, Behe argues that systems such as the bacterial flagellum display obvious signs of having been designed. According to Behe, an irreducibly complex system is one "composed of several well-matched, interacting parts that contribute to the basic function, wherein the removal of any one of the parts causes the system to effectively cease functioning" (1996: 39). This is essentially the feature to which Paley appeals in arguing for design. Behe extends Paley's argument to suggest that not only do biological systems display evidence of design, but that Darwin did not provide a viable alternative explanation. According to Behe, since an irreducibly complex system cannot function without its full set of parts, it cannot be produced in a Darwinian stepwise manner from a sequence of predecessor systems of increasing fitness.[4]

Even with the triumph of Darwin, Paley's work continues to haunt discussions of biological complexity and adaptation. Contemporary defenders of evolutionary theory frequently use Paley's work as a foil for Darwin's theory. The title of Richard Dawkins' classic, *The Blind Watchmaker* (1986), is of course a reference to Paley, and Dawkins spends some time responding to Paley's favourite example of the eye. Even as a staunch Darwinian, Dawkins attributes continuing relevance to Paley's work, even describing himself as a 'neo-Paleyist'.

Indeed, the status of Paley's argument continues to be relevant to how evolutionary theory is defended, as it matters whether the work of a designer stands as

3. For an overview of the fine-tuning design argument and various critical responses, see Leslie (1989).
4. Behe's arguments have received numerous searching criticisms. Recent ones are found in: Petto & Godfrey (2007); Kitcher (2007).

a possible alternative to natural selection. Elliot Sober (2008) argues that despite the intuitive grip that Paley's arguments have had on people, even before the Darwinian alternative was available Paley failed to provide any good evidence for design. If Sober is correct, then in defending Darwin there is no need to enter into further comparative evaluations between Paley's and Darwin's proposals. The case for Darwin's theory stands on its own merits. Others, like Dawkins, do not think that Paley's arguments can be so easily dismissed, and believe that it took Darwin's work decisively to refute Paley's argument, making it "possible to be an intellectually fulfilled atheist" (Dawkins 1986: 37). According to Dawkins, while Paley's conclusion was ultimately unsatisfactory, he was right that the complex functional organization that he found in nature cried out for explanation, and that it was unsatisfactory to be left with no alternative while rejecting Paley's conclusion. If Dawkins is right, the burden is on the defender of the theory of natural selection to show that Darwin provided a far *superior* explanation of the data than Paley did. Stephen J. Gould (1980) argues in this manner, as did Darwin himself in *On the Origin of Species* ([1859] 1998), pointing to cases of apparent sub-optimal design. Such cases, they argue, are better explained by the interplay of random mutation and natural selection than by Paley's designer.

FURTHER READING

Clarke, M. 1974. *Paley: Evidences for the Man*. Toronto: SPCK.

Gould, S. J. 1993. "Darwin and Paley Meet the Invisible Hand". In his *Eight Little Piggies: Reflections in Natural History*, 138–52. New York: W. W. Norton.

Le Mahieu, D. 1976. *The Mind of William Paley: A Philosopher and His Age*. Lincoln, NE: University of Nebraska Press.

Nuovo, V. 1992. "Rethinking Paley". *Synthese* **91**: 29–51.

Oppy, G. 2006. *Arguing about Gods*. Cambridge: Cambridge University Press.

Paley, E. [1825] 1970. *An Account of the Life and Writings of William Paley*. Farnborough: Gregg.

Sober, E. 2003. "The Design Argument". In *God and Design: The Teleological Argument and Modern Science*, N. Manson (ed.), 27–54. London: Routledge.

On ARGUMENT FROM DESIGN see also Vol. 4, Ch. 12; Vol. 5, Ch. 17. On INTELLIGENT DESIGN see also Vol. 1, Chs 4, 8; Vol. 4, Chs 11, 12. On NATURAL RELIGION/THEOLOGY see also Chs 4, 6, 7, 11, 12, 13, 19; Vol. 4, Chs 8, 12; Vol. 5, Ch. 23. On UTILITARIANISM see also Vol. 4, Ch. 11.

CHRONOLOGY

1501 Establishment of Safavid Dynasty in Iran.

1504 Death of Isabella, Queen of Spain, sponsor of Columbus' voyages.

1506 Death of Josetsu, Buddhist monk and Japanese master of ink painting.

1509 Birth of **John Calvin**, one of the foremost theologians of the Protestant Reformation.

1512 Death of Americo Vespucci, the Spanish merchant and navigator who gave his name to the American continent.
Michelangelo, Italian sculptor and painter, finishes painting the ceiling of the Sistine Chapel.

1517 **Martin Luther** initiates the Protestant Reformation by nailing his Ninety-Five Theses to the door of the Castle Church in Wittenberg, Germany.

1519 Death of Leonardo da Vinci, Florentine artist, scientist and inventor, often regarded as the very model of the 'Renaissance Man'.
Cortez commences the Spanish conquest of Mexico.

1521 Death of Ferdinand Magellan, Portuguese navigator who led the first European circumnavigation of the globe.
The Diet of Worms addresses the Protestant Reformation, with **Luther** refusing to repudiate his writings and (according to tradition) declaring, "Here I stand. I can do no other".

1524 Death of Vasco de Gama, Portuguese navigator and the first European to travel to India around the Cape of Good Hope.
Start of the Peasant's War in the Holy Roman Empire, involving about 300,000 peasant insurgents.

1526 Foundation of the Mughal Empire by Babur.

1527 Death of **Niccolò Machiavelli**, Italian Renaissance political philosopher and author of *The Prince*.
Sacking of Rome marks the end of the Italian Renaissance.

1531 The Church of England breaks away from the Roman Catholic Church and recognizes King Henry VIII as its head.

1532 Francisco Pizarro leads the Spanish conquest of the Incan Empire.

1533 Birth of **Michel de Montaigne**, French writer best known for his *Essays*.

1536 Death of **Erasmus** (*see* Vol. 2, Ch. 19).

1540 Thomas Cromwell, Vicar General and chief advisor to Henry VIII, is beheaded for treason.
Ignatius Loyola's Society of Jesus (the Jesuits) receives papal confirmation and goes on to become a dominant force in the Catholic Counter-Reformation.

1541 Death of Paracelsus, Swiss physician who pioneered the application of chemistry to medicine.

1543 Death of Copernicus, advocate of the heliocentric theory (the Copernican Revolution).
The Nanban trade period begins with the arrival of Portuguese traders in Japan.

1545 The opening of the Council of Trent inaugurates the Counter-Reformation.

1546 Death of **Luther**.

1547 Death of Henry VIII.

1548 Birth of **Francisco Suárez**, prominent Scholastic philosopher and theologian.

1550 The Modern English (language) period begins.

1550–51 The Valladolid debate (in Spain) is held, concerning the proper treatment of the natives of the New World.

1556 An earthquake in Shaanxi, China kills about 830,000 people.

1557 Death of Jacques Cartier, French navigator who explored the St Lawrence River.
The Inquisition in Rome under Pope Pius IV issues the first *Index librorum prohibitorum* (List of prohibited books), a list of books Catholics are forbidden to read or possess.

1558 Death of Charles V, King of Spain and Holy Roman emperor, who struggled to hold his empire together against the growing forces of Protestantism and increasing Turkish and French pressure.
Start of the Livonian War between Poland, Sweden, Denmark and Russia.

1561 Guido de Bres writes the Belgic Confession of Faith.

1562 The French wars of religion between Catholics and Huguenots (French Protestants) start.

1564 Death of **Calvin**.

1566 Death of Suleiman the Magnificent, sultan at the pinnacle of the Ottoman Empire.

1569 The Union of Lublin establishes the Polish–Lithuanian Commonwealth.

1571 Spanish missionaries are murdered by Indians at the site of Jamestown settlement, Virginia.

1572 Catherine de' Medici instigates the St Bartholomew's Day massacre of thousands of Huguenots.
The Danish astronomer Tycho Brahe observes supernova SN 1572.

1577 Francis Drake, the English navigator who would later play a key role in the defeat of the Spanish Armada, commences his journey of circumnavigation.

1579 The Union of Utrecht unifies the northern Netherlands.

1580 Philip II unifies Spain and Portugal.

1582 Adoption of the Gregorian calendar in Catholic countries.

1583 Birth of **Lord Herbert of Cherbury**, English diplomat and philosopher, considered the father of English deism.

1584 Death of Ivan 'the Terrible', the first Russian to assume the title 'tsar'.

1588 Birth of **Thomas Hobbes**, English philosopher who devised social contract theory.
Defeat of the Spanish Armada by England.

1589 Repulsion of the English fleet by Spain.
William Shakespeare, English playwright and poet, considered the greatest dramatist of all time, writes his first play.

1592 Death of **Montaigne**.
Korea, with the aid of the Ming dynasty, repels the Japanese invasion.

1593 Death of Li Shih-Chen, the Chinese scientist who compiled a fifty-volume work on pharmacology, botany, zoology, minerology and metallurgy.

1594 Death of Gerardus Mercator, Flemish cartographer.

1596 Birth of **René Descartes**, French philosopher and mathematician, often referred to as the 'father of modern philosophy'.

1598 Death of Philip II, King of Spain, leader of the Spanish struggle against Protestantism.
Edict of Nantes ends the French wars of religion.
Russia descends into anarchy during the Time of Troubles.

1600 Giordano Bruno, Italian philosopher, is burned as a heretic in Rome.
Chartering of the British East India Company, a joint-stock trading company that traded with the Indian subcontinent and China.

1601 Elizabethan Poor Law appoints parishes as administrators of poverty relief.

1603 Death of William Gilbert, English scientist who pioneered investigations into magnetism and electrical attraction.
Death of Elizabeth, Queen of England, whose forty-five-year reign saw England established as the leading Protestant power.

1605 Death of Akbar the Great, Mogul emperor of India, noted for his 'Edict of toleration for all religions'.
The gunpowder plot intended to kill the king, his family and most of the Protestant aristocracy by blowing up the Houses of Parliament during the State Opening on 5 November fails in England.

1609 Johann Carolus publishes *Relation*, the first newspaper, in Germany.

1610 Galileo observes the moons of Jupiter.

1611 Publication of the King James Bible.

1612 Pendle witch trials in England, with ten people found guilty and executed by hanging.

1613 The Time of Troubles ends in Russia with the establishment of the House of Romanov.

1614 John Napier introduces logarithms to simplify arithmetical calculations.
Death of El Greco, innovative Cretan artist who spent most of his life in Toledo, Spain.

1616 Death of Shakespeare.

1617 Birth of **Ralph Cudworth**, English philosopher and leading exponent of Cambridge Platonism.
Death of **Suárez**.

1618 Execution of Walter Raleigh, English adventurer who was accused of treason by King James I.

The Manchus commence their invasion of China.
The Synod of Dort, a Dutch Reformed assembly, approves the 'Five Points of Calvinism'.

1620 Puritan Pilgrims arrive at Plymouth Rock in Massachusetts, founding colonies at Plymouth, Salem and Boston.

1623 Birth of **Blaise Pascal**, French mathematician, scientist and religious philosopher.

1625 Foundation of New Amsterdam (later New York City) by the Dutch East India Company.

1626 Death of Francis Bacon, English philosopher who played a significant role in the rise of empiricism.
Completion of St Peter's Basilica in the Vatican.

1630 Death of Johannes Kepler, German physicist who made significant contributions to optics and astronomy.

1632 Birth of **Baruch Spinoza**, Dutch philosopher and theologian, expelled from the Jewish community in Amsterdam for his unpopular views.
Birth of **John Locke**, English empiricist philosopher and political theorist.
Death of King Gustav II Adolph, under whom Sweden became a major European power.
Construction starts on the Taj Mahal.

1633 The Inquisition compels Galileo to renounce Copernican theories.

1640 Torture is outlawed in England.

1641 Foreigners are expelled from Japan, and nobody is permitted to enter or leave the country.
Start of the English Civil War.

1642 Death of Galileo, Italian scientist who made immense contributions to physics, astronomy and scientific philosophy.
Death of Cardinal Richelieu, French statesman who founded the French Academy.
Dutch explorer Abel Tasman makes the first recorded European sighting of New Zealand.

1643 Evangelista Torricelli invents the mercury barometer.

1644 The Ming dynasty in China is overthrown in a civil war.

1645 Death of Mary Ward, English Roman Catholic nun recognized as a pioneer in the education of women.
Death of Hugo Grotius, Protestant natural law theorist.

1646 Birth of **Gottfried Wilhelm Leibniz**, German rational philosopher and mathematician, discoverer (separately from Newton) of calculus.

1648 Death of **Lord Herbert of Cherbury**.

1650 Death of **Descartes**.

1652 Cape Town is established by the Dutch East India Company.

1657 Death of William Harvey, English physician noted for his discovery of the circulatory system and the pumping activity of the heart.

1658 Death of Oliver Cromwell, English statesman who became first Chairman of the new British Republic after the English Civil War.

1660 Restoration of the monarchy in England at the end of the English Commonwealth.
Foundation of the Royal Society of London.

1662 Death of **Pascal**.

1664 British troops capture New Amsterdam and rename it New York.

1666 Great Fire of London.

1671 Death of Margaret Brent, first woman landholder in Maryland, denied permission to vote in the Maryland Assembly.

1675 Birth of **Samuel Clarke**, English philosopher and theologian and exponent of Newtonian natural science.

1676 Antoni van Leeuwenhoek discovers bacteria.

1677 Death of **Spinoza**.

1679 Death of **Hobbes**.

1682 La Salle explores the length of the Mississippi River.
Peter I ('Peter the Great') becomes tsar of Russia, launching a wide-ranging program of modernization.

1683 China conquers the kingdom of Tungning and annexes Taiwan.

1685 Birth of **George Berkeley**, Anglican bishop and philosopher, famous for his defence of idealism in metaphysics.
The Edict of Fontainebleau outlaws Protestantism in France.

1691 Death of Robert Boyle, British natural philosopher and early advocate of the use of experimental methods in the study of nature.

1692 Salem witchcraft trials in Massachusetts.

1693 Death of Marie La Fayette, French writer, traditionally designated the originator of the modern novel.

1694 Birth of **Voltaire**, controversial and influential writer of the French Enlightenment.

1702 Death of William of Orange, who was made King of England to ward off the threat of a permanent Catholic dynasty.

1703 Birth of **Jonathan Edwards**, pastor and philosophical theologian who played a leading role in the religious revival in the British American colonies known as the Great Awakening.
Founding of city of St Petersburg by Peter the Great (the capital of Russia was transferred from Moscow to St Petersburg in 1712).

1704 Death of **Locke**.

1705 Death of Jakob Bernoulli, a Swiss mathematician who made important contributions to probability theory and analytic geometry.

1710 Birth of **Thomas Reid**, a philosopher of the Scottish Enlightenment.

1711 Birth of **David Hume**, leading philosopher of the eighteenth century, known especially for his empiricism and sceptical views on religion.

1713 Birth of **Denis Diderot**, prominent French philosopher of the Enlightenment best known for his editorship of the *Encyclopédie*.
British slave trade to Spanish America begins.

1715 Death of Louis XIV, the 'Sun King', who ruled France for seventy-two years.

1716 Death of **Leibniz**.

1717 Birth of Jean le Ron d'Alembert, mathematician and co-editor with **Diderot** of the *Encyclopédie*.

1718 Death of William Penn, Quaker founder of the American Commonwealth of Pennsylvania.
Foundation of the city of New Orleans.

1720 Collapse of South Sea Company shares.

1722 Death of **Toland**.
Death of K'ang Hsi, Chinese emperor, military commander, scholar and statesman who encouraged the introduction of Western education in China.

1724 Birth of **Immanuel Kant**, foremost thinker of the Enlightenment, whose *Critique of Pure Reason* ushered in modern philosophy.

1727 Death of Isaac Newton, the English mathematician and natural philosopher best known for his work on gravitation, optics and the calculus.

1729 Birth of **Gotthold Ephraim Lessing**, German dramatist, literary critic and philosopher, considered the founder of modern German literature.
Death of **Clarke**.
Death of Thomas Newcomen, the English inventor who produced the first effective steam engine.

1730 Development of the sextant by John Hadley and Thomas Godfrey.

1733 Death of **Tindal**.

1740 Development of modern steel by Benjamin Huntsman.

1741 European discovery of Alaska by Vitus Bering.

1742 Death of Edmund Halley, English astronomer who predicted the return of 'Halley's Comet'.

1743 Birth of **William Paley**, best known for his teleological argument for the existence of God.

1745 Invention of the Leyden jar, the first electrical capacitor, by Ewald von Keist.

1749 Death of Gabrielle du Châtelet, French mathematician and scholar who translated Newton's *Principia*.

1750 Approximate peak of the Little Ice Age.
Death of Johann Sebastian Bach, the great German Baroque composer.

1751 First stage of publication of the French *Encyclopédie*, one of the chief works of the Enlightenment, edited by **Diderot** and d'Alembert.
China invades Tibet and secures control over the succession of the Dalai Lama.

1753 Death of **Berkeley**.

1755 Death of Montesquieu, pivotal figure in the French Enlightenment.
Lisbon earthquake sees death of between 60,000 and 100,000 people.
Publication of Samuel Johnson's English dictionary.

1757 Battle of Plassey initiates British rule in India.

1758 Death of **Edwards**.
Publication of **Voltaire**'s *Candide*.

1759 Death of George Frederick Handel, great German Baroque composer.

1762 Birth of **Johann Gottlieb Fichte** (*see* Vol. 4, Ch. 2), German idealist philosopher.

1764 Creation of the Spinning Jenny by James Hargreaves initiates the Industrial Revolution in Britain.

1768 Birth of **Friedrich Schleiermacher** (*see* Vol. 4, Ch. 3), influential German Protestant theologian.
Ghurkhas conquer Nepal.

1770 Birth of **G. W. F. Hegel**, major German idealist philosopher (*see* Vol. 4, Ch. 4).
The Bengal famine is responsible for the deaths of an estimated ten million people.

1772 Partitions of Poland end the Polish–Lithuanian Commonwealth.

1775 Birth of **Friedrich Wilhelm Joseph Schelling** (*see* Vol. 4, Ch. 5), German idealist philosopher.
The American War of Independence begins, lasting until 1783.

1776 Death of **Hume**.
American Declaration of Independence is issued, giving birth to the United States of America.

1778 Death of **Voltaire**.
Death of Jean Jacques Rousseau, French philosopher who helped to spark the French Revolution.

1779 Discovery of photosynthesis by Dutch scientist Jan Ingenhouse.
Commencement of the Xhosa wars in South Africa.

1780 Death of Maria Theresa, Holy Roman Empress, Queen of Hungary and Bohemia.

1781 Death of **Lessing**.

1785 Commencement of the Northwest Indian War between the United States and a confederation of native Americans.

1786 Death of Frederick the Great, King of Prussia, military commander, writer and composer.

1787 Foundation of Freetown in Sierra Leone by freed London slaves.

1788 Birth of **Arthur Schopenhauer** (*see* Vol. 4, Ch. 6), 'philosopher of pessimism'.
First European settlement in Australia.

1789 Start of the French Revolution with the storming of the Bastille.

1790 Death of Adam Smith, acclaimed Scottish economist whose recommendation of free markets and free trade in *The Wealth of Nations* was to have great influence in the West.

1791 Beginning of the Haitian revolution, which leads to the establishment of the first free, black republic.
Death of Wolfgang Amadeus Mozart, masterly Austrian composer.

1792 Foundation of New York Stock and Exchange Board.

1793 Banning of slavery in Upper Canada.
Louis XVI and Marie Antoinette are executed in Paris, marking the start of the 'Reign of Terror' in France.

1795 Pinckney's Treaty grants the Mississippi Territory to the United States.

1796 Death of **Reid**.
Britain ejects the Dutch from Ceylon.
Death of Catherine the Great, Empress of Russia.

1798 Birth of **Auguste Comte** (*see* Vol. 4, Ch. 7), French philosopher and founder of positivism.
Publication of Edward Jenner's treatise on smallpox vaccination.

1799 Dissolution of the Dutch East India Company.
Napoleon Bonaparte becomes First Consul of France.
Discovery of the Rosetta Stone, which enables Egyptian hieroglyphs to be deciphered.
Death of George Washington, first president of the United States of America.

BIBLIOGRAPHY

Adams, E. 2001. "Calvin's View of Natural Knowledge of God". *International Journal of Systematic Theology* **3**: 280–92.

Adams, R. 1994. *Leibniz: Determinist, Theist, Idealist*. Oxford: Oxford University Press.

Alexander, H. (ed.) 1956. *The Leibniz–Clarke Correspondence*. Manchester: Manchester University Press.

Allison, H. 1966. *Lessing and the Enlightenment: His Philosophy of Religion in Relation to Eighteenth-Century Thought*. Ann Arbor, MI: University of Michigan Press.

Althusser, L. 1999. *Machiavelli and Us*, G. Elliot (trans.). London: Verso.

Annet, P. 1746. *Deism Fairly Stated and Vindicated*. London.

Anstey, P. (ed.) 2003. *The Philosophy of John Locke: New Perspectives*. London: Routledge.

Antognazza, M. 2006. "Revealed Religion: The Continental European Debate". In *The Cambridge History of Eighteenth-Century Philosophy*, K. Haakonssen (ed.), vol. 2, 666-82. Cambridge: Cambridge University Press.

Aquinas, T. 1964. *Summa theologiae*, Blackfriars (trans.). New York: McGraw-Hill.

Aquinas, T. 2006. *Summa theologiae, Questions on God*, B. Davies & B. Leftow (eds). Cambridge: Cambridge University Press.

Aristotle 1984. *On the Soul*. In *The Complete Works of Aristotle*, J. Barnes (ed.), vol. 1, 641–92. Princeton, NJ: Princeton University Press.

Aristotle 1995. *The Complete Works of Aristotle*, J. Barnes (ed.), vol. 2. Princeton, NJ: Princeton University Press.

Ayers, M. 1996. "Introduction". In his *Philosophical Works including the Works on Vision*, G. Berkeley (ed.), xv–xxxix. London: Everyman.

Bacon, F. 2002. *Francis Bacon: The Major Works*, B. Vickers (ed.). New York: Oxford University Press.

Bacon, F. 2004. *The "Instauratio Magna, Part II: Novum Organum" and Associated Texts*, G. Rees & M. Wakely (eds & trans.), The Oxford Francis Bacon, vol. XI. Oxford: Clarendon Press.

Badir, M. 1974. *Voltaire et l'Islam*. Banbury: SVEC/Voltaire Foundation.

Bagley, P. (ed.) 1999. *Piety, Peace, and the Freedom to Philosophize*. Dordrecht: Kluwer.

Barber, W. 1955. *Leibniz in France*. Oxford: Clarendon Press.

Barker, S. 1983. "Hume on the Logic of Design". *Hume Studies* **9**: 1–18.

Barth, K. & E. Brunner 2002. *Natural Theology: Comprising "Nature and Grace" by Professor Emil Brunner and the Reply "No!" by Dr. Karl Barth*, P. Fraenkel (trans.). Eugene, OR: Wipf & Stock Publishers.

Barth, P. 1935. *Das Problem der naturlichen Theologie bei Calvin*, Theologische Existenz Heute 18. Munich: Kaiser.

Battles, F. 1996. *Interpreting John Calvin*. Grand Rapids, MI: Baker Books.

Baudelaire, C. [1857] 1991. *Les fleurs du mal*. Paris: Flammarion.

Bayle, P. 1696–1740. *Dictionnaire historique et critique*. Amsterdam.

Bayle, P. 1965. *Historical and Critical Dictionary: Selections*. Indianapolis, IN: Hackett.

Beck, L. 1960. *A Commentary on Kant's "Critique of Practical Reason"*. Chicago, IL: University of Chicago Press.

Behe, M. 1996. *Darwin's Black Box: The Biochemical Challenge to Evolution*. New York: Free Press.

Bell, D. 1984. *Spinoza in Germany: From 1670 to the Age of Goethe*. London: Institute of Germanic Studies.

Belleforest, F. 1570. *L'histoire universelle du monde, contenant l'entière description & situation des quatre parties de la terre, la division & estendue d'une chacun region & provinces d'icelles: Ensemble l'origine & particulières mœurs, loix, coustumes, religion, & ceremonies de toutes les nations, et peuples par qui elles sont habitées* Paris: G. Mallot.

Berkeley, G. 1948–57. *The Works of George Berkeley Bishop of Cloyne*, 9 vols, A. Luce & T. Jessop (eds). London: Nelson.

Berkouwer, G. 1979. *General Revelation*. Grand Rapids, MI: Eerdmans.

Berlin, I. 1982. "The Originality of Machiavelli". In *Against the Current: Essays in the History of Ideas* , H. Hardy (ed.), 25–79. New York: Penguin.

Berlin, I. 2002. *Freedom and its Betrayal*. London: Chatto & Windus.

Berman, D. 1981. "Cognitive Theology and Emotive Mysteries in Berkeley's *Alciphron*". *Proceedings of the Royal Irish Academy* **81c**(7): 219–29.

Besterman, T. 1962. *Voltaire Essays and Another*. Oxford: Oxford University Press.

Besterman, T. 1967. "Voltaire's God. *Studies on Voltaire and the Eighteenth Century* **55**: 23–41.

Beversluis, J. 1995. "Reforming the 'Reformed' Objection to Natural Theology". *Faith and Philosophy* **12**: 189–206.

Blount, C. 1695. *The Oracles of Reason, Miscellaneous Works*. London.

Blumenfeld, D. 1995. "Leibniz's Ontological and Cosmological Argument". In *The Cambridge Companion to Leibniz*, N. Jolley (ed.), 353–81. Cambridge: Cambridge University Press.

Boemus, J. 1520. *Omnium gentium mores, leges et ritus ex multis clarissimis rerum scriptoribus*. Lyon: J. Tornaesium & G. Gazeium (2nd edn 1556).

Boemus, J. 1556. *Omnium gentium mores, leges et ritus, ex multis clarissimis rerum scriptoribus a Joanne Boëmo, nuper collecti et novissime recogniti. Tribus libris absolutum opus, Aphricam, Asiam et Europam describentibus*. Lyon: J. Tornaesium and G. Gazeium.

Bollacher, M. 1978. *Lessing: Vernunft und Geschichte*. Tübingen: Niemeyer.

Bonnet, C. 1770. *Contemplation de la nature*. Amsterdam: Marc-Michel Rey.

Boswell, J. [1777] 1947. "An Account of My Last Interview with David Hume, Esq.". In D. Hume, *Dialogues Concerning Natural Religion*, N. Smith (ed.), 76–9. New York: Thomas Nelson.

Bourdieu, P. 1997. *Méditations pascaliennes*. Paris: Seuil.

Bourdieu, P. 2000. *Pascalian Meditations*, R. Nice (trans.). Oxford: Polity Press in association with Blackwell.

Bouwsma, W. 1992. "Calvin and the Renaissance Crisis of Knowing". In *Calvin and Calvinism, Vol. 7: The Organizational Structure of Calvin's Theology*, R. Gamble (ed.), 226–47. New York: Garland.

Boyle, R. [1691] 2000. *The Christian Virtuoso*. In *The Works of Robert Boyle*, M. Hunter & E. Davis (eds), vol. 11, 281–327. London: Pickering & Chatto.

Boyle, R. [1688] 1999–2000. *A Disquisition about the Final Causes of Natural Things*. In *The Works of Robert Boyle*, M. Hunter & E. Davis (eds), vol. 11, 79–151. London: Pickering & Chatto.

Brooks, R. 1964. *Voltaire and Leibniz*. Geneva: Droz.
Brougham, H. 1845. *Lives of Men of Letters and Science Who Flourished in the Time of George III*. London: C. Knight.
Brunschvigg, L. 1905. *Le Recueil original des Pensées*. Paris: Hachette.
Butler, J. 1736. *The Analogy of Religion*. Dublin.
Calvin, J. 1960. *Institutes of the Christian Religion*, 2 vols, J. McNeill (ed.), F. Battles (trans.) [translated from the 1559 Latin edition]. Philadelphia, PA: Westminster Press.
Calvin, J. 1979a. *Commentary upon the Acts of the Apostles: II, Acts 14–28*, H. Beveridge (ed.), C. Fetherstone (trans.), Calvin's Commentaries, vol. 19. Grand Rapids, MI: Baker Book House.
Calvin, J. 1979b. *Commentaries on the Epistle of Paul the Apostle to the Romans*, J. Owen (ed. & trans.), Calvin's Commentaries, vol. 19. Grand Rapids, MI: Baker Book House.
Calvin, J. 1979c. *Commentary on the Book of Psalms*, J. Anderson (trans.), Calvin's Commentaries, vols 4–6. Grand Rapids, MI: Baker Book House.
Calvin, J. 1979d. *Commentaries on the First Book of Moses called Genesis*, J. King (trans.), Calvin's Commentaries, vol. 1. Grand Rapids, MI: Baker Book House.
Calvin, J. 1979e. *Commentaries on the Epistle of Paul the Apostle to the Hebrews*, J. Owen (trans.), Calvin's Commentaries, vol. 22. Grand Rapids, MI: Baker Book House.
Carey, D. 2006. *Locke, Shaftesbury, and Hutcheson: Contesting Diversity in the Enlightenment and Beyond*. Cambridge: Cambridge University Press.
Cassirer, E. 1946. *The Myth of the State*, New Haven, CT: Yale University Press.
Catholic Encyclopedia n.d. "Encyclopedists", www.newadvent.org/cathen/05418a.htm (accessed June 2009).
Chappell, V. (ed.) 1994. *The Cambridge Companion to Locke*. Cambridge: Cambridge University Press.
Chaudon, L. 1759. *Dictionnaire anti-philosophique*. Avignon: Veuve Girard & François Seguin.
Chouillet, J. 1977. *Diderot*. Paris: SEDES.
Chubb, T. 1741. *A Discourse of Miracles*. London.
Clarke, S. 1711. *A Discourse concerning the Unchangeable Obligations of Natural Religion and the Truth and Certainty of the Christian Revelation*, 3rd edn. London.
Coby, J. 1999. *Machiavelli's Romans: Liberty and Greatness in the Discourses on Livy*. New York: Lexington Books.
Cohen, H. 1980. *Hermann Cohens Jüdischen Schriften*. New York: Arno Press.
Coleridge, S. 1955. *Coleridge on the Seventeenth Century*, R. Brinkley (ed.). Durham, NC: Duke University Press.
Collins, A. 1713. *A Discourse of Free-Thinking*. London.
Collins, A. 1717. *A Philosophical Enquiry into Human Liberty*. London.
Collins, A. 1724. *A Discourse of the Grounds and Reasons of the Christian Religion*. London.
Compayré, G. 1879. "Montaigne". In *Histoire critique des doctrines d'éducation en France depuis le XVIe siècle*, G. Compayré (ed.), 88–112. Paris: Hachette.
Conche, M. 1996. "La signification de Dieu". In *Montaigne et la philosophie*, M. Conche (ed.), 129–41. Paris: PUF.
Cotoni, M. 1984. *L'Exégèse du Nouveau Testament dans la philosophie française du dix-huitième siècle*. Oxford: Voltaire Foundation.
Cottingham, J. 1985. "Cartesian Trialism". *Mind* **94**: 218–30.
Crisp, O. 2003. "How 'Occasional' was Edward's Occasionalism". In *Jonathan Edwards: Philosophical Theologian*, P. Helm & O. Crisp (eds), 61–77. Aldershot: Ashgate.
Cudworth, R. n.d. *British Library Additional Manuscripts, 4978–4983*.
Cudworth, R. 1664. *A Sermon Preached to the Honourable Society of Lincolnes-Inne*. London.
Cudworth, R. 1678. *The True Intellectual System of the Universe: The First Part; Wherein, All the Reason and Philosophy of Atheism is Confuted; and Its Impossibility Demonstrated*. London.

Cudworth, R. 1969. "A Sermon Preached before the House of Commons. March 31, 1647". In *The Cambridge Platonists*, C. Patrides (ed.), 90–127. London: Edward Arnold.

Cudworth, R. 1996. *A Treatise Concerning Eternal and Immutable Reality and A Treatise on Freewill*, S. Hutton (ed.). Cambridge: Cambridge University Press.

Cuneo, T. & R. Van Woudenberg (eds) 2004. *The Cambridge Companion to Thomas Reid*. Cambridge: Cambridge University Press.

Curley, E. 1972. "The Roots of Contingency". In *Leibniz: A Collection of Critical Essays*, H. Frankfurt (ed.), 69–97. New York: Doubleday.

d'Alembert, J. 1995. *Preliminary Discourse to the Encyclopedia of Diderot*, R. Schwab (ed. & trans.). Chicago, IL: University of Chicago Press. [First published in French in 1751.]

Daniels, N. 1989. *Thomas Reid's Inquiry: The Geometry of Visibles and The Case for Realism*. Stanford, CA: Stanford University Press.

Darwall, S. 1995. *The British Moralists and the Internal "Ought": 1640–1740*. Cambridge: Cambridge University Press.

Darwin, C. [1859] 1998. *On the Origin of Species*, G. Beer (ed.). Oxford: Oxford University Press.

Darwin, C. [1893] 2000. *The Autobiography of Charles Darwin*, F. Darwin (ed.). New York: Prometheus.

Dawkins, R. 1986. *The Blind Watchmaker: Why the Evidence of Evolution Reveals a Universe without Design*. New York: W. W. Norton.

De Bary, P. 2002. *Thomas Reid and Scepticism: His Reliabilist Response*. London: Routledge.

De Beer, E. 1976–89. *The Correspondence of John Locke*, 8 vols. Oxford: Clarendon Press.

De Dijn, H., F. Mignini *et al.* (eds) 1995. *Studia Spinozana: Spinoza's Philosophy of Religion*. Würzburg: Könighausen & Neumann.

Delattre, R. 1968. *Beauty and Sensibility in the Thought of Jonathan Edwards*. New Haven, CT: Yale University Press.

Descartes, R. 1976. *Discours de la Méthode. Texte et commentaire*, 5th edn, E. Gilson (ed.). Paris: Vrin.

Descartes, R. 1984. *The Philosophical Writings of Descartes, Vol. 2*, J. Cottingham, R. Stoothoff & D. Murdoch (trans.). Cambridge: Cambridge University Press.

Descartes, R. 1985. *The Philosophical Writings of Descartes, Vol. 1*, J. Cottingham, R. Stoothoff & D. Murdoch (trans.). Cambridge: Cambridge University Press.

Descartes, R. 1991. *The Philosophical Writings of Descartes, Vol. 3: The Correspondence*, J. Cottingham, R. Stoothoff, D. Murdoch & A. Kenny (trans.). Cambridge: Cambridge University Press.

Diderot, D. 1875. *Œuvres complètes de Diderot*, 20 vols, J. Assézat & M. Tourneux (eds). Paris: Garnier.

Diderot, D. 1975– . *Œuvres complètes de Diderot*, H. Dieckmann, J. Proust & J. Varloot (eds). Paris: Hermann.

Diderot, D. 2000. *Lettre sur les aveugles*, M. Hobson & S. Harvey (eds). Paris: Garnier Flammarion.

Diderot, D. 2004. "Prière". *Recherches sur Diderot et sur l'Encyclopédie* **36**: 174–7.

Dieter, T. 2001. *Der junge Luther und Aristoteles*. Berlin: de Gruyter.

Dowey, Jr, E. 1994. *The Knowledge of God in Calvin's Theology*, 3rd edn. Grand Rapids, MI: Eerdmans.

Earman, J. 2000. *Hume's Abject Failure: The Argument against Miracles*. New York: Oxford University Press.

Edwards, J. 1959. *The Works of Jonathan Edwards, vol. 2: Religious Affections*, J. Smith (ed.). New Haven, CT: Yale University Press.

Edwards, J. 1970. *The Works of Jonathan Edwards, vol. 3: Original Sin*, C. Holbrook (ed.). New Haven, CT: Yale University Press.

Edwards, J. 1980. *The Works of Jonathan Edwards, vol. 6: Scientific and Philosophical Writings*, W. Anderson (ed.). New Haven, CT: Yale University Press.
Edwards, J. 1989. *The Works of Jonathan Edwards, vol. 8: Ethical Writings*, P. Ramsey (ed.). New Haven, CT: Yale University Press.
Edwards, J. 1994. *The Works of Jonathan Edwards, vol. 13: The "Miscellanies" a-500*, T. Schafer (ed.). New Haven, CT: Yale University Press.
Edwards, J. 1998. *The Works of Jonathan Edwards, vol. 16: Letters and Personal Writings*, G. Claghorn (ed.). New Haven, CT: Yale University Press.
Edwards, J. 2000. *The Works of Jonathan Edwards, vol. 18: The "Miscellanies" 501–832*, A. Chamberlain (ed.). New Haven, CT: Yale University Press.
Edwards, J. 2002a. *The Works of Jonathan Edwards, vol. 20: The "Miscellanies" 833–1152*, A. Pauw (ed.). New Haven, CT: Yale University Press.
Edwards, J. 2002b. *The Works of Jonathan Edwards, vol. 21: Writings on the Trinity, Grace, and Faith*, S. Lee (ed.). New Haven, CT: Yale University Press.
Ferre, F. 1962. "Introduction". In W. Paley, *Natural Theology: Selections*, xi–xxxii. Indianapolis, IN: Bobbs-Merrill.
Flasch, K. 1989. *Aufklärung im Mittelalter? Die Verurteilung von 1277. Das Dokument des Bischofs von Paris eingeleitet, übersetzt und erklärt von Kurt Flasch*. Mainz: Dieterichsche Verlagsbuchhandlung.
Fleming, P. 2006. "Berkeley's Immaterialist Account of Action". *Journal of the History of Philosophy* **44**: 415–29.
Fogelin, R. 2003. *A Defense of Hume on Miracles*. Princeton, NJ: Princeton University Press.
Fontana, B. 1999. "Love of Country and Love of God: The Political Uses of Religion in Machiavelli". *Journal of the History of Ideas* **60**: 639–58.
Frank, G. 2003. *Die Vernunft des Gottesgedankens. Religionsphilosophische Studien zur frühen Neuzeit*. Stuttgart-Bad Cannstatt: frommann-holzboog.
Frankfurt, H. (ed.) 1972. *Leibniz: A Collection of Critical Essays*. New York: Doubleday.
Galileo 1957. *Discoveries and Opinions of Galileo*, S. Drake (trans.). New York: Anchor/Doubleday.
Gamble, R. (ed.) 1992. *Calvin and Calvinism*, vol. 7. New York: Garland.
Gay, P. 1967. *The Enlightenment: An Interpretation, vol. 1: The Rise of Modern Paganism*. London: Weidenfeld & Nicholson.
Gibbon, E. [1776] 2000. *The History of the Decline and Fall of the Roman Empire*, D. Womersley (ed.). Harmondsworth: Penguin.
Gould, S. J. 1980. *The Panda's Thumb: More Reflections in Natural History*. New York: W. W. Norton.
Grafton, A. & L. Jardine 1986. *From Humanism to Humanities: Education and the Liberal Arts in Fifteenth- and Sixteenth-Century Europe*. London: Duckworth.
Grant, E. 1981. *Much Ado about Nothing: Theories of Space and Vacuum from the Middle Ages to the Scientific Revolution*. Cambridge: Cambridge University Press.
Greig, J. (ed.) 1932. *Letters of David Hume*, vol. 1. Oxford: Clarendon Press.
Hanna, B. 1964. "Les Débuts intellectuels de Denis Diderot", 2 vols. Unpublished PhD thesis, University of Montreal.
Harris, J. 2003. "Answering Bayle's Question: Religious Belief in the Moral Philosophy of the Scottish Enlightenment". In *Oxford Studies in Early Modern Philosophy*, D. Garber & S. Nadler (eds), vol. 1, 229–53. Oxford: Oxford University Press.
Harrison, J. & P. Laslett 1971. *The Library of John Locke*, 2nd edn. Oxford: Clarendon Press.
Harrison, P. 1990. *"Religion" and the Religions in the English Enlightenment*. Cambridge: Cambridge University Press.
Harrison, P. 2000. "The Influence of Cartesian Cosmology in England". In *Descartes' Natural Philosophy*, S. Gaukroger, J. Schuster & J. Sutton (eds), 168–92. London: Routledge.

Harrison, P. 2005. "Physico-theology and the Mixed Sciences: The Role of Theology in Early Modern Natural Philosophy". In *The Science of Nature in the Seventeenth Century: Patterns of Change in Early Modern Natural Philosophy*, P. Anstey & J. Schuster (eds), 165–83. Dordrecht: Springer.
Häyry, M. & H. Häyry 1994. "Obedience to Rules and Berkeley's Theological Utilitarianism". *Utilitas* **6**: 233–42.
Hazard, P. 1935. *La Crise de la conscience européenne*, 2 vols. Paris: Boivin.
Hegel, G. 1982. *Vorlesungen über die Geschichte der Philosophie III*. Frankfurt: Suhrkamp.
Heidegger, M. 1995. *Phänomenologie des religiösen Lebens*, Gesamtausgabe 60. Frankfurt: Vittorio Klostermann.
Helm, P. 1997. *Faith and Understanding*. Grand Rapids, MI: Eerdmans.
Helm, P. 2004a. *John Calvin's Ideas*. Oxford: Clarendon Press.
Helm, P. 2004b. "Reid and 'Reformed' Epistemology". In *Thomas Reid: Context, Influence and Significance*, J. Houston (ed.), 103–22. Edinburgh: Dunedin Academic Press.
Helm, P. & O. Crisp (eds) 2003. *Jonathan Edwards: Philosophical Theologian*. Aldershot: Ashgate.
Helmer, C. 1999. *The Trinity and Martin Luther: A Study on the Relationship between Genre, Language and the Trinity in Luther's Works (1523–1546)*. Mainz: Philipp von Zabern.
Herbert, E. (Lord Herbert of Cherbury) 1645. *De religione Laici*. London.
Herbert, E. (Lord Herbert of Cherbury) 1663. *De religione Gentilium*. Amsterdam.
Herbert, E. (Lord Herbert of Cherbury) 1937. *De veritate*, H. Carre (trans.). Bristol: University of Bristol Press. Originally published (Paris, 1624).
Hertzberg, A. 1968. *The French Enlightenment and the Jews*. New York: Columbia University Press.
Hilgenfeld, H. 1971. *Mittelalterlich-traditionelle Elemente in Luthers Abendmahlsschriften*. Zürich: Theologischer Verlag Zürich.
Hobart, M. 1995. "The Analytical Vision and Organisation of Knowledge in the *Encyclopédie*". *Studies on Voltaire* **327**: 153–82.
Hobbes, T. 1651. *Leviathan*. London.
Hobbes, T. 1968. *Leviathan*, C. Macpherson (ed.). Harmondsworth: Penguin.
Hobbes, T. 1990. *Behemoth; or, The Long Parliament*, F. Tönnies (ed.). Chicago, IL: University of Chicago Press.
Hobbes, T. [1651] 1994. *Leviathan*. Indianapolis, IN: Hackett.
Hödl, L. 1987. "'... sie reden, als ob es zwei gegensätzliche Wahrheiten gäbe'. Legende und Wirklichkeit der mittelalterlichen Theorie von der doppelten Wahrheit". In *Philosophie im Mittelalter. Entwicklungslinien und Paradigmen*, J. Beckmann *et al.* (eds), 225–43. Hamburg: Meiner.
Hoitenga, D. 1991. *Faith and Reason from Plato to Plantinga: An Introduction to Reformed Epistemology*. Albany, NY: SUNY Press.
Hooke, R. 1665. *Micrographia*. London.
Houston, J. (ed.) 2004. *Thomas Reid: Context, Influence and Significance*. Edinburgh: Dunedin Academic Press.
Hugh of Saint-Victor 1951. *On the Sacraments of the Christian Faith*, R. Deferrari (trans.). Cambridge: Medieval Academy of America.
Hulliung, M. 1983. *Citizen Machiavelli*. Princeton, NJ: Princeton University Press.
Hume, D. 1757. "The Natural History of Religion". In his *Four Dissertations*, 1–117. London: A. Millar.
Hume, D. [1739] 1888. *A Treatise of Human Nature*, L. Selby-Bigge (ed.). Oxford: Clarendon Press. [Reprinted from the original edition.]
Hume, D. 1896. *A Treatise of Human Nature*, L. Selby-Bigge (ed.). Oxford: Oxford University Press.

Hume, D. [1748] 1975. *An Enquiry Concerning Human Understanding*. In his *Enquiries Concerning Human Understanding and Concerning the Principles of Morals*, L. Selby-Bigge (ed.), 3rd edn, P. Nidditch (rev.). Oxford: Clarendon Press. [Reprinted from the 1777 edition.]

Hume, D. [1779] 1993. *Dialogues Concerning Natural Religion and The Natural History of Religion*, J. Gaskin (ed.). Oxford: Oxford University Press.

Hume, D. [1777] 1998a. "Of the Immortality of the Soul". In his *Dialogues Concerning Natural Religion*, 2nd edn, R. Popkin (ed.), 91–7. Indianapolis, IN: Hackett.

Hume, D. [1779] 1998b. *Dialogues Concerning Natural Religion*, J. Gaskin (ed.). Oxford: Oxford University Press.

Hume, D. [1748] 2000. *An Enquiry Concerning Human Understanding*, T. Beauchamp (ed.). Oxford: Clarendon Press.

Hunter, M. & E. Davis (eds) 2000. *The Works of Robert Boyle*, 14 vols. London: Pickering & Chatto.

Hunter, M. & D. Wootton (eds) 1992. *Atheism from the Reformation to the Enlightenment*. Oxford: Clarendon Press.

Israel, J. 2001. *Radical Enlightenment: Philosophy and the Making of Modernity, 1650–1750*. Oxford: Oxford University Press.

Israel, J. 2006a. *Enlightenment Contested: Philosophy, Modernity, and the Emancipation of Man 1670–1752*. Oxford: Oxford University Press.

Israel, J. 2006b. "Enlightenment! Which Enlightenment?". *Journal of the History of Ideas* **67**: 523–45.

James, E. 1984. "Voltaire and the *Ethics* of Spinoza". *Studies on Voltaire and the Eighteenth Century* **228**: 67–87.

Jansen, C. 1640. *Augustinus*. Rouen: Berthelin.

Jaspers, K. 1995. *The Great Philosophers, Vol. 4: The Disturbers: Descartes, Pascal, Lessing, Kierkegaard, Nietzsche. Philosophers in Other Realms: Einstein, Weber, Marx*. L. Ehrlich & M. Ermarth (eds), E. Ehrlich (trans.). New York: Harcourt Brace.

Jesseph, D. 2005. "Berkeley, God, and Explanation". In *Early Modern Philosophy: Mind, Matter, and Metaphysics*, C. Mercer & E. O'Neill (eds), 183–205. Oxford: Oxford University Press.

Johnson, S. [1755] 1975. *A Dictionary of the English Language*. London: Times Books.

Jolley, N. (ed.) 1995. *The Cambridge Companion to Leibniz*. Cambridge: Cambridge University Press.

Jolley, N. 1998. "The Relation Between Theology and Philosophy". In *The Cambridge History of Seventeenth-Century Philosophy*, D. Garber & M. Ayers (eds), vol. 1, 363–92. Cambridge: Cambridge University Press.

Kauffman, S. 1993. *Origins of Order: Self-organization and Selection in Evolution*. Oxford: Oxford University Press.

Kant, I. 1900– . *Kant's Gesammelte Schriften*, von der Königlich Preußischen Akademie der Wissenschaften (ed.). Berlin: Walter de Gruyter.

Kant, I. [1781/87] 1992– . *The Cambridge Edition of the Works of Immanuel Kant*. Cambridge: Cambridge University Press.

Kant, I. 1996. *Critique of Pure Reason*. Indianapolis, IN: Hackett.

Kisiel, T. 1993. *The Genesis of Heidegger's "Being and Time"*. Berkeley, CA: University of California Press.

Kitcher, P. 2007. *Living with Darwin: Evolution, Design, and the Future of Faith*. Oxford: Oxford University Press.

Koch, F. 1928. "Lessing und der Irrationalismus". *Deutsche Vierteljahrsschrift für Literaturwissenschaft und Geistesgeschichte* **6**: 114–43.

Kolb, R. & T. Wengert (eds) 2000. *The Book of Concord: The Confessions of the Evangelical Lutheran Church*. Minneapolis, MN: Fortress Press.

Kramar, E. & M. Latzer (eds) 2001. *Evil in Early Modern Philosophy*. Toronto: University of Toronto Press.

Lange, F. 1879. *The History of Materialism*, 3 vols. London: Hübner.

Lanson, G. 1929. *Les Essais de Montaigne, étude et analyse par Gustave Lanson*. Paris: Mellottée.

LeCerf, A. 1949. *Introduction to Reformed Dogmatics*. London: Lutterworth Press.

Lee, S. 1988. *The Philosophical Theology of Jonathan Edwards*. Princeton, NJ: Princeton University Press.

Lehrer, K. 1989. *Thomas Reid*. New York: Routledge.

Lehrer, K. & B. Warner 2000. "Reid, God and Epistemology". *American Catholic Philosophical Quarterly* **74**: 357–72.

Leibniz, G. 1969. *Gottfried Wilhelm Leibniz: Philosophical Papers and Letters*, 2nd edn, L. Loemker (ed. & trans.). Dordrecht: Reidel.

Leibniz, G. 1973. *Philosophical Writings*, M. Morris & G. Parkinson (eds & trans.). London: Dent.

Leibniz, G. 1982. *New Essays on Human Understanding*, P. Remnant & J. Bennett (eds & trans.). Cambridge: Cambridge University Press.

Leibniz, G. 1985. *Theodicy*, E. Huggard (trans.). La Salle, IL: Open Court.

Leibniz, G. 1989. *Philosophical Essays*, R. Ariew & D. Garber (eds & trans.). Indianapolis, IN: Hackett.

Leibniz, G. 1994. *Writings on China*, D. Cook & H. Rosemont (trans.). Chicago, IL: Open Court.

Leibniz, G. 2005. *Confessio Philosophi: Papers Concerning the Problem of Evil, 1671–1678*, R. Sleigh, Jr (ed. & trans.). New Haven, CT: Yale University Press.

Leibniz, G. 2007. *The Leibniz–Des Bosses Correspondence*, B. Look & D. Rutherford (trans.). New Haven, CT: Yale University Press.

Leland. J. 1754. *A View of the Principal Deistical Writers*. London.

Le Mahieu, D. 1976. *The Mind of William Paley: A Philosopher and His Age*. Lincoln, NE: University of Nebraska Press.

Leslie, J. 1989. *Universes*. London: Routledge.

Lessing, G. 1886–1924. *Sämtliche Schriften*, K. Lachmann & F. Muncker (eds). Stuttgart: Göschen.

Lessing, G. 1955. *Nathan the Wise*, B. Morgan (trans.). New York: Ungar.

Lessing, G. 1956. *Theological Writings*, H. Chadwick (ed. & trans.). London: Black.

Lessing, G. 1985–2003. *Werke und Briefe*, 12 vols, W. Barner *et al.* (eds). Frankfurt: Deutscher Klassiker Verlag.

Lessing, G. 2005. *Philosophical and Theological Writings*, H. B. Nisbet (ed. & trans.). Cambridge: Cambridge University Press.

Lestringant, F. 1990. *Le Huguenot et le Sauvage, L'Amérique et la controverse coloniale, en France, au temps des Guerres de Religion (1555–1589)*. Paris: Aux amateurs de Livres, diffusion Klincksieck.

Lévy-Strauss, C. 1981. "En relisant Montaigne". In his *Histoire de lynx*, ch. 18. Paris: Plon.

Livy (Titus Livius) 1960. *The Early History of Rome*. In *The History of Rome from its Foundations*, A. De Sélincourt (trans.), Books I–V. Harmondsworth: Penguin.

Locke, J. 1690. *Two Treatises of Government*. London.

Locke, J. 1697. *A Second Vindication of the Reasonableness of Christianity*. London: A. and J. Churchill.

Locke, J. 1961. *An Essay Concerning Human Understanding*, J. Yolton (ed.). London: J. M. Dent & Sons.

Locke, J. [1690] 1975. *An Essay Concerning Human Understanding*, P. Nidditch (ed.). Oxford: Clarendon Press.

Locke, J. 1987. *A Paraphrase and Notes on the Epistles of St Paul*, 2 vols, A. Wainwright (ed.). Oxford: Clarendon Press.
Long, P. 1959. *A Summary Catalogue of the Lovelace Collection of the Papers of John Locke in the Bodleian Library*. Oxford: Oxford University Press.
Loofs, F. 1913. "Lessings Stellung zum Christentum". *Theologische Studien und Kritiken* **86**: 68–86.
Look, B. & D. Rutherford 2007. "Introduction". In *The Leibniz–Des Bosses Correspondence*, B. Look & D. Rutherford (trans.), xix–lxxix. New Haven, CT: Yale University Press.
Lovejoy, A. 1908. "Kant and the English Platonists". In *Essays Philosophical and Psychological: In Honor of William James*, by his colleagues at Columbia University, 263–302. New York: Longmans, Green.
Lucretius Carsus, Titus 2007. *The Nature of Things*, A. Stallings (trans.). Harmondsworth: Penguin.
Luther, M. [1525] 1823. *On the Bondage of the Will*. London.
Luther, M. 1883–2005. *D. Martin Luthers Werke, Kritische Gesamtausgabe*, 71 vols, J. Knaake *et al.* (eds). Weimar: Hermann Böhlaus Nachfolger.
Luther, M. 1955–86. *Luther's Works*, American Edition, 55 vols, J. Pelikan (general ed., vols 1–30), H. Lehmann (general ed., vols 31–55). St. Louis, MO: Concordia Publishing House/ Philadelphia, PA: Fortress Press.
Machiavelli, N. [1531] 1970. *Discourses on the First Ten Books of Titus Livy*, L. Walker (trans.). New York: Penguin.
Machiavelli, N. [1532] 1988. *The Prince*, Q. Skinner & R. Price (eds). Cambridge: Cambridge University Press.
Machiavelli, N. 1992. "The Exhortation to Penitence". In *The Prince*, 2nd edn, R. Adams (ed. & trans.). New York: W. W. Norton.
Machiavelli, N. [1521] 2001. *The Art of War*, E. Farneworth (trans.). Cambridge: Da Capo Press.
MacIntosh, J. (ed.) 2005. *Boyle on Atheism*. Toronto: University of Toronto Press.
Maimonides, M. 1963. *The Guide of the Perplexed*. Chicago, IL: University of Chicago Press.
Malcolm, N. 2002. *Aspects of Hobbes*. Oxford: Clarendon Press.
Mandeville, B. [1714] 1988. *The Fable of the Bees or Private Vices, Publick Benefits*, 2 vols, F. Kaye (ed.). Indianapolis, IN: Liberty Fund.
Mansfield, H. 1979. *Machiavelli's New Modes and Orders: A Study of the Discourses on Livy*. Ithaca, NY: Cornell University Press.
Maritain, J. 1944. *The Dream of Descartes Together with Some Other Essays*, M. Andison (trans.). New York: Philosophical Library.
Mason, J. & R. Wokler (eds) 1992. *Diderot: Political Writings*. Cambridge: Cambridge University Press.
May, G. 1954. *Diderot et "La Religieuse"*. New Haven, CT: Yale University Press.
McManners, J. 1998. *The Church and Society in Eighteenth-Century France*, 2 vols. Oxford: Oxford University Press.
Melanchthon, P. [1532] 1965. *Romerbrief – Kommentar*, G. Ebeling & R. Schafer (eds). In *Melanchthons Werke in Auswahl*, vol. 5. Gütersloh: C. Bertelsmann.
Melanchthon, P. [1540] 1992. *Commentary on Romans*, F. Kramer (trans.). St. Louis, MO: Concordia Publishing House.
Mendelssohn, M. 1997. *Philosophical Writings*, D. Dahlstrom (ed. & trans.). Cambridge: Cambridge University Press.
Mill, J. S. 1859. *On Liberty*. London.
Montaigne, M. 1924. *Les Essais*, 3 vols, P. Villey (ed.). Paris: PUF.
Montaigne, M. 1948. *The Complete Works: Essays, Travel Journal, Letters*, D. Frame (trans.). Stanford, CA: Stanford University Press.
More, H. 1660. *An Explanation of the Grand Mystery of Godliness*. London.

More, H. 1969. *The Complete Poems of Dr Henry More (1614–1687)*, A. Grosart (ed.). Hildesheim: Georg Olms.

Moreau, P. 1996. "Spinoza's Reception and Influence". In *The Cambridge Companion to Spinoza*, D. Garrett (ed.), 408–33. Cambridge: Cambridge University Press.

Morin, R. 1975. *Les "Pensées philosophiques" de Diderot devant leurs principaux contradicteurs au XVIIIe siécle*. Paris: Les Belles Lettres.

Moroney, S. 2000. *The Noetic Effects of Sin: A Historical and Contemporary Exploration of How Sin Affects our Thinking*. Lanham, MD: Lexington Books.

Muller, R. 2003a. *Post-Reformation Reformed Dogmatics: Volume 1: Prolegomena to Theology*, 2nd edn. Grand Rapids, MI: Baker Book House.

Muller, R. 2003b. *Post-Reformation Reformed Dogmatics: Volume 3: The Divine Essence and Attributes*. Grand Rapids, MI: Baker Book House.

Mungello, D. 1977. *Leibniz and Confucianism: The Search for Accord*. Honolulu, HI: University Press of Hawaii.

Münster, S. 1575. *La cosmographie universelle de tout le monde, comprenant la Grèce, avec les descriptions anciennes et modernes, tant du plant que noms des villes et régions comme de l'histoire et descrivant les deux asies selon leur estendue, raretez, richesses et histoire de l'estat des royaumes outre ce qui en a esté cy devant descouvert. Plus y est adiuostée l'Affrique, autant doctement que veritablement. Comme aussi y est descripte briefvement et entierement l'histoire geographique de toutes les terres decouvertes vers l'Occident, et outre l'Equateur, et és partie septentrionales, avec les isles, peuples, nations, et leurs loix, religions et façons de vivre. Ainsi ce qui est de rare tant au plat pays, qu'ès isles plus eslonguees et moins cogneues des nostres*, F. de Belleforest (ed.). Paris: Michel Sonnius.

Murphey, M. 1961. *The Development of Peirce's Philosophy*. Cambridge, MA: Harvard University Press.

Murray, M. 2005. "Leibniz on the Problem of Evil". *Stanford Encyclopedia of Philosophy* (spring 2005 edn), E. Zalta (ed.), http://plato.stanford.edu/archives/spr2005/entries/leibniz-evil/ (accessed May 2009).

Nadler, S. 1999. *Spinoza: A Life*. Cambridge: Cambridge University Press.

Nadler, S. 2001. *Spinoza's Heresy: Immortality and the Jewish Mind*. New York: Oxford University Press.

Najemy, J. 1999. "Papirius and the Chickens, or Machiavelli on the Necessity of Interpreting Religion". *Journal of the History of Ideas* **604**: 659–81.

Navarre, M. 1558. *L'Heptaméron des nouvelles*, P. Boiastuau (ed.). Paris.

Nisbet, H. 1978. "Lessing and Pierre Bayle". In *Tradition and Creation: Essays in Honour of Elizabeth Mary Wilkinson*, C. P. Magill, B. A. Rowley & C. J. Smith (eds), 13–29. Leeds: Maney.

Nisbet, H. 1999. "The Rationalisation of the Holy Trinity from Lessing to Hegel". *Lessing Yearbook* **31**: 65–89.

Nuovo, V. 1992. "Rethinking Paley". *Synthese* **91**: 29–51.

Nuovo, V. (ed.) 2002. *John Locke: Writings on Religion*. Oxford: Clarendon Press.

Oppy, G. 2006. *Arguing about Gods*. Cambridge: Cambridge University Press.

Owen, D. 1999. *Hume's Reason* Oxford: Clarendon Press.

Paine, T. 1794. *The Age of Reason*. Paris.

Paley, W. [1790] 1860a. *Horae Paulinae: Or, the Truth of the Scripture History of St. Paul Evinced By a Comparison of the Epistles Which Bear His Name with the Acts of the Apostles and with One Another*. New York: American Tract Society.

Paley, W. [1794] 1860b. *A View of the Evidences of Christianity*, with annotations by R. Whatley. New York: J. Miller.

Paley, W. [1785] 2002. *The Principles of Moral and Political Philosophy*. Indianapolis, IN: Liberty Fund.

Paley, W. [1802] 2006. *Natural Theology: or Evidence of the Existence and Attributes of the Deity,*

Collected from the Appearances of Nature, M. Eddy & D. Knight (eds). Oxford: Oxford University Press.

Parker, T. 1959. *Calvin's Doctrine of the Knowledge of God*. Grand Rapids, MI: Eerdmans.

Pascal, B. 1931. *Pensées*. London: Dent & Sons.

Pascal, B. 1991. *Pensées*, P. Sellier (ed.). Paris: Classiques Garnier.

Pascal, B. 1995. *Pensées*, rev. edn, A. J. Krailsheimer (intro. and trans.). Harmondsworth: Penguin.

Patrides, C. (ed.) 1969. *The Cambridge Platonists*. London: Edward Arnold.

Perkins, F. 2004. *Leibniz and China*. Cambridge: Cambridge University Press.

Petto, A. & L. Godfrey (eds) 2007. *Scientists Confront Intelligent Design and Creationism*. New York: W. W. Norton.

Plantinga, A. 1967. *God and Other Minds*. Ithaca, NY: Cornell University Press.

Plantinga, A. 1980. "The Reformed Objection to Natural Theology". *Proceedings of the American Catholic Philosophical Association* **15**: 49–62.

Plantinga, A. 1993. *Warrant and Proper Function*. New York: Oxford University Press.

Plantinga, A. 2000. *Warranted Christian Belief*. New York: Oxford University Press.

Platt, J. 1982. *Reformed Thought and Scholasticism: The Arguments for the Existence of God in Dutch Theology, 1575–1650*. Leiden: Brill.

Pocock, J. 1975. *The Machiavellian Moment: Florentine Political Thought and the Atlantic Republican Tradition*. Princeton, MJ: Princeton University Press.

Pomeau, R. 1956. *La Religion de Voltaire*. Paris: Nizet.

Pomeau, R. 1985. *D'Arouet à Voltaire 1694–1734*. Oxford: Voltaire Foundation.

Pomeau, R. 1994a. *Ecraser l'infâme 1759–1770*. Oxford: Voltaire Foundation.

Pomeau, R. 1994b. *On a voulu l'enterrer 1770–1791*. Oxford: Voltaire Foundation.

Pons, G. 1964. *Gotthold Ephraim Lessing et le Christianisme*. Paris: Didier.

Popkin, R. 1965. "Introduction". In *Historical and Critical Dictionary: Selections*, P. Bayle, viii–xxx. New York: Bobbs-Merrill.

Popkin, R. 1979. *The History of Scepticism from Erasmus to Spinoza*. Berkeley, CA: University of California Press.

Poppi, A. 1988. "Fate, Fortune, Providence and Human Freedom". In *The Cambridge History of Renaissance Philosophy*, C. Schmitt & Q. Skinner (eds), 641–67. Cambridge: Cambridge University Press.

Porteau, P. 1935. *Montaigne et la vie pédagogique de son temps*. Paris: Droz.

Postema, G. 1992. "Calvin and the Renaissance Crisis of Knowing". In *Calvin and Calvinism, Vol. 7: The Organizational Structure of Calvin's Theology*, R. Gamble (ed.), 135–46. New York: Garland.

Preus, S. J. 1979. "Machiavelli's Functional Analysis of Religion: Context and Object". *Journal of the History of Ideas* **40**: 171–90.

Preus, S. J. 2001. *Spinoza and the Irrelevance of Biblical Authority*. Cambridge: Cambridge University Press.

Proust, J. 1962. *Diderot et l'Encyclopédie*. Paris: A. Colin.

Ray, J. [1691] 1977. *The Wisdom of God Manifested in the Works of the Creation*. New York: Arno Press.

Reid, T. 1981. *Thomas Reid's "Lectures on Natural Theology"*, E. Duncan (ed.). Washington, DC: University Press of America.

Reid, T. 1989. *The Philosophical Orations of Thomas Reid*, D. Todd (ed.), S. Sullivan (trans.). Carbondale, IL: Southern Illinois University Press.

Reid, T. 1997. *An Inquiry into the Human Mind on the Principles of Common Sense*, D. Brookes (ed.). University Park, PA: Pennsylvania State University Press.

Reid, T. 2002a. *Essays on the Intellectual Powers of Man*, D. Brookes (ed.). University Park, PA: Pennsylvania State University Press.

Reid, T. 2002b. *The Correspondence of Thomas Reid*, P. Wood (ed.). University Park, PA: Pennsylvania State University Press.

Renwick, J. 1974. *Marmontel, Voltaire and the 'Bélisaire' Affair*, Studies on Voltaire and the Eighteenth Century, vol. 121. Oxford: Voltaire Foundation.

Ross, G. 1984. *Leibniz*. Oxford: Oxford University Press.

Rowe, W. 1991. *Thomas Reid on Freedom and Morality*. Ithaca, NY: Cornell University Press.

Russell, B. 1937. *A Critical Exposition of the Philosophy of Leibniz, with an Appendix of Leading Passages*, 2nd edn. London: Allen & Unwin.

Russell, B. 1946. *History of Western Philosophy*. London: Allen & Unwin.

Schmaltz, T. 2002. *Radical Cartesianism: The French Reception of Descartes*. Cambridge: Cambridge University Press.

Schneewind, J. (ed.) 1990. *Moral Philosophy from Montaigne to Kant: An Anthology*, 2 vols. Cambridge: Cambridge University Press.

Scholz, H. (ed.) 1916. *Die Hauptschriften zum Pantheismusstreit zwischen Jacobi und Mendelssohn*. Berlin: Kantgesellschaft.

Schwarz, R. 1966. "Gott ist Mensch. Zur Lehre von der Person Christi bei den Ockhamisten und bei Luther". *Zeitschrift für Theologie und Kirche* **63**: 289–351.

Schwarzbach, B. 1971. *Voltaire's Old Testament Criticism*. Geneva: Droz.

Schwarzbach, B. 1998. "Voltaire et les juifs: bilan et plaidoyer". *Studies on Voltaire and the Eighteenth Century* **358**: 27–91.

Skinner, Q. 1981. *Machiavelli*. New York: Hill & Wang.

Sleigh, R., Jr 2001. "Remarks on Leibniz's Treatment of the Problem of Evil". In *Evil in Early Modern Philosophy*, E. Kramar & M. Latzer (eds), 163–79. Toronto: University of Toronto Press.

Sleigh, R., Jr, V. Chappell & M. Della Rocca 1998. "Determinism and Human Freedom". In *The Cambridge History of Seventeenth-Century Philosophy*, D. Garber & M. Ayers (eds), vol. 2, 1195–1278. Cambridge: Cambridge University Press.

Smith, J. (ed.) 2006. *The Problem of Animal Generation in Early Modern Philosophy*. Cambridge: Cambridge University Press.

Sober, E. 1993. *Philosophy of Biology*. Boulder, CO: Westview Press.

Sober, E. 2008. *Evidence and Evolution*. Cambridge: Cambridge University Press.

Socinus, F. 1611. *De Auctoritate S. Scripturae: Opusculum his temporibus nostris utilissimum* Steinfurt; translated as *An Argument for the Authority of Holy Scripture; from the Latin of Socinus, after the Steinfurt Copy*, E. Combe (trans.) (London: W. Meadows, 1731).

Spinoza, B. 1951. *Theologico-Political Treatise*. In *The Chief Works*, R. Elwes (ed.), vol. 1. New York: Dover.

Spinoza, B. 1958. *The Political Works*. Oxford: Clarendon Press.

Spinoza, B. 1985. *The Collected Works*. Princeton, NJ: Princeton University Press.

Spinoza, B. 1991. *Tractatus Theologico-Politicus*, S. Shirley (trans.). Leiden: Brill.

Steinmetz, D. 1995. *Calvin in Context*. New York: Oxford University Press.

Stewart, M. 1981. "Locke's Professional Contacts with Boyle". *Locke Newsletter* **12**: 19–44.

Stewart, M. (ed.) 2000. *English Philosophy in the Age of Locke*. Oxford: Clarendon Press.

Stewart, M. 2004. "Rational Religion and Common Sense". In *Thomas Reid: Context, Influence and Significance*, J. Houston (ed.), 123–60. Edinburgh: Dunedin Academic Press.

Stewart, M. 2006. "Revealed Religion: The British Debate". In *The Cambridge History of Eighteenth-Century Philosophy*, K. Haakonssen (ed.), vol. 2, 683–709. Cambridge: Cambridge University Press.

Stillingfleet, E. 1697. *A Discourse in Vindication of the Doctrine of the Trinity*. London.

Strauss, L. 1952. *Persecution and the Art of Writing*. Glencoe, IL: Free Press.

Strauss, L. 1958. *Thoughts on Machiavelli*. Chicago, IL: University of Chicago Press.

Suárez, F. 1597. *Disputationes metaphysicae*. Salamanca.

Suárez, F. 1856–77. *Disputationes metaphysicae*. In *Opera omnia*, Vivès (ed.), vols 25–6. Paris.
Suárez, F. 2004. *The Metaphysical Demonstration of the Existence of God: Metaphysical Disputations 28–29* (Dist. XXVIII–XXIX), J. Doyle (ed. & trans.). South Bend, IN: Indiana University Press.
Sudduth, M. 1995. "The Prospects for 'Mediate' Natural Theology in John Calvin". *Religious Studies* **31**: 53–68.
Sudduth, M. 1998. "Calvin, Plantinga, and the Natural Knowledge of God: A Response to Beversluius". *Faith and Philosophy* **15**: 92–103.
Sudduth, M. (forthcoming). *The Reformed Objection to Natural Theology*. London: Ashgate.
Sullivan, V. 1996. *Machiavelli's Three Romes: Religion, Human Liberty, and Politics Reformed*. DeKalb, IL: Northern Illinois University Press.
Sutcliffe, A. 1998. "Myth, Origins, Identity: Voltaire, the Jews and the Enlightenment Notion of Tolerance". *Eighteenth Century Theory and Interpretation* **39**: 107–26.
Swinburne, R. 2004. *The Existence of God*, 2nd edn. Oxford: Clarendon Press.
Thielicke, H. 1957. *Offenbarung, Vernunft und Existenz: Studien zur Religionsphilosophie Lessings*, 3rd edn. Gütersloh: Bertelsmann.
Tindal, M. 1730. *Christianity as Old as the Creation*. London.
Todorov, T. 2000. *Éloge de l'individu*. Paris: Adam Biro.
Toland, J. 1696. *Christianity not Mysterious*. London.
Toland, J. 1704. *Letters to Serena*. London.
Torrey, N. 1930. *Voltaire and the English Deists*. New Haven, CT: Yale University Press.
Trousson, R. 1997. *Images de Diderot en France 1784–1913*. Paris: Champion.
Tuggy, D. 2000. "Thomas Reid on Causation". *Reid Studies* **3**: 3–28.
Tuggy, D. 2004. "Reid's Philosophy of Religion". In *The Cambridge Companion to Thomas Reid*, T. Cuneo & R. Van Woudenberg (eds), 289–312. Cambridge: Cambridge University Press.
Vaillot, R. 1988. *Avec Mme Du Châtelet 1734–49 (With Mme Du Châtelet 1734–49)*. Oxford: Voltaire Foundation.
Vallée, G. (ed.) 1988. *The Spinoza Conversations between Lessing and Jacobi: Text with Excerpts from the Ensuing Controversy*, G. Vallée, J. Lawson & C. Chapple (trans.). Lanham, MD: University Press of America.
Vatter, M. 2000. *Between Form and Event: Machiavelli's Theory of Political Freedom*. Dordrecht: Kluwer.
Venturi, F. 1939. *Jeunesse de Diderot 1713–1753*. Paris: Skira.
Verbeek, T. 1992. *Descartes and the Dutch: Early Reactions to Cartesian Philosophy, 1637–1650*. Carbondale, IL: Southern Illinois University Press.
Villey, P. 1933. *Les sources et l'évolution des Essais de Montaigne*. Paris: Hachette.
Viret, P. 1564. *Instruction Chrétienne*. Geneva.
Viroli, M. 1998. *Machiavelli*. New York: Oxford University Press.
Voltaire 1743. *Lettres philosophiques*. Rouen.
Voltaire 1759. *Candide*. Geneva.
Voltaire 1877–82. *Œuvres complètes de Voltaire*, L. Moland (ed.). Paris: Garnier.
Voltaire 1968–77. *Correspondence and Related Documents*, T. Besterman (ed.). Oeuvres complètes de Voltaire, 85–135. Oxford: Voltaire Foundation.
Warfield, B. 2000. *Calvin and Calvinism*, The Works of Benjamin Breckinridge Warfield, vol. 5. Grand Rapids, MI: Baker Book House.
Watson, R. 1982. "Transubstantiation among the Cartesians". In *Problems of Cartesianism*, T. Lennon, J. Nicholas & J. Davis (eds), 127–48. Kingston: McGill-Queens University Press.
Webster, C. 2002. *The Great Instauration Science, Medicine and Reform (1626–1660)*, 2nd edn. Bern: Peter Lang.
Wendel, F. 1963. *Calvin: The Origin and Development of His Thought*, P. Mairet (trans.). London: Collins.

Werner, S. 1971. "Diderot's *Encyclopédie* article 'Agnus Scythicus'". *Studies on Voltaire* **79**: 79–92.

Wessell, L. 1977. *G. E. Lessing's Theology: A Reinterpretation*. Mouton: The Hague.

Wheen, F. 2004. *How Mumbo-Jumbo Conquered the World*. London: Harper Perennial.

Whichcote, B. 1753. "Eight Letters of Dr Anthony Tuckney and Benjamin Whichcote". In his *Moral and Religious Aphorisms*, S. Salter (ed.). London.

Whichcote, B. 1930. *Moral and Religious Aphorisms*, W. Inge (ed.). London: Elkin Matthews & Marrot.

White, G. 1994. *Luther as Nominalist: A Study of the Logical Methods used in Martin Luther's Disputations in the Light of their Medieval Background*. Helsinki: Luther-Agricola-Society.

Willey, B. 1957. *The Seventeenth Century Background: Studies in the Thought of the Age in relation to Poetry and Religion*. London: Chatto & Windus.

Winnett, A. 1974. *Peter Browne: Provost, Bishop, Metaphysician*. London: SPCK.

Wojcik, J. 1997. *Robert Boyle and the Limits of Reason*. Cambridge: Cambridge University Press.

Wolterstorff, N. 1983. "Thomas Reid and Rationality". In *Rationality in the Calvinian Tradition*, H. Hart, J. van der Hoeven & N. Wolterstorff (eds), 43–69. Lanham, MD: University Press of America.

Wolterstorff, N. 2004. "God and Darkness in Reid". In *Thomas Reid: Context, Influence and Significance*, J. Houston (ed.), 77–102. Edinburgh: Dunedin Academic Press.

Yaffe, G. 2004. *Manifest Activity*. New York: Oxford University Press.

Yolton, J. 1983. *Thinking Matter: Materialism in Eighteenth-Century Britain*. Minneapolis, MN: University of Minnesota Press.

Yolton, J. 1991. *Locke and French Materialism*.Oxford: Oxford University Press.

INDEX

Aberdeen Philosophical Society 235
alchemy 12
Allen, Ethan 213
American deists 213, 220
Annet, Peter
  deism 212, 215
  Deism Fairly Stated and Vindicated 214
Aquinas, Thomas
  criticism of his theology by Montaigne 67
  on divine foreknowledge and human freedom 173
Arian heresy 119
Aristotelian cosmology 12
Aristotle
  On the Soul 15
  on rational capacities 103
Arminians, on free will and divine providence 8
Arnauld, Antoine 4
Ashley-Cooper, Anthony *see* Shaftesbury, Earl of (Anthony Ashley-Cooper)
atheism
  and avoidance of persecution 213
  Cudworth's attack on 116–17, 120
  distinguished from deism 213
  forms of 120
  meaning of the term 7
  and virtue 11–12
atomical atheism 120
Augustinianism 128
authoritarianism, in religion 99

Bacon, Francis
  on Machiavelli 19
  value of theory 102
Bañez, Domingo 174, 175
Barrow, Isaac 154
Bayle, Pierre
  attack on Spinoza 142
  deism 7
  Dictionnaire Historique et Critique (Critical and historical dictionary) 212
  influence on Voltaire 198
  on problem of evil 8, 206–7
  on religious toleration 12
Behe, Michael 311
Benedict XVI (Pope) 137
Berkeley, George
  Alciphron, the Minute Philosopher 183, 186, 187, 189
  arguments for the existence of God 184–8
  biographical details 183
  contribution to philosophy of religion 183–4, 194
  A Discourse Addressed to Magistrates and Men in Authority 188
  eschatological dimension of his ethics 189–91
  An Essay Towards a New Theory of Vision 183, 186–7
  on God and morality 188–91
  on God's attributes 191
  influence and significance 183–4
  on meaningfulness of the term God's grace 192–3

on meaningfulness of term 'original sin' 194
metaphysical system 184–5
opposition to ethical egotism, sensual hedonism, relativism and secularism 188–9
Passive Obedience 183, 189–90
on propositions regarding Christian mysteries 194
on religious language 191–4
Siris: A Chain of Philosophical Reflections and Inquiries 183
theory of visual perception 187
Three Dialogues between Hylas and Philonous 183, 184, 185–6
A Treatise Concerning The Principles of Human Knowledge 183, 184, 185
Blount, Charles
deism 212, 215
The Oracles of Reason 214
Bolingbroke, Henry St John (Lord) 198, 212
Bosseut, Jacques-Bénigne 136
Bourdieu, Pierre 129
Bovelle, Charles de, influence of Sebond 67
Boyle Lectures, for defence of Christian Faith 6, 121
Boyle, Robert
on Christianity and experimental natural philosophy as perfect complements 154
Disquisition about the Final Causes of Natural Things 17
influence on Locke 153–4
'physico-theology' 6
on space 15
British deism
course of 219–22
key figures 212, 213, 215–19
legacy 219–22
Brunschvigg, Leon 130
Buffon, Comte de 17
Butler, Joseph 220, 235
The Analogy of Religion 220

Calas, Jean 198
Calvin, John
account of natural knowledge of God compared to Melanchthon's 54–5
ambivalence towards philosophical theology 48–9
contribution to philosophy of religion 47, 49, 63
educational background and writings 47–8
exegesis of Scripture 50
immediacy and theistic inferences 55–6
influence and significance 47, 63
'innumerable evidences' and theistic inferences 53–4
Institutes of the Christian Religion 48, 49–50
interpretations of his account of the natural knowledge of God 51–2
on limited scope of propositional knowledge of God 59–60
limits and reconstruction of natural theology 59–62
on meaning of 'knowledge of God' 57–8
on natural knowledge of God 49–51
on noetic effects of sin 56–9
retention of epistemic elements in humanity's natural knowledge of God 58–9
on rhetorical and demonstrative types of natural theology 52–3
theistic arguments 52–6
on unregenerate and regenerate natural theology 60–62
Calvinism, forms of 114
Cambridge Platonists
on the mind's creative activity in cognitive processes 227
opposition to scholastic education 113, 114
reaction to English Calvinism 114–16
Camus, Albert 129
Cardanus, Hieronymus 291–2
Cartesianism, *see* Descartes, Rene
Cartestian vortex theory 12–13
Catholic Church
censorship 15, 265
Rites Controversy 168
Celsus 173
censorship
by Catholic Church 15, 265
in France under *ancien régime* 265
Chillingworth, William 154
Christian virtuosos
character of 154
emergence of 6
Christianity

changes and challenges in early modern period 1
dominance in Europe in early modern period 1
sectarian strife 149
tensions with Judaism 149
Christianity *see also* Catholic Church
Christina (Queen of Sweden) 102
Chubb, Thomas 212, 220
chymistry 12
civil authority, relation to ecclesiastical authority 9–10, 150–51
Clarke, Samuel 121, 213, 235
Collins, Anthony 155, 188, 191, 213
concept containment theory of truth 170
Copernicanism 102
Copernicus 12, 104
Cordemoy, Géraud de 13
Cordier, Mathurin 48
cosmo-plastic atheism 120
cosmological argument for God's existence *see* theistic proofs
Council of Trent 69, 173
Cudworth, Ralph
attack on atheism and determinism 116–17, 120
attack on doctrine of predestination 120–21
biographical details 113
contribution to philosophy of religion 113, 117, 124
defence of human agency and free will 115–16
definition of the Trinity 119
doctrine of Plastic Nature of Reality 120–21
epistemology 122–3
eternal and immutable morality 121–3
ethics 121–4
on free will and divine providence 123–4
on "God's freeman" 124
humanism 113, 116
on the immanent Trinity 118–19
influence of Plotinus 114, 117–18
intellectual origins 114
on mind's creative activity in cognitive processes 227
on natural law theory 9
Neoplatonic reaction against English Calvinism 114–16
philosophical influence and significance 113, 124
on presence of God within creation 119–21
proof of existence of God 117–18
on rational participation in religious life 115–16
Sermon Preached before the Honourable House of Commons 115
Treatise Concerning Eternal and Immutable Morality 121–3
True Intellectual System of the Universe 113, 116–17, 123
cultural relativism 71

Darwin, Charles
criticisms of his evolutionary theory 311
On the Origin of Species 312
theory of natural selection 309
Dawkins, Richard, *The Blind Watchmaker* 311–12
deism
definition 211, 212
demise 220
distinction from atheism 231
faith and history 221–2
God and creation 174
and historical-critical study of religion 218
legacy 219–22
nature of 214
opposition to revelation and revealed religion 211
reason and religious truth 211, 214
rejection of divine intervention and miracles 215, 220–21
religious diversity and pluralism 221
rise in eighteenth century 7, 11, 198, 211, 212–13
support for natural religion 211, 214
deists
in antiquity 212
differing beliefs 213–14
in Europe 212–13
and freethinking 213
important American deists 213
important British religious thinkers 212
non-uniformity of religious philosophy 213
shared percepts 214
used as a pejorative term 213

deists *see also* British deism, key figures
Descartes, René
  advocacy of vivisection 110
  biographical details 101–2
  charges of dissimulation and atheism 107–8
  cogito ('I think') insight 106–7
  conception of matter as homogeneous 108
  conception of morality 110–11
  criticism of Aristotelianism 104–5, 108
  criticism of syllogistic method 140–45
  Discourse on Method 102, 105, 109
  on divine preordination and human freedom 175
  doctrine of the *bête machine* 16
  God's relation to nature 4
  on human body as a mechanism 109–10
  on human mastery of nature 107–8
  matter theory and doctrine of transubstantiation 14–15
  Meditations on First Philosophy 102, 106–7, 110
  metaphysics 103, 107
  method of doubt 106–7
  method for the pursuit of truth 105–6
  on mind–body unity 110
  Le Monde 102, 107
  on natural laws 109
  on nature as a mechanical system 109
  need for theoretical knowledge with specific applications 102–3
  ontological proof for existence of God 117–18
  Passions of the Soul 102, 110
  philosophical influence and significance 101, 111
  Principles of Philosophy 102
  reason and the equality of minds 102–4
  reduction of sensible qualities in nature to unique geometric representations 108–9
  secular conception of wisdom 102–3
  theory of mind 15–16
  treatment of Copernicanism 102, 107
  vortex theory 12–13
Diderot, Denis
  atheistic reputation 263–4
  biographical details 264–5
  De la Suffisance de la religion naturelle (On the sufficiency of natural religion) 267
  deistic and anti-fanatical outlook 266–7
  Encyclopédie 2, 265, 269–70
  Les Eleuthéromanes (Those zealous for freedom) 273–4
  The Father of a Family 271
  hostility to Christianity 273–4
  ideas on religion after 1760 271–4
  ideas on religion before 1760 265–9
  imprisonment for his views 265
  influence and significance 263–4
  influence of Spinoza on theological context of his time 266
  Jacques le fataliste et son maître (James the fatalist and his master) 274
  Letter sur les aveugles (Letter on the blind) 268–9, 272
  man–machine doctrine 16
  Pensées philosophiques (Philosophical thoughts) 266–7
  the "Prayer" 270
  La Promenade du sceptique (The sceptic's walk) 267
  Rameau's nephew 271–3
  La Religieuse (The nun) 271–2
  Rêve de d'Alembert (D'Alembert's dream) 273
  Supplement to Bougainville's voyage 273
  utilitarian definition of morality 266
  willingness to believe in God 270
  writings 265–6
divine providence, and free will 123–4, 172–6, 206–8
'doctrine of the double truth' 39–40
Dominicans 174, 175

early modern period
  defined 2
  historiography 2–3
  relations between philosophy and religion 18
  terminology, disciplinary categories and boundaries 2–3
ecclesiastical authority
  and free judgement 68–9
  relation to civil authority 9–10
  and state-controlled religion 150–51
Edwards, Jonathan
  biographical details 223
  concept of beauty 226
  contribution to philosophy of religion 223

defence of occasionalism 5
dispositional ontology 223–5
Dissertation Concerning the End for Which God Created the World 233
Dissertation Concerning the Nature of True Virtue 233
doctrine of the will 232–3
on 'habits' and 'laws' 224–5
on imagination, knowledge and the sense of the heart 7, 227–30
influence of Cambridge Platonists 227–8
influence of Locke 224, 227
philosophical influence and significance 223
relational ontology 225–7
religious empistemology 230
theological ethics 233
theory of imagination 228–30
on the Trinity and the end for which God created the world 230–32
Elizabeth (Princess of Bohemia) 16, 102
English providentialism 206
English Romanticism 229
Epicurean atomism 12
epistemic impairment 5
epistemology, reading back into early modern thought 2
Erastianism 150–51
ethical rationalism 121
Eucharist doctrine, conflict between philosophy and theology 43–4
Euthyphro dilemma 8, 9–10, 169
evil
and free will 8–9
Leibniz's conception of problem 176–9
logical problem distinguished from evidential problem 177

faith and history 221–2
faith and reason
continuum of views during early modern period 5–7
doctrinal divisions 6
the Fall
and epistemic impairment 5
and the human condition 136–7
Ficioni, Marcilio 114, 117
fideism 5
Florentine Neoplatonism 114
foundationalism 240
Fourth Lateran Council (1215) 42
Franklin, Benjamin 213
free will
causal determination and the problem of evil 8–9
and divine providence 123–4, 172–6, 206–8
and ethical knowledge 123–4
freethinking 66, 155, 188–9, 193, 198, 199, 213
French scepticism 68, 70, 74, 136, 198
Freneau, Philip 213

Galileo
Letter to the Grand Duchess Christina 6
punishment for supporting Copernican hypothesis 102, 107
God's beauty 226
God's essence and attributes 179
absolute perfection 84, 158
Berkeley on achieving a direct and proper notion of 191
Edward's reformulation 230–32
immutability 85–6, 159
infinite nature and omnipotence 84, 158
invisibility, incomprehensibility and ineffabilty 86–7
omnipresence/immenseness 85, 158
as pure act and simple 84–5
Tindal's deist account 218–19
God's relation to nature, debates during early modern period 4–5
Goeze, Johann Melchior 295–7
great chain of being 16–17
Great Tew Circle 114
Grotius, Hugo 67, 154

Hales, John 154
Heidegger, Martin, on Luther's *Heidelberg Disputation* 36
Herbert, Lord of Cherbury 114
concept of God 216
concept of human nature 216
epistemology 216
five Common Notions (or Catholic Articles) of Religion 214, 215, 216
on revelation 216–17
as source of deistic ideas and themes for eighteenth-century deists 215–17
De veritate (Concerning truth) 215–16, 217
High Calvinism 114

history and creation, in early modern period 12–13
Hobbes, Thomas
 anti-clericalism 99
 argument for hierarchy of responsibility 98
 authoritarianism in religion 99
 biographical details 89
 De cive (The citizen) 89
 compatibilism 98
 distinction between prudence and sapience 92
 on laws of nature 92–3
 Leviathan 10, 89, 90–91
 on materiality of the soul 16
 method 92
 on miracles 93–4
 on natural reason and laws of nature 91–3
 on 'naturalness' of religion and religious impulse 89–90, 96
 on personal revelation and prophecy 93–4
 place of religion in his political theory 90–91
 reconciling natural divine law and a sovereign's law 96–7
 on relation between civil and ecclesiastical authority 10, 90–91, 95–6
 on religious education 96
 scriptural interpretations 94
 sincerity of his religious beliefs 98–9
 on sources of religious knowledge 93–4
 The Elements of Law 89
Hooker, Richard 114, 154
Hugh of Saint-Victor 107
human freedom
 compatiblist position 8, 173
 and divine providence and foreknowledge 172–6
human freedom *see also* free will
humanism 71–2, 212
Hume, David
 attacks on religious belief 236
 contribution to philosophy of religion 249, 260–61
 and the design argument 250–53, 305–7
 on desire 11
 Dialogues Concerning Natural Religion 237, 250, 254, 256, 305–6
 dismissal of cosmological argument 258–9
 empiricism 249
 An Enquiry concerning Human Understanding 6, 220, 236, 251
 evidentialism 249
 "The Natural History of Religion" 3
 influence of Newton 261
 as a non-believer 250
 "Of the Immortality of the Soul" 259
 "Of Miracles" 257–8
 Philo's reversal regarding the design argument 255–6
 on the problem of evil 254–5
 on reason and religious belief 249–50
 scepticism 249
 on the soul 259–60
 as a threat to integrity of Christian doctrine 235
 A Treatise on Human Nature 236, 249
 on trustworthiness of proofs of miracles 257–8
Hume, David *see also* Reid, Thomas
Hutcheson, Francis, moral sense theory 11, 233
hylopathian atheism 120
hylozoic atheism 120

Index librorum prohibitorum (List of prohibited books) 15
innatist theory of human knowledge 123
Islam
 criticism by Montaigne 73
 as a 'false relgion' 137
 Lessing's account 292
 Locke's account 163
 Voltaire's account 205–6

Jacobi, Friedrich Heinrich 300
Jansen, Cornelius
 Augustinius 128
 controversy 128
Jansenism 127–8, 204
Jefferson, Thomas 213
Jesuits
 on divine providence and foreknowledge and human freedom 174
 and Rites Controversy 168
Judaism
 Cardanus' account 292
 Christian tensions with 149

Lessing's account 298, 299
Locke's account 163
Spinoza's account 149
Voltaire's assessment 204–5

Kant, Immanuel
on achievement of an ethical commonwealth 286–8
biographical details 277
criticism of traditional theoretical proofs of God's existence 3, 278–9
Critique of the Power of Judgement 283–5
Critique of Pure Reason 3, 278, 279–80, 282
deism 213
on the ethical state of nature 286
on freedom, autonomy and the moral law 280–82
on the highest good and moral law 281–2, 284
his position with regard to God's existence 284–5
on human beings as ends in creation 284
"Ideas for a Universal History From a Cosmopolitan Point of View" 286
on limits of philosophy and philosophical methods 278, 288
moral motivation and the categorical imperative 11
moral philosophy and the possibility of speaking about God 280
on need for philosophical agnosticism 279, 288
The One Possible Basis for a Demonstration of the Existence of God 278
Opus postumum 288
physico-theological argument for God's existence 277
Principiorum primorum cognitionis metaphysicae nova dilucidatio (A new elucidation of the first principles of metaphysical cognition) 277
principle of the power of judgment and the moral law 283
Religion Within the Boundaries of Mere Reason 285–7
on teleology in nature 283–4
Kepler, Johannes 12, 104
King, William
debate with Pierre Bayle regarding dispensations of divine providence 206–7
On Evil 170
De origine male (On the origin of evil) 206–7
knowledge
debates about the nature and scope of 5–7
innatist theory 123
Koran, George Sale's English translation 206

La Mettrie, Julien Offray de 16
attack on Descartes' metaphysics 107
Lacan, Jacques 129
Lafuma, Louis 130–31, 135
latitudinarianism 154, 199
Laudian Church of England 153
Leibniz, Gottfried Wilhelm
biographical details 167–9, 180
concept containment theory of truth 170
development of calculus 167
Discourse on Metaphysics 169, 180
dissimulation or sincerity 180
on divine providence and foreknowledge and human freedom 172–6
ecumenical work 167
influence and significance 167, 169
metaphysics 170, 180
Monadology 180
on natural theology 170–72
on natural theology of the Chinese 168–9
New Essays on Human Understanding 169–70
philosophical system 169–70
philosophical theology 172–6
on principle of contradiction 170
on principles governing reason 169
Theodicy 168, 172, 176
theodicy and problems of evil 176–9, 206–7
theory of formal atoms or monads
Leibniz–Bayle dialogue 207
Leibnizianism 206–8
Leland, John 213
Lenclos, Ninon de 199
Lessing, Gotthold Ephraim 213

Axioms 296
biographical details 289
The Christianity of Reason 292
collaboration with Moses Mendelssohn 292
contribution to philosophy of religion 289–91
debate over his Spinozism 300
deism 293
development of his thought in 1750s and 1760s 291–3
The Education of the Human Race 292, 297–301
on historical arguments for truth of revealed religion 294–7
influence of Leibniz 293–4
influence and significance 289
Leibniz on Eternal Punishment 294
major influences 291
Nathan the Wise 293, 297
Necessary Answer to a Very Unnecessary Question 296
On the Manner of the Propagation and Dissemination of the Christian Religion 292–3
On the Origin of Revealed Religion 293
On the Reality of Things Outside God 292
progressive rationalism 292
on reason and revelation 292, 297–301
Reimarus controversy 293, 295
rejection of the transcendence of God 292–3
A Rejoinder 290
religious tolerance 291–2
revision of his attitude towards orthodoxy 293–4
Spinoza only put Leibniz on the Track of Pre-established Harmony 292
Thoughts on the Moravians 291
Vindication of Hieronymus Cardanus 291–2
in Wolfenbüttel 293–7
libertarianism 175
Linnaeus, Carl 17
Lisbon earthquake (1755) 18, 208
Locke, John
biographical details 153–6
Christian beliefs 155–6
contribution to philosophy of religion 156
Essay Concerning Human Understanding 123, 155, 156, 217, 227, 268
Letter Concerning Toleration 12, 155
moderate theological influences 154
on moral religion 159–61
on natural religion 156
on nature of free human agency 160–61
on the nature of the soul 16
"Of Faith and Reason, and their Distinct Provinces" 7
ontological argument for existence of God 156–9
on personal identity 161
The Reasonableness of Christianity 155, 162, 164
on revelation 161–3, 220–21
tendency towards deism and freethinking 155
theory of morality 159–61
theory of punishment 160
tutelage and influence of Robert Boyle 153–4
Two Treatises on Government 10, 154
on the variety of faith and the perfection of the mind 164–5
warranting Christianity 163–4
Way of Ideas 217
Lombard, Peter, conflict with Joachim of Fiore over essence of God 42
Luther, Martin
on achievements of reason 38
Bondage of the Will 8
on civil versus ecclesiastical authority 9–10
on conflict between reason and theology 40–44
contribution to philosophy of religion 33–4
criticism of Aristotle 33–4
on defining human beings 38–9
doctine of justification and freedom 37–8
and the doctrine of the double truth 39–40
on existence of a common concept of God 34–5
existential theology 35
Heidelberg Disputations 35
De homine (On humankind) 38–9
on immortality and God's relation to human beings 39

influence and significance 33–4
on need to distinguish between realms of philosophy and theology 40–44
on philosophy and theological anthropology 38–9
structural motif of his theology 37–8
theology of glory versus theology of the cross 35–6
Treatise on Christian Liberty 37
"The Word Was Made Flesh" 39

Machiavelli, Niccolò
The Art of War 23*n*, 27
on the cause of greatness in republics 25–8
Christianity contrasted to pagan religion 23–5
'civil religion' 21–3
on civil versus ecclesiastical authority 9
crisis of republics and the politics of religion 21–3
debate over his view of religion 19, 28–31
Discourses on the First Ten Books of Titus Livy 19, 21–3, 26, 27, 28–30
exercise of power as the religion of politics 19–21
influence and significance 19
pragmatic approach to religiosity and moral character 19–21, 28
The Prince 19–21
religion as a disciplinary mode of education 26–7
religion as force for "producing good men" 27–8
secular function of religion 21–3, 26–8
Malebranche, Nicolas 4
man–machine doctrine 16
Mandeville, Bernard 188, 189
matter theory
and doctrine of transubstantiation 14–15
matter as homogeneous 108
mechanical philosophy
and God and Nature 4
human body as a mechanism 109–10
impact on metaphysics 13–14
medieval semantic theory 42
Mendelssohn, Moses, *Philosophical Dialogues* 292
metaphysics
Descartes' conception 103
doctrine of justification and freedom 37–8
impact of mechanical philosophy 13–14
radical change during early modern period 13–17
reading back into early modern thought 2
Middleton, Conyers 212
Mill, John Stuart, *On Liberty* 12
millenarian doctrines 13
mind–body interaction/unity 16, 110
mind–body distinction 15–16
minute philosophers 188
miracles
focus on nature and credibility of 6
Hume's essay on trustworthiness of proofs 257–8
rejection by deists 215, 220–21
moderate English religious thought 114, 154
Molina, Luis de, theory of freedom 8, 174–5, 176
Montaigne, Michel de
against spiritual arrogance 72–3
"Apology of Raymond Sebond" 66–7, 69, 72, 73
background and writings 65–6
censorship of his work 69
as a citizen of the world 72
contribution to philosophy of religion 73–4
Copernican philosophy of religion 73–4
criticism of Aristotelian philosophy and Thomist theology 67
criticism of natural theology 66–8
cultural relativism 71
Essays 65–6, 69, 71, 73
on free judgement and the authority of the Church 68–9
humanist approach to religion 71–2
influence and significance 65
personal religious convictions 70–71
pragmatic approach to religion 70
on religion as custom 66, 70
scepticism and faith 68, 70, 74, 136
moral evil 246
moral knowledge, debates over sources of 10–12
moral motivation, shift from theological to psychologistic context 11–12

moral and political philosophy, key themes interwoven with religion in early modern period 7–12
moral relativism 11
moral sense theory 11, 233
morality, and Euthyphro dilemma 8, 9–10
Moravians 291
More, Henry 107
Morgan, Thomas 212

natural evil 246
natural law theory
  Descartes' contribution 109
  development of 8–9
  tension between intellectualists and voluntarists 9, 160
natural philosophy
  role of witnesses and testimony 6
  terminology 2
natural religion 156, 189
  core of 214
  faith and history 221–2
  as once lived 217–18
  and role of Jesus 219
natural theology
  Calvin's reconstruction 59–62
  criticism by Montaigne 66–8
  faith and reason 5–7
  regenerate and unregenerate 60–62
  rhetorical and demonstrative theistic arguments 52–3
  of Suárez 76–7
nature, human mastery of 107–8
Neoplatonism in England *see* Cambridge Platonists
Newton, Isaac
  absolute theory of space 15
  development of calculus 167
Newtonianism 12
Nicholas of Cusa, influence of Sebond 67
nomic occasionalism 4

occasionalism 4–5, 174
Ockham's razor 254
ontological argument for God's existence *see* theistic proofs
Origen 173

Paine, Thomas 213
  The Age of Reason 220
Paley, William 156
  argument from design for existence of God 304–10
  biographical details and major works 303–4
  contemporary relevance of his arguments 310–12
  contribution to philosophy of religion 304
  evolutionary ideas 309–10
  Horae Paulinae 303
  influence and significance 304
  Natural Theology: Or Evidence of the Existence and Attributes of the Deity, Collected from the Appearances of Nature 304–10
  The Principles of Moral and Political Philosophy 303
  A View of the Evidences of Christianity 303
  watch analogy 304, 305
Paracelsus 12
paranormal phenomena, interest in 16
Pascal, Blaise
  anthropology and the enigma of the human condition 135–7
  Apology for the Christian Religion 128, 130
  attack on sceptics and atheists 132
  biographical details 127–9, 140
  contribution to philosophy of religion 129
  Conversation with M. de Sacy on Epictetus and Montaigne 127
  "Discourse on the Machine" or 'the wager' 133–5
  and doctrine of the Fall 136–7
  exegetical proofs 138–9
  on false religion 137
  his spirituality 140
  on immortality of the soul 132
  influence and significance 129
  Mémorial 127
  Pensées 128, 129, 130–31
  preface to the *Apology* 132–3
  Provincial Letters 127–8, 129
  on true conversion 139
Patrick, Simon 154
Peirce, Charles Sanders 224
personal identity, debates about nature of 16, 18

Peyrére, Isaac de la 212
philosophy, need to distinguish from theology 40–44
philosophy of religion
Cudworth's contribution 113, 117
Montaigne's Copernican perspective 73–4
Reid's attempt to change focus of discussion to epistemology of religious belief 237–8
physico-theological argument for God's existence *see* theistic proofs
Plantinga, Alvin 238, 241, 242, 244
Plastic Nature of Reality, doctrine of 120–21
Pope, Alexander 206
predestination, Cudworth's attack on doctrine 120
properties, theory of
radical transformation during early modern period 14
theological implications of radical changes 14–117
prophecy 93–4
Protestant theology, distinction between rhetorical and demonstrative theistic arguments 52–3
providentialism 198
providentialism theory 206
Pyrrhonian scepticism 216

qualities, theory of, reorientation of 14–15

rational theology, and theistic proofs 3–4
Ray, John, *The Wisdom of God Manifested in the Works of Creation* 304
reason
conflict with theology 40–44
and the equality of minds 102–4
reformed epistemology 240–41, 242
Reformed theology, Calvin's contributions 47, 63
Reid, Thomas
arguments for God's existence 242–5
biographical details 235
contribution to philosophy of religion 235–8, 247
Essays on the Active Powers of Man 236
Essays on the Intellectual Powers of Man 236, 242–3
on human freedom 246
influences on his philosophy of religion 235–7
An Inquiry into the Human Mind on the Principles of Common Sense 236
Lectures on Natural Theology 236
method and focus on questions *de jure* 238
philosophical influence and significance 235
philosophy of mind and theory of perception 236
on the problem of evil 245–6
on rationality and belief in God 240–42
relationship to Hume 236–7
on role of God in Reid's philosophical system 238–9
Reimarus, Hermann Samuel
Apology or Defense of the Rational Worshippers of God 295
controversy 289, 293, 295–6
religion
as custom 66
as a disciplinary mode of education 26–7
as force for "producing good men" 27–8
humanist approach 71–2
politics of 21–3
pragmatic approach to 19–21, 28, 70
relations with philosophy in early modern period 18
religious diversity and pluralism 221
religious intolerance 264
religious language, Berkeley's reflections 191–4
religious schism 150–51
religious toleration
Spinoza's prudential arguement 151
support for 12, 71
versus authoritartianism 99
revelation and revealed religion 93–4
deist's opposition to 217
reasonableness of 161–3
Voltaire's attack on doctrines 203
Rites Controversy 168
Rousseau, Jean-Jacques 213
Russell, Bertrand 180

scepticism, and fallibility of the senses 5
scholastic Aristotelianism 12, 13, 14
scholasticism, shedding of 17
Schumann, Johann Daniel, *On the Proof of the Spirit and the Power* 296

science, reading back into early modern thought 2
Scottish Enlightenment 235
Scripture
 debates over historical status of Gospels 296
 as source of moral knowledge 10–11
Sebond, Raymond 66–7
 Theologia naturalis sive liber creaturarum (Natural theology or the book of creatures) 67
secularism, and ecclesiastical authority 9–10
Sellier, Phillipe 131, 135
Shaftesbury, Earl of (Anthony Ashley-Cooper) 154, 227
 Essay Concerning Virtue and Merit 266
sin, noetic effects of 56–9
Socinianism 119, 177, 199
Socinus, Faustus, *De Auctoritate Sacrae Scripturae* (Concerning the authority of sacred Scripture) 163
soul, the
 immateriality of 15–16
 immortality of 15–16
 materiality of 16
 mortality of 16, 259–60
 tripartite division 15
sovereign states, and relation between civil and ecclesiastical authority 9–10
space, theories of
 absolute versus relative conceptions of space 15
 relation of space to God 15
special revelation, in faith and reason 6–7
species, nature of, debates during early modern period 17
Spinoza, Baruch
 accusations of atheism 145, 147
 articles of universal faith 214
 attack on traditional allegorical method of interpreting Scripture 143–4
 biographical details 141–2
 conception of God and morality 145–7
 contribution to philosophy of religion 142
 critique of religion 142–5
 denial of God's transcendence 4
 on epistemological inadequacy of knowledge found in revelation 143–4
 Ethics 141, 142, 144, 145
 expulsion from Jewish community 142
 historical and philological analysis of Scripture 144–5
 influence and significance 142
 on internal and external religion 147–50
 on the metaphysics of God 144
 on psychosocial origin of religious belief 143
 on religion and politics 150–51
 on religious toleration 151
 Short Treatise on God, Man and His Well-Being 141
 Theological-Political Treatise (*Tractatus Theologico-Politicus*) 142, 143, 144, 145, 147, 151, 214
 view of religion 147–50
state-controlled religion 150–51
Stillingfleet, Edward 14, 16
strong foundationalism 240
Suárez, Francisco
 a posteriori demonstration of existence of God 80–81
 a priori demonstration of existence of God 81–3
 absolute perfection of God 84
 biographical details 75–6
 contribution to philosophy of religion 75–6
 Disputationes metaphysicae (Metaphysical disputations) 13, 75–6, 77, 83–4
 epistemological principles guiding his analysis of God's essence and attributes 83
 God as pure act and simple 84–5
 his natural theology 76–7
 immutability of God 85–6
 infinite nature and omnipotence of God 84
 invisibility, incomprehensibility and ineffability of God 86–7
 metaphysical argument for existence of God 77–80
 omnipresence of God 85
 on problem of divine freedom and immutability 86
substance/attribute ontology 14–15
syllogismus expositorius 41–2
syllogistic method 104–5

Taylor, Charles 129
Tempier, Stephan 39

theistic proofs
a posteriori argument of Suárez 80–81
a priori argument by Suárez 81–3
argument from eternal truths by Leibniz 172
Calvin's arguments 52–6
contemporary relevance of Paley's arguments 310–12
cosmological and teleological arguments of Leibniz 171
Cudworth's extension of Descartes ontological proof 117–18
divine language argument of Berkeley 186–7
exegetical proofs by Pascal 138–9
Hume on the design argument 250–53, 255–6
Hume's dismissal of cosmological argument 258–9
Kant's criticism of traditional theoretical proofs of God's existence 3, 278–9
Locke's proof of existence and attributes of God 156–9
metaphysical argument for existence of a first cause 77–80
ontological argument by Leibniz 171–2
ontological arguments by Berkeley 185–6
Paley's argument from design 304–10
Pascal's 'wager' 133–5
and rational theology 3–4
Reid's cosmological argument 242–5
theocentric theory of knowledge 241
theodicy, and problems of evil 176–9
theology, need to distinguish from philosophy 40–44
theology of glory, versus theology of the cross 35–6
theoretical knowledge, and practical application 102
theory of mind 15–16
Tillotson, John 154
Tindal, Matthew
Christianity as Old as the Creation 218–19
deism 212, 214
on essence and attributes of God 218–19
Toland, John 155, 188, 191, 212
Christianity not Mysterious 217
influence of Locke's Way of Ideas 217
Letters to Serena 217–18
on natural religion 217–18
on revelation 217
Torricelli, Evangelista 15
transubstantiation, and Cartesian matter theory 14–15
Trinitarian doctrine
Cudworth's immanent interpretation 118–19
Edwards' social analogy 231
and the *syllogismus expositorius* 41–2
truth, concept containment theory 170
Tuckney, Anthony 115
Turnbull, George 235

unbelief, philosophical development of various forms 7
universities, method of teaching in medieval period 104
Usingen, Arnoldi von, *Exercitium Physicorum* (Exercises in physics) 39–40
Ussher, James, age of the earth 13

Viret, Pierre, *Instruction Chrétienne* (Christian teaching) 212
vivisection 110
Voetius, Gisbertus 107
Voltaire, Francois-Marie Arouet de
De l'Alcoran ou de Mahomet (On the Koran or Muhammad) 205
Anti-Pascal 204, 207
attack on doctrine of Trinity 203
attack on doctrines of revelation 203–4
attacks on Catholic Church 202, 204
attacks on Judaism 204–5
attitude towards Islam 205–6
biographical details 197–200, 208–9
Candide, ou l'optimisme (Candide, or optimism) 8, 18, 206, 208
commitment to deism and natural religion 199, 200–201, 204
contribution to philosophy of religion 197–8
conversion to Newtonianism 200
as a dangerous dissident and unbeliever 199–200
Dîner du comte de Boulainvilliers 204
Dieu et les hommes (God and humanity) 203, 205
on difficulties regarding God's existence 200–201
education 199

Elements de la philosophie de Newton 200, 201, 207
English Letters 129
Entretiens chinois (Chinese conversations) 209
Epitre a l'auteur des Troi Imposteurs (Epistle to the author of the three imposters) 202
Examen important de milord Bolingbroke (Lord Bolingbroke's important inquiry) 205
Du Fanatisme (On fanaticism) 206
Le Fanatisme, ou Mahomet le prophète (Fanaticism, or the Prophet Muhammad) 205
on free will, providence and the problem of evil 206–8
his 'public' God 202–3
Histoire de l'éstablissement du christianisme (History of the foundation of Christianity) 203–4
influence of Leibniz 206–8
influence and significance 197–8
Letters Concerning the English Nation/ Lettres philosphiques 199, 265
philosophical influences 198
Philosophical Letters 134
Poème dur le désastre de Lisbonne 208
Poème sur la loi naturelle (Poem on natural law) 203
position as public enemy of the Church 203
La Profession de foi des théistes (The theist profession of faith) 204
on religious intolerance and fanaticism 198
religious philosophy 204–5, 208–9
Sermon des cinquante (A sermon to the fifty) 203, 204
Sermon du rabbin Akib (Rabbi Akib's sermon) 205
Sur le théisme (On theism) 201
theism 200–201, 204–5
Traite de métaphysique (Treatise on metaphysics) 199–200, 201, 202
Treatise on toleration on the occasion of Jean Calas' death 198
Un Chrétien contre six juifs (A Christian against six Jews) 205

Whichcote, Benjamin 114, 115–16
wisdom, Descartes' secular conception 102–3
witchcraft 16
Wolff, Christian-Freidrich 207
Woolston, Thomas 212